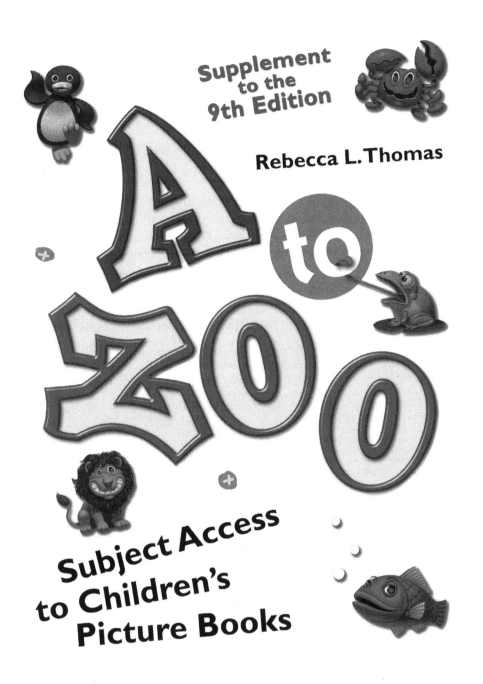

Supplement
to the
9th Edition

Rebecca L. Thomas

A to Zoo

Subject Access
to Children's
Picture Books

Children's and Young Adult Literature Reference
Catherine Barr, Series Editor

 LIBRARIES
UNLIMITED™
An Imprint of ABC-CLIO, LLC
Santa Barbara, California • Denver, Colorado

Library of Congress Cataloging-in-Publication Data is available at www.loc.gov.

ISBN: 978-1-61069-819-1
EISBN: 978-1-61069-820-7

20 19 18 17 16   1 2 3 4 5

This book is also available as an eBook.

Libraries Unlimited
An Imprint of ABC-CLIO, LLC

ABC-CLIO, LLC
130 Cremona Drive, P.O. Box 1911
Santa Barbara, California 93116-1911
www.abc-clio.com

This book is printed on acid-free paper ∞
Manufactured in the United States of America

Contents

Preface

This supplement to the 9th edition of *A to Zoo* (Libraries Unlimited, 2014) provides users with subject access to picture books published in 2014 and 2015. It includes more than 1,400 titles cataloged under more than 600 subjects, and will be useful for public and school librarians developing collections, preparing bibliographies and classroom units, and reader's advisory. Its arrangement is the same as that of the main edition, and the familiar subject headings are used.

Rebecca L. Thomas has been a school librarian, university teacher, and author in the field of children's literature. With this supplement, she continues the work of Carolyn W. Lima and John Lima.

Several library collections served as guides in the selection process, including the San Diego Public Library—the collection that served as the original resource for early editions of *A to Zoo*. Also examined was the catalog of the CLEVNET libraries in Ohio, which includes the Cleveland Public Library along with numerous independent libraries in northeastern Ohio, and the collections of the Cuyahoga County Public Library system. School library collections were also explored, including those of the Shaker Heights (Ohio) City schools and other schools in northeastern Ohio.

HOW TO USE THIS BOOK

A to Zoo can be used to obtain information about children's picture books in two ways: to learn the titles, authors, and illustrators of books on a particular subject, such as "dragons" or "weddings"; or to ascertain the subject (or subjects) when only the title, author and title, or illustrator and title are known. For example, if the title *The Day the Crayons Came Home* is known, this volume will enable the user to discover that *The Day the Crayons Came Home* is written by Drew Daywalt, illustrated by Oliver Jeffers, published by Philomel in 2015, and that the subject areas are: Behavior – lost & found possessions. Concepts – color. Letters, cards.

For ease and convenience of reference use, *A to Zoo* is divided into five sections:

Subject Headings
Subject Guide
Bibliographic Guide
Title Index
Illustrator Index

SUBJECT HEADINGS: This section contains an alphabetical list of the subjects cataloged in this book. The subject headings reflect the established terms used commonly in public libraries, originally based on questions asked by parents and teachers and then modified and adapted by librarians. To facilitate reference use, and because subjects are requested in a variety of terms, the list of subject headings contains numerous cross-references. Subheadings are arranged alphabetically under each general topic, for example:

> Animals (general topic)
> Animals – apes *see* Animals – chimpanzees; Animals – gorillas; Animals – monkeys (cross reference)
> Animals – babies (subheading)
> Animals – badgers (subheading)

SUBJECT GUIDE: This guide to 1,430 picture books for preschool children through second graders is cataloged under 640 subjects. The guide reflects the arrangement in the Subject Headings—alphabetical by subject heading and subheading. Many books, of course, relate to more than one subject, and this comprehensive list provides a means of identifying all those books that may contain any information or material on a particular subject.

If, for example, the user wants books on snakes, the Subject Headings section will show that Reptiles is a subject classification. A look in the Subject Guide reveals that under Reptiles – snakes there are 4 titles listed alphabetically by author, plus an additional 17 titles under 4 related subheadings. For ease of access to the extensive list of subjects, many headings are organized in groupings:

Activities	Emotions	Musical instruments
Anatomy	Ethnic groups in the U.S.	Mythical creatures
Animals	Family life	Religion
Behavior	Foreign lands	Reptiles
Birds	Format, unusual	Royalty
Careers	Holidays	Seasons
Character traits	Illness	Senses
Clothing	Indians of North	Sports
Concepts	America	Toys
Disabilities	Insects	Weather

Using the list of Subject Headings, a teacher can examine the general subject Activities and see topics such as driving, flying, hiking, running, traveling, and walking to select books for a program on motion. Or a parent can look through the list of Careers to plan a home-schooling lesson on jobs and work. A librarian might explore the books in Ethnic Groups in the U.S. and find African Americans and then organize programming for Black History Month.

Two of the most-used groupings in the Subject Headings list are Behavior and Character Traits. These two areas contain subheadings such as Behavior – boredom, Behavior – bullying, teasing, Behavior – fighting, arguing, Behavior – sharing, Character traits – helpfulness, Character traits – individuality, Character traits – shyness, and Character traits – vanity. They are the "go to" headings for programs on character development and conduct. Cross-references have been generated for all of the subheadings for Behavior and Character Traits.

BIBLIOGRAPHIC GUIDE: Each book is listed with full bibliographic information. This section is arranged alphabetically by author, or by title when the author is unknown, or by uniform (classic) title. Each entry contains bibliographic information in order: author, title, illustrator, publisher and date of publication, miscellaneous notes when given, International Standard Book Number (ISBN), and subjects, listed according to the alphabetical classification in the Subject Headings section.

The user can consult the Bibliographic Guide to find complete data on each of the titles listed in the Subject Guide. Turning from the Subject Guide heading of Machines to consult the Bibliographic Guide, for example, the user will find the following entry:

> **Burleigh, Robert.** *Zoom! zoom! sounds of things that go in the city* ill. by Tad Carpenter. Simon & Schuster/Paula Wiseman, 2014. ISBN 978-144248315-6 Subj: Automobiles. Cities, towns. Machines. Noise, sounds. Rhyming text.

In the case of joint authors, the second author is listed in alphabetical order, followed by the book title and the name of the primary author or main entry. The user can then locate the primary author for complete bibliographic information. For example:

> **Hamilton, Emma Walton.** *The very fairy princess: a spooky, sparkly Halloween* (Andrews, Julie)

Bibliographic information for this title will be found in the Bibliographic Guide section under Andrews, Julie.

Titles for an author who is both a single author and a joint author are interfiled alphabetically. Where the author is not known, the entry is listed alphabetically by title with complete bibliographic information following the same format as given above.

TITLE INDEX: This section contains an alphabetical list of all titles in the book with authors in parentheses where appropriate, followed by the page number of the full listing in the Bibliographic Guide, such as:

> *Daddy hugs* (Tafuri, Nancy), 120

Ultimately, the Title Index guides the reader to the full bibliographic information in the Bibliographic Index.

ILLUSTRATOR INDEX: This section contains an alphabetical list of illustrators with titles, author names in parentheses, and the page number of the full listing in the Bibliographic Guide. For example:

> **Blackall, Sophie.** *And two boys booed* (Viorst, Judith), 123

Titles listed under an illustrator's name appear in alphabetical sequence. When the author is the same as the illustrator the author's name is not repeated.

Acknowledgments

The author wishes to express her thanks for the assistance provided by many people in bringing this book together. Special thanks to Christine McNaull whose knowledge of the database, sorting, and formatting was essential. Series editor Catherine Barr provided guidance and support throughout the process. Thanks also to Barbara Ittner of Libraries Unlimited. My family and friends provided me with time and encouragement to complete this book.

Subject Headings

Main headings, subheadings, and cross-references are arranged alphabetically and provide a quick reference to the subjects used in the Subject Guide section, where author and title names appear under appropriate headings. For more information on how subjects are grouped, see Preface p. vii.

ABC books
Abused children *see* Child abuse
Accidents
Activities
Activities – babysitting
Activities – baking, cooking
Activities – ballooning
Activities – bargaining *see*
   Activities – trading
Activities – bartering *see*
   Activities – trading
Activities – bathing
Activities – cooking *see* Activities
   – baking, cooking
Activities – dancing
Activities – digging
Activities – drawing
Activities – driving
Activities – eating *see* Food
Activities – flying
Activities – gardening *see*
   Gardens, gardening
Activities – hiking
Activities – kissing *see* Kissing
Activities – knitting
Activities – making things
Activities – painting *see also*
   Careers – artists
Activities – picnicking
Activities – playing
Activities – reading *see* Books,
   reading
Activities – running
Activities – sewing
Activities – singing
Activities – storytelling
Activities – swapping *see*
   Activities – trading
Activities – swimming *see* Sports
   – swimming
Activities – trading
Activities – traveling
Activities – vacationing
Activities – walking
Activities – whistling
Activities – working

Activities – writing
Adoption
Aged *see* Old age
Airplanes, airports
Alaska
Aliens
Alphabet books *see* ABC books
Ambition *see* Character traits –
   ambition
American Indians *see* Indians of
   North America
Amusement parks *see* Parks –
   amusement
Anatomy
Anatomy – ears
Anatomy – eyes
Anatomy – hands
Anatomy – skin
Anatomy – tails
Anatomy – teeth *see* Teeth
Anatomy – thumbs *see* Thumb
   sucking
Anatomy – toes
Angels
Animals *see also* Birds; Frogs &
   toads; Reptiles
Animals – apes *see* Animals
   – chimpanzees; Animals –
   gorillas; Animals – monkeys
Animals – babies
Animals – badgers
Animals – bats
Animals – bears
Animals – beavers
Animals – brush wolves *see*
   Animals – coyotes
Animals – bulls, cows
Animals – caribou *see* Animals –
   reindeer
Animals – cats
Animals – chimpanzees
Animals – cows *see* Animals –
   bulls, cows
Animals – coyotes
Animals – deer
Animals – dogs

Animals – donkeys
Animals – elephants
Animals – endangered animals
Animals – foxes
Animals – giraffes
Animals – gnus
Animals – goats
Animals – gorillas
Animals – groundhogs
Animals – guinea pigs
Animals – hamsters
Animals – hedgehogs
Animals – hippopotamuses
Animals – horses, ponies
Animals – hyenas
Animals – jaguars
Animals – kindness to *see*
   Character traits – kindness to
   animals
Animals – koalas
Animals – lemurs
Animals – leopards
Animals – lions
Animals – llamas
Animals – meerkats
Animals – mice
Animals – migration *see*
   Migration
Animals – moles
Animals – monkeys
Animals – moose
Animals – muskrats
Animals – octopuses *see*
   Octopuses
Animals – opossums *see* Animals
   – possums
Animals – orangutans
Animals – otters
Animals – pandas
Animals – panthers *see* Animals
   – leopards
Animals – pigs
Animals – platypuses
Animals – polar bears
Animals – possums

Animals – prairie wolves *see* Animals – coyotes
Animals – rabbits
Animals – raccoons
Animals – reindeer
Animals – rhinoceros
Animals – seals
Animals – service animals
Animals – sheep
Animals – shrews
Animals – skunks
Animals – sloths
Animals – slugs
Animals – snow leopards *see* Animals – leopards
Animals – squid *see* Squid
Animals – squirrels
Animals – swine *see* Animals – pigs
Animals – tapirs
Animals – tigers
Animals – voles
Animals – walruses
Animals – warthogs
Animals – weasels
Animals – whales
Animals – wolves
Animals – woolly mammoths
Animals – worms
Animals – zebras
Anti-violence *see* Violence, nonviolence
Apartments *see* Homes, houses
Appearance *see* Character traits – appearance
Arachnids *see* Spiders
Arithmetic *see* Counting, numbers
Art
Assertiveness *see* Character traits – assertiveness
Astrology *see* Zodiac
Astronauts *see* Careers – astronauts; Space & space ships
Astronomy
Authors *see* Careers – writers
Authors, children *see* Children as authors
Automobiles
Autumn *see* Seasons – fall
Award-winning books *see* Caldecott award books; Caldecott award honor books

Babies, new *see* Family life – new sibling
Babies, toddlers
Bad day *see* Behavior – bad day, bad mood
Bad mood *see* Behavior – bad day, bad mood

Ballerinas *see* Ballet; Careers – dancers
Ballet
Balloons *see* Toys – balloons
Bayous *see* Swamps
Beaches *see* Sea & seashore – beaches
Beasts *see* Monsters
Bedtime
Behavior
Behavior – arguing *see* Behavior – fighting, arguing
Behavior – bad day, bad mood
Behavior – boasting, showing off
Behavior – boredom
Behavior – bossy
Behavior – bullying, teasing
Behavior – collecting things
Behavior – dissatisfaction
Behavior – fighting, arguing
Behavior – forgetfulness
Behavior – forgiving
Behavior – gossip, rumors
Behavior – greed
Behavior – growing up
Behavior – hiding
Behavior – hiding things
Behavior – hurrying
Behavior – indecision
Behavior – lost
Behavior – lost & found possessions
Behavior – lying
Behavior – messy
Behavior – misbehavior
Behavior – mistakes
Behavior – misunderstanding
Behavior – naughty *see* Behavior – misbehavior
Behavior – needing someone
Behavior – potty training *see* Toilet training
Behavior – promptness, tardiness
Behavior – resourcefulness
Behavior – rumors *see* Behavior – gossip, rumors
Behavior – running away
Behavior – secrets
Behavior – seeking better things
Behavior – sharing
Behavior – solitude
Behavior – stealing
Behavior – talking to strangers
Behavior – tardiness *see* Behavior – promptness, tardiness
Behavior – teasing *see* Behavior – bullying, teasing

Behavior – toilet training *see* Toilet training
Behavior – trickery
Behavior – unnoticed, unseen
Behavior – wishing
Behavior – worrying
Being different *see* Character traits – being different
Bereavement *see* Death; Emotions – grief
Bible *see* Religion
Bigotry *see* Prejudice
Birds
Birds – bluebirds
Birds – chickens, roosters
Birds – crows
Birds – cuckoos
Birds – ducks
Birds – geese
Birds – guinea fowl
Birds – owls
Birds – parakeets, parrots
Birds – peacocks, peahens
Birds – penguins
Birds – pigeons
Birds – plovers
Birds – puffins
Birds – ravens
Birds – robins
Birds – sparrows
Birds – toucans
Birds – turkeys
Birds – woodpeckers
Birth
Birthdays
Blindness *see* Disabilities – blindness; Senses – sight
Board books *see* Format, unusual – board books
Boasting *see* Behavior – boasting, showing off
Boats, ships
Boogy man *see* Monsters
Books, reading *see also* Libraries
Boredom *see* Behavior – boredom
Bossy *see* Behavior – bossy
Bravery *see* Character traits – bravery
Brothers *see* Family life – brothers; Family life – brothers & sisters; Sibling rivalry
Bubbles
Bugs *see* Insects
Bulldozers *see* Machines
Bullying *see* Behavior – bullying, teasing
Burros *see* Animals – donkeys
Buses

Cabs *see* Taxis

Cafés *see* Restaurants
Caldecott award books
Caldecott award honor books
Camouflages *see* Disguises
Camping *see* Camps, camping
Camps, camping
Cards *see* Letters, cards
Careers
Careers – actors
Careers – airplane pilots
Careers – artists *see also*
  Activities – painting; Art
Careers – astronauts
Careers – astronomers
Careers – authors *see* Careers –
  writers
Careers – bus drivers
Careers – chefs, cooks
Careers – clergy
Careers – composers
Careers – construction workers
Careers – cooks *see* Careers –
  chefs, cooks
Careers – dancers
Careers – detectives
Careers – doctors
Careers – engineers
Careers – farmers
Careers – firefighters
Careers – fishermen
Careers – garbage collectors *see*
  Careers – sanitation workers
Careers – inventors
Careers – librarians
Careers – mail carriers *see*
  Careers – postal workers
Careers – mechanics
Careers – meteorologists
Careers – military
Careers – musicians
Careers – naturalists
Careers – nurses
Careers – opera singers *see*
  Careers – singers
Careers – painters *see* Careers
  – artists
Careers – photographers
Careers – physicians *see* Careers
  – doctors
Careers – postal workers
Careers – preachers *see* Careers
  – clergy
Careers – ranchers
Careers – sailors *see* Careers –
  military
Careers – sanitation workers
Careers – scientists
Careers – sheriffs
Careers – shoemakers
Careers – singers
Careers – soldiers *see* Careers –
  military

Careers – tailors
Careers – teachers
Careers – weather reporters *see*
  Careers – meteorologists
Careers – writers
Careers – zookeepers
Caribou *see* Animals – reindeer
Carnivals *see* Fairs, festivals
Cars *see* Automobiles
Caterpillars *see* Insects –
  butterflies, caterpillars
Cave dwellers
Chanukah *see* Holidays –
  Hanukkah
Character traits
Character traits – ambition
Character traits – appearance
Character traits – assertiveness
Character traits – being
  different
Character traits – bravery
Character traits – cleanliness
Character traits – cleverness
Character traits – clumsiness
Character traits –
  compromising
Character traits – confidence
Character traits – cooperation
Character traits – courage *see*
  Character traits – bravery
Character traits – cruelty to
  animals *see* Character traits –
  kindness to animals
Character traits – curiosity
Character traits – fortune *see*
  Character traits – luck
Character traits – freedom
Character traits – generosity
Character traits – helpfulness
Character traits – hopefulness
Character traits – incentive *see*
  Character traits – ambition
Character traits – individuality
Character traits – kindness
Character traits – kindness to
  animals
Character traits – loyalty
Character traits – luck
Character traits – meanness
Character traits – optimism
Character traits – orderliness
Character traits – ostracism
  see Character traits – being
  different
Character traits – patience
Character traits –
  perfectionism
Character traits – perseverance
Character traits – persistence
Character traits – questioning
Character traits – responsibility
Character traits – selfishness

Character traits – shyness
Character traits – smallness
Character traits – vanity
Character traits – willfulness
Character traits – wisdom
Cherubs *see* Angels
Chickens *see* Birds – chickens,
  roosters
Child abuse
Children as authors
Circular tales
Circus
Cities, towns
Cleanliness *see* Character traits
  – cleanliness
Cleverness *see* Character traits –
  cleverness
Cloaks *see* Clothing – coats
Clocks, watches
Clothing
Clothing – coats
Clothing – costumes
Clothing – dresses
Clothing – hats
Clothing – scarves
Clothing – shoes
Clothing – socks
Clothing – underwear
Clowns, jesters
Clubs, gangs
Clumsiness *see* Character traits
  – clumsiness
Cold *see* Concepts – cold & heat
Collecting things *see* Behavior –
  collecting things
Communication
Communities, neighborhoods
Competition *see* Contests;
  Sibling rivalry
Compromising *see* Character
  traits – compromising
Computers
Concepts
Concepts – change
Concepts – cold & heat
Concepts – color
Concepts – counting *see*
  Counting, numbers
Concepts – opposites
Concepts – patterns
Concepts – self *see* Self-concept
Concepts – shape
Concepts – size
Concepts – speed
Confidence *see* Character traits
  – confidence
Conservation *see* Ecology
Contests
Cooking *see* Activities – baking,
  cooking
Cooks *see* Careers – chefs, cooks

Cooperation *see* Character traits – cooperation
Counting, numbers
Countries, foreign *see* Foreign lands
Country
Courage *see* Character traits – bravery
Cowboys, cowgirls
Cows *see* Animals – bulls, cows
Crafts *see* Activities – making things
Creation
Creatures *see* Monsters; Mythical creatures
Crime
Crippled *see* Disabilities – physical disabilities
Crocodiles *see* Reptiles – alligators, crocodiles
Cruelty to animals *see* Character traits – kindness to animals
Crustaceans – crabs
Crying *see* Emotions
Cumulative tales
Curiosity *see* Character traits – curiosity
Currency *see* Money

Dark *see* Night
Darkness – fear *see* Emotions – fear
Dawn *see* Morning
Day
Day care *see* School – nursery
Daydreams *see* Dreams
Days of the week, months of the year
Deafness *see* Anatomy – ears
Death
Demons *see* Monsters
Department stores *see* Stores
Detective stories *see* Careers – detectives; Mystery stories; Problem solving
Dictionaries
Diggers *see* Careers – construction workers; Machines
Diners *see* Restaurants
Dinosaurs
Disabilities
Disabilities – Asperger's
Disabilities – autism
Disabilities – blindness *see also* Anatomy – eyes
Disabilities – physical disabilities
Disabilities – stuttering
Diseases *see* Illness
Disguises

Dissatisfaction *see* Behavior – dissatisfaction
Divorce
Dragons
Dreams
Dwellings *see* Homes, houses
Dying *see* Death

Ears *see* Anatomy – ears
Earth
Eating *see* Food
Ecology
Education *see* School
Eggs
Elderly *see* Old age
Emotions
Emotions – anger
Emotions – embarrassment
Emotions – envy, jealousy
Emotions – fear
Emotions – grief
Emotions – happiness
Emotions – jealousy *see* Emotions – envy, jealousy
Emotions – loneliness
Emotions – love
Emotions – sadness
Emotions – unhappiness *see* Emotions – happiness; Emotions – sadness
Engineered books *see* Format, unusual – toy & movable books
Entertainment *see* Theater
Entrepreneur *see* Money
Environment *see* Ecology
Eskimos *see also* Indians of North America – Inuit
Ethnic groups in the U.S.
Ethnic groups in the U.S. – African Americans
Ethnic groups in the U.S. – Black Americans *see* Ethnic groups in the U.S. – African Americans
Ethnic groups in the U.S. – Cambodian Americans
Ethnic groups in the U.S. – Chinese Americans
Ethnic groups in the U.S. – Guatemalan Americans
Ethnic groups in the U.S. – Hispanic Americans
Ethnic groups in the U.S. – Irish Americans
Ethnic groups in the U.S. – Japanese Americans
Ethnic groups in the U.S. – Jewish Americans *see* Jewish culture
Ethnic groups in the U.S. – Korean Americans

Ethnic groups in the U.S. – Mexican Americans
Ethnic groups in the U.S. – Puerto Rican Americans
Ethnic groups in the U.S. – Somali Americans
Etiquette
Exercise *see* Health & fitness – exercise
Experiments *see* Science
Extraterrestrial beings *see* Aliens
Eye glasses *see* Glasses
Eyes *see* Anatomy – eyes; Glasses; Disabilities – blindness; Senses – sight

Fables *see* Folk & fairy tales
Fairies
Fairs, festivals
Fairy tales *see* Folk & fairy tales
Family life
Family life – brothers *see also* Family life; Family life – brothers & sisters; Sibling rivalry
Family life – brothers & sisters
Family life – cousins
Family life – daughters
Family life – fathers
Family life – grandfathers
Family life – grandmothers
Family life – grandparents
Family life – mothers
Family life – new sibling
Family life – parents
Family life – same-sex parents
Family life – single-parent families
Family life – sisters *see also* Family life; Family life – brothers & sisters; Sibling rivalry
Family life – stepchildren *see* Divorce; Family life – stepfamilies
Family life – stepfamilies
Family life – stepparents *see* Divorce; Family life – stepfamilies
Farms
Feathers
Feeling *see* Senses – touch
Feelings *see* Emotions
Fighting, arguing *see* Behavior – fighting, arguing
Fingers *see* Anatomy – hands
Fire
Fire engines *see* Careers – firefighters; Trucks
Fish
Fish – sharks

Fitness *see* Health & fitness
Flowers
Fold-out books *see* Format, unusual – toy & movable books
Folk & fairy tales
Food
Foreign lands
Foreign lands – Africa
Foreign lands – Arctic
Foreign lands – Argentina
Foreign lands – Austria
Foreign lands – Bavaria *see* Foreign lands – Austria
Foreign lands – Brazil
Foreign lands – Burkina Faso
Foreign lands – Cambodia
Foreign lands – Canada
Foreign lands – China
Foreign lands – Costa Rica
Foreign lands – Cuba
Foreign lands – Denmark
Foreign lands – Dominican Republic
Foreign lands – Egypt
Foreign lands – England
Foreign lands – France
Foreign lands – Galapagos Islands
Foreign lands – Gambia
Foreign lands – Ghana
Foreign lands – India
Foreign lands – Kenya
Foreign lands – Latin America
Foreign lands – Mexico
Foreign lands – Nepal
Foreign lands – Nigeria
Foreign lands – Pakistan
Foreign lands – Russia
Foreign lands – Scotland
Foreign lands – South Africa
Foreign lands – Tanzania
Foreign lands – Vietnam
Foreign lands – Zimbabwe
Foreign languages
Forest, woods
Forgetfulness *see* Behavior – forgetfulness
Forgiving *see* Behavior – forgiving
Format, unusual
Format, unusual – board books
Format, unusual – graphic novels
Format, unusual – toy & movable books
Fortune *see* Character traits – luck
Fossils
Freedom *see* Character traits – freedom
Friendship

Frogs & toads
Frontier life *see* U.S. history – frontier & pioneer life
Furniture – beds

Games
Gangs *see* Clubs, gangs
Garage sales, rummage sales
Garbage collectors *see* Careers – sanitation workers
Gardens, gardening
Gender roles
Generosity *see* Character traits – generosity
Ghosts
Giants
Gifts
Glasses
Gossip *see* Behavior – gossip, rumors
Grammar *see* Language
Graphic novels *see* Format, unusual – graphic novels
Greed *see* Behavior – greed
Grocery stores *see* Stores
Growing up *see* Behavior – growing up

Habits *see* Thumb sucking
Hair
Handicaps *see* Disabilities
Hares *see* Animals – rabbits
Health & fitness
Health & fitness – exercise
Hearing *see* Anatomy – ears
Heat *see* Concepts – cold & heat
Heavy equipment *see* Machines
Helpfulness *see* Character traits – helpfulness
Hens *see* Birds – chickens, roosters
Hibernation
Hiccups
Hiding *see* Behavior – hiding
Hiding things *see* Behavior – hiding things
Hogs *see* Animals – pigs
Holidays
Holidays – Chanukah *see* Holidays – Hanukkah
Holidays – Chinese New Year
Holidays – Christmas
Holidays – Day of the Dead
Holidays – Easter
Holidays – Groundhog Day
Holidays – Halloween
Holidays – Hanukkah
Holidays – Juneteenth
Holidays – Martin Luther King Day
Holidays – Mother's Day

Holidays – Passover
Holidays – Ramadan
Holidays – Sukkot
Holidays – Thanksgiving
Holidays – Tu B'Shevat
Holidays – Valentine's Day
Holocaust
Homes, houses
Homework
Homosexuality
Honey bees *see* Insects – bees
Hope *see* Character traits – hopefulness
Hopefulness *see* Character traits – hopefulness
Hot air balloons *see* Activities – ballooning
Houses *see* Homes, houses
Hugging
Humorous stories
Hurrying *see* Behavior – hurrying
Hygiene *see also* Character traits – cleanliness; Health & fitness

Identity *see* Self-concept
Illness
Illness – allergies
Illness – Alzheimer's
Illness – cold (disease)
Illness – mental illness
Imagination
Imagination – imaginary friends
Immigrants
Incentive *see* Character traits – ambition
Indecision *see* Behavior – indecision
Indians of North America – Inuit
Indians of North America – Pueblo
Indians, American *see* Indians of North America
Individuality *see* Character traits – individuality
Insects
Insects – ants
Insects – bees
Insects – butterflies, caterpillars
Insects – fleas
Insects – flies
Insects – grasshoppers
Insects – moths
Internet *see* Technology
Inventions
Islands

Jackets *see* Clothing – coats
Jealousy *see* Emotions – envy, jealousy
Jesters *see* Clowns, jesters
Jewish culture
Jobs *see* Careers
Jokes *see* Riddles & jokes
Jungle

Kindness *see* Character traits – kindness
Kindness to animals *see* Character traits – kindness to animals
Kissing
Kites
Knights

Lakes, ponds
Lambs *see* Animals – babies; Animals – sheep
Language
Language – sign language *see* Sign language
Languages, foreign *see* Foreign languages
Law *see* Crime
Legends *see* Folk & fairy tales
Letters, cards
Libraries *see also* Books, reading
Light, lights
Littleness *see* Character traits – smallness
Lost *see* Behavior – lost
Lost & found possessions *see* Behavior – lost & found possessions
Loyalty *see* Character traits – loyalty
Luck *see* Character traits – luck
Lullabies
Lying *see* Behavior – lying

Machines
Magic
Mail *see* Careers – postal workers; Letters, cards
Mail carriers *see* Careers – postal workers; Letters, cards
Manners *see* Etiquette
Maps
Markets *see* Stores
Marriages *see* Weddings
Masks
Math *see* Counting, numbers
Mazes
Meanness *see* Character traits – meanness
Mechanical men *see* Robots
Memories, memory

Messy *see* Behavior – messy
Metamorphosis
Middle Ages
Migration
Mimes *see* Clowns, jesters
Ministers *see* Careers – clergy
Minorities *see* Ethnic groups in the U.S.
Misbehavior *see* Behavior – misbehavior
Mistakes *see* Behavior – mistakes
Misunderstanding *see* Behavior – misunderstanding
Money
Monsters
Months of the year *see* Days of the week, months of the year
Moon
Morning
Mother Goose *see* Nursery rhymes
Motion pictures *see* Theater
Mountains
Moving
Multi-ethnic *see* Ethnic groups in the U.S.
Multiple births – twins
Mummies
Museums
Music
Musical instruments
Musical instruments – bands
Musical instruments – drums
Musical instruments – Fiddles *see* Musical instruments – violins
Musical instruments – guitars
Musical instruments – orchestras
Musical instruments – pianos
Musical instruments – trombones
Musical instruments – violins
Mystery stories
Mythical creatures
Mythical creatures – aliens *see* Aliens
Mythical creatures – mermaids, mermen
Mythical creatures – trolls
Mythical creatures – unicorns

Napping *see* Sleep
Native Americans *see* Indians of North America
Nature
Naughty *see* Behavior – misbehavior
Needing someone *see* Behavior – needing someone

Negotiation *see* Activities – trading
Neighborhoods *see* Communities, neighborhoods
Night
Ninja *see* Sports – martial arts
No text *see* Wordless
Noise, sounds
North Pole *see* Foreign lands – Arctic
Noses *see* Senses – smell
Numbers *see* Counting, numbers
Nursery rhymes
Nursery school *see* School – nursery
Nutrition *see* Food; Health & fitness

Occupations *see* Careers
Oceans *see* Sea & seashore
Octopuses
Odors *see* Senses – smell
Old age
Olympics *see* Sports – Olympics
Opossums *see* Animals – possums
Optimism *see* Character traits – optimism
Orderliness *see* Character traits – orderliness
Outer space *see* Space & space ships

Pageants *see* Theater
Painters *see* Activities – painting; Careers – artists
Panthers *see* Animals – leopards
Parades
Parks
Parks – amusement
Parrots *see* Birds – parakeets, parrots
Participation
Parties
Patience *see* Character traits – patience
Peace *see* Violence, nonviolence
Peahens *see* Birds – peacocks, peahens
Pen pals
Perfectionism *see* Character traits – perfectionism
Perseverance *see* Character traits – perseverance
Persistence *see* Character traits – persistence
Pets
Physicians *see* Careers – doctors
Picture puzzles

Pilgrims

Pioneer life *see* U.S. history – frontier & pioneer life

Pirates

Planes *see* Airplanes, airports

Planets

Plants

Plays *see* Theater

Pockets *see* Clothing

Poetry

Pollution *see* Ecology

Poltergeists *see* Ghosts

Ponds *see* Lakes, ponds

Ponies *see* Animals – horses, ponies

Poor *see* Poverty

Pop-up books *see* Format, unusual – toy & movable books

Potty training *see* Toilet training

Poverty

Prairie wolves *see* Animals – coyotes

Prayers *see* Religion

Preachers *see* Careers – clergy

Pregnancy *see* Birth

Prehistoric man *see* Cave dwellers

Prejudice

Preschool *see* School – nursery

Pretending *see* Imagination

Priests *see* Careers – clergy

Problem solving

Promptness, tardiness *see* Behavior – promptness, tardiness

Punctuality *see* Behavior – promptness, tardiness

Questioning *see* Character traits – questioning

Quilts

Rabbis *see* Careers – clergy

Race relations *see* Prejudice

Racially mixed *see* Ethnic groups in the U.S.

Railroads *see* Trains

Reading *see* Books, reading

Recycling *see* Ecology

Religion

Religion – Islam

Religion – Nativity

Religion – Noah

Remembering *see* Memories, memory

Repetitive stories *see* Cumulative tales

Reptiles

Reptiles – alligators, crocodiles

Reptiles – lizards

Reptiles – snakes

Reptiles – turtles, tortoises

Resourcefulness *see* Behavior – resourcefulness

Responsibility *see* Character traits – responsibility

Rest *see* Sleep

Restaurants

Rhyming text

Riddles & jokes

Riots *see* Violence, nonviolence

Roads

Robbers *see* Crime

Robots

Rockets *see* Space & space ships

Rocks

Roosters *see* Birds – chickens, roosters

Royalty

Royalty – kings

Royalty – princes

Royalty – princesses

Royalty – queens

Rummage sales *see* Garage sales, rummage sales

Rumors *see* Behavior – gossip, rumors

Running *see* Activities – running; Sports – racing

Running away *see* Behavior – running away

Safety

Santa Claus

Scarecrows

School

School – field trips

School – first day

School – nursery

School teachers *see* Careers – teachers

Science

Sea & seashore

Sea & seashore – beaches

Sea serpents *see* Monsters; Mythical creatures

Seashore *see* Sea & seashore – beaches

Seasons

Seasons – fall

Seasons – spring

Seasons – summer

Seasons – winter

Secrets *see* Behavior – secrets

Seeds

Seeing *see* Anatomy – eyes; Glasses; Disabilities – blindness; Senses – sight

Seeing eye dogs *see* Animals – service animals

Seeking better things *see* Behavior – seeking better things

Self-concept

Self-esteem *see* Self-concept

Self-image *see* Self-concept

Self-reliance *see* Character traits – confidence

Selfishness *see* Character traits – selfishness

Senses

Senses – sight

Senses – smell

Senses – touch

Sex instruction

Sex roles *see* Gender roles

Shaped books *see* Format, unusual

Sharing *see* Behavior – sharing

Shells *see* Sea & seashore

Ships *see* Boats, ships

Shops *see* Stores

Showing off *see* Behavior – boasting, showing off

Shows *see* Theater

Shyness *see* Character traits – shyness

Sibling rivalry

Siblings *see* Family life – brothers; Family life – brothers & sisters; Family life – sisters; Family life – stepfamilies; Sibling rivalry

Sickness *see* Health & fitness; Illness

Sight *see* Anatomy – eyes; Glasses; Disabilities – blindness; Senses – sight

Sign language

Singers *see* Careers – singers

Sisters *see* Family life – brothers & sisters; Family life – sisters; Sibling rivalry

Skating *see* Sports – ice skating; Sports – hockey

Sky

Slavery

Sleep

Sleep – snoring

Sleepovers

Sleight-of-hand *see* Magic

Smallness *see* Character traits – smallness

Smell *see* Senses – smell

Snoring *see* Noise, sounds; Sleep – snoring

Snow *see* Weather – blizzards; Weather – snow

Snow plows *see* Machines

Snowmen

Soldiers *see* Careers – military

Solitude *see* Behavior – solitude

Songs

Sounds *see* Noise, sounds
Space & space ships
Spectacles *see* Glasses
Speech *see* Disabilities – stuttering; Language
Spiders
Split page books *see* Format, unusual
Spooks *see* Ghosts
Sports
Sports – baseball
Sports – bicycling
Sports – camping *see* Camps, camping
Sports – fishing
Sports – football
Sports – gymnastics
Sports – hiking
Sports – hockey
Sports – hunting
Sports – ice skating
Sports – martial arts
Sports – Olympics
Sports – racing
Sports – sledding
Sports – soccer
Sports – swimming
Squid
Stage *see* Theater
Stars
Stealing *see* Behavior – stealing; Crime
Steam shovels *see* Machines
Steamrollers *see* Machines
Step families *see* Divorce; Family life – stepfamilies
Stepchildren *see* Divorce; Family life – stepfamilies
Stepparents *see* Divorce; Family life – stepfamilies
Stones *see* Rocks
Stores
Stories in rhyme *see* Rhyming text
Strangers *see* Behavior – talking to strangers
Streets *see* Roads
Submarines *see* Boats, ships
Subway *see* Trains
Sun
Swamps
Swapping *see* Activities – trading

Talent shows *see* Theater
Talking to strangers *see* Behavior – talking to strangers
Tall tales
Tardiness *see* Behavior – promptness, tardiness
Taxis

Teasing *see* Behavior – bullying, teasing
Technology
Teddy bears *see* Toys – bears
Teeth
Television
Telling stories *see* Activities – storytelling
Telling time *see* Clocks, watches; Time
Temper tantrums *see* Emotions – anger
Texas
Textless *see* Wordless
Theater
Thieves *see* Crime
Thumb sucking
Thunder *see* Weather – lightning, thunder; Weather – storms
Time
Toads *see* Frogs & toads
Toddlers *see* Babies, toddlers
Toilet training
Tools
Tooth fairy *see* Fairies; Teeth
Tortoises *see* Reptiles – turtles, tortoises
Towns *see* Cities, towns
Toy & movable books *see* Format, unusual – toy & movable books
Toys
Toys – balloons
Toys – bears
Toys – blocks
Toys – dolls
Toys – teddy bears *see* Toys – bears
Tractors
Traffic, traffic signs
Trains
Transportation
Trees
Trickery *see* Behavior – trickery
Tricks *see* Magic
Trucks
TV *see* Television
Twins *see* Multiple births – twins

U.S. history
U.S. history – frontier & pioneer life
Unhappiness *see* Emotions – happiness; Emotions – sadness
Unnoticed, unseen *see* Behavior – unnoticed, unseen
Unseen *see* Behavior – unnoticed, unseen
Unusual format *see* Format, unusual

Vanity *see* Character traits – vanity
Vikings
Violence, nonviolence

War
Washing machines *see* Machines
Watches *see* Clocks, watches
Water
Weather
Weather – blizzards
Weather – floods
Weather – hurricanes
Weather – lightning, thunder
Weather – rain
Weather – rainbows
Weather – snow
Weather – storms
Weather – thunder *see* Weather – lightning, thunder
Weather – wind
Weather reporters *see* Careers – meteorologists
Weddings
Weekdays *see* Days of the week, months of the year
West *see* U.S. history – frontier & pioneer life
Wheelchairs *see* Disabilities – physical disabilities
Wildlife rescue *see* Character traits – kindness to animals
Willfulness *see* Character traits – willfulness
Wisdom *see* Character traits – wisdom
Wishing *see* Behavior – wishing
Witches
Woodchucks *see* Animals – groundhogs
Woods *see* Forest, woods
Word games *see* Language
Wordless
Working *see* Activities – working; Careers
World
Worrying *see* Behavior – worrying
Wrecking machines *see* Machines
Writers *see* Careers – writers; Children as authors
Writing letters *see* Letters, cards

Yeti *see* Monsters
Yoga *see* Health & fitness – exercise

Zodiac
Zombies *see* Monsters
Zoos

Subject Guide

This is a subject-arranged guide to picture books. Under appropriate subject headings and subheadings, titles appear alphabetically by author name, or by title when author is unknown. Complete bibliographic information for each title cited will be found in the Bibliographic Guide.

ABC books

American Museum of Natural History. *ABC insects*
Bunting, Eve. *P is for pirate*
Clayton, Dallas. *A is for awesome*
Cooper, Elisha. *8, an animal alphabet*
Crowther, Robert. *Robert Crowther's pop-up dinosaur ABC*
Escoffier, Michael. *Take away the A*
Falkenstern, Lisa. *Professor Whiskerton presents Steampunk ABC*
Gutierrez, Elisa. *Letter lunch*
Hatanaka, Kellen. *Work*
Hills, Tad. *R is for Rocket*
Johnson, Stephen T. *Alphabet school*
Joyce, William. *The Numberlys*
Katz, Susan B. *ABC school's for me!*
Lewis, J. Patrick. *M is for monster*
Lobel, Anita. *Playful pigs from A to Z*
Olivera, Ramon. *ABCs on wings*
Raschka, Chris. *Alphabetabum*
Rosenthal, Amy Krouse. *Awake beautiful child*
Roussen, Jean. *Beautiful birds*
Saaf, Donald. *The ABC animal orchestra*
Schoonmaker, Elizabeth. *Square cat ABC*
Scieszka, Jon. *Race from A to Z*
Vamos, Samantha R. *Alphabet trains*
Viano, Hannah. *B is for bear*
Watkins, Adam F. *R is for robot*
White, Teagan. *Adventures with barefoot critters*

Abused children *see* Child abuse

Accidents

Byous, Shawn. *Because I stubbed my toe*
Stower, Adam. *Slam!*

Activities

Gibson, Amy. *By day, by night*

Vogel, Vin. *The thing about yetis*

Activities – babysitting

Reagan, Jean. *How to babysit a grandma*

Activities – baking, cooking

Anderson, Brian. *Monster chefs*
Argueta, Jorge. *Salsa*
Bee, William. *Stanley's diner*
Burfoot, Ella. *How to bake a book*
Denise, Anika. *Baking day at Grandma's*
Dunbar, Joyce. *Pat-a-cake baby*
Edwards, Michelle. *Max makes a cake*
Jenkins, Emily. *A fine dessert*
Kyle, Tracey. *Gazpacho for Nacho*
Livingston, A. A. *B. Bear and Lolly: catch that cookie!*
Manzano, Sonia. *Miracle on 133rd Street*
Martin, Jacqueline Briggs. *Alice Waters and the trip to delicious*
May, Eleanor. *Albert the muffin-maker*
Miller, Pat Zietlow. *Sharing the bread*
Parenteau, Shirley. *Bears and a birthday*
Peppa Pig and the vegetable garden
Tegen, Katherine. *Pink cupcake magic*

Activities – ballooning

Migy. *And away we go!*
Stead, Philip C. *Sebastian and the balloon*

Activities – bargaining *see* Activities – trading

Activities – bartering *see* Activities – trading

Activities – bathing

Anderson, Derek. *Ten pigs*
Barnett, Mac. *President Taft is stuck in the bath*
Feeney, Tatyana. *Small Elephant's bathtime*
Gershator, Phillis. *Time for a bath*
Mack, Jeff. *Who needs a bath?*
Parenteau, Shirley. *Bears in the bath*
Robinson, Michelle. *How to wash a woolly mammoth*
Russo, Marisabina. *Little Bird takes a bath*
Teckentrup, Britta. *Get out of my bath!*
Willems, Mo. *The pigeon needs a bath*

Activities – cooking *see* Activities – baking, cooking

Activities – dancing

Bloom, Suzanne. *Bear can dance!*
Capucilli, Alyssa Satin. *Tulip loves Rex*
Federle, Tim. *Tommy can't stop!*
Feiffer, Jules. *Rupert can dance*
Isadora, Rachel. *Bea in The Nutcracker*
Kirwan, Wednesday. *Baby loves to boogie!*
Litwin, Eric. *The Nuts: sing and dance in your polka-dot pants*
Proimos, James. *Waddle! waddle!*
Ray, Mary Lyn. *Deer dancer*
Riecherter, Daryn. *The Cambodian dancer*
Schofield-Morrison, Connie. *I got the rhythm*
Sif, Birgitta. *Frances Dean who loved to dance and dance*
Singer, Marilyn. *Tallulah's tap shoes*
Teague, Mark. *The sky is falling!*
Zapf, Marlena. *Underpants dance*

Activities – digging

Barnett, Mac. *Sam and Dave dig a hole*

Activities – drawing

Becker, Aaron. *Quest*
Browne, Anthony. *The little Bear book*
Carlin, Laura. *A world of your own*
Colón, Raúl. *Draw!*
Davies, Matt. *Ben draws trouble*
Dominguez, Angela. *Knit together*
Florian, Douglas. *How to draw a dragon*
Light, Kelly. *Louise loves art*
McPhail, David. *Andrew draws*
 Beatrix Potter and her paint box
Myers, Christopher. *My pen*
Russell, Natalie. *Lost for words*
Stubbs, Lisa. *Lily and Bear*

Activities – driving

Hatanaka, Kellen. *Drive*

Activities – eating *see* Food

Activities – flying

Bently, Peter. *Those magnificent sheep in their flying machine*
Biddulph, Rob. *Blown away*
Bloom, Suzanne. *Bear can dance!*
Dudley, Rebecca. *Hank has a dream*
Judge, Lita. *Flight school*
Leiter, Richard. *The flying hand of Marco B.*
Paul, Alison. *The plan*
Ryan, Candace. *Ewe and Aye*

Activities – gardening *see* Gardens, gardening

Activities – hiking

Kwan, James. *Dear Yeti*

Activities – kissing *see* Kissing

Activities – knitting

Dominguez, Angela. *Knit together*
Pomranz, Craig. *Made by Raffi*

Activities – making things

Bright, Rachel. *Love Monster and the perfect present*
Cocca-Leffler, Maryann. *A homemade together Christmas*
Hall, Kirsten. *The jacket*
Kenney, Sean. *Cool creations in 101 pieces*
Meshon, Aaron. *Tools rule!*

Activities – painting *see also* Careers – artists

Arnold, Tedd. *Vincent paints his house*
Bang, Molly. *When Sophie's feelings are really, really hurt*
Engle, Margarita. *The sky painter*
Hawkes, Kevin. *Remy and Lulu*
McPhail, David. *Beatrix Potter and her paint box*
Rhodes-Pitts, Sharifa. *Jake makes a world*

Activities – picnicking

Burningham, John. *Picnic*
Phillipps, J. C. *The Simples love a picnic*

Activities – playing

Abbot, Judi. *Train!*
Atteberry, Kevan. *Bunnies!!!*
Bertier, Anne. *Wednesday*
Best, Cari. *A perfect day for digging*
Border, Terry. *Peanut Butter and Cupcake!*
Chung, Arree. *Ninja!*
Clanton, Ben. *Rex wrecks it!*
Crum, Shutta. *Uh-oh!*
Dewdney, Anna. *Nelly Gnu and Daddy too*
Escoffier, Michael. *The day I lost my superpowers*
Garland, Sally Anne. *Share*
Gill, Deirdre. *Outside*
Gomi, Taro. *The great day*
Hannigan, Katherine. *Gwendolyn Grace*
Jenkins, Emily. *Toys meet snow*
Landström, Lena. *Pom and Pim*
 Where is Pim?
Litwin, Eric. *The Nuts*
 The Nuts: sing and dance in your polka-dot pants
Lobel, Anita. *Playful pigs from A to Z*
Lundquist, Mary. *Cat and Bunny*
McCarty, Peter. *First snow*
McClure, Nikki. *In*
McQuinn, Anna. *Leo loves baby time*
Martin, David. *Peep and Ducky: rainy day*
Murguia, Bethanie Deeney. *Zoe's jungle*
Nordling, Lee. *Shehewe*
Phelan, Matt. *Druthers*
Pilutti, Deb. *Ten rules of being a superhero*
Sattler, Jennifer. *Pig kahuna pirates!*
Schaefer, Lola M. *One busy day*
Soman, David. *Ladybug Girl and the best ever playdate*
Thomas, Shelley Moore. *No, no, kitten!*
Wohnoutka, Mike. *Little puppy and the big green monster*

Activities – reading *see* Books, reading

Activities – running

Best, Cari. *My three best friends and me, Zulay*

Activities – sewing

Brown, Monica. *Maya's blanket*
Herkert, Barbara. *Sewing stories*
Luxbacher, Irene. *Mr. Frank*

Activities – singing

Barrett, Ron. *Cats got talent*
Litwin, Eric. *The Nuts: sing and dance in your polka-dot pants*

Activities – storytelling

Benton, Jim. *The end (almost)*
Bottner, Barbara. *Miss Brooks' Story Nook (where tales are told and ogres are welcome)*
Dotlich, Rebecca Kai. *One day, the end*
Gay, Marie-Louise. *Any questions?*
Luján, Jorge. *Moví la mano / I moved my hand*
McQuinn, Anna. *Leo loves baby time*
Muth, Jon J. *Zen socks*
O'Leary, Sara. *This is Sadie*
Virján, Emma J. *What this story needs is a pig in a wig*
Zagarenski, Pamela. *The whisper*

Activities – swapping *see* Activities – trading

Activities – swimming *see* Sports – swimming

Activities – trading

Bram, Elizabeth. *Rufus the writer*
Lodding, Linda Ravin. *A gift for Mama*
Ormerod, Jan. *The baby swap*
Pham, LeUyen. *A piece of cake*
Pryor, Katherine. *Zora's zucchini*

Activities – traveling

Ashman, Linda. *Over the river and through the wood*
Buitrago, Jairo. *Two white rabbits*
Cousins, Lucy. *Maisy goes on a plane*
Holabird, Katharine. *Angelina's Cinderella*
Lloyd-Jones, Sally. *Poor Doreen*
Luzzati, Emanuele. *Three little owls*
Miller, Pat Zietlow. *Wherever you go*
Na, Il Sung. *Welcome home, Bear*
Stead, Philip C. *Sebastian and the balloon Special delivery*
Yoon, Salina. *Penguin's big adventure*

Activities – vacationing

Larsen, Andrew. *See you next year*
Latimer, Alex. *Stay! a top dog story*
Pearlman, Robb. *Groundhog's day off*
Soffer, Gilad. *Duck's vacation*

Activities – walking

Lawson, Jonarno. *Sidewalk flowers*

Activities – whistling

Spinelli, Jerry. *Mama Seeton's whistle*

Activities – working

Aesop. *The grasshopper and the ants*

Activities – writing

Auch, Mary Jane. *The buk buk buk festival*
Bram, Elizabeth. *Rufus the writer*
Dotlich, Rebecca Kai. *One day, the end*
Graham, Joan Bransfield. *The poem that will not end*
Joyce, William. *Billy's booger*
McNamara, Margaret. *A poem in your pocket*
Palatini, Margie. *Under a pig tree*
Polacco, Patricia. *An A from Miss Keller*
Saltzberg, Barney. *Inside this book (are three books)*
Sís, Peter. *Ice cream summer*
Tullet, Hervé. *Help! we need a title!*

Adoption

Dyckman, Ame. *Wolfie the bunny*
Gliori, Debi. *Dragon's extraordinary egg*
Tupper Ling, Nancy. *The story I'll tell*

Aged *see* Old age

Airplanes, airports

Bently, Peter. *Those magnificent sheep in their flying machine*
Cousins, Lucy. *Maisy goes on a plane*
Floca, Brian. *Five trucks*
Green, Rod. *Giant vehicles*
Light, Steve. *Planes go*
Olivera, Ramon. *ABCs on wings*
Paul, Alison. *The plan*
Poletti, Frances. *Miss Todd and her wonderful flying machine*

Alaska

London, Jonathan. *Little Puffin's first flight*

Aliens

Dolan, Elys. *Nuts in space*
Sanders, Rob. *Outer space bedtime race*
Sauer, Tammi. *Your alien*
Slack, Michael. *Wazdot?*

Alphabet books *see* ABC books

Ambition *see* Character traits – ambition

American Indians *see* Indians of North America

Amusement parks *see* Parks – amusement

Anatomy

Bottner, Barbara. *Feet go to sleep*
Harrington, Tim. *Nose to toes, you are yummy!*
Jenkins, Steve. *Creature features*
Kudlinski, Kathleen V. *Boy, were we wrong about the human body!*

Anatomy – ears

McCarthy, Meghan. *Earmuffs for everyone!*

Anatomy – eyes

Jenkins, Steve. *Eye to eye*

Anatomy – hands

Otoshi, Kathryn. *Beautiful hands*
Shannon, George. *Hands say love*

Anatomy – skin

Manushkin, Fran. *Happy in our skin*

Anatomy – tails

Sandu, Anca. *Churchill's tale of tails*

Anatomy – teeth *see* Teeth

Anatomy – thumbs *see* Thumb sucking

Anatomy – toes

Byous, Shawn. *Because I stubbed my toe*
Hood, Susan. *Tickly toes*

Angels

McGhee, Alison. *Star bright*

Animals *see also* Birds; Frogs & toads; Reptiles

Arndt, Michael. *Cat says meow and other animalopoeia*
Arnold, Marsha Diane. *Lost. found*
Arnold, Tedd. *Vincent paints his house*
Aston, Dianna Hutts. *A nest is noisy*
Barner, Bob. *Sea bones*
Barton, Byron. *My bus*
Beaumont, Karen. *Wild about us!*
Berkes, Marianne. *Over on a mountain*
Biddulph, Rob. *Blown away*
Bijsterbosch, Anita. *Whose hat is that?*
Bleiman, Andrew. *1-2-3 zooborns!*
Boyd, Lizi. *Big bear little chair*
Brett, Jan. *The animals' Santa*
    The turnip
Bunting, Eve. *Whose shoe?*
Burningham, John. *The way to the zoo*
Cabrera, Jane. *Row, row, row your boat*
Carle, Eric, et al. *What's your favorite animal?*
Chapman, Jane. *No more cuddles!*
Chicken Little. *Brave Chicken Little*
Chiew, Suzanne. *When you need a friend*
Colón, Raúl. *Draw!*
Cooper, Elisha. *8, an animal alphabet*
Cronin, Doreen. *Boom Snot Twitty*

Boom, Snot, Twitty, this way that way
    Click, clack, ho! ho! ho!
Deak, Erzsi. *Pumpkin time!*
dePaola, Tomie. *Jack*
Duke, Kate. *In the rainforest*
Ferri, Giuliano. *Peekaboo*
FitzSimmons, David. *Curious critters, vol. 2*
Florian, Douglas. *I love my hat*
Franco, Betsy. *A spectacular selection of sea critters*
Freeman, Tor. *Olive and the embarrassing gift*
Gehl, Laura. *One big pair of underwear*
Hacohen, Dean. *Who's hungry?*
Harrington, Tim. *Nose to toes, you are yummy!*
Henkes, Kevin. *Waiting*
Hillenbrand, Will. *Down by the barn*
Hissey, Jane. *Jolly snow*
Jenkins, Steve. *Creature features*
    Eye to eye
    How to swallow a pig
Johnston, Tony. *Winter is coming*
Kang, Anna. *That's not mine*
Kasza, Keiko. *Finders keepers*
Kennedy, Anne Vittur. *The farmer's away! baa! neigh!*
Kirk, Daniel. *The thing about spring*
Kohara, Kazuno. *The Midnight Library*
Lang, Suzanne. *Families, families, families!*
Latham, Irene. *Dear Wandering Wildebeest*
Lawler, Janet. *Love is real*
Lehrhaupt, Adam. *Please, open this book!*
Litton, Jonthan. *Snip snap*
Ljungkvist, Laura. *Search and spot: animals!*
Long, Ethan. *In, over, and on (the farm)*
Long, Loren. *Little tree*
Low, William. *Daytime nighttime*
McFarland, Clive. *A bed for Bear*
McGowan, Jayme. *One bear extraordinaire*
Mack, Jeff. *Duck in the fridge*
Marino, Gianna. *Night animals*
Messner, Kate. *Tree of wonder*
Metzger, Steve. *Waiting for Santa*
Migy. *And away we go!*
Milgrim, David. *Wild feelings*
Minor, Wendell. *Daylight starlight wildlife*
Miyakoshi, Akiko. *The tea party in the woods*
Monfreid, Dorothée de. *The cake*
Moüy, Iris de. *Naptime*
Murphy, Mary. *Say hello like this!*
Nelson, Kadir. *Baby Bear*
    If you plant a seed
Old MacDonald had a farm. *Pete the Cat: Old MacDonald had a farm*
Pajalunga, Lorena V. *Yoga for kids*
Pearce, Clemency. *Three little words*
Petty, Dev. *I don't want to be a frog*
Pham, LeUyen. *A piece of cake*
Posada, Mia. *Who was here?*
Robinson, Michelle. *There's a lion in my cornflakes*
Rose, Caroline Starr. *Over in the wetlands*
Rosenthal, Betsy R. *An ambush of tigers*
Rowand, Phyllis. *It is night*
Saaf, Donald. *The ABC animal orchestra*
Sassi, Laura. *Goodnight, Ark*
Sauer, Tammi. *Ginny Louise and the school showdown*
Scheffler, Axel. *Axel Scheffler's Flip flap safari*
Schneider, Josh. *Everybody sleeps (but not Fred)*
Sheehy, Shawn. *Welcome to the neighborwood*
Sherry, Kevin. *Turtle Island*
Shuttlewood, Craig. *Who's in the tree?*

Sidman, Joyce. *Winter bees and other poems of the cold*
Sierra, Judy. *E-I-E-I-O*
Sill, Cathryn. *Forests*
Smallman, Steve. *Hiccupotamus*
Stewart, Melissa. *Beneath the sun*
Stewart, Whitney. *Meditation is an open sky*
Stockdale, Susan. *Spectacular spots*
Stoop, Naoko. *Red Knit Cap Girl and the reading tree*
Sturm, James. *Sleepless knight*
Surplice, Holly. *Peek-a-boo Bunny*
Swenson, Jamie A. *If you were a dog*
Tafuri, Nancy. *Daddy hugs*
Teague, Mark. *The sky is falling!*
Teckentrup, Britta. *Busy bunny days*
    Get out of my bath!
    The odd one out
    Where's the pair?
Thornhill, Jan. *Winter's coming*
Viano, Hannah. *B is for bear*
Virján, Emma J. *What this story needs is a pig in a wig*
Waldron, Kevin. *Panda-monium at Peek Zoo*
Walsh, Joanna. *I love Mom*
Wells, Rosemary. *Stella's Starliner*
White, Teagan. *Adventures with barefoot critters*
Willis, Jeanne. *Boa's bad birthday*
Wilson, Karma. *Bear sees colors*
Won, Brian. *Hooray for hat!*
Wood, Audrey. *The full moon at the napping house*
Zoboli, Giovanna. *The big book of slumber*
Zommer, Yuval. *The big blue thing on the hill*

Animals – apes *see* Animals – chimpanzees; Animals – gorillas; Animals – monkeys

Animals – babies

Cronin, Doreen. *Click, clack, peep!*
Faulconer, Maria. *A mom for Umande*
Howatt, Sandra J. *Sleepyheads*
Jackson, Ellen. *Beastly babies*
Judge, Lita. *Born in the wild*
Kirwan, Wednesday. *Baby loves to boogie!*
McPhail, David. *Baby Pig Pig talks*
Magoon, Scott. *Breathe*
National Wildlife Federation. *My first book of baby animals*
Yuly, Toni. *Night owl*

Animals – badgers

Chiew, Suzanne. *When you need a friend*

Animals – bats

Lies, Brian. *Bats in the band*

Animals – bears

Arnold, Marsha Diane. *Lost. found*
Asch, Frank. *Pizza*
Becker, Bonny. *A library book for Bear*
Beebe, Katy. *Brother Hugo and the bear*
Benton, Jim. *The end (almost)*
Berger, Carin. *Finding spring*
Biedrzycki, David. *Breaking news: bear alert*
Blackstone, Stella. *Bear's school day*
Blecha, Aaron. *Goodnight, Grizzle Grump!*
Bloom, Suzanne. *Alone together*

Bear can dance!
Brett, Jeannie. *Wild about bears*
Browne, Anthony. *The little Bear book*
Capucilli, Alyssa Satin. *Not this bear*
Carnesi, Monica. *Sleepover with Beatrice and Bear*
Carroll, James Christopher. *Papa's backpack*
Chaud, Benjamin. *The bear's sea escape*
    The bear's surprise
Davis, Jon. *Small Blue and the deep dark night*
Denise, Anika. *Baking day at Grandma's*
Desbordes, Astrid. *Edmond, the moonlit party*
Dodd, Emma. *The entertainer*
    When I grow up
Duval, Kathy. *A bear's year*
Foreman, Michael. *I love you, too!*
Gavin, Ciara. *Room for Bear*
Gehrmann, Katja. *Goose the bear*
Gravett, Emily. *Bear and Hare: snow!*
    Bear and Hare go fishing
Higgins, Ryan T. *Mother Bruce*
Hillenbrand, Will. *All for a dime! a Bear and Mole story*
Hudson, Katy. *Bear and Duck*
Imai, Ayano. *Mr. Brown's fantastic hat*
James, Ann. *Bird and Bear*
John, Jory. *Goodnight already!*
    I love you already!
Johnson, Mariana Ruiz. *I know a bear*
Katz, Susan B. *ABC school's for me!*
Liu, Cynthea. *Bike on, Bear!*
Livingston, A. A. *B. Bear and Lolly: off to school*
    B. Bear and Lolly: catch that cookie!
McFarland, Clive. *A bed for Bear*
McGowan, Jayme. *One bear extraordinaire*
Mack, Jeff. *Who needs a bath?*
    Who wants a hug?
Mattick, Lindsay. *Finding Winnie*
Mitton, Tony. *Snowy Bear*
Na, Il Sung. *Welcome home, Bear*
Nelson, Kadir. *Baby Bear*
Oldland, Nicholas. *Walk on the wild side*
Parenteau, Shirley. *Bears and a birthday*
    Bears in the bath
Percival, Tom. *Herman's letter*
Pilutti, Deb. *Bear and Squirrel are friends . . . yes, really!*
Pinder, Eric. *How to share with a bear*
Pinkwater, Daniel. *Bear and Bunny*
Prasadam-Halls, Smriti. *I love you night and day*
Ruzzier, Sergio. *Too busy*
Sarcone-Roach, Julia. *The bear ate your sandwich*
Skofield, James. *Bear and Bird*
Soman, David. *Three bears in a boat*
Stubbs, Lisa. *Lily and Bear*
The three bears *Goatilocks and the three bears*
Walker, Sally M. *Winnie*
Wilson, Karma. *Bear counts*
    Bear sees colors
Yoon, Salina. *Found*
    Stormy night

Animals – beavers

Bagley, Jessixa. *Boats for Papa*
Oldland, Nicholas. *Walk on the wild side*

Animals – brush wolves *see* Animals – coyotes

Animals – bulls, cows

Drummond, Ree. *Charlie and the new baby*
Esbaum, Jill. *I am cow, hear me moo!*
Raschka, Chris. *Cowy cow*

Animals – caribou *see* Animals – reindeer

Animals – cats

Allenby, Victoria. *Nat the cat can sleep like that*
Barrett, Ron. *Cats got talent*
Borando, Silvia. *Black cat, white cat*
Bramsen, Carin. *Just a duck?*
Busch, Miriam. *Lion, lion*
Dean, James. *Pete the Cat: twinkle, twinkle, little star*
   Pete the Cat and his magic sunglasses
   Pete the Cat and the bedtime blues
   Pete the Cat and the new guy
Ewert, Marcus. *Mummy cat*
Feiffer, Jules. *Rupert can dance*
Fox, Diane. *The cat, the dog, Little Red, the exploding eggs, the wolf, and Grandma*
Friedman, Laurie. *Ruby Valentine and the sweet surprise*
Gall, Chris. *Dog vs. Cat*
Gerstein, Mordicai. *The night world*
Gorbachev, Valeri. *Cats are cats*
Gravett, Emily. *Matilda's cat*
Gray, Kes. *Frog on a log?*
Grey, Mini. *Space Dog*
Hancocks, Helen. *Penguin in peril*
Harper, Charise Mericle. *Superlove*
Harrison, Hannah E. *Bernice gets carried away*
Hernandez, Leeza. *Cat napped*
Imai, Ayano. *Puss and boots*
Leathers, Philippa. *How to catch a mouse*
Lundquist, Mary. *Cat and Bunny*
Mader, C. Roger. *Tiptop cat*
Muncaster, Harriet. *I am a witch's cat*
Newgarden, Mark. *Bow-Wow's nightmare neighbors*
Newman, Lesléa. *Ketzel, the cat who composed*
Olien, Jessica. *Shark Detective!*
Pinkwater, Daniel. *Beautiful Yetta's Hanukkah kitten*
Pizzoli, Greg. *Templeton gets his wish*
Potter, Alicia. *Miss Hazeltine's Home for Shy and Fearful Cats*
Preston-Gannon, Frann. *Pepper and Poe*
Reeve, Rosie. *Training Tallulah*
Saab, Julie. *Little Lola*
Sanderson, Ruth. *A castle full of cats*
Schoonmaker, Elizabeth. *Square cat ABC*
Schwarz, Viviane. *Is there a dog in this book?*
Scotton, Rob. *Scaredy-cat, Splat!*
Stower, Adam. *Naughty kitty!*
Thomas, Shelley Moore. *No, no, kitten!*
Trimmer, Christian. *Simon's new bed*
Trukhan, Ekaterina. *Me and my cat*
Underwood, Deborah. *Here comes Santa Cat*
   Here comes the Easter Cat
   Here comes the Tooth Fairy Cat
   Here comes Valentine Cat
Verde, Susan. *You and me*
Vere, Ed. *Max the brave*
Wardlaw, Lee. *Won Ton and Chopstick*
Webb, Holly. *Little puppy lost*
Weeks, Sarah. *Glamourpuss*

Animals – chimpanzees

Browne, Anthony. *Willy's stories*

Animals – cows *see* Animals – bulls, cows

Animals – coyotes

Appelt, Kathi. *When Otis courted Mama*

Animals – deer

Ray, Mary Lyn. *Deer dancer*

Animals – dogs

Adderson, Caroline. *Norman, speak!*
Agee, Jon. *It's only Stanley*
Appelt, Kathi. *Mogie*
Barclay, Eric. *Counting dogs*
Bateman, Teresa. *Job wanted*
Beaumont, Karen. *Crybaby*
Bee, William. *Digger Dog*
Berger, Lou. *Dream dog*
Berry, Lynne. *Pig and Pug*
Bowles, Paula. *Messy Jesse*
Brenning, Juli. *Maggi and Milo*
Bridwell, Norman. *Clifford celebrates Hanukkah*
Brown, Alison. *Eddie and Dog*
Byrne, Richard. *This book just ate my dog!*
Capucilli, Alyssa Satin. *Tulip loves Rex*
Chichester Clark, Emma. *Love is my favorite thing*
Corderoy, Tracey. *Just right for two*
Cronin, Doreen. *Smick!*
Cyrus, Kurt. *Motor Dog*
Day, Alexandra. *Carl's Halloween*
DiPucchio, Kelly. *Dog days of school*
   Gaston
Drummond, Ree. *Charlie and the new baby*
Fergus, Maureen. *Buddy and Earl*
Fischer, Ellen. *Latke, the lucky dog*
Fox, Diane. *The cat, the dog, Little Red, the exploding eggs, the wolf, and Grandma*
Fox, Mem. *Nellie Belle*
Gall, Chris. *Dog vs. Cat*
Gianferrari, Maria. *Penny and Jelly*
Goodrich, Carter. *Mister Bud wears the cone*
Gordon, Domenica More. *Archie's vacation*
Grey, Mini. *Space Dog*
Hall, Kirsten. *The jacket*
Harrison, Hannah E. *Extraordinary Jane*
Hawkes, Kevin. *Remy and Lulu*
Hills, Tad. *R is for Rocket*
Horvath, James. *Work, dogs, work*
Huneck, Stephen. *Sally goes to heaven*
Hurley, Jorey. *Fetch*
Ismail, Yasmeen. *Time for bed, Fred!*
Jenkins, Emily. *The fun book of scary stuff*
Kellogg, Steven. *Pinkerton, behave!*
Kenah, Katharine. *Ferry tail*
Kennedy, Anne Vittur. *Ragweed's farm dog handbook*
Ko, Sangmi. *A dog wearing shoes*
Lane, Nathan. *Naughty Mabel*
Latimer, Alex. *Stay! a top dog story*
London, Jonathan. *Froggy gets a doggy*
McCarty, Peter. *First snow*
McCully, Emily Arnold. *Strongheart*
McDonald, Megan. *Shoe dog*
McPhail, David. *Bad dog*

Montalván, Luis Carlos. *Tuesday tucks me in*
Murray, Alison. *Hickory dickory dog*
Newgarden, Mark. *Bow-Wow's nightmare neighbors*
Norman, Kim. *Puddle pug*
Paul, Ruth. *Bad dog, Flash*
    Go home Flash
Pizzoli, Greg. *Number one Sam*
Provensen, Alice. *Murphy in the city*
Ray, Mary Lyn. *Goodnight, good dog*
    A lucky author has a dog
Regan, Dian Curtis. *Space Boy and his dog*
Rudge, Leila. *A perfect place for Ted*
Samuels, Barbara. *Fred's beds*
Sarcone-Roach, Julia. *The bear ate your sandwich*
Sattler, Jennifer. *A Chick 'n' Pug Christmas*
Schindel, John. *The babies and doggies book*
Schneider, Josh. *Princess Sparkle-Heart gets a makeover*
Schwarz, Viviane. *Is there a dog in this book?*
Seeger, Laura Vaccaro. *Dog and Bear: tricks and treats*
Shaw, Nancy. *Sheep go to sleep*
Shyba, Jessica. *Naptime with Theo and Beau*
Singleton, Linda Joy. *Snow dog, sand dog*
Spires, Ashley. *The most magnificent thing*
Stainton, Sue. *I love dogs!*
Stanton, Karen. *Monday, Wednesday, and every other weekend*
Stein, David Ezra. *I'm my own dog*
Thompson, Laurie Ann. *My dog is the best*
Torrey, Richard. *My dog, Bob*
Trimmer, Christian. *Simon's new bed*
Trukhan, Ekaterina. *Patrick wants a dog!*
Underwood, Deborah. *Here comes Valentine Cat*
Wardlaw, Lee. *Won Ton and Chopstick*
Webb, Holly. *Little puppy lost*
Weeks, Sarah. *Glamourpuss*
Wegman, William. *Flo and Wendell explore*
Weingarten, Gene. *Me and dog*
Winters, Kari-Lynn. *Bad pirate*
Wohnoutka, Mike. *Little puppy and the big green monster*

Animals – donkeys

Bell, Cece. *I yam a donkey!*
Daly, Niki. *Thank you, Jackson*
Kornell, Max. *Me first*

Animals – elephants

Abbot, Judi. *Train!*
Brunhoff, Laurent de. *Babar on Paradise Island*
Buzzeo, Toni. *My Bibi always remembers*
    A passion for elephants
Chase, Kit. *Oliver's tree*
Cordell, Matthew. *Wish*
Curato, Mike. *Little Elliot, big city*
    Little Elliot, big family
Dodd, Emma. *Always*
Engler, Michael. *Elephantastic!*
Feeney, Tatyana. *Small Elephant's bathtime*
Fox, Mem. *Baby bedtime*
Gude, Paul. *When Elephant met Giraffe*
Javaherbin, Mina. *Elephant in the dark*
Knapman, Timothy. *Soon*
Koehler, Fred. *How to cheer up Dad*
McKee, David. *Elmer and Butterfly*
    Elmer and the flood

    Elmer and the monster
    Elmer and the whales
Mantchev, Lisa. *Strictly no elephants*
Perepeczko, Jenny. *Moses*
Stead, Philip C. *Special delivery*
Teckentrup, Britta. *Get out of my bath!*
van Lieshout, Maria. *Hopper and Wilson fetch a star*
Warnes, Tim. *The great cheese robbery*
Won, Brian. *Hooray for hat!*
Young, Cybèle. *Nancy knows*

Animals – endangered animals

Cline-Ransome, Lesa. *Whale trails, before and now*
Cotton, Katie. *Counting lions*

Animals – foxes

Bloom, Suzanne. *Alone together*
    Bear can dance!
Camcam, Princesse. *Fox's garden*
Husband, Amy. *The noisy foxes*
Migy. *And away we go!*
Pierce, Christa. *Did you know that I love you?*
Rankin, Laura. *Ruthie and the (not so) very busy day*
Stoeke, Janet Morgan. *Oh no! a fox!*
Subramaniam, Manasi. *The fox and the crow*
Wahl, Phoebe. *Sonya's chickens*

Animals – giraffes

Averbeck, Jim. *One word from Sophia*
Bender, Rebecca. *Giraffe meets Bird*
Flory, Neil. *The short giraffe*
Gude, Paul. *When Elephant met Giraffe*
O'Neill, Gemma. *Oh dear, Geoffrey!*
Sirett, Dawn. *Happy birthday Sophie!*

Animals – gnus

Dewdney, Anna. *Nelly Gnu and Daddy too*

Animals – goats

The three bears *Goatilocks and the three bears*
Yaccarino, Dan. *Billy and Goat at the state fair*

Animals – gorillas

Antony, Steve. *Betty goes bananas*
Applegate, Katherine. *Ivan*
Fairgray, Richard. *Gorillas in our midst*
Faulconer, Maria. *A mom for Umande*
Graves, Keith. *Second banana*
Mack, Jeff. *Look!*

Animals – groundhogs

Pearlman, Robb. *Groundhog's day off*

Animals – guinea pigs

Wells, Rosemary. *Felix stands tall*

Animals – hamsters

Bee, William. *Stanley the builder*
    Stanley the farmer
    Stanley's diner
    Stanley's garage

Lord, Cynthia. *Hot Rod Hamster: monster truck mania!*
Van Allsburg, Chris. *The misadventures of Sweetie Pie*

Animals – hedgehogs

Fergus, Maureen. *Buddy and Earl*
Sauer, Tammi. *Ginny Louise and the school showdown*

Animals – hippopotamuses

Fliess, Sue. *Books for me!*
London, Jonathan. *Hippos are huge!*
Smallman, Steve. *Hiccupotamus*

Animals – horses, ponies

Beaton, Kate. *The princess and the pony*
Lewin, Betsy. *Good night, Knight*

Animals – hyenas

Jantzen, Doug. *Henry Hyena, why won't you laugh?*

Animals – jaguars

Rabinowitz, Alan. *A boy and a jaguar*

Animals – kindness to *see* Character traits – kindness to animals

Animals – koalas

Dodd, Emma. *Everything*
Ferrell, Sean. *I don't like Koala*

Animals – lemurs

Preston-Gannon, Frann. *How to lose a lemur*
Ryan, Candace. *Ewe and Aye*

Animals – leopards

Landau, Orna. *Leopardpox!*

Animals – lions

Busch, Miriam. *Lion, lion*
Dubuc, Marianne. *The lion and the bird*
O'Neill, Gemma. *Monty's magnificent mane*

Animals – llamas

Dewdney, Anna. *Llama Llama Gram and Grandpa*

Animals – meerkats

O'Neill, Gemma. *Monty's magnificent mane*

Animals – mice

Alexander, Claire. *Monkey and the little one*
Bardhan-Quallen, Sudipta. *Snoring Beauty*
Becker, Bonny. *A library book for Bear*
Bright, Rachel. *Side by side*
Buehner, Caralyn. *Merry Christmas, Mr. Mouse*
Bunting, Eve. *Whose shoe?*
Burton, LeVar. *The rhino who swallowed a storm*
Christie, R. Gregory. *Mousetropolis*
Corderoy, Tracey. *I want my daddy*

Just right for two
Cousins, Lucy. *Count with Maisy, cheep, cheep, cheep!*
    Maisy goes on a plane
    Maisy goes to the movies
    Maisy plays soccer
    Maisy's Christmas tree
Curato, Mike. *Little Elliot, big city*
    Little Elliot, big family
Donofrio, Beverly. *Where's Mommy?*
Dubuc, Marianne. *Mr. Postmouse's rounds*
Falkenstern, Lisa. *Professor Whiskerton presents Steampunk ABC*
Fleming, Denise. *Go, shapes, go!*
Freedman, Deborah. *By Mouse and Frog*
Gore, Emily. *And Nick*
Grey, Mini. *Hermelin the detective mouse*
    Space Dog
Hodgkinson, Jo. *A big day for Migs*
Holabird, Katharine. *Angelina's big city ballet*
    Angelina's Cinderella
Horácek, Petr. *The mouse who ate the moon*
    A surprise for Tiny Mouse
Johnston, Tony. *First grade, here I come!*
Leathers, Philippa. *How to catch a mouse*
Long, Ethan. *Me and my big mouse*
May, Eleanor. *Albert the muffin-maker*
Molk, Laurel. *Eeny, Meeny, Miney, Mo and Flo!*
Moore, Clement Clarke. *The night before Christmas*
    'Twas the night before Christmas
Pham, LeUyen. *A piece of cake*
Puttock, Simon. *Mouse's first night at Moonlight School*
Rudy, Maggie. *I wish I had a pet*
Ruzzier, Sergio. *Two mice*
Scheffler, Axel. *Pip and Posy: the bedtime frog*
Schertle, Alice. *Such a little mouse*
Schoonmaker, Elizabeth. *Square cat ABC*
Stills, Caroline. *Mice mischief*
Tupera, Tupera. *Polar Bear's underwear*
Underwood, Deborah. *Here comes the Tooth Fairy Cat*
van Lieshout, Maria. *Hopper and Wilson fetch a star*
Walsh, Ellen Stoll. *Where is Jumper?*
Warnes, Tim. *The great cheese robbery*
Wells, Rosemary. *Sophie's terrible twos*
    Use your words, Sophie!
Wilson, Karma. *Bear counts*

Animals – migration *see* Migration

Animals – moles

Bee, William. *Stanley the farmer*
Hillenbrand, Will. *All for a dime! a Bear and Mole story*
Kuhlmann, Torben. *Moletown*
Pilcher, Steve. *Over there*

Animals – monkeys

Alexander, Claire. *Monkey and the little one*
Bloom, C. P. *The Monkey goes bananas*
Brown, Marc. *Monkey*
Choldenko, Gennifer. *Putting the monkeys to bed*
Dodd, Emma. *More and more*
Graves, Keith. *Second banana*
Hamburg, Jennifer. *Monkey and Duck quack up!*
Price, Ben Joel. *Earth space moon base*
Sebe, Masayuki. *100 hungry monkeys!*

Sehgal, Kabir. *A bucket of blessings*

Animals – moose

Bingham, Kelly. *Circle, square, Moose*
Morris, Richard T. *This is a moose*
Oldland, Nicholas. *Walk on the wild side*
Plourde, Lynn. *Merry Moosey Christmas*

Animals – muskrats

Chaconas, Dori. *Cork and Fuzz: merry merry holly
    holly*

Animals – octopuses *see* Octopuses

Animals – opossums *see* Animals – possums

Animals – orangutans

Engle, Margarita. *Orangutanka*

Animals – otters

Garton, Sam. *I am Otter*
    Otter in space
    Otter loves Halloween
London, Jonathan. *Ollie's first year*

Animals – pandas

Antony, Steve. *Please, Mr. Panda*
Dillard, Sarah. *First day at Zoo School*
Gaiman, Neil. *Chu's day at the beach*
    Chu's first day of school
Henn, Sophy. *Pom Pom Panda gets the grumps*
Latimer, Miriam. *Dear Panda*
Muth, Jon J. *Hi, Koo!*
    Zen socks
Saltzberg, Barney. *Chengdu could not, would not,
    fall asleep*
Yim, Natasha. *Goldy Luck and the three pandas*

Animals – panthers *see* Animals – leopards

Animals – pigs

Anderson, Derek. *Ten pigs*
Berry, Lynne. *Pig and Pug*
Cocca-Leffler, Maryann. *A homemade together
    Christmas*
Côté, Geneviève. *Goodnight, you*
    Starring me and you
Griswell, Kim T. *Rufus goes to sea*
Helakoski, Leslie. *Big pigs*
Kirk, Daniel. *Ten thank-you letters*
Latimer, Alex. *Pig and small*
Lobel, Anita. *Playful pigs from A to Z*
Maccarone, Grace. *The three little pigs count to 100*
McPhail, David. *Baby Pig Pig talks*
Norman, Kim. *Puddle pug*
Palatini, Margie. *Under a pig tree*
Peppa Pig and the vegetable garden
Sandu, Anca. *Churchill's tale of tails*
Sattler, Jennifer. *Pig kahuna: who's that pig?*
    Pig kahuna pirates!

Animals – platypuses

Dean, James. *Pete the Cat and the new guy*

Animals – polar bears

Bogan, Paulette. *Virgil and Owen*
Heder, Thyra. *The bear report*
Kimmel, Eric A. *Simon and the bear*
Tupera, Tupera. *Polar Bear's underwear*
Yoon, Salina. *Penguin's big adventure*

Animals – possums

Chaconas, Dori. *Cork and Fuzz: merry merry holly
    holly*
Marino, Gianna. *Night animals*

Animals – prairie wolves *see* Animals –
    coyotes

Animals – rabbits

Atteberry, Kevan. *Bunnies!!!*
Beck, Robert. *A bunny in the ballet*
Brett, Jan. *The animals' Santa*
Carnesi, Monica. *Sleepover with Beatrice and Bear*
Catrow, David. *Fun in the sun*
Chase, Kit. *Oliver's tree*
Côté, Geneviève. *Goodnight, you*
    Starring me and you
Davis, Jon. *Small Blue and the deep dark night*
DeLaporte, Bérengère. *Superfab saves the day*
Dyckman, Ame. *Wolfie the bunny*
Engle, Margarita. *Tiny rabbit's big wish*
Fleming, Candace. *Tippy-tippy-tippy, splash!*
Galbraith, Kathryn O. *Two bunny buddies*
Garland, Sally Anne. *Share*
Gershator, Phillis. *Time for a bath*
Gravett, Emily. *Bear and Hare: snow!*
    Bear and Hare go fishing
Hillenbrand, Will. *Snowman's story*
Kaplan, Michael B. *Betty Bunny loves Easter*
    Betty Bunny wants a goal
Kirk, Daniel. *Ten thank-you letters*
Lloyd-Jones, Sally. *Bunny's first spring*
Lobe, Mira. *Hoppelpopp and the best bunny*
Lobel, Anita. *Taking care of Mama Rabbit*
Lundquist, Mary. *Cat and Bunny*
Maloney, Brenna. *Ready Rabbit gets ready!*
May, Robert L. *Rudolph shines again*
Miller, Pat Zietlow. *Wherever you go*
Olson, Jennifer Gray. *Ninja bunny*
Oskarsson, Bardur. *The flat rabbit*
Patricelli, Leslie. *Hop! hop!*
Pinkwater, Daniel. *Bear and Bunny*
Prasadam-Halls, Smriti. *I love you night and day*
Russo, Marisabina. *Sophie sleeps over*
Scheffler, Axel. *Pip and Posy: the bedtime frog*
Sterling, Cheryl. *Some bunny to talk to*
Sternberg, Julie. *Bedtime at Bessie and Lil's*
Surplice, Holly. *Peek-a-boo Bunny*
Teckentrup, Britta. *Busy bunny days*
Thornhill, Jan. *Winter's coming*
Trasler, Janee. *Mimi and Bear in the snow*
Wells, Rosemary. *Max and Ruby at the Warthogs'
    wedding*
Weninger, Brigitte. *Davy loves his mommy*
    Happy Easter, Davy!

Animals – raccoons

Castillo, Lauren. *The troublemaker*
Percival, Tom. *Herman's letter*
Plant, David J. *Hungry Roscoe*

Animals – reindeer

May, Robert L. *Rudolph shines again*
Plourde, Lynn. *Merry Moosey Christmas*

Animals – rhinoceros

Burton, LeVar. *The rhino who swallowed a storm*
Coat, Janik. *Rhymoceros*
Ross, Tony. *Rita's rhino*

Animals – seals

Cox, Lynne. *Elizabeth, queen of the seas*

Animals – service animals

Appelt, Kathi. *Mogie*
Montalván, Luis Carlos. *Tuesday tucks me in*

Animals – sheep

Bently, Peter. *Those magnificent sheep in their flying machine*
Cabrera, Jane. *Baa, baa, black sheep*
Chin, Oliver. *The year of the sheep*
Dumont, Jean-François. *The sheep go on strike*
Ryan, Candace. *Ewe and Aye*
Shaw, Nancy. *Sheep go to sleep*
Twohy, Mike. *Wake up, Rupert!*

Animals – shrews

Macaulay, David. *How machines work: zoo break!*
Pilcher, Steve. *Over there*

Animals – skunks

Barnett, Mac. *The skunk*
Hillenbrand, Will. *All for a dime! a Bear and Mole story*
Mack, Jeff. *Who needs a bath?*
　Who wants a hug?

Animals – sloths

Berger, Samantha. *Snoozefest at the Nuzzledome*
Macaulay, David. *How machines work: zoo break!*
Offill, Jenny. *Sparky!*

Animals – slugs

Willis, Jeanne. *Slug needs a hug!*

Animals – snow leopards *see* Animals – leopards

Animals – squid *see* Squid

Animals – squirrels

Desbordes, Astrid. *Edmond, the moonlit party*
Hall, Pamela. *Miss you like crazy*
Kasza, Keiko. *Finders keepers*
McClurkan, Rob. *Aw, nuts!*
Ohi, Debbie Ridpath. *Where are my books?*
OHora, Zachariah. *My cousin Momo*
Pilutti, Deb. *Bear and Squirrel are friends . . . yes, really!*
Rose, Nancy. *Merry Christmas, squirrels!*
　The secret life of squirrels

Animals – swine *see* Animals – pigs

Animals – tapirs

Russell, Natalie. *Lost for words*

Animals – tigers

Gorbachev, Valeri. *Cats are cats*
Stower, Adam. *Naughty kitty!*
Turnbull, Victoria. *The sea tiger*

Animals – voles

Bright, Rachel. *Side by side*

Animals – walruses

Savage, Stephen. *Where's Walrus? and Penguin?*

Animals – warthogs

Wallace, Nancy Elizabeth. *Water! water! water!*

Animals – weasels

Dolan, Elys. *Weasels*
Ruzzier, Sergio. *A letter for Leo*

Animals – whales

Burleigh, Robert. *Trapped! a whale's rescue*
Cline-Ransome, Lesa. *Whale trails, before and now*
Heinz, Brian. *Mocha Dick*
McKee, David. *Elmer and the whales*
Magoon, Scott. *Breathe*
Marino, Gianna. *Following Papa's song*
Yolen, Jane. *The stranded whale*

Animals – wolves

Anderson, Derek. *Ten pigs*
Carey, Lorraine. *Cinderella's stepsister and the big bad wolf*
Chapman, Jared. *Steve, raised by wolves*
Dyckman, Ame. *Wolfie the bunny*
Elya, Susan Middleton. *Little Roja Riding Hood*
Heapy, Teresa. *Very little Red Riding Hood*
Lazar, Tara. *Little Red Gliding Hood*
London, Jonathan. *The seasons of Little Wolf*
Ramadier, Cédric. *Help! the wolf is coming!*
Schwartz, Corey Rosen. *Ninja Red Riding Hood*
Ts'o, Pauline. *Whispers of the wolf*

Animals – woolly mammoths

Elliott, David. *This Orq. (He say "ugh!")*
　This Orq. (He cave boy.)
Robinson, Michelle. *How to wash a woolly mammoth*

Animals – worms

Donaldson, Julia. *Superworm*

Animals – zebras

Bingham, Kelly. *Circle, square, Moose*
Rudolph, Shaina. *All my stripes*

Anti-violence *see* Violence, nonviolence

Apartments *see* Homes, houses

Appearance *see* Character traits – appearance

Arachnids *see* Spiders

Arithmetic *see* Counting, numbers

Art

Bang, Molly. *When Sophie's feelings are really, really hurt*
Burleigh, Robert. *Edward Hopper paints his world*
Carle, Eric, et al. *What's your favorite animal?*
Carlin, Laura. *A world of your own*
Daly, Cathleen. *Emily's blue period*
Ehlert, Lois. *The scraps book*
Engle, Margarita. *The sky painter*
Herkert, Barbara. *Sewing stories*
Hutchins, Hazel. *Snap!*
Light, Kelly. *Louise loves art*
MacLachlan, Patricia. *The iridescence of birds*
McPhail, David. *Beatrix Potter and her paint box*
Menchin, Scott. *Grandma in blue with red hat*
Morales, Yuyi. *Viva Frida*
Otoshi, Kathryn. *Beautiful hands*
Rhodes-Pitts, Sharifa. *Jake makes a world*
Rosenstock, Barb. *The noisy paint box*
Winter, Jeanette. *Mr. Cornell's dream boxes*
Young, Cybèle. *Some things I've lost*

Assertiveness *see* Character traits – assertiveness

Astrology *see* Zodiac

Astronauts *see* Careers – astronauts; Space & space ships

Astronomy

Sisson, Stephanie Roth. *Star stuff*

Authors *see* Careers – writers

Authors, children *see* Children as authors

Automobiles

Bee, William. *Stanley's garage*

Burleigh, Robert. *Zoom! zoom!*
Deneux, Xavier. *Vehicles*
Dotlich, Rebecca Kai. *Race car count*
Leiter, Richard. *The flying hand of Marco B.*
Pizzoli, Greg. *Number one Sam*
Sehgal, Kabir. *The wheels on the tuk tuk*
Shulevitz, Uri. *Troto and the trucks*

Autumn *see* Seasons – fall

Award-winning books *see* Caldecott award books; Caldecott award honor books

Babies, new *see* Family life – new sibling

Babies, toddlers

Ajmera, Maya. *Global baby boys*
    Global baby girls
Beaumont, Karen. *Crybaby*
Blackall, Sophie. *The baby tree*
Cordell, Matthew. *Wish*
Crum, Shutta. *Uh-oh!*
DiPucchio, Kelly. *Zombie in love 2 + 1*
DiTerlizzi, Angela. *Baby love*
Dunbar, Joyce. *Pat-a-cake baby*
Enersen, Adele. *Vincent and the night*
Fox, Mem. *Baby bedtime*
Gerber, Carole. *Tuck-in time*
Good, Jason. *Must. push. buttons!*
Hale, Bruce. *Big Bad Baby*
Heos, Bridget. *Mustache Baby meets his match*
Hood, Susan. *Mission: new baby*
    Tickly toes
Horácek, Petr. *Time for bed*
Isadora, Rachel. *Bea in The Nutcracker*
Kirwan, Wednesday. *Baby loves to boogie!*
Krensky, Stephen. *I am so brave!*
McPike, Elizabeth. *Little sleepyhead*
McQuinn, Anna. *Leo loves baby time*
Myers, Anna. *Tumbleweed Baby*
O'Connell, Rebecca. *Baby party*
Oliver, Lin. *Little poems for tiny ears*
Palatini, Margie. *No nap! yes nap!*
Roberts, Jillian. *Where do babies come from? our first talk about birth*
Rosenthal, Amy Krouse. *Little Miss, big sis*
Salerno, Steven. *Wild child*
Schindel, John. *The babies and doggies book*
Shields, Carol Diggory. *Baby's got the blues*
Ward, Lindsay. *Henry finds his word*
Weinstone, David. *Music class today!*
Yum, Hyewon. *The twins' little sister*
Zeltser, David. *Ninja baby*

Bad day *see* Behavior – bad day, bad mood

Bad mood *see* Behavior – bad day, bad mood

Ballerinas *see* Ballet; Careers – dancers

Ballet

Beck, Robert. *A bunny in the ballet*
Copeland, Misty. *Firebird*
Dempsey, Kristy. *A dance like starlight*
Holabird, Katharine. *Angelina's big city ballet*
    Angelina's Cinderella
Isadora, Rachel. *Bea in The Nutcracker*
Mayhew, James. *Ella Bella ballerina and A*
    Midsummer Night's Dream
Membrino, Anna. *I want to be a ballerina*
Singer, Marilyn. *Tallulah's tap shoes*

Balloons *see* Toys – balloons

Bayous *see* Swamps

Beaches *see* Sea & seashore – beaches

Beasts *see* Monsters

Bedtime

Allenby, Victoria. *Nat the cat can sleep like that*
Balmes, Santi. *I will fight monsters for you*
Beaumont, Karen. *Crybaby*
Bolden, Tonya. *Beautiful moon*
Bottner, Barbara. *Feet go to sleep*
Choldenko, Gennifer. *Putting the monkeys to bed*
Crowe, Caroline. *Pirates in pajamas*
Dahl, Michael. *Goodnight football*
Dean, James. *Pete the Cat and the bedtime blues*
Enersen, Adele. *Vincent and the night*
Farrell, Darren. *Thank you, Octopus*
Foreman, Michael. *I love you, too!*
Fox, Mem. *Baby bedtime*
Fredrickson, Lane. *Monster trouble!*
Gerber, Carole. *Tuck-in time*
Horácek, Petr. *Time for bed*
Howatt, Sandra J. *Sleepyheads*
Ismail, Yasmeen. *Time for bed, Fred!*
John, Jory. *Goodnight already!*
Litwin, Eric. *The Nuts*
McDonnell, Patrick. *Thank you and good night*
McFarland, Clive. *A bed for Bear*
Mack, Jeff. *Duck in the fridge*
McPike, Elizabeth. *Little sleepyhead*
Manceau, Edouard. *Tickle monster*
Matheson, Christie. *Touch the brightest star*
Potter, Giselle. *Tell me what to dream about*
Ray, Mary Lyn. *Go to sleep, little farm*
    Goodnight, good dog
Roques, Dominique. *Sleep tight, Anna Banana!*
Roscoe, Lily. *The night parade*
Rosen, Michael. *Send for a superhero!*
Rowand, Phyllis. *It is night*
Saltzberg, Barney. *Chengdu could not, would not,*
    fall asleep
Sanders, Rob. *Outer space bedtime race*
Sassi, Laura. *Goodnight, Ark*

Scheffler, Axel. *Pip and Posy: the bedtime frog*
Schneider, Josh. *Everybody sleeps (but not Fred)*
Schubert, Ingrid. *There is a crocodile under my bed*
Shaw, Nancy. *Sheep go to sleep*
Simon, Francesca. *Hello, Moon!*
Smith, Danna. *Mother Goose's pajama party*
Sperring, Mark. *Max and the won't go to bed show*
Staniszewski, Anna. *Power down, Little Robot*
Stein, David Ezra. *Tad and Dad*
Sternberg, Julie. *Bedtime at Bessie and Lil's*
Tarpley, Todd. *Beep! beep! go to sleep!*
Yarlett, Emma. *Orion and the Dark*
Yolen, Jane. *You nest here with me*
Yoon, Salina. *Stormy night*
Zoboli, Giovanna. *The big book of slumber*

Behavior

Dillon, Leo. *If kids ran the world*
Good, Jason. *Must. push. buttons!*
Rockliff, Mara. *The Grudge Keeper*

Behavior – arguing *see* Behavior – fighting, arguing

Behavior – bad day, bad mood

Dean, James. *Pete the Cat and his magic sunglasses*
Delacroix, Sibylle. *Prickly Jenny*
Harrison, Hannah E. *Bernice gets carried away*
Henn, Sophy. *Pom Pom Panda gets the grumps*
Higgins, Ryan T. *Mother Bruce*
Koehler, Fred. *How to cheer up Dad*
Rankin, Laura. *Ruthie and the (not so) very busy day*
Sattler, Jennifer. *Pig kahuna pirates!*
Smallman, Steve. *Scowl*
Wells, Rosemary. *Sophie's terrible twos*
Won, Brian. *Hooray for hat!*

Behavior – boasting, showing off

Bertier, Anne. *Wednesday*

Behavior – boredom

Fergus, Maureen. *Buddy and Earl*
Knapman, Timothy. *A monster moved in!*
Pennypacker, Sara. *Meet the Dullards*
Phelan, Matt. *Druthers*

Behavior – bossy

Bogan, Paulette. *Virgil and Owen*
dePaola, Tomie. *Strega Nona does it again*
Watkins, Rowboat. *Rude cakes*

Behavior – bullying, teasing

Brown-Wood, JaNay. *Imani's moon*
Cocca-Leffler, Maryann. *Janine*
De Kinder, Jan. *Red*
Elliott, David. *This Orq. (He say "ugh!")*
Frankel, Erin. *Nobody!*
Hoffman, Sarah. *Jacob's new dress*
Jantzen, Doug. *Henry Hyena, why won't you laugh?*
Levy, Janice. *Thomas the toadilly terrible bully*
Lynch, Jane. *Marlene, Marlene, Queen of Mean*
Pfister, Marcus. *The little moon raven*
Roberts, Justin. *The smallest girl in the smallest grade*

Sauer, Tammi. *Ginny Louise and the school showdown*
Shulevitz, Uri. *Troto and the trucks*
Wells, Rosemary. *Felix stands tall*
   Stella's Starliner

Behavior – collecting things

Corderoy, Tracey. *Just right for two*
Wellington, Monica. *My leaf book*

Behavior – dissatisfaction

Clarkson, Stephanie. *Sleeping Cinderella and other*
   princess mix-ups
DiPucchio, Kelly. *Dog days of school*
Pearlman, Robb. *Groundhog's day off*
Petty, Dev. *I don't want to be a frog*

Behavior – fighting, arguing

Bedford, David. *Two tough crocs*
Galbraith, Kathryn O. *Two bunny buddies*
Jeffers, Oliver. *The Hueys in It wasn't me*
Kang, Anna. *That's not mine*
   You are (not) small
Kaplan, Bruce Eric. *Meaniehead*
Kornell, Max. *Me first*
Monfreid, Dorothée de. *The cake*
Moüy, Iris de. *Naptime*
Nichols, Lori. *Maple and Willow together*
Otoshi, Kathryn. *Two*

Behavior – forgetfulness

Shepherd, Jessica. *Grandma*
Young, Cybèle. *Nancy knows*

Behavior – forgiving

Rockliff, Mara. *The Grudge Keeper*

Behavior – gossip, rumors

Chicken Little. *Brave Chicken Little*
Rosenberg, Liz. *What James said*

Behavior – greed

McClurkan, Rob. *Aw, nuts!*
Muth, Jon J. *Zen socks*
Rolli, Jennifer Hanson. *Just one more*
Stewart, Whitney. *A catfish tale*

Behavior – growing up

Bailey, Linda. *When Santa was a baby*
Dodd, Emma. *When I grow up*
Krensky, Stephen. *I am so brave!*
Murguia, Bethanie Deeney. *I feel five!*
Urban, Linda. *Little Red Henry*

Behavior – hiding

Joosse, Barbara. *Evermore dragon*
Surplice, Holly. *Peek-a-boo Bunny*
Walsh, Ellen Stoll. *Where is Jumper?*

Behavior – hiding things

Ross, Tony. *Rita's rhino*

Behavior – hurrying

Portis, Antoinette. *Wait*

Behavior – indecision

Seuss, Dr. *What pet should I get?*

Behavior – lost

Frazee, Marla. *The farmer and the clown*
Goodrich, Carter. *We forgot Brock!*
Grimm, Jacob and Wilhelm. *Hansel and Gretel*
Hakte, Ben. *Julia's house for lost creatures*
May, Robert L. *Rudolph shines again*
Nelson, Kadir. *Baby Bear*
Norman, Kim. *Puddle pug*
Preston-Gannon, Frann. *How to lose a lemur*
Webb, Holly. *Little puppy lost*

Behavior – lost & found possessions

Antony, Steve. *The Queen's hat*
Arnold, Marsha Diane. *Lost. found*
Bunting, Eve. *Whose shoe?*
Busch, Miriam. *Lion, lion*
Castillo, Lauren. *The troublemaker*
Davies, Matt. *Ben draws trouble*
Daywalt, Drew. *The day the crayons came home*
Fisman, Karen. *Nonna's Hanukkah surprise*
Garton, Sam. *I am Otter*
Grey, Mini. *Hermelin the detective mouse*
Hernandez, Leeza. *Cat napped*
Jackson, Alison. *When the wind blew*
Kasza, Keiko. *Finders keepers*
Ko, Sangmi. *A dog wearing shoes*
Landström, Lena. *Where is Pim?*
Light, Steve. *Have you seen my monster?*
Miyares, Daniel. *Float*
Ohi, Debbie Ridpath. *Where are my books?*
Olien, Jessica. *Shark Detective!*
Singer, Isaac Bashevis. *The parakeet named Dreidel*
Sturm, James. *Sleepless knight*
Trasler, Janee. *Mimi and Bear in the snow*
Tupera, Tupera. *Polar Bear's underwear*
Wells, Rosemary. *Max and Ruby at the Warthogs'*
   wedding
Yoon, Salina. *Found*
Young, Cybèle. *Some things I've lost*

Behavior – lying

Duddle, Johnny. *Gigantosaurus*
Miller, John. *Winston and George*

Behavior – messy

Bowles, Paula. *Messy Jesse*
Coats, Lucy. *Captain Beastlie's pirate party*
Garton, Sam. *I am Otter*
Gershator, Phillis. *Time for a bath*
Helakoski, Leslie. *Big pigs*
Hodgkinson, Leigh. *Troll swap*
Lester, Helen. *The loch mess monster*
McDonnell, Patrick. *A perfectly messed-up story*
Reynolds, Aaron. *Here comes Destructosaurus!*
Winstead, Rosie. *Sprout helps out*

Behavior – misbehavior

Bardhan-Quallen, Sudipta. *Tyrannosaurus wrecks!*
Bingham, Kelly. *Circle, square, Moose*
Castillo, Lauren. *The troublemaker*
Clanton, Ben. *Rex wrecks it!*
Cullen, Lynn. *Dear Mr. Washington*
Enersen, Adele. *Vincent and the night*
Feeney, Tatyana. *Small Elephant's bathtime*
Goodrich, Carter. *Mister Bud wears the cone*
Grant, Jacob. *Little Bird's bad word*
Hale, Bruce. *Big Bad Baby*
Hodgkinson, Jo. *A big day for Migs*
Houran, Lori Haskins. *A dozen cousins*
Ismail, Yasmeen. *Time for bed, Fred!*
Kellogg, Steven. *Pinkerton, behave!*
Koehler, Fred. *How to cheer up Dad*
Lane, Nathan. *Naughty Mabel*
LaReau, Kara. *No slurping, no burping!*
Mack, Jeff. *Duck in the fridge*
McPhail, David. *Bad dog*
Palatini, Margie. *No nap! yes nap!*
Parsley, Elise. *If you ever want to bring an alligator to school, don't!*
Paul, Ruth. *Bad dog, Flash*
    Go home Flash
Richards, Dan. *The problem with not being scared of monsters*
Schneider, Josh. *Everybody sleeps (but not Fred)*
Shea, Bob. *Dinosaur vs. Mommy*
Soman, David. *Three bears in a boat*
Sternberg, Julie. *Bedtime at Bessie and Lil's*
Tougas, Chris. *Dojo Daycare*
Underwood, Deborah. *Here comes Santa Cat*
Viorst, Judith. *Alexander, who's trying his best to be the best boy ever*
Wells, Rosemary. *Sophie's terrible twos*

Behavior – mistakes

Parr, Todd. *It's okay to make mistakes*

Behavior – misunderstanding

Brown, Peter. *My teacher is a monster! (no, I am not)*
Rosenberg, Liz. *What James said*

Behavior – naughty *see* Behavior – misbehavior

Behavior – needing someone

Rudge, Leila. *A perfect place for Ted*
Sterling, Cheryl. *Some bunny to talk to*

Behavior – potty training *see* Toilet training

Behavior – promptness, tardiness

Cali, Davide. *A funny thing happened on the way to school . . .*
Perl, Erica S. *Totally tardy Marty*

Behavior – resourcefulness

Brown, Monica. *Maya's blanket*
Cali, Davide. *I didn't do my homework because . . .*
Chapman, Jared. *Pirate, Viking, and Scientist*
Chase, Kit. *Oliver's tree*

Hakte, Ben. *Julia's house for lost creatures*
Heine, Theresa. *Chandra's magic light*
Imai, Ayano. *Puss and boots*
Macaulay, David. *How machines work: zoo break!*
McKee, David. *Elmer and the flood*
Paul, Alison. *The plan*
Pryor, Katherine. *Zora's zucchini*
Reynolds, Peter H. *Going places*
Singleton, Linda Joy. *Snow dog, sand dog*
Spires, Ashley. *The most magnificent thing*
Young, Cybèle. *Some things I've lost*
Zapf, Marlena. *Underpants dance*

Behavior – rumors *see* Behavior – gossip, rumors

Behavior – running away

Durand, Hallie. *Catch that cookie!*
Kenah, Katharine. *Ferry tail*
Savage, Stephen. *Where's Walrus? and Penguin?*

Behavior – secrets

Brandt, Lois. *Maddi's fridge*

Behavior – seeking better things

Buitrago, Jairo. *Two white rabbits*
Kimmel, Elizabeth Cody. *A taste of freedom*
Paul, Miranda. *One plastic bag*
Stone, Tanya Lee. *The house that Jane built*

Behavior – sharing

Antony, Steve. *Please, Mr. Panda*
Deedman, Heidi. *Too many toys!*
dePaola, Tomie. *Look and be grateful*
Garland, Sally Anne. *Share*
Gehl, Laura. *One big pair of underwear*
The gingerbread boy. *The Gingerbread Man loose at Christmas*
Heap, Sue. *Mine!*
Kang, Anna. *That's not mine*
Kirk, Daniel. *You are not my friend, but I miss you*
Messner, Kate. *How to read a story*
Miller, Pat Zietlow. *Sharing the bread*
Miyares, Daniel. *Pardon me!*
Muth, Jon J. *Zen socks*
Pinder, Eric. *How to share with a bear*
Rockliff, Mara. *Chik chak Shabbat*
Stoop, Naoko. *Red Knit Cap Girl and the reading tree*
Trimmer, Christian. *Simon's new bed*
Yim, Natasha. *Goldy Luck and the three pandas*

Behavior – solitude

Bloom, Suzanne. *Alone together*
McKee, David. *Elmer and the flood*

Behavior – stealing

Davies, Nicola. *The promise*
Hancocks, Helen. *Penguin in peril*
Watts, Bernadette. *The golden plate*

Behavior – talking to strangers

Heapy, Teresa. *Very little Red Riding Hood*

Schwartz, Corey Rosen. *Ninja Red Riding Hood*

Behavior – tardiness *see* Behavior – promptness, tardiness

Behavior – teasing *see* Behavior – bullying, teasing

Behavior – toilet training *see* Toilet training

Behavior – trickery

Chicken Little. *Brave Chicken Little*
Miller, John. *Winston and George*
Niemann, Christoph. *The potato king*
Subramaniam, Manasi. *The fox and the crow*
Teague, Mark. *The sky is falling!*

Behavior – unnoticed, unseen

Rudge, Leila. *A perfect place for Ted*

Behavior – wishing

Cordell, Matthew. *Wish*
DiPucchio, Kelly. *Dog days of school*
Nolen, Jerdine. *Irene's wish*
Pizzoli, Greg. *Templeton gets his wish*
Rosenthal, Amy Krouse. *I wish you more*

Behavior – worrying

Andrews, Julie. *The very fairy princess: graduation girl!*
Brown, Marc. *Monkey*
Browne, Anthony. *What if . . . ?*
Bunting, Eve. *Yard sale*
Diesen, Deborah. *The pout-pout fish goes to school*
Gaiman, Neil. *Chu's first day of school*
Gordon, Domenica More. *Archie's vacation*
Latimer, Miriam. *Dear Panda*
Marino, Gianna. *Following Papa's song*
Sterling, Cheryl. *Some bunny to talk to*

Being different *see* Character traits – being different

Bereavement *see* Death; Emotions – grief

Bible *see* Religion

Bigotry *see* Prejudice

Birds

Anholt, Laurence. *Two nests*
Aston, Dianna Hutts. *A nest is noisy*
Barnett, Mac. *Telephone*
Bender, Rebecca. *Giraffe meets Bird*
Berne, Jennifer. *Calvin, look out!*
DePalma, Mary Newell. *Two little birds*
Dubuc, Marianne. *The lion and the bird*
Elliott, David. *On the wing*

Engle, Margarita. *The sky painter*
Esbaum, Jill. *I hatched!*
Frost, Helen. *Sweep up the sun*
Grant, Jacob. *Little Bird's bad word*
Gray, Rita. *Have you heard the nesting bird?*
Han, Eun-sun. *The flying birds*
Haughton, Chris. *Shh! we have a plan*
Himmelman, John. *Noisy bird sing-along*
Imai, Ayano. *Mr. Brown's fantastic hat*
James, Ann. *Bird and Bear*
Könnecke, Ole. *You can do it, Bert!*
Miyares, Daniel. *Pardon me!*
Pierce, Christa. *Did you know that I love you?*
Portis, Antoinette. *Froodle*
Reynolds, Aaron. *Nerdy birdy*
Rose, Caroline Starr. *Over in the wetlands*
Roussen, Jean. *Beautiful birds*
Russo, Marisabina. *Little Bird takes a bath*
Ruzzier, Sergio. *A letter for Leo*
Skofield, James. *Bear and Bird*
Stewart, Melissa. *Feathers*
Ward, Jennifer. *Mama built a little nest*
Yolen, Jane. *You nest here with me*
Yuly, Toni. *Early bird*

Birds – bluebirds

Martin, David. *Peep and Ducky: rainy day*
Yankey, Lindsey. *Bluebird*

Birds – chickens, roosters

Alakija, Polly. *Counting chickens*
Auch, Mary Jane. *The buk buk buk festival*
Brett, Jan. *Cinders*
Chicken Little. *Brave Chicken Little*
Cousins, Lucy. *Count with Maisy, cheep, cheep, cheep!*
Cronin, Doreen. *Smick!*
Kishira, Mayuko. *Who's next door?*
Mathers, Petra. *When Aunt Mattie got her wings*
Paschkis, Julie. *P. Zonka lays an egg*
Pinkwater, Daniel. *Beautiful Yetta's Hanukkah kitten*
Sattler, Jennifer. *A Chick 'n' Pug Christmas*
Stanton, Elizabeth Rose. *Henny*
Stoeke, Janet Morgan. *Oh no! a fox!*
Teague, Mark. *The sky is falling!*
Twohy, Mike. *Wake up, Rupert!*
Wahl, Phoebe. *Sonya's chickens*
Walker, Anna. *Peggy*

Birds – crows

Appelt, Kathi. *Counting crows*
Subramaniam, Manasi. *The fox and the crow*

Birds – cuckoos

Roberton, Fiona. *Cuckoo!*

Birds – ducks

Bramsen, Carin. *Just a duck?*
Cronin, Doreen. *Click, clack, ho! ho! ho!*
  Click, clack, peep!
Gavin, Ciara. *Room for Bear*
Gerstein, Mordicai. *You can't have too many friends!*
Hamburg, Jennifer. *Monkey and Duck quack up!*
Hills, Tad. *Duck and Goose go to the beach*
Himmelman, John. *Duck to the rescue*
Hudson, Katy. *Bear and Duck*

John, Jory. *Goodnight already!*
    I love you already!
Long, Ethan. *The Wing Wing brothers geometry palooza!*
Lurie, Susan. *Swim, duck, swim!*
Mack, Jeff. *Duck in the fridge*
Martin, David. *Peep and Ducky: rainy day*
Mathers, Petra. *When Aunt Mattie got her wings*
Soffer, Gilad. *Duck's vacation*
Wells, Rosemary. *A visit to Dr. Duck*
Wilson, Karma. *Duddle Puck*

Birds – geese

Bloom, Suzanne. *Alone together*
    Bear can dance!
Dumont, Jean-François. *The geese march in step*
Dunrea, Olivier. *Gemma and Gus*
Gehrmann, Katja. *Goose the bear*
Higgins, Ryan T. *Mother Bruce*
Hills, Tad. *Duck and Goose go to the beach*
Wall, Laura. *Goose*
    Goose goes to school

Birds – guinea fowl

Ward, Helen. *Spots in a box*

Birds – owls

Boiger, Alexandra. *Max and Marla*
Chase, Kit. *Oliver's tree*
Desbordes, Astrid. *Edmond, the moonlit party*
Dodd, Emma. *Happy*
Kishira, Mayuko. *Who's next door?*
Luzzati, Emanuele. *Three little owls*
McClure, Nikki. *In*
Schatell, Brian. *Owl boy*
Smallman, Steve. *Scowl*
Srinivasan, Divya. *Little Owl's day*
Taylor, Sean. *Hoot owl, master of disguise*
Yuly, Toni. *Night owl*

Birds – parakeets, parrots

Friedman, Laurie. *Ruby Valentine and the sweet surprise*
Judge, Lita. *Good morning to me!*
Medina, Meg. *Mango, Abuela, and me*
Singer, Isaac Bashevis. *The parakeet named Dreidel*

Birds – peacocks, peahens

Sehgal, Kabir. *A bucket of blessings*

Birds – penguins

Ashdown, Rebecca. *Bob and Flo*
Bentley, Tadgh. *Little Penguin gets the hiccups*
Biddulph, Rob. *Blown away*
Bogan, Paulette. *Virgil and Owen*
Clayton, Dallas. *Lily the unicorn*
Corderoy, Tracey. *The magical snow garden*
Gliori, Debi. *Dragon's extraordinary egg*
Guion, Melissa. *Baby penguins love their Mama*
Hancocks, Helen. *Penguin in peril*
Idle, Molly. *Flora and the penguin*
Judge, Lita. *Flight school*
Lester, Helen. *Tacky and the haunted igloo*
Proimos, James. *Waddle! waddle!*

Rash, Andy. *Archie the daredevil penguin*
Muñoz Ryan, Pam. *Tony Baloney: buddy trouble*
Savage, Stephen. *Where's Walrus? and Penguin?*
Yoon, Salina. *Penguin and Pumpkin*
    Penguin's big adventure

Birds – pigeons

Willems, Mo. *The pigeon needs a bath*

Birds – plovers

Miller, John. *Winston and George*

Birds – puffins

London, Jonathan. *Little Puffin's first flight*

Birds – ravens

Pfister, Marcus. *The little moon raven*

Birds – robins

Hurley, Jorey. *Nest*
Rockwell, Anne. *My spring robin*

Birds – sparrows

Sheehan, Kevin. *The dandelion's tale*

Birds – toucans

Antony, Steve. *Betty goes bananas*

Birds – turkeys

Kenah, Katharine. *The very stuffed turkey*

Birds – woodpeckers

Sayre, April Pulley. *Woodpecker wham!*

Birth

Roberts, Jillian. *Where do babies come from? our first talk about birth*

Birthdays

Averbeck, Jim. *One word from Sophia*
Bach, Annie. *Monster party!*
Chapin, Tom. *The backwards birthday party*
Coats, Lucy. *Captain Beastlie's pirate party*
Dodd, Emma. *The entertainer*
Fleming, Candace. *Bulldozer's big day*
Godin, Thelma Lynne. *The hula-hoopin' queen*
Harrison, Hannah E. *Bernice gets carried away*
London, Jonathan. *Froggy's birthday wish*
Mann, Jennifer K. *Two speckled eggs*
Monroe, Chris. *Bug on a bike*
Murguia, Bethanie Deeney. *I feel five!*
Parenteau, Shirley. *Bears and a birthday*
Pham, LeUyen. *A piece of cake*
Robinson, Sharon. *Under the same sun*
Samuels, Barbara. *Fred's beds*
Sirett, Dawn. *Happy birthday Sophie!*
Viva, Frank. *Outstanding in the rain*
Wells, Rosemary. *Sophie's terrible twos*
Willis, Jeanne. *Boa's bad birthday*

Blindness *see* Disabilities – blindness; Senses – sight

Board books *see* Format, unusual – board books

Boasting *see* Behavior – boasting, showing off

Boats, ships

Bagley, Jessixa. *Boats for Papa*
Brunhoff, Laurent de. *Babar on Paradise Island*
Cabrera, Jane. *Row, row, row your boat*
Garland, Michael. *Tugboat*
Greenwood, Mark. *The Mayflower*
Kenah, Katharine. *Ferry tail*
Lyon, George Ella. *Boats float!*
Miyares, Daniel. *Float*
Ruzzier, Sergio. *Two mice*
Soman, David. *Three bears in a boat*
Virján, Emma J. *What this story needs is a pig in a wig*

Boogy man *see* Monsters

Books, reading *see also* Libraries

Auch, Mary Jane. *The buk buk buk festival*
Becker, Bonny. *A library book for Bear*
Beebe, Katy. *Brother Hugo and the bear*
Benton, Jim. *The end (almost)*
Berne, Jennifer. *Calvin, look out!*
Blatt, Jane. *Books always everywhere*
Brown, Monica. *Maya's blanket*
Browne, Anthony. *Willy's stories*
Bryant, Jen. *The right word*
Burfoot, Ella. *How to bake a book*
Byrne, Richard. *This book just ate my dog!*
Cabrera, Jane. *Baa, baa, black sheep*
Dotlich, Rebecca Kai. *One day, the end*
Driscoll, Amanda. *Duncan the story dragon*
Ehlert, Lois. *The scraps book*
Fliess, Sue. *Books for me!*
Fox, Diane. *The cat, the dog, Little Red, the exploding eggs, the wolf, and Grandma*
Gay, Marie-Louise. *Any questions?*
Griswell, Kim T. *Rufus goes to sea*
Hall, Kirsten. *The jacket*
Hopkins, Lee Bennett. *Jumping off library shelves*
John, Jory. *I will chomp you!*
Joyce, William. *Billy's booger*
Kerley, Barbara. *A home for Mr. Emerson*
Kohara, Kazuno. *The Midnight Library*
Lammle, Leslie. *Princess wannabe*
Lehrhaupt, Adam. *Please, open this book!*
McDonnell, Patrick. *A perfectly messed-up story*
Mack, Jeff. *Duck in the fridge*
    Look!
Mattick, Lindsay. *Finding Winnie*
Messner, Kate. *How to read a story*
Morrison, Toni. *Please, Louise*
Nelson, Vaunda Micheaux. *The book itch*
Novak, B. J. *The book with no pictures*
Ohi, Debbie Ridpath. *Where are my books?*
O'Leary, Sara. *This is Sadie*
Palatini, Margie. *Under a pig tree*
Rosen, Michael. *Send for a superhero!*

Saltzberg, Barney. *Inside this book (are three books)*
Slade, Suzanne. *With books and bricks*
Staake, Bob. *My pet book*
Stoop, Naoko. *Red Knit Cap Girl and the reading tree*
Tullet, Hervé. *Help! we need a title!*
Van Biesen, Koen. *Roger is reading a book*
Walker, Sally M. *Winnie*
Zagarenski, Pamela. *The whisper*

Boredom *see* Behavior – boredom

Bossy *see* Behavior – bossy

Bravery *see* Character traits – bravery

Brothers *see* Family life – brothers; Family life – brothers & sisters; Sibling rivalry

Bubbles

Rubin, Adam. *Big bad bubble*

Bugs *see* Insects

Bulldozers *see* Machines

Bullying *see* Behavior – bullying, teasing

Burros *see* Animals – donkeys

Buses

Barton, Byron. *My bus*
Cuyler, Margery. *The little school bus*
de la Peña, Matt. *Last stop on Market Street*
Deneux, Xavier. *Vehicles*
Rosen, Michael. *The bus is for us!*

Cabs *see* Taxis

Cafés *see* Restaurants

Caldecott award books

Mattick, Lindsay. *Finding Winnie*
Santat, Dan. *The adventures of Beekle*

Caldecott award honor books

Andrews, Troy. *Trombone Shorty*

Barnett, Mac. *Sam and Dave dig a hole*
Bryant, Jen. *The right word*
Castillo, Lauren. *Nana in the city*
de la Peña, Matt. *Last stop on Market Street*
Henkes, Kevin. *Waiting*
Morales, Yuyi. *Viva Frida*
Rosenstock, Barb. *The noisy paint box*
Tamaki, Mariko. *This one summer*
Weatherford, Carole Boston. *Voice of freedom*

Camouflages *see* Disguises

Camping *see* Camps, camping

Camps, camping

Côté, Geneviève. *Goodnight, you*
Coyle, Carmela LaVigna. *Do princesses make happy campers?*
Idle, Molly. *Camp Rex*
Manning, Jane. *Millie Fierce sleeps out*
Powell-Tuck, Maudie. *Pirates aren't afraid of the dark!*
Schatell, Brian. *Owl boy*
Singer, Marilyn. *I'm gonna climb a mountain in my patent leather shoes*
Sturm, James. *Sleepless knight*
Wegman, William. *Flo and Wendell explore*
Williams, Brenda. *Outdoor opposites*

Cards *see* Letters, cards

Careers

Hatanaka, Kellen. *Work*

Careers – actors

McCully, Emily Arnold. *Strongheart*

Careers – airplane pilots

Poletti, Frances. *Miss Todd and her wonderful flying machine*
Sís, Peter. *The pilot and the Little Prince*

Careers – artists *see also* Activities – painting; Art

Arnold, Tedd. *Vincent paints his house*
Burleigh, Robert. *Edward Hopper paints his world*
Ehlert, Lois. *The scraps book*
Engle, Margarita. *The sky painter*
Hanson, Faye. *The wonder*
Hawkes, Kevin. *Remy and Lulu*
MacLachlan, Patricia. *The iridescence of birds*
McPhail, David. *Beatrix Potter and her paint box*
Morales, Yuyi. *Viva Frida*
Rhodes-Pitts, Sharifa. *Jake makes a world*
Rosenstock, Barb. *The noisy paint box*
Winter, Jeanette. *Mr. Cornell's dream boxes*

Careers – astronauts

Grey, Mini. *Space Dog*
Houran, Lori Haskins. *A trip into space*
Price, Ben Joel. *Earth space moon base*

Careers – astronomers

Sisson, Stephanie Roth. *Star stuff*

Careers – authors *see* Careers – writers

Careers – bus drivers

Anstee, Ashlyn. *Are we there, Yeti?*

Careers – chefs, cooks

Anderson, Brian. *Monster chefs*
Martin, Jacqueline Briggs. *Alice Waters and the trip to delicious*
Slegers, Liesbet. *Chefs and what they do*

Careers – clergy

Beebe, Katy. *Brother Hugo and the bear*

Careers – composers

Newman, Lesléa. *Ketzel, the cat who composed*

Careers – construction workers

Bee, William. *Stanley the builder*
Buzzeo, Toni. *Whose tools?*
Horvath, James. *Work, dogs, work*
Sutton, Sally. *Construction*

Careers – cooks *see* Careers – chefs, cooks

Careers – dancers

Copeland, Misty. *Firebird*
Dempsey, Kristy. *A dance like starlight*
Membrino, Anna. *I want to be a ballerina*

Careers – detectives

Grey, Mini. *Hermelin the detective mouse*
Olien, Jessica. *Shark Detective!*
Young, Jessica. *Spy Guy*

Careers – doctors

Wells, Rosemary. *A visit to Dr. Duck*

Careers – engineers

Davis, Kathryn Gibbs. *Mr. Ferris and his wheel*
Kraft, Betsy Harvey. *The fantastic Ferris wheel*
Underwood, Deborah. *Interstellar Cinderella*

Careers – farmers

Bee, William. *Stanley the farmer*
Florian, Douglas. *I love my hat*
Frazee, Marla. *The farmer and the clown*
Old MacDonald had a farm. *Pete the Cat: Old MacDonald had a farm*
Preston-Gannon, Frann. *Dinosaur farm*
Raschka, Chris. *Give and take*

Careers – firefighters

Austin, Mike. *Fire Engine No. 9*

McMullan, Kate. *I'm brave!*

Careers – fishermen

Van, Muon. *In a village by the sea*

Careers – garbage collectors *see* Careers – sanitation workers

Careers – inventors

Davis, Kathryn Gibbs. *Mr. Ferris and his wheel*
Kraft, Betsy Harvey. *The fantastic Ferris wheel*
McCarthy, Meghan. *Earmuffs for everyone!*

Careers – librarians

Bottner, Barbara. *Miss Brooks' Story Nook (where tales are told and ogres are welcome)*

Careers – mail carriers *see* Careers – postal workers

Careers – mechanics

Bee, William. *Stanley's garage*

Careers – meteorologists

Kudlinski, Kathleen V. *Boy, were we wrong about the weather!*

Careers – military

Carroll, James Christopher. *Papa's backpack*
Montalván, Luis Carlos. *Tuesday tucks me in*
Ruth, Greg. *Coming home*
Walker, Sally M. *Winnie*

Careers – musicians

Andrews, Troy. *Trombone Shorty*
Golio, Gary. *Bird and Diz*
Richards, Keith. *Gus and me*
Ringgold, Faith. *Harlem Renaissance party*
Winter, Jonah. *How Jelly Roll Morton invented jazz*

Careers – naturalists

Smith, Matthew Clark. *Small wonders*

Careers – nurses

Demi. *Florence Nightingale*
Polacco, Patricia. *Clara and Davie*

Careers – opera singers *see* Careers – singers

Careers – painters *see* Careers – artists

Careers – photographers

Weatherford, Carole Boston. *Gordon Parks*

Careers – physicians *see* Careers – doctors

Careers – postal workers

Dubuc, Marianne. *Mr. Postmouse's rounds*
Ruzzier, Sergio. *A letter for Leo*

Careers – preachers *see* Careers – clergy

Careers – ranchers

Drummond, Ree. *Charlie and the new baby*

Careers – sailors *see* Careers – military

Careers – sanitation workers

Savage, Stephen. *Supertruck*

Careers – scientists

Buzzeo, Toni. *A passion for elephants*
Chapman, Jared. *Pirate, Viking, and Scientist*
Houran, Lori Haskins. *How to spy on a shark*
Kudlinski, Kathleen V. *Boy, were we wrong about the weather!*
Meltzer, Brad. *I am Albert Einstein*
Rabinowitz, Alan. *A boy and a jaguar*

Careers – sheriffs

Shea, Bob. *Kid Sheriff and the terrible Toads*

Careers – shoemakers

Imai, Ayano. *Puss and boots*

Careers – singers

Nolan, Nina. *Mahalia Jackson*
Weatherford, Carole Boston. *Leontyne Price*

Careers – soldiers *see* Careers – military

Careers – tailors

Aylesworth, Jim. *My grandfather's coat*
Luxbacher, Irene. *Mr. Frank*

Careers – teachers

Brown, Peter. *My teacher is a monster! (no, I am not)*
Mann, Jennifer K. *I will never get a star on Mrs. Benson's blackboard*
Polacco, Patricia. *An A from Miss Keller*
 Mr. Wayne's masterpiece
Trent, Tereai. *The girl who buried her dreams in a can*

Careers – weather reporters *see* Careers – meteorologists

Careers – writers

Bram, Elizabeth. *Rufus the writer*
Freedman, Deborah. *By Mouse and Frog*
Gay, Marie-Louise. *Any questions?*
Joyce, William. *Billy's booger*, ill. by William Joyce
 Billy's booger, ill. by William Joyce
Kerley, Barbara. *A home for Mr. Emerson*

McNamara, Margaret. *A poem in your pocket*
McPhail, David. *Beatrix Potter and her paint box*
Palatini, Margie. *Under a pig tree*
Ray, Mary Lyn. *A lucky author has a dog*
Ringgold, Faith. *Harlem Renaissance party*
Sís, Peter. *The pilot and the Little Prince*
Tullet, Hervé. *Help! we need a title!*

Careers – zookeepers

Savage, Stephen. *Where's Walrus? and Penguin?*
Waldron, Kevin. *Panda-monium at Peek Zoo*

Caribou *see* Animals – reindeer

Carnivals *see* Fairs, festivals

Cars *see* Automobiles

Caterpillars *see* Insects – butterflies, caterpillars

Cave dwellers

Elliott, David. *This Orq. (He say "ugh!")*
   This Orq. (He cave boy.)

Chanukah *see* Holidays – Hanukkah

Character traits

Kirk, Daniel. *Ten thank-you letters*
Martin, Emily Winfield. *The wonderful things you will be*

Character traits – ambition

Czajak, Paul. *Monster needs your vote*
Spires, Ashley. *The most magnificent thing*

Character traits – appearance

Beaumont, Karen. *Wild about us!*
Cohen, Jeff. *Eva and Sadie and the worst haircut ever!*
Hall, Michael. *Red: a crayon's story*
Heos, Bridget. *Mustache Baby meets his match*
Jenkins, Steve. *Creature features*
Jones, Ursula. *Beauty and the beast*
Landau, Orna. *Leopardpox!*
Lee, H. Chuku. *Beauty and the beast*
O'Neill, Gemma. *Monty's magnificent mane*
Raschka, Chris. *Crabby crab*
Willis, Jeanne. *Slug needs a hug!*

Character traits – assertiveness

Czajak, Paul. *Monster needs your vote*
Manning, Jane. *Millie Fierce sleeps out*
Wells, Rosemary. *Felix stands tall*

Character traits – being different

Carlson, Nancy. *Armond goes to a party*
Chapman, Jared. *Steve, raised by wolves*
Dean, James. *Pete the Cat and the new guy*
De Kinder, Jan. *Red*
DiPucchio, Kelly. *Gaston*

Dumont, Jean-François. *The geese march in step*
Gall, Chris. *Dog vs. Cat*
Gehrmann, Katja. *Goose the bear*
Gliori, Debi. *Dragon's extraordinary egg*
Hall, Michael. *Red: a crayon's story*
Herthel, Jessica. *I am Jazz*
Landau, Orna. *Leopardpox!*
Mann, Jennifer K. *Two speckled eggs*
Mantchev, Lisa. *Strictly no elephants*
Merino, Gemma. *The crocodile who didn't like water*
OHora, Zachariah. *My cousin Momo*
Paschkis, Julie. *P. Zonka lays an egg*
Pomranz, Craig. *Made by Raffi*
Smallman, Steve. *Scowl*
Stanton, Elizabeth Rose. *Henny*
Tarpley, Todd. *My grandma's a ninja*
Ward, Helen. *Spots in a box*
Wilson, Karma. *Duddle Puck*

Character traits – bravery

Elvgren, Jennifer. *The whispering town*
Esbaum, Jill. *I am cow, hear me moo!*
Joyce, William. *Jack Frost*
Kirk, David. *Oh so brave dragon*
McGhee, Alison. *The sweetest witch around*
McMullan, Kate. *I'm brave!*
Mader, C. Roger. *Tiptop cat*
Newgarden, Mark. *Bow-Wow's nightmare neighbors*
Pfister, Marcus. *The little moon raven*
Stein, Peter. *Little Red's riding 'hood*
Tonatiuh, Duncan. *Separate is never equal*
Vere, Ed. *Max the brave*
Winter, Jeanette. *Malala, a brave girl from Pakistan / Iqbal, a brave boy from Pakistan*

Character traits – cleanliness

Best, Cari. *A perfect day for digging*
Bunting, Eve. *Washday*
Krall, Dan. *Sick Simon*
Watt, Mélanie. *Bug in a vacuum*

Character traits – cleverness

Glaser, Linda. *Stone soup with matzoh balls*
Imai, Ayano. *Puss and boots*
Reynolds, Peter H. *Going places*
Singleton, Linda Joy. *Snow dog, sand dog*

Character traits – clumsiness

O'Neill, Gemma. *Oh dear, Geoffrey!*

Character traits – compromising

Bender, Rebecca. *Giraffe meets Bird*
Côté, Geneviève. *Starring me and you*
Dumont, Jean-François. *The sheep go on strike*
Freedman, Deborah. *By Mouse and Frog*
Gude, Paul. *When Elephant met Giraffe*
O'Connor, Jane. *Fancy Nancy and the wedding of the century*
Trimmer, Christian. *Simon's new bed*

Character traits – confidence

Diesen, Deborah. *The pout-pout fish goes to school*
Könnecke, Ole. *You can do it, Bert!*
Krumwiede, Lana. *Just Itzy*

Sif, Birgitta. *Frances Dean who loved to dance and dance*
Viorst, Judith. *And two boys booed*
Yankey, Lindsey. *Bluebird*

Character traits – cooperation

Bender, Rebecca. *Giraffe meets Bird*
Bertier, Anne. *Wednesday*
Brett, Jan. *The turnip*
Chin, Oliver. *The year of the sheep*
Clanton, Ben. *Rex wrecks it!*
Dominguez, Angela. *Knit together*
Flory, Neil. *The short giraffe*
Freedman, Deborah. *By Mouse and Frog*
Ishida, Sanae. *Little Kunoichi, the ninja girl*
Lobe, Mira. *Hoppelpopp and the best bunny*
Manzano, Sonia. *Miracle on 133rd Street*
Meshon, Aaron. *Tools rule!*
Nelson, Kadir. *If you plant a seed*
Pham, LeUyen. *A piece of cake*
Reynolds, Peter H. *Going places*
Ryan, Candace. *Ewe and Aye*
Singer, Marilyn. *Tallulah's tap shoes*
Zommer, Yuval. *The big blue thing on the hill*

Character traits – courage *see* Character
traits – bravery

Character traits – cruelty to animals *see*
Character traits – kindness to animals

Character traits – curiosity

Buzzeo, Toni. *My Bibi always remembers*
Campbell, K.G. *The mermaid and the shoe*
McGhee, Alison. *The sweetest witch around*
Meltzer, Brad. *I am Albert Einstein*

Character traits – fortune *see* Character traits
– luck

Character traits – freedom

Cooper, Floyd. *Juneteenth for Mazie*
Elvgren, Jennifer. *The whispering town*
Winter, Jeanette. *Malala, a brave girl from Pakistan / Iqbal, a brave boy from Pakistan*
Woelfle, Gretchen. *Mumbet's Declaration of Independence*

Character traits – generosity

Biedrzycki, David. *Me and my dragon: Christmas spirit*
Spinelli, Eileen. *Thankful*
Underwood, Deborah. *Here comes Santa Cat*

Character traits – helpfulness

Bloom, Suzanne. *Bear can dance!*
Brandt, Lois. *Maddi's fridge*
Brisson, Pat. *Before we eat*
Chiew, Suzanne. *When you need a friend*
Curato, Mike. *Little Elliot, big city*
de la Peña, Matt. *Last stop on Market Street*
Dillon, Leo. *If kids ran the world*

Donaldson, Julia. *Superworm*
Isabella, Jude. *The red bicycle*
Kwan, James. *Dear Yeti*
Lum, Kate. *Princesses are not just pretty*
McKee, David. *Elmer and Butterfly*
McLellan, Stephanie Simpson. *Tweezle into everything*
May, Robert L. *Rudolph shines again*
Otoshi, Kathryn. *Beautiful hands*
Rocco, John. *Blizzard*
Stone, Tanya Lee. *The house that Jane built*
Winstead, Rosie. *Sprout helps out*
Winters, Kari-Lynn. *Bad pirate*

Character traits – hopefulness

Cordell, Matthew. *Wish*
Davies, Nicola. *The promise*
Krensky, Stephen. *The last Christmas tree*

Character traits – incentive *see* Character
traits – ambition

Character traits – individuality

Auerbach, Adam. *Edda*
Beaumont, Karen. *Wild about us!*
Bloom, Suzanne. *Alone together*
Bradley, Sandra. *Henry Holton takes the ice*
Chapman, Jared. *Steve, raised by wolves*
Cocca-Leffler, Maryann. *Janine*
Desbordes, Astrid. *Edmond, the moonlit party*
DiPucchio, Kelly. *Gaston*
Dumont, Jean-François. *The geese march in step*
Gore, Emily. *And Nick*
Gutman, Dan. *Rappy the raptor*
Hodgkinson, Leigh. *Troll swap*
Jeffers, Oliver. *The Hueys in It wasn't me*
John, Jory. *I love you already!*
McPhail, David. *Brothers*
Mann, Jennifer K. *I will never get a star on Mrs. Benson's blackboard*
Meltzer, Brad. *I am Albert Einstein*
OHora, Zachariah. *My cousin Momo*
Portis, Antoinette. *Froodle*
Rim, Sujean. *Birdie's big-girl hair*
Rudge, Leila. *A perfect place for Ted*
Russell, Natalie. *Lost for words*
Stanton, Elizabeth Rose. *Henny*
Stein, David Ezra. *I'm my own dog*
Tarpley, Todd. *My grandma's a ninja*
Tillman, Nancy. *You're here for a reason*
Ward, Helen. *Spots in a box*

Character traits – kindness

Brandt, Lois. *Maddi's fridge*
de la Peña, Matt. *Last stop on Market Street*
dePaola, Tomie. *Look and be grateful*
Fields, Terri. *One good deed*
Idle, Molly. *Flora and the penguin*
Jantzen, Doug. *Henry Hyena, why won't you laugh?*
Kirk, Daniel. *Ten thank-you letters*
McDonnell, Patrick. *Thank you and good night*
Muth, Jon J. *Zen socks*
Nelson, Kadir. *If you plant a seed*
Reynolds, Aaron. *Nerdy birdy*
Roberts, Justin. *The smallest girl in the smallest grade*
Sauer, Tammi. *Ginny Louise and the school showdown*

Simon, Richard. *Oskar and the eight blessings*
Spinelli, Eileen. *Thankful*
Watkins, Rowboat. *Rude cakes*

Character traits – kindness to animals

Adderson, Caroline. *Norman, speak!*
Applegate, Katherine. *Ivan*
Burleigh, Robert. *Trapped! a whale's rescue*
Camcam, Princesse. *Fox's garden*
Capucilli, Alyssa Satin. *Tulip loves Rex*
Cox, Lynne. *Elizabeth, queen of the seas*
Daly, Niki. *Thank you, Jackson*
Dubuc, Marianne. *The lion and the bird*
Faulconer, Maria. *A mom for Umande*
Fischer, Ellen. *Latke, the lucky dog*
Hernandez, Leeza. *Cat napped*
Jay, Alison. *Out of the blue*
Johnson, Mariana Ruiz. *I know a bear*
Ko, Sangmi. *A dog wearing shoes*
McDonald, Megan. *Shoe dog*
Newman, Lesléa. *Ketzel, the cat who composed*
Perepeczko, Jenny. *Moses*
Ts'o, Pauline. *Whispers of the wolf*
Van Allsburg, Chris. *The misadventures of Sweetie Pie*

Character traits – loyalty

Jones, Ursula. *Beauty and the beast*
Lee, H. Chuku. *Beauty and the beast*

Character traits – luck

Borden, Louise. *Kindergarten luck*
Landström, Lena. *Pom and Pim*

Character traits – meanness

Sauer, Tammi. *Ginny Louise and the school showdown*

Character traits – optimism

Krosoczka, Jarrett J. *It's tough to lose your balloon*
Lloyd-Jones, Sally. *Poor Doreen*
Otoshi, Kathryn. *Beautiful hands*
Sauer, Tammi. *Ginny Louise and the school showdown*

Character traits – orderliness

Hodgkinson, Leigh. *Troll swap*
McDonnell, Patrick. *A perfectly messed-up story*

Character traits – ostracism *see* Character
traits – being different

Character traits – patience

Alakija, Polly. *Counting chickens*
Elliott, David. *Nobody's perfect*
Hannigan, Katherine. *Gwendolyn Grace*
Henkes, Kevin. *Waiting*
Muth, Jon J. *Zen socks*
Portis, Antoinette. *Wait*
Schwartz, Amy. *I can't wait!*
Usher, Sam. *Snow*

Character traits – perfectionism

Elliott, David. *Nobody's perfect*

Character traits – perseverance

Beck, Robert. *A bunny in the ballet*
Braun, Sebastien. *Whoosh and Chug!*
Corderoy, Tracey. *The magical snow garden*
Judge, Lita. *Flight school*
Kaplan, Michael B. *Betty Bunny wants a goal*
Kimmel, Elizabeth Cody. *A taste of freedom*
Krumwiede, Lana. *Just Itzy*
Polacco, Patricia. *Fiona's lace*
Singer, Marilyn. *Tallulah's tap shoes*
Slade, Suzanne. *With books and bricks*
Young, Jessica. *Spy Guy*

Character traits – persistence

Bandy, Michael S. *Granddaddy's turn*
Bloom, C. P. *The Monkey goes bananas*
Boiger, Alexandra. *Max and Marla*
Brown-Wood, JaNay. *Imani's moon*
Ishida, Sanae. *Little Kunoichi, the ninja girl*
Koehler, Lora. *The little snowplow*
Krull, Kathleen. *Hillary Rodham Clinton*
Liu, Cynthea. *Bike on, Bear!*
Ray, Mary Lyn. *A violin for Elva*
Spires, Ashley. *The most magnificent thing*
Uegaki, Chieri. *Hana Hashimoto, sixth violin*

Character traits – questioning

Blackall, Sophie. *The baby tree*
Campbell, K.G. *The mermaid and the shoe*
Chang, Victoria. *Is Mommy?*
Coyle, Carmela LaVigna. *Do princesses make happy
campers?*
Gay, Marie-Louise. *Any questions?*
Jenkins, Steve. *How to swallow a pig*
Waber, Bernard. *Ask me*

Character traits – responsibility

Godin, Thelma Lynne. *The hula-hoopin' queen*
Hakte, Ben. *Julia's house for lost creatures*
Rudy, Maggie. *I wish I had a pet*
Muñoz Ryan, Pam. *Tony Baloney: buddy trouble*
Twohy, Mike. *Wake up, Rupert!*
Watts, Bernadette. *The golden plate*
Yoon, Salina. *Found*

Character traits – selfishness

Rolli, Jennifer Hanson. *Just one more*
Watkins, Rowboat. *Rude cakes*
Winters, Kari-Lynn. *Bad pirate*

Character traits – shyness

Desbordes, Astrid. *Edmond, the moonlit party*
Hodgkinson, Jo. *A big day for Migs*
Polacco, Patricia. *Mr. Wayne's masterpiece*
Pomranz, Craig. *Made by Raffi*
Potter, Alicia. *Miss Hazeltine's Home for Shy and
Fearful Cats*
Puttock, Simon. *Mouse's first night at Moonlight
School*
Sattler, Jennifer. *Pig kahuna: who's that pig?*
Turnbull, Victoria. *The sea tiger*
Weinstone, David. *Music class today!*
Winter, Jeanette. *Mr. Cornell's dream boxes*

Character traits – smallness

Baguley, Elizabeth. *Ready, steady, ghost!*
Bentley, Jonathan. *Little big*
Brown-Wood, JaNay. *Imani's moon*
Cohen, Laurie. *The flea*
Curato, Mike. *Little Elliot, big city*
Engle, Margarita. *Tiny rabbit's big wish*
Flory, Neil. *The short giraffe*
Gore, Emily. *And Nick*
Heapy, Teresa. *Very little Red Riding Hood*
Kang, Anna. *You are (not) small*
Kimura, Ken. *999 frogs and a little brother*
Koehler, Lora. *The little snowplow*
Latimer, Alex. *Pig and small*
Pham, LeUyen. *There's no such thing as little*
Roberts, Justin. *The smallest girl in the smallest grade*
Shulevitz, Uri. *Troto and the trucks*

Character traits – vanity

DeLaporte, Bérengère. *Superfab saves the day*
dePaola, Tomie. *Strega Nona does it again*
DiPucchio, Kelly. *Everyone loves bacon*
Lum, Kate. *Princesses are not just pretty*
Weeks, Sarah. *Glamourpuss*

Character traits – willfulness

Fox, Mem. *Nellie Belle*
Maloney, Brenna. *Ready Rabbit gets ready!*
Torrey, Richard. *Ally-Saurus and the first day of school*

Character traits – wisdom

dePaola, Tomie. *Look and be grateful*
French, Vivian. *The most wonderful thing in the world*

Cherubs *see* Angels

Chickens *see* Birds – chickens, roosters

Child abuse

International Center for Assault Prevention. *My body belongs to me from my head to my toes*
Starishevsky, Jill. *My body belongs to me*

Children as authors

Saltzberg, Barney. *Inside this book (are three books)*

Circular tales

Lodding, Linda Ravin. *A gift for Mama*
Virján, Emma J. *What this story needs is a pig in a wig*

Circus

Barton, Byron. *My bike*
Chaud, Benjamin. *The bear's surprise*
Frazee, Marla. *The farmer and the clown*
Graves, Keith. *Second banana*
Harrison, Hannah E. *Extraordinary Jane*
Stills, Caroline. *Mice mischief*

Cities, towns

Bluemle, Elizabeth. *Tap tap boom boom*
Brown, Marc. *In New York*
Burleigh, Robert. *Zoom! zoom!*
Castillo, Lauren. *Nana in the city*
Christie, R. Gregory. *Mousetropolis*
Curato, Mike. *Little Elliot, big city*
de la Peña, Matt. *Last stop on Market Street*
Kuhlmann, Torben. *Moletown*
Lendroth, Susan. *Old Manhattan has some farms*
Light, Steve. *Have you seen my dragon?*
Provensen, Alice. *Murphy in the city*
Russo, Marisabina. *Little Bird takes a bath*
Sarcone-Roach, Julia. *The bear ate your sandwich*
Shuttlewood, Craig. *Through the town*
Teckentrup, Britta. *Busy bunny days*
Walker, Anna. *Peggy*

Cleanliness *see* Character traits – cleanliness

Cleverness *see* Character traits – cleverness

Cloaks *see* Clothing – coats

Clocks, watches

Chast, Roz. *Around the clock!*

Clothing

Black, Michael Ian. *Naked!*
Florian, Douglas. *I love my hat*
Hennessy, B. G. *A Christmas wish for Corduroy*
Luxbacher, Irene. *Mr. Frank*

Clothing – coats

Aylesworth, Jim. *My grandfather's coat*

Clothing – costumes

Andrews, Julie. *The very fairy princess: a spooky, sparkly Halloween*
Day, Alexandra. *Carl's Halloween*
DeLaporte, Bérengère. *Superfab saves the day*
Lester, Helen. *Tacky and the haunted igloo*
Milgrim, David. *Wild feelings*
Patricelli, Leslie. *Boo!*
Pinder, Eric. *How to share with a bear*
Scotton, Rob. *Scaredy-cat, Splat!*
Soman, David. *Ladybug Girl and the dress-up dilemma*

Clothing – dresses

Baldacchino, Christine. *Morris Micklewhite and the tangerine dress*
Hoffman, Sarah. *Jacob's new dress*

Clothing – hats

Antony, Steve. *The Queen's hat*
Bijsterbosch, Anita. *Whose hat is that?*
Freeman, Tor. *Olive and the embarrassing gift*
Hillenbrand, Will. *Snowman's story*
Imai, Ayano. *Mr. Brown's fantastic hat*

Kasza, Keiko. *Finders keepers*
Won, Brian. *Hooray for hat!*

Clothing – scarves

Arnold, Marsha Diane. *Lost. found*

Clothing – shoes

Bunting, Eve. *Whose shoe?*
Campbell, K.G. *The mermaid and the shoe*
Ko, Sangmi. *A dog wearing shoes*
McDonald, Megan. *Shoe dog*
Meyer, Susan Lynn. *New shoes*

Clothing – socks

Sohn, Tania. *Socks!*

Clothing – underwear

Chapman, Jared. *Vegetables in underwear*
Doodler, Todd H. *Veggies with wedgies*
Tupera, Tupera. *Polar Bear's underwear*
Zapf, Marlena. *Underpants dance*

Clowns, jesters

Barton, Byron. *My bike*
Frazee, Marla. *The farmer and the clown*
Jones, Ursula. *The princess who had no kingdom*

Clubs, gangs

Long, Ethan. *Fright club*

Clumsiness *see* Character traits – clumsiness

Cold *see* Concepts – cold & heat

Collecting things *see* Behavior – collecting
   things

Communication

Allen, Kathryn Madeline. *Show me happy*
Barnett, Mac. *Telephone*
Chrustowski, Rick. *Bee dance*
Roberton, Fiona. *Cuckoo!*
Wells, Rosemary. *Use your words, Sophie!*

Communities, neighborhoods

Grey, Mini. *Hermelin the detective mouse*
Manzano, Sonia. *Miracle on 133rd Street*
Ritchie, Scot. *Look where we live!*
Rockliff, Mara. *Chik chak Shabbat*

Competition *see* Contests; Sibling rivalry

Compromising *see* Character traits –
   compromising

Computers

Saltzberg, Barney. *Tea with Grandpa*

Wallmark, Laurie. *Ada Byron Lovelace and the
   thinking machine*

Concepts

Fisher, Valorie. *I can do it myself*
Pham, LeUyen. *There's no such thing as little*
Ward, Helen. *Spots in a box*

Concepts – change

Aregui, Matthias. *Before after*
Kirk, Daniel. *The thing about spring*
Long, Loren. *Little tree*
Young, Cybèle. *Some things I've lost*

Concepts – cold & heat

Stewart, Melissa. *Beneath the sun*

Concepts – color

Arnold, Tedd. *Vincent paints his house*
Baker, Keith. *Little green peas*
Bass, Jennifer Vogel. *Edible colors*
Boldt, Mike. *Colors versus shapes*
Chernesky, Felicia Sanzari. *Sugar white snow and
   evergreens*
Daywalt, Drew. *The day the crayons came home*
Hall, Michael. *It's an orange aardvark!*
   Red: a crayon's story
Horacek, Judy. *Yellow is my color star*
Hutchins, Hazel. *Snap!*
Paschkis, Julie. *P. Zonka lays an egg*
Patricelli, Leslie. *Hop! hop!*
Siddals, Mary McKenna. *Shivery shades of Halloween*
Steggall, Susan. *Colors*
Thong, Roseanne Greenfield. *Green is a chile pepper*
Tullet, Hervé. *Mix it up!*
Wilson, Karma. *Bear sees colors*

Concepts – counting *see* Counting, numbers

Concepts – opposites

Boyd, Lizi. *Big bear little chair*
Chernesky, Felicia Sanzari. *Sun above and blooms
   below*
Hatanaka, Kellen. *Drive*
Rosenthal, Marc. *Big bot, small bot*
Williams, Brenda. *Outdoor opposites*

Concepts – patterns

Goldstone, Bruce. *I see a pattern here*
Previn, Stacey. *Find spot!*

Concepts – self *see* Self-concept

Concepts – shape

Adler, David A. *Triangles*
Antony, Steve. *Green lizards vs. red rectangles*
Banks, Kate. *Max's math*
Bertier, Anne. *Wednesday*
Bingham, Kelly. *Circle, square, Moose*
Boldt, Mike. *Colors versus shapes*
Fleming, Denise. *Go, shapes, go!*

Light, Steve. *Have you seen my monster?*
Maccarone, Grace. *The three little pigs count to 100*
O'Connell, Rebecca. *Baby party*
Previn, Stacey. *Find spot!*
Rosenthal, Amy Krouse. *Friendshape*

Concepts – size

Bentley, Jonathan. *Little big*
Boyd, Lizi. *Big bear little chair*
Cohen, Laurie. *The flea*
Cole, Henry. *Big bug*
Engle, Margarita. *Tiny rabbit's big wish*
Gavin, Ciara. *Room for Bear*
Helakoski, Leslie. *Big pigs*
Kang, Anna. *You are (not) small*
Kimura, Ken. *999 frogs and a little brother*
Latimer, Alex. *Pig and small*
Long, Ethan. *Me and my big mouse*
Miura, Taro. *The big princess*
Roberts, Justin. *The smallest girl in the smallest grade*

Concepts – speed

Braun, Sebastien. *Whoosh and Chug!*
Rozier, Lucy Margaret. *Jackrabbit McCabe and the electric telegraph*

Confidence *see* Character traits – confidence

Conservation *see* Ecology

Contests

Bee, William. *Worst in show*
Godin, Thelma Lynne. *The hula-hoopin' queen*
Hamburg, Jennifer. *Monkey and Duck quack up!*
Heos, Bridget. *Mustache Baby meets his match*
Ishida, Sanae. *Little Kunoichi, the ninja girl*
Joyce, William. *Billy's booger*
Lazar, Tara. *Little Red Gliding Hood*
Lobe, Mira. *Hoppelpopp and the best bunny*
Lum, Kate. *Princesses are not just pretty*
Oldland, Nicholas. *Walk on the wild side*
Paul, Ellis. *The night the lights went out on Christmas*
Pizzoli, Greg. *Number one Sam*
Reynolds, Peter H. *Going places*
Rozier, Lucy Margaret. *Jackrabbit McCabe and the electric telegraph*
Sayres, Brianna Caplan. *Tiara Saurus Rex*
Shulevitz, Uri. *Troto and the trucks*

Cooking *see* Activities – baking, cooking

Cooks *see* Careers – chefs, cooks

Cooperation *see* Character traits – cooperation

Counting, numbers

Adler, David A. *Triangles*
Alakija, Polly. *Counting chickens*
Anderson, Derek. *Ten pigs*
Appelt, Kathi. *Counting crows*
Banks, Kate. *Max's math*

Barclay, Eric. *Counting dogs*
Barton, Byron. *My bus*
Bass, Jennifer Vogel. *Edible numbers*
Berkes, Marianne. *Over on a mountain*
Bleiman, Andrew. *1-2-3 zooborns!*
Buitrago, Jairo. *Two white rabbits*
Chernesky, Felicia Sanzari. *Cheers for a dozen ears*
Cooper, Elisha. *8, an animal alphabet*
Cotton, Katie. *Counting lions*
Cousins, Lucy. *Count with Maisy, cheep, cheep, cheep!*
Day, Nancy Raines. *What in the world?*
Dotlich, Rebecca Kai. *Race car count*
Einhorn, Edward. *Fractions in disguise*
Fisher, Valorie. *I can do it myself*
Formento, Alison. *These rocks count!*
Franceschelli, Christopher. *Countablock*
Gehl, Laura. *One big pair of underwear*
Han, Eun-sun. *The flying birds*
Jacobs, Paul DuBois. *Count on the subway*
Jane, Pamela. *Little elfie one*
Jeffers, Oliver. *The Hueys in None the number*
Joyce, William. *The Numberlys*
Ketteman, Helen. *At the old haunted house*
Light, Steve. *Have you seen my dragon?*
Long, Ethan. *The Wing Wing brothers geometry palooza!*
Maccarone, Grace. *The three little pigs count to 100*
McGrath, Barbara Barbieri. *Teddy bear addition*
May, Eleanor. *Albert the muffin-maker*
Otoshi, Kathryn. *Two*
Pallotta, Jerry. *Butterfly counting*
Preston-Gannon, Frann. *Deep deep sea*
Savage, Stephen. *Seven orange pumpkins*
Sebe, Masayuki. *100 hungry monkeys!*
Shannon, George. *One family*
Stills, Caroline. *Mice mischief*
Wallmark, Laurie. *Ada Byron Lovelace and the thinking machine*
Wilson, Karma. *Bear counts*

Countries, foreign *see* Foreign lands

Country

Christie, R. Gregory. *Mousetropolis*

Courage *see* Character traits – bravery

Cowboys, cowgirls

Little old lady who swallowed a fly. *There once was a cowpoke who swallowed an ant*
Perkins, Maripat. *Rodeo Red*
Sadler, Marilyn. *Alice from Dallas*

Cows *see* Animals – bulls, cows

Crafts *see* Activities – making things

Creation

Bible. Old Testament. Genesis. *Let there be light*

Creatures *see* Monsters; Mythical creatures

Crime

Hancocks, Helen. *Penguin in peril*
Shea, Bob. *Kid Sheriff and the terrible Toads*
Warnes, Tim. *The great cheese robbery*
Young, Jessica. *Spy Guy*

Crippled *see* Disabilities – physical disabilities

Crocodiles *see* Reptiles – alligators, crocodiles

Cruelty to animals *see* Character traits –
kindness to animals

Crustaceans – crabs

Raschka, Chris. *Crabby crab*

Crying *see* Emotions

Cumulative tales

Brendler, Carol. *Not very scary*
Brett, Jan. *The turnip*
Chicken Little. *Brave Chicken Little*
Colandro, Lucille. *There was an old lady who
swallowed a frog!*
dePaola, Tomie. *Jack*
Klostermann, Penny Parker. *There was an old
dragon who swallowed a knight*
Lendroth, Susan. *Old Manhattan has some farms*
Little old lady who swallowed a fly. *There once was a
cowpoke who swallowed an ant*
There was an old lady who swallowed a fly
There was an old mummy who swallowed a spider
Monroe, Chris. *Bug on a bike*
Old MacDonald had a farm. *Pete the Cat: Old
MacDonald had a farm*
The twelve days of Christmas. English folk song..
The twelve days of Christmas
Verburg, Bonnie. *The tree house that Jack built*
Wood, Audrey. *The full moon at the napping house*

Curiosity *see* Character traits – curiosity

Currency *see* Money

Dark *see* Night

Darkness – fear *see* Emotions – fear

Dawn *see* Morning

Day

Borando, Silvia. *Black cat, white cat*
Chast, Roz. *Around the clock!*
Gomi, Taro. *The great day*
Graham, Bob. *How the sun got to Coco's house*
Low, William. *Daytime nighttime*
Minor, Wendell. *Daylight starlight wildlife*
Rosenthal, Amy Krouse. *Awake beautiful child*
Srinivasan, Divya. *Little Owl's day*

Day care *see* School – nursery

Daydreams *see* Dreams

Days of the week, months of the year

Alakija, Polly. *Counting chickens*
Guion, Melissa. *Baby penguins love their Mama*
Leduc, Emilie. *All year round*
Preston-Gannon, Frann. *Pepper and Poe*

Deafness *see* Anatomy – ears

Death

Bagley, Jessixa. *Boats for Papa*
Hole, Stian. *Anna's heaven*
Huneck, Stephen. *Sally goes to heaven*
Mathers, Petra. *When Aunt Mattie got her wings*
Mora, Pat. *The remembering day / El día de los
muertos*
Oskarsson, Bardur. *The flat rabbit*
Polacco, Patricia. *An A from Miss Keller*
Skofield, James. *Bear and Bird*
Wahl, Phoebe. *Sonya's chickens*
Yolen, Jane. *The stranded whale*

Demons *see* Monsters

Department stores *see* Stores

Detective stories *see* Careers – detectives;
Mystery stories; Problem solving

Dictionaries

Fern, Tracey. *W is for Webster*

Diggers *see* Careers – construction workers;
Machines

Diners *see* Restaurants

Dinosaurs

Bailey, Linda. *If you happen to have a dinosaur*
Bardhan-Quallen, Sudipta. *Tyrannosaurus wrecks!*
Clanton, Ben. *Rex wrecks it!*
Climo, Liz. *Rory the dinosaur: me and my dad*

Crowther, Robert. *Robert Crowther's pop-up dinosaur ABC*
Dale, Penny. *Dinosaur rocket!*
DiSiena, Laura Lyn. *Dinosaurs live on!*
Duddle, Johnny. *Gigantosaurus*
Franceschelli, Christopher. *Dinoblock*
Gall, Chris. *Dinotrux dig the beach*
Gutman, Dan. *Rappy the raptor*
Halpern, Shari. *Dinosaur parade*
Idle, Molly. *Camp Rex*
    Sea Rex
O'Connor, George. *If I had a raptor*
    If I had a triceratops
Pett, Mark. *Lizard from the park*
Preston-Gannon, Frann. *Dinosaur farm*
Roderick, Stacey. *Dinosaurs from head to tail*
Sayres, Brianna Caplan. *Tiara Saurus Rex*
Shea, Bob. *Dinosaur vs. Mommy*
    Dinosaur vs. school
    Kid Sheriff and the terrible Toads
Weinberg, Steven. *Rex finds an egg! egg! egg!*
Wheeler, Lisa. *Dino-boarding*
    Dino-swimming
Yolen, Jane. *How do dinosaurs stay safe?*

Disabilities

Montalván, Luis Carlos. *Tuesday tucks me in*
Stockdale, Sean. *Max the champion*

Disabilities – Asperger's

Carlson, Nancy. *Armond goes to a party*

Disabilities – autism

Carlson, Nancy. *Armond goes to a party*
Rudolph, Shaina. *All my stripes*

Disabilities – blindness *see also* Anatomy – eyes

Best, Cari. *My three best friends and me, Zulay*

Disabilities – physical disabilities

Thompson, Laurie Ann. *Emmanuel's dream*

Disabilities – stuttering

Rabinowitz, Alan. *A boy and a jaguar*

Diseases *see* Illness

Disguises

Fairgray, Richard. *Gorillas in our midst*
Stockdale, Susan. *Spectacular spots*
Taylor, Sean. *Hoot owl, master of disguise*

Dissatisfaction *see* Behavior – dissatisfaction

Divorce

Appelt, Kathi. *When Otis courted Mama*
Daly, Cathleen. *Emily's blue period*
Stanton, Karen. *Monday, Wednesday, and every other weekend*

Dragons

Biedrzycki, David. *Me and my dragon: Christmas spirit*
Brunhoff, Laurent de. *Babar on Paradise Island*
Driscoll, Amanda. *Duncan the story dragon*
Florian, Douglas. *How to draw a dragon*
Gliori, Debi. *Dragon's extraordinary egg*
Hoban, Russell. *Ace Dragon Ltd*
Joosse, Barbara. *Evermore dragon*
Kirk, David. *Oh so brave dragon*
Klostermann, Penny Parker. *There was an old dragon who swallowed a knight*
Light, Steve. *Have you seen my dragon?*
Merino, Gemma. *The crocodile who didn't like water*
Sabuda, Robert. *The dragon and the knight*

Dreams

Bar-el, Dan. *A fish named Glub*
Dudley, Rebecca. *Hank has a dream*
Hanson, Faye. *The wonder*
Martin, Emily Winfield. *Day dreamers*
Potter, Giselle. *Tell me what to dream about*
Winter, Jeanette. *Mr. Cornell's dream boxes*

Dwellings *see* Homes, houses

Dying *see* Death

Ears *see* Anatomy – ears

Earth

Bang, Molly. *Buried sunlight*
Gifford, Peggy. *The great big green*

Eating *see* Food

Ecology

Austin, Mike. *Junkyard*
Isabella, Jude. *The red bicycle*
Karas, G. Brian. *As an oak tree grows*
Kuhlmann, Torben. *Moletown*
Messner, Kate. *Tree of wonder*
Paul, Miranda. *One plastic bag*
Prevot, Franck. *Wangari Maathai*
Rabinowitz, Alan. *A boy and a jaguar*
Sill, Cathryn. *Forests*
Wallace, Nancy Elizabeth. *Water! water! water!*

Education *see* School

Eggs

Higgins, Ryan T. *Mother Bruce*
Kaplan, Michael B. *Betty Bunny loves Easter*
Paschkis, Julie. *P. Zonka lays an egg*
Patricelli, Leslie. *Hop! hop!*
Schmid, Paul. *Oliver and his egg*
Weinberg, Steven. *Rex finds an egg! egg! egg!*

Elderly *see* Old age

Emotions

Allen, Kathryn Madeline. *Show me happy*
Bang, Molly. *When Sophie's feelings are really, really hurt*
Beaumont, Karen. *Crybaby*
Côté, Geneviève. *Starring me and you*
Daly, Cathleen. *Emily's blue period*
Krosoczka, Jarrett J. *It's tough to lose your balloon*
Milgrim, David. *Wild feelings*
Rockliff, Mara. *The Grudge Keeper*
Smith, A. J. *Even monsters*
Sterling, Cheryl. *Some bunny to talk to*
Stewart, Whitney. *Meditation is an open sky*
Watts, Bernadette. *The golden plate*
Yoon, Salina. *Found*

Emotions – anger

Antony, Steve. *Betty goes bananas*
Henn, Sophy. *Pom Pom Panda gets the grumps*
McDonnell, Patrick. *A perfectly messed-up story*
Rankin, Laura. *Ruthie and the (not so) very busy day*
Reynolds, Aaron. *Here comes Destructosaurus!*
Spires, Ashley. *The most magnificent thing*

Emotions – embarrassment

Carlson, Nancy. *Sometimes you barf*
Freeman, Tor. *Olive and the embarrassing gift*
Vernick, Audrey. *First grade dropout*

Emotions – envy, jealousy

Child, Lauren. *The new small person*
Drummond, Ree. *Charlie and the new baby*
Ormerod, Jan. *The baby swap*
Schneider, Josh. *Princess Sparkle-Heart gets a makeover*
Weeks, Sarah. *Glamourpuss*
Yankey, Lindsey. *Sun and Moon*

Emotions – fear

Baguley, Elizabeth. *Ready, steady, ghost!*
Balmes, Santi. *I will fight monsters for you*
Brendler, Carol. *Not very scary*
Castillo, Lauren. *Nana in the city*
Clayton, Dallas. *Lily the unicorn*
Côté, Geneviève. *Goodnight, you*
Davies, Nicola. *I (don't) like snakes*
Davis, Jon. *Small Blue and the deep dark night*
Esbaum, Jill. *I am cow, hear me moo!*
Garton, Sam. *Otter loves Halloween*
Jenkins, Emily. *The fun book of scary stuff*
Kirk, David. *Oh so brave dragon*
Lester, Helen. *Tacky and the haunted igloo*
Liniers. *What there is before there is anything there*

McKee, David. *Elmer and the monster*
Mader, C. Roger. *Tiptop cat*
Manceau, Edouard. *Tickle monster*
Marino, Gianna. *Night animals*
Morrison, Toni. *Please, Louise*
Polacco, Patricia. *Mr. Wayne's masterpiece*
Potter, Alicia. *Miss Hazeltine's Home for Shy and Fearful Cats*
Powell-Tuck, Maudie. *Pirates aren't afraid of the dark!*
Rash, Andy. *Archie the daredevil penguin*
Rim, Sujean. *Birdie's first day of school*
Rubin, Adam. *Big bad bubble*
Viorst, Judith. *And two boys booed*
Warnes, Tim. *The great cheese robbery*
Wells, Rosemary. *A visit to Dr. Duck*
Yarlett, Emma. *Orion and the Dark*
Yoon, Salina. *Stormy night*

Emotions – grief

Bagley, Jessixa. *Boats for Papa*
Hole, Stian. *Anna's heaven*
Parr, Todd. *The goodbye book*
Polacco, Patricia. *An A from Miss Keller*
Skofield, James. *Bear and Bird*

Emotions – happiness

Schwartz, Amy. *100 things that make me happy*
Williams, Pharrell. *Happy!*

Emotions – jealousy *see* Emotions – envy, jealousy

Emotions – loneliness

Barnett, Mac. *Leo: a ghost story*
Colfer, Eoin. *Imaginary Fred*
Corderoy, Tracey. *Just right for two*
Curato, Mike. *Little Elliot, big family*
Emberley, Rebecca. *Spare parts*
Ferry, Beth. *Stick and Stone*
Imai, Ayano. *Mr. Brown's fantastic hat*
Nichols, Lori. *Maple and Willow apart*
Pilcher, Steve. *Over there*
Pizzoli, Greg. *Templeton gets his wish*
Ruzzier, Sergio. *A letter for Leo*
Sherry, Kevin. *Turtle Island*
Wall, Laura. *Goose*

Emotions – love

Chichester Clark, Emma. *Love is my favorite thing*
Denise, Anika. *Baking day at Grandma's*
DiTerlizzi, Angela. *Baby love*
Dodd, Emma. *Always*
  Everything
  Happy
  More and more
Foreman, Michael. *I love you, too!*
Jones, Ursula. *Beauty and the beast*
Lawler, Janet. *Love is real*
Lee, H. Chuku. *Beauty and the beast*
McPhail, David. *Brothers*
Massini, Sarah. *Love always everywhere*
Pearce, Clemency. *Three little words*
Pierce, Christa. *Did you know that I love you?*
Prasadam-Halls, Smriti. *I love you night and day*
Salzano, Tammi. *I love you just the way you are*

Shannon, George. *Hands say love*
Tupper Ling, Nancy. *The story I'll tell*
Wood, Douglas. *When a grandpa says "I love you"*

Emotions – sadness

Bang, Molly. *When Sophie's feelings are really, really hurt*
Carroll, James Christopher. *Papa's backpack*
Kobald, Irena. *My two blankets*
Parr, Todd. *The goodbye book*
Paul, Alison. *The plan*
Yolen, Jane. *The stranded whale*

Emotions – unhappiness *see* Emotions – happiness; Emotions – sadness

Engineered books *see* Format, unusual – toy & movable books

Entertainment *see* Theater

Entrepreneur *see* Money

Environment *see* Ecology

Eskimos *see also* Indians of North America – Inuit

Ethnic groups in the U.S.

Averbeck, Jim. *One word from Sophia*
de la Peña, Matt. *Last stop on Market Street*
Diggs, Taye. *Mixed me!*
Faruqi, Reem. *Lailah's lunchbox*
Manushkin, Fran. *Happy in our skin*
Petricic, Dusan. *My family tree and me*
Shannon, George. *One family*

Ethnic groups in the U.S. – African Americans

Andrews, Troy. *Trombone Shorty*
Bandy, Michael S. *Granddaddy's turn*
Bass, Hester. *Seeds of freedom*
Best, Cari. *My three best friends and me, Zulay*
Bolden, Tonya. *Beautiful moon*
Busch, Miriam. *Lion, lion*
Child, Lauren. *The new small person*
Cline-Ransome, Lesa. *Freedom's school*
Cooper, Floyd. *Juneteenth for Mazie*
Copeland, Misty. *Firebird*
Dempsey, Kristy. *A dance like starlight*
Fredrickson, Lane. *Monster trouble!*
Godin, Thelma Lynne. *The hula-hoopin' queen*
Golio, Gary. *Bird and Diz*
Herkert, Barbara. *Sewing stories*
Johnson, Angela. *All different now*
Krensky, Stephen. *I am so brave!*
McQuinn, Anna. *Leo loves baby time*
    Lola plants a garden
Meltzer, Brad. *I am Rosa Parks*
Meyer, Susan Lynn. *New shoes*
Nelson, Vaunda Micheaux. *The book itch*

Nolan, Nina. *Mahalia Jackson*
Nolen, Jerdine. *Irene's wish*
O'Connor, George. *If I had a raptor*
Rappaport, Doreen. *Frederick's journey*
Raschka, Chris. *The cosmobiography of Sun Ra*
Rhodes-Pitts, Sharifa. *Jake makes a world*
Ringgold, Faith. *Harlem Renaissance party*
Russell-Brown, Katheryn. *Little Melba and her big trombone*
Schofield-Morrison, Connie. *I got the rhythm*
Slade, Suzanne. *Friends for freedom*
    With books and bricks
Smith, Charles R. *28 days*
Watkins, Angela Farris. *Love will see you through*
Weatherford, Carole Boston. *Gordon Parks*
    Leontyne Price
    Sugar Hill
    Voice of freedom
Winter, Jonah. *How Jelly Roll Morton invented jazz*
    Lillian's right to vote
Woelfle, Gretchen. *Mumbet's Declaration of Independence*

Ethnic groups in the U.S. – Black Americans *see* Ethnic groups in the U.S. – African Americans

Ethnic groups in the U.S. – Cambodian Americans

Riecherter, Daryn. *The Cambodian dancer*

Ethnic groups in the U.S. – Chinese Americans

Petricic, Dusan. *My family tree and me*

Ethnic groups in the U.S. – Guatemalan Americans

O'Brien, Anne Sibley. *I'm new here*

Ethnic groups in the U.S. – Hispanic Americans

Kyle, Tracey. *Gazpacho for Nacho*
Thong, Roseanne Greenfield. *Green is a chile pepper*

Ethnic groups in the U.S. – Irish Americans

Polacco, Patricia. *Fiona's lace*

Ethnic groups in the U.S. – Japanese Americans

Uegaki, Chieri. *Hana Hashimoto, sixth violin*

Ethnic groups in the U.S. – Jewish Americans *see* Jewish culture

Ethnic groups in the U.S. – Korean Americans

O'Brien, Anne Sibley. *I'm new here*

Ethnic groups in the U.S. – Mexican Americans

Mora, Pat. *I pledge allegiance*
Tonatiuh, Duncan. *Separate is never equal*

Ethnic groups in the U.S. – Puerto Rican Americans

Manzano, Sonia. *Miracle on 133rd Street*

Ethnic groups in the U.S. – Somali Americans

O'Brien, Anne Sibley. *I'm new here*

Etiquette

Antony, Steve. *Please, Mr. Panda*
Cullen, Lynn. *Dear Mr. Washington*
Daly, Niki. *Thank you, Jackson*
Delaunois, Angèle. *Magic little words*
Holt, Kimberly Willis. *Dinner with the Highbrows*
Lane, Nathan. *Naughty Mabel*
LaReau, Kara. *No slurping, no burping!*
Riehle, Mary Ann McCabe. *The little kids' table*
Watkins, Rowboat. *Rude cakes*
Weninger, Brigitte. *Davy loves his mommy*

Exercise *see* Health & fitness – exercise

Experiments *see* Science

Extraterrestrial beings *see* Aliens

Eye glasses *see* Glasses

Eyes *see* Anatomy – eyes; Glasses; Disabilities – blindness; Senses – sight

Fables *see* Folk & fairy tales

Fairies

Coombs, Kate. *The tooth fairy wars*
Grimm, Jacob and Wilhelm. *Sleeping beauty*
Underwood, Deborah. *Here comes the Tooth Fairy Cat*

Fairs, festivals

Berger, Samantha. *Snoozefest at the Nuzzledome*
Davis, Kathryn Gibbs. *Mr. Ferris and his wheel*

Kraft, Betsy Harvey. *The fantastic Ferris wheel*
Light, Steve. *Have you seen my monster?*
Lord, Cynthia. *Hot Rod Hamster: monster truck mania!*
Yaccarino, Dan. *Billy and Goat at the state fair*

Fairy tales *see* Folk & fairy tales

Family life

Ashman, Linda. *Over the river and through the wood*
Averbeck, Jim. *One word from Sophia*
Barash, Chris. *Is it Hanukkah yet?*
Bean, Jonathan. *This is my home, this is my school*
Chaud, Benjamin. *The bear's surprise*
Cordell, Matthew. *Wish*
Curato, Mike. *Little Elliot, big family*
Elliott, David. *Nobody's perfect*
Fearing, Mark. *The great Thanksgiving escape*
Federle, Tim. *Tommy can't stop!*
Hannigan, Katherine. *Gwendolyn Grace*
Kaplan, Michael B. *Betty Bunny wants a goal*
Lang, Suzanne. *Families, families, families!*
Lloyd-Jones, Sally. *The house that's your home*
Lobel, Anita. *Taking care of Mama Rabbit*
Luxbacher, Irene. *Mr. Frank*
Mackintosh, David. *Lucky*
McLellan, Stephanie Simpson. *Tweezle into everything*
Manushkin, Fran. *Happy in our skin*
Miller, Pat Zietlow. *Sharing the bread*
Mora, Pat. *I pledge allegiance*
Myers, Anna. *Tumbleweed Baby*
Pennypacker, Sara. *Meet the Dullards*
Petricic, Dusan. *My family tree and me*
Phillipps, J. C. *The Simples love a picnic*
Pizzoli, Greg. *Templeton gets his wish*
Robinson, Sharon. *Under the same sun*
Rotner, Shelley. *Families*
Sauer, Tammi. *Your alien*
Schwartz, Amy. *I can't wait!*
Shannon, George. *One family*
Spinelli, Jerry. *Mama Seeton's whistle*
Stille, Ljuba. *Mia's thumb*
Sweeney, Linda Booth. *When the wind blows*
Teckentrup, Britta. *Busy bunny days*
Tuell, Todd. *Ninja, ninja, never stop!*
Urban, Linda. *Little Red Henry*
Van, Muon. *In a village by the sea*
Viorst, Judith. *Alexander, who's trying his best to be the best boy ever*
Wells, Rosemary. *Sophie's terrible twos*
   Stella's Starliner
Winstead, Rosie. *Sprout helps out*
Yoon, Salina. *Stormy night*

Family life – brothers *see also* Family life; Family life – brothers & sisters; Sibling rivalry

Bentley, Jonathan. *Little big*
Child, Lauren. *The new small person*
Fraser, Mary Ann. *No Yeti yet*
Gore, Emily. *And Nick*
Long, Ethan. *The Wing Wing brothers geometry palooza!*
McPhail, David. *Brothers*
Pinder, Eric. *How to share with a bear*
Sattler, Jennifer. *Pig kahuna pirates!*

Yoon, Salina. *Penguin and Pumpkin*

Family life – brothers & sisters

Berry, Lynne. *Squid Kid the Magnificent*
Cullen, Lynn. *Dear Mr. Washington*
Dunrea, Olivier. *Gemma and Gus*
Feeney, Tatyana. *Little Frog's tadpole trouble*
Gill, Timothy. *Flip and Fin: we rule the school!*
Hood, Susan. *Mission: new baby*
Javaherbin, Mina. *Soccer star*
Judge, Chris. *Tin*
Kaplan, Bruce Eric. *Meaniehead*
Kornell, Max. *Me first*
Light, Kelly. *Louise loves art*
Lobe, Mira. *Hoppelpopp and the best bunny*
Molk, Laurel. *Eeny, Meeny, Miney, Mo and Flo!*
Muth, Jon J. *Zen socks*
Offill, Jenny. *While you were napping*
Ormerod, Jan. *The baby swap*
Perkins, Maripat. *Rodeo Red*
Powell-Tuck, Maudie. *Pirates aren't afraid of the dark!*
Regan, Dian Curtis. *Space Boy and his dog*
Muñoz Ryan, Pam. *Tony Baloney: buddy trouble*
Saltzberg, Barney. *Inside this book (are three books)*
Schaefer, Lola M. *One busy day*
Singer, Marilyn. *I'm gonna climb a mountain in my patent leather shoes*
Snicket, Lemony. *29 myths on the Swinster Pharmacy*
Wegman, William. *Flo and Wendell explore*
Winthrop, Elizabeth. *Lucy and Henry are twins*

Family life – cousins

Brownlee, Sophia Grace. *Show time with Sophia Grace and Rosie*
Garland, Sally Anne. *Share*
Holabird, Katharine. *Angelina's big city ballet*
Houran, Lori Haskins. *A dozen cousins*
McCarty, Peter. *First snow*
McKee, David. *Elmer and the whales*
OHora, Zachariah. *My cousin Momo*
Perret, Delphine. *Pedro and George*
Rose, Nancy. *Merry Christmas, squirrels!*
The secret life of squirrels

Family life – daughters

Buitrago, Jairo. *Two white rabbits*
Dominguez, Angela. *Knit together*
Newman, Lesléa. *Heather has two mommies*
Paul, Alison. *The plan*
Waber, Bernard. *Ask me*
Winters, Kari-Lynn. *Bad pirate*

Family life – fathers

Buitrago, Jairo. *Two white rabbits*
Carroll, James Christopher. *Papa's backpack*
Chaud, Benjamin. *The bear's sea escape*
Climo, Liz. *Rory the dinosaur: me and my dad*
Corderoy, Tracey. *I want my daddy*
Dewdney, Anna. *Nelly Gnu and Daddy too*
Foreman, Michael. *I love you, too!*
Grant, Jacob. *Little Bird's bad word*
Hole, Stian. *Anna's heaven*
Holub, Joan. *Mighty dads*
Koehler, Fred. *How to cheer up Dad*
LaReau, Kara. *No slurping, no burping!*
Lawson, Jonarno. *Sidewalk flowers*

Mack, Jeff. *Duck in the fridge*
Marino, Gianna. *Following Papa's song*
Nolen, Jerdine. *Irene's wish*
Paul, Alison. *The plan*
Phelan, Matt. *Druthers*
Reagan, Jean. *How to surprise a dad*
Stein, David Ezra. *Tad and Dad*
Tafuri, Nancy. *Daddy hugs*
Waber, Bernard. *Ask me*
Winters, Kari-Lynn. *Bad pirate*
Wohnoutka, Mike. *Dad's first day*
Young, Jessica. *Spy Guy*

Family life – grandfathers

Aylesworth, Jim. *My grandfather's coat*
Bandy, Michael S. *Granddaddy's turn*
Dorros, Arthur. *Abuelo*
Latimer, Alex. *Stay! a top dog story*
Muller, Gerda. *How does my garden grow?*
Richards, Keith. *Gus and me*
Saltzberg, Barney. *Tea with Grandpa*
Sís, Peter. *Ice cream summer*
Uegaki, Chieri. *Hana Hashimoto, sixth violin*
Usher, Sam. *Snow*
Wood, Douglas. *When a grandpa says "I love you"*

Family life – grandmothers

Bissonette, Aimée. *North woods girl*
Bunting, Eve. *Washday*
Buzzeo, Toni. *My Bibi always remembers*
Castillo, Lauren. *Nana in the city*
de la Peña, Matt. *Last stop on Market Street*
Denise, Anika. *Baking day at Grandma's*
Elya, Susan Middleton. *Little Roja Riding Hood*
Fisman, Karen. *Nonna's Hanukkah surprise*
Heapy, Teresa. *Very little Red Riding Hood*
MacGregor, Roy. *The highest number in the world*
Medina, Meg. *Mango, Abuela, and me*
Menchin, Scott. *Grandma in blue with red hat*
Mora, Pat. *The remembering day / El día de los muertos*
Reagan, Jean. *How to babysit a grandma*
Robinson, Sharon. *Under the same sun*
Sadler, Marilyn. *Tony Baroni loves macaroni*
Shepherd, Jessica. *Grandma*
Tarpley, Todd. *My grandma's a ninja*
Van Laan, Nancy. *Forget me not*
Wood, Audrey. *The full moon at the napping house*

Family life – grandparents

Dewdney, Anna. *Llama Llama Gram and Grandpa*
Orloff, Karen Kaufman. *I wanna go home*

Family life – mothers

Appelt, Kathi. *When Otis courted Mama*
Bagley, Jessixa. *Boats for Papa*
Chang, Victoria. *Is Mommy?*
Dodd, Emma. *Everything*
Happy
Dominguez, Angela. *Knit together*
Guion, Melissa. *Baby penguins love their Mama*
Hall, Pamela. *Miss you like crazy*
Knapman, Timothy. *Soon*
Landau, Orna. *Leopardpox!*
Lobel, Anita. *Taking care of Mama Rabbit*
Napoli, Donna Jo. *Hands and hearts*

Newman, Lesléa. *Heather has two mommies*
Portis, Antoinette. *Wait*
Rim, Sujean. *Birdie's big-girl hair*
Rudolph, Shaina. *All my stripes*
Ruth, Greg. *Coming home*
Salzano, Tammi. *I love you just the way you are*
Shea, Bob. *Dinosaur vs. Mommy*
Spinelli, Jerry. *Mama Seeton's whistle*
Tupper Ling, Nancy. *The story I'll tell*
Van Slyke, Rebecca. *Mom school*
Walsh, Joanna. *I love Mom*
Weninger, Brigitte. *Davy loves his mommy*
Willis, Jeanne. *Slug needs a hug!*

Family life – new sibling

Chaud, Benjamin. *The bear's surprise*
Feeney, Tatyana. *Little Frog's tadpole trouble*
Nichols, Lori. *Maple*
Ormerod, Jan. *The baby swap*
Perkins, Maripat. *Rodeo Red*
Rosenthal, Amy Krouse. *Little Miss, big sis*
Wells, Rosemary. *Use your words, Sophie!*
Zeltser, David. *Ninja baby*

Family life – parents

Bently, Peter. *Meet the parents*
DiTerlizzi, Angela. *Baby love*
Gerber, Carole. *Tuck-in time*
Martin, Emily Winfield. *The wonderful things you will be*

Family life – same-sex parents

Newman, Lesléa. *Heather has two mommies*
Rotner, Shelley. *Families*
Schiffer, Miriam B. *Stella brings the family*

Family life – single-parent families

Rotner, Shelley. *Families*

Family life – sisters *see also* Family life; Family life – brothers & sisters; Sibling rivalry

Cohen, Jeff. *Eva and Sadie and the best classroom ever!*
  Eva and Sadie and the worst haircut ever!
Heine, Theresa. *Chandra's magic light*
McGhee, Alison. *The sweetest witch around*
Membrino, Anna. *I want to be a ballerina*
Murguia, Bethanie Deeney. *Zoe's jungle*
Nichols, Lori. *Maple and Willow apart*
  Maple and Willow together
Potter, Giselle. *Tell me what to dream about*
Rosenthal, Amy Krouse. *Little Miss, big sis*
Wells, Rosemary. *Use your words, Sophie!*
Yum, Hyewon. *The twins' little sister*
Zapf, Marlena. *Underpants dance*

Family life – stepchildren *see* Divorce; Family life – stepfamilies

Family life – stepfamilies

Appelt, Kathi. *When Otis courted Mama*

Carey, Lorraine. *Cinderella's stepsister and the big bad wolf*
Rotner, Shelley. *Families*
Underwood, Deborah. *Interstellar Cinderella*

Family life – stepparents *see* Divorce; Family life – stepfamilies

Farms

Bateman, Teresa. *Job wanted*
Bee, William. *Stanley the farmer*
Brett, Jan. *The turnip*
Chernesky, Felicia Sanzari. *Cheers for a dozen ears*
  From apple trees to cider, please!
  Sun above and blooms below
Clement, Nathan. *Big tractor*
Cole, Henry. *Big bug*
Cronin, Doreen. *Click, clack, peep!*
Deak, Erzsi. *Pumpkin time!*
Detlefsen, Lisl H. *Time for cranberries*
Doodler, Todd H. *Veggies with wedgies*
Dumont, Jean-François. *The sheep go on strike*
Hillenbrand, Will. *Down by the barn*
Kennedy, Anne Vittur. *The farmer's away! baa! neigh!*
  Ragweed's farm dog handbook
Lendroth, Susan. *Old Manhattan has some farms*
Long, Ethan. *In, over, and on (the farm)*
Long, Loren. *Otis and the scarecrow*
Munro, Roxie. *Market maze*
Old MacDonald had a farm. *Pete the Cat: Old MacDonald had a farm*
Preston-Gannon, Frann. *Dinosaur farm*
Raschka, Chris. *Give and take*
Ray, Mary Lyn. *Go to sleep, little farm*
Sierra, Judy. *E-I-E-I-O*
Sims, Nat. *Peekaboo barn*
Slack, Michael. *Wazdot?*
Teckentrup, Britta. *Busy bunny days*
Tougas, Chris. *Dojo daytrip*
Twohy, Mike. *Wake up, Rupert!*
Wahl, Phoebe. *Sonya's chickens*
Wilson, Karma. *Duddle Puck*
Yaccarino, Dan. *Doug unplugs on the farm*
Yoon, Salina. *Penguin and Pumpkin*

Feathers

Stewart, Melissa. *Feathers*

Feeling *see* Senses – touch

Feelings *see* Emotions

Fighting, arguing *see* Behavior – fighting, arguing

Fingers *see* Anatomy – hands

Fire

Heos, Bridget. *Be safe around fire*

Fire engines *see* Careers – firefighters; Trucks

Fish

Bar-el, Dan. *A fish named Glub*
Diesen, Deborah. *The not very merry pout-pout fish*
    The pout-pout fish goes to school
Lloyd-Jones, Sally. *Poor Doreen*

Fish – sharks

Bloom, C. P. *The Monkey goes bananas*
Gill, Timothy. *Flip and Fin: we rule the school!*
Houran, Lori Haskins. *How to spy on a shark*
Olien, Jessica. *Shark Detective!*
Waters, John F. *Sharks have six senses*

Fitness *see* Health & fitness

Flowers

Lawson, Jonarno. *Sidewalk flowers*
McQuinn, Anna. *Lola plants a garden*
Rockwell, Anne. *My spring robin*

Fold-out books *see* Format, unusual – toy &
    movable books

Folk & fairy tales

Aesop. *The grasshopper and the ants*
Auerbach, Adam. *Edda*
Brett, Jan. *Cinders*
    The turnip
Carey, Lorraine. *Cinderella's stepsister and the big*
    bad wolf
Chicken Little. *Brave Chicken Little*
Christie, R. Gregory. *Mousetropolis*
Christopher, Neil. *On the shoulder of a giant*
Clarkson, Stephanie. *Sleeping Cinderella and other*
    princess mix-ups
Durand, Hallie. *Catch that cookie!*
Elya, Susan Middleton. *Little Roja Riding Hood*
Fox, Diane. *The cat, the dog, Little Red, the exploding*
    eggs, the wolf, and Grandma
French, Vivian. *The most wonderful thing in the world*
The gingerbread boy. *The Gingerbread Man loose at*
    Christmas
Glaser, Linda. *Stone soup with matzoh balls*
Grimm, Jacob and Wilhelm. *Hansel and Gretel*
    Sleeping beauty
Heapy, Teresa. *Very little Red Riding Hood*
Imai, Ayano. *Puss and boots*
Javaherbin, Mina. *Elephant in the dark*
Jones, Ursula. *Beauty and the beast*
    The princess who had no kingdom
Joyce, William. *A bean, a stalk, and a boy named Jack*
Lazar, Tara. *Little Red Gliding Hood*
Lee, H. Chuku. *Beauty and the beast*
Little old lady who swallowed a fly. *There once was a*
    cowpoke who swallowed an ant
    There was an old lady who swallowed a fly
Livingston, A. A. B. *Bear and Lolly: off to school*
    B. Bear and Lolly: catch that cookie!
Maccarone, Grace. *The three little pigs count to 100*
Sabuda, Robert. *The dragon and the knight*
Schwartz, Corey Rosen. *Ninja Red Riding Hood*

Sehgal, Kabir. *A bucket of blessings*
Stein, Peter. *Little Red's riding 'hood*
Stewart, Whitney. *A catfish tale*
Subramaniam, Manasi. *The fox and the crow*
Teague, Mark. *The sky is falling!*
The three bears *Goatilocks and the three bears*
Underwood, Deborah. *Interstellar Cinderella*
Yim, Natasha. *Goldy Luck and the three pandas*

Food

Antony, Steve. *Betty goes bananas*
Asch, Frank. *Pizza*
Baker, Keith. *Little green peas*
Bass, Jennifer Vogel. *Edible colors*
    Edible numbers
Border, Terry. *Peanut Butter and Cupcake!*
Brandt, Lois. *Maddi's fridge*
Brisson, Pat. *Before we eat*
Chapman, Jared. *Vegetables in underwear*
Chernesky, Felicia Sanzari. *Cheers for a dozen ears*
    From apple trees to cider, please!
Detlefsen, Lisl H. *Time for cranberries*
DiPucchio, Kelly. *Everyone loves bacon*
Dolan, Elys. *Nuts in space*
Doodler, Todd H. *Veggies with wedgies*
Edwards, Michelle. *Max makes a cake*
Freedman, Claire. *Spider sandwiches*
Gibbons, Gail. *The fruits we eat*
The gingerbread boy. *The Gingerbread Man loose at*
    Christmas
Glaser, Linda. *Stone soup with matzoh balls*
Gutierrez, Elisa. *Letter lunch*
Hacohen, Dean. *Who's hungry?*
Harris, Robie H. *What's so yummy?*
Holt, Kimberly Willis. *Dinner with the Highbrows*
Jenkins, Emily. *A fine dessert*
John, Jory. *I will chomp you!*
Kenah, Katharine. *The very stuffed turkey*
Kyle, Tracey. *Gazpacho for Nacho*
LaReau, Kara. *No slurping, no burping!*
Lewin, Betsy. *Good night, Knight*
Livingston, A. A. B. *Bear and Lolly: catch that cookie!*
McGee, Joe. *Peanut butter and brains*
Martin, Jacqueline Briggs. *Alice Waters and the trip*
    to delicious
Miller, Pat Zietlow. *Sharing the bread*
Monfreid, Dorothée de. *The cake*
Niemann, Christoph. *The potato king*
Palatini, Margie. *Under a pig tree*
Pham, LeUyen. *A piece of cake*
Pryor, Katherine. *Zora's zucchini*
Riehle, Mary Ann McCabe. *The little kids' table*
Robinson, Michelle. *There's a lion in my cornflakes*
Rockliff, Mara. *Chik chak Shabbat*
Rockwell, Lizzy. *Plants feed me*
Ruddell, Deborah. *The popcorn astronauts*
Sadler, Marilyn. *Tony Baroni loves macaroni*
Sarcone-Roach, Julia. *The bear ate your sandwich*
Scanlon, Elizabeth Garton. *The good-pie party*
Sebe, Masayuki. *100 hungry monkeys!*
Shaw, Stephanie. *A cookie for Santa*
Sís, Peter. *Ice cream summer*
Tegen, Katherine. *Pink cupcake magic*
Todd, Mark. *Food trucks!*
Watkins, Rowboat. *Rude cakes*

Foreign lands

Niemann, Christoph. *The potato king*
Tupper Ling, Nancy. *The story I'll tell*

Foreign lands – Africa

Alakija, Polly. *Counting chickens*
Atinuke. *Double trouble for Anna Hibiscus!*
Brown-Wood, JaNay. *Imani's moon*
Buzzeo, Toni. *My Bibi always remembers*
Latham, Irene. *Dear Wandering Wildebeest*
Lee, H. Chuku. *Beauty and the beast*
London, Jonathan. *Hippos are huge!*
O'Neill, Gemma. *Oh dear, Geoffrey!*

Foreign lands – Arctic

Heder, Thyra. *The bear report*
Yoon, Salina. *Penguin's big adventure*

Foreign lands – Argentina

Dorros, Arthur. *Abuelo*

Foreign lands – Austria

Lodding, Linda Ravin. *A gift for Mama*

Foreign lands – Bavaria *see* Foreign lands – Austria

Foreign lands – Brazil

Javaherbin, Mina. *Soccer star*

Foreign lands – Burkina Faso

Isabella, Jude. *The red bicycle*

Foreign lands – Cambodia

Riecherter, Daryn. *The Cambodian dancer*

Foreign lands – Canada

MacGregor, Roy. *The highest number in the world*
Walker, Sally M. *Winnie*

Foreign lands – China

Hyde, Heidi Smith. *Shanghai Sukkah*

Foreign lands – Costa Rica

Burns, Loree Griffin. *Handle with care*

Foreign lands – Cuba

Engle, Margarita. *Drum dream girl*

Foreign lands – Denmark

Elvgren, Jennifer. *The whispering town*

Foreign lands – Dominican Republic

Tavares, Matt. *Growing up Pedro*

Foreign lands – Egypt

Ewert, Marcus. *Mummy cat*

Foreign lands – England

Antony, Steve. *The Queen's hat*
Whelan, Gloria. *Queen Victoria's bathing machine*

Foreign lands – France

Hawkes, Kevin. *Remy and Lulu*
Mader, C. Roger. *Tiptop cat*
Muller, Gerda. *How does my garden grow?*
Sís, Peter. *The pilot and the Little Prince*
Smith, Matthew Clark. *Small wonders*

Foreign lands – Galapagos Islands

George, Jean Craighead. *Galápagos George*

Foreign lands – Gambia

Paul, Miranda. *One plastic bag*

Foreign lands – Ghana

Thompson, Laurie Ann. *Emmanuel's dream*

Foreign lands – India

Javaherbin, Mina. *Elephant in the dark*
Kimmel, Elizabeth Cody. *A taste of freedom*
Sehgal, Kabir. *A bucket of blessings*
    The wheels on the tuk tuk

Foreign lands – Kenya

Prevot, Franck. *Wangari Maathai*

Foreign lands – Latin America

Argueta, Jorge. *Salsa*
Thong, Roseanne Greenfield. *Día de los muertos*
    'Twas nochebuena

Foreign lands – Mexico

Mora, Pat. *The remembering day / El día de los muertos*
Morales, Yuyi. *Viva Frida*

Foreign lands – Nepal

Heine, Theresa. *Chandra's magic light*

Foreign lands – Nigeria

Onyefulu, Ifeoma. *Ife's first haircut*

Foreign lands – Pakistan

Winter, Jeanette. *Malala, a brave girl from Pakistan / Iqbal, a brave boy from Pakistan*

Foreign lands – Russia

Brett, Jan. *The turnip*

Foreign lands – Scotland

Lester, Helen. *The loch mess monster*

Foreign lands – South Africa

Bildner, Phil. *The soccer fence*
Daly, Niki. *Thank you, Jackson*

Foreign lands – Tanzania

Robinson, Sharon. *Under the same sun*

Foreign lands – Vietnam

Van, Muon. *In a village by the sea*

Foreign lands – Zimbabwe

Trent, Tereai. *The girl who buried her dreams in a can*

Foreign languages

Adderson, Caroline. *Norman, speak!*
Argueta, Jorge. *Salsa*
Brown, Monica. *Maya's blanket*
Dorros, Arthur. *Abuelo*
Elya, Susan Middleton. *Little Roja Riding Hood*
Kyle, Tracey. *Gazpacho for Nacho*
Luján, Jorge. *Moví la mano / I moved my hand*
Medina, Meg. *Mango, Abuela, and me*
Mora, Pat. *I pledge allegiance*
    The remembering day / El día de los muertos
    Water rolls, water rises / el agua ruda, el agua sube
Morales, Yuyi. *Viva Frida*
Pinkwater, Daniel. *Beautiful Yetta's Hanukkah kitten*
Thong, Roseanne Greenfield. *Día de los muertos*
    'Twas nochebuena

Forest, woods

Bissonette, Aimée. *North woods girl*
Grimm, Jacob and Wilhelm. *Hansel and Gretel*
Johnston, Tony. *Winter is coming*
Lyon, George Ella. *What forest knows*
McFarland, Clive. *A bed for Bear*
Miyakoshi, Akiko. *The tea party in the woods*
Sill, Cathryn. *Forests*
Srinivasan, Divya. *Little Owl's day*

Forgetfulness *see* Behavior – forgetfulness

Forgiving *see* Behavior – forgiving

Format, unusual

Joyce, William. *The Numberlys*
Tullet, Hervé. *Mix it up!*

Format, unusual – board books

Ajmera, Maya. *Global baby boys*
    Global baby girls
American Museum of Natural History. *ABC insects*
Barclay, Eric. *Counting dogs*
Barrett, Mary Brigid. *All fall down*
    Pat-a-cake
Coat, Janik. *Rhymoceros*
Cousins, Lucy. *Maisy's Christmas tree*

Davis, Sarah. *My first trucks*
Ferri, Giuliano. *Peekaboo*
Franceschelli, Christopher. *Dinoblock*
Hood, Susan. *Tickly toes*
Horácek, Petr. *A surprise for Tiny Mouse*
    Time for bed
Jones, Christianne C. *The Santa shimmy*
Kirwan, Wednesday. *Baby loves to boogie!*
Krensky, Stephen. *I am so brave!*
Lemke, Donald. *Book-o-beards*
Light, Steve. *Planes go*
McPhail, David. *Baby Pig Pig talks*
National Wildlife Federation. *My first book of baby
    animals*
Patricelli, Leslie. *Boo!*
    Hop! hop!
Preston-Gannon, Frann. *Deep deep sea*
Ramadier, Cédric. *Help! the wolf is coming!*
Riggs, Kate. *Time to build*
Savage, Stephen. *Seven orange pumpkins*
Schindel, John. *The babies and doggies book*
Shuttlewood, Craig. *Through the town*
Sims, Nat. *Peekaboo barn*
Wells, Rosemary. *A visit to Dr. Duck*
Wick, Walter. *Can you see what I see? Christmas*

Format, unusual – graphic novels

Nordling, Lee. *Shehewe*
Sturm, James. *Sleepless knight*
Tamaki, Mariko. *This one summer*

Format, unusual – toy & movable books

Buzzeo, Toni. *Whose tools?*
Cousins, Lucy. *Count with Maisy, cheep, cheep, cheep!*
Crowther, Robert. *Robert Crowther's pop-up dinosaur
    ABC*
Deneux, Xavier. *Vehicles*
Ferri, Giuliano. *Peekaboo*
Franceschelli, Christopher. *Countablock*
Graves, Keith. *The monsterator*
Green, Rod. *Giant vehicles*
Hacohen, Dean. *Who's hungry?*
Hall, Michael. *It's an orange aardvark!*
Horácek, Petr. *The mouse who ate the moon*
    A surprise for Tiny Mouse
Idle, Molly. *Flora and the penguin*
Lemke, Donald. *Book-o-beards*
Litton, Jonthan. *Snip snap*
Macaulay, David. *How machines work: zoo break!*
Murphy, Mary. *Say hello like this!*
Pham, LeUyen. *There's no such thing as little*
Previn, Stacey. *Find spot!*
Rosenthal, Marc. *Big bot, small bot*
Rubin, Adam. *Robo-Sauce*
Sabuda, Robert. *The dragon and the knight*
Scheffler, Axel. *Axel Scheffler's Flip flap safari*
Schwarz, Viviane. *Is there a dog in this book?*
Sheehy, Shawn. *Welcome to the neighborwood*
Shuttlewood, Craig. *Who's in the tree?*
Sims, Nat. *Peekaboo barn*
Sirett, Dawn. *Happy birthday Sophie!*
Teckentrup, Britta. *Get out of my bath!*
Tupera, Tupera. *Polar Bear's underwear*
Viorst, Judith. *And two boys booed*
Viva, Frank. *Outstanding in the rain*
Wells, Rosemary. *Max and Ruby at the Warthogs'
    wedding*

Wick, Walter. *Hey, Seymour!*
Young, Cybèle. *Some things I've lost*

Fortune *see* Character traits – luck

Fossils

DiSiena, Laura Lyn. *Dinosaurs live on!*

Freedom *see* Character traits – freedom

Friendship

Alexander, Claire. *Monkey and the little one*
Ashdown, Rebecca. *Bob and Flo*
Barnett, Mac. *Leo: a ghost story*
Barrett, Ron. *Cats got talent*
Becker, Bonny. *A library book for Bear*
Bender, Rebecca. *Giraffe meets Bird*
Bertier, Anne. *Wednesday*
Bloom, Suzanne. *Alone together*
Bogan, Paulette. *Virgil and Owen*
Borando, Silvia. *Black cat, white cat*
Border, Terry. *Peanut Butter and Cupcake!*
Bramsen, Carin. *Just a duck?*
Bright, Rachel. *Love Monster and the perfect present*
    Side by side
Brown, Alison. *Eddie and Dog*
Burningham, John. *Picnic*
Carnesi, Monica. *Sleepover with Beatrice and Bear*
Chaconas, Dori. *Cork and Fuzz: merry merry holly holly*
Chapman, Jared. *Pirate, Viking, and Scientist*
Chase, Kit. *Oliver's tree*
Chiew, Suzanne. *When you need a friend*
Clayton, Dallas. *Lily the unicorn*
Colfer, Eoin. *Imaginary Fred*
Corderoy, Tracey. *Just right for two*
Côté, Geneviève. *Bob's hungry ghost*
    Starring me and you
Cousins, Lucy. *Maisy plays soccer*
Cronin, Doreen. *Boom Snot Twitty*
    Boom, Snot, Twitty, this way that way
    Smick!
Curato, Mike. *Little Elliot, big city*
Donofrio, Beverly. *Where's Mommy?*
Dubuc, Marianne. *The lion and the bird*
Emberley, Rebecca. *Spare parts*
Engler, Michael. *Elephantastic!*
Fergus, Maureen. *Buddy and Earl*
Ferry, Beth. *Stick and Stone*
Freeman, Tor. *Olive and the embarrassing gift*
Galbraith, Kathryn O. *Two bunny buddies*
Gall, Chris. *Dog vs. Cat*
Garton, Sam. *I am Otter*
Gerstein, Mordicai. *You can't have too many friends!*
Gianferrari, Maria. *Penny and Jelly*
Goodrich, Carter. *We forgot Brock!*
Gravett, Emily. *Bear and Hare: snow!*
Grey, Mini. *Space Dog*
Gude, Paul. *When Elephant met Giraffe*
Harris, Robie H. *Turtle and me*
Hills, Tad. *Duck and Goose go to the beach*
Hudson, Katy. *Bear and Duck*
Hyde, Heidi Smith. *Shanghai Sukkah*
Imai, Ayano. *Mr. Brown's fantastic hat*
James, Ann. *Bird and Bear*
John, Jory. *I love you already!*

Joosse, Barbara. *Evermore dragon*
Kenah, Katharine. *The very stuffed turkey*
Kerley, Barbara. *With a friend by your side*
Kimura, Ken. *999 frogs and a little brother*
Kirk, Daniel. *You are not my friend, but I miss you*
Kirk, David. *Oh so brave dragon*
Knudsen, Michelle. *Marilyn's monster*
Landström, Lena. *Pom and Pim*
    Where is Pim?
Latimer, Alex. *Pig and small*
Latimer, Miriam. *Dear Panda*
Levy, Janice. *Thomas the toadilly terrible bully*
Livingston, A. A. *B. Bear and Lolly: off to school*
Lundquist, Mary. *Cat and Bunny*
McDonnell, Patrick. *Thank you and good night*
Mann, Jennifer K. *Two speckled eggs*
Martin, David. *Peep and Ducky: rainy day*
Newman, Lesléa. *Ketzel, the cat who composed*
Nichols, Lori. *Maple*
    Maple and Willow together
Oldland, Nicholas. *Walk on the wild side*
Olson, Jennifer Gray. *Ninja bunny*
O'Neill, Gemma. *Monty's magnificent mane*
    Oh dear, Geoffrey!
Otoshi, Kathryn. *Two*
Percival, Tom. *Herman's letter*
Perl, Erica S. *Totally tardy Marty*
Pett, Mark. *Lizard from the park*
Pilcher, Steve. *Over there*
Pilutti, Deb. *Bear and Squirrel are friends . . . yes, really!*
Pinkwater, Daniel. *Bear and Bunny*
Preston-Gannon, Frann. *How to lose a lemur*
Proimos, James. *Waddle! waddle!*
Reynolds, Aaron. *Nerdy birdy*
Richards, Dan. *The problem with not being scared of monsters*
Rosenberg, Liz. *What James said*
Rosenthal, Amy Krouse. *Friendshape*
    Uni the unicorn
Russo, Marisabina. *Sophie sleeps over*
Ruzzier, Sergio. *A letter for Leo*
    Too busy
Sadler, Marilyn. *Alice from Dallas*
Sandu, Anca. *Churchill's tale of tails*
Santat, Dan. *The adventures of Beekle*
Sauer, Tammi. *Your alien*
Scanlon, Elizabeth Garton. *The good-pie party*
Schmid, Paul. *Oliver and his egg*
Schneider, Josh. *Princess Sparkle-Heart gets a makeover*
Schwartz, Amy. *I can't wait!*
Seeger, Laura Vaccaro. *Dog and Bear: tricks and treats*
Sheehan, Kevin. *The dandelion's tale*
Sherry, Kevin. *Turtle Island*
Slade, Suzanne. *Friends for freedom*
Soman, David. *Ladybug Girl and the best ever playdate*
Stead, Philip C. *Lenny and Lucy*
Trukhan, Ekaterina. *Me and my cat*
Ts'o, Pauline. *Whispers of the wolf*
Turnbull, Victoria. *The sea tiger*
Underwood, Deborah. *Bad bye, good bye*
van Lieshout, Maria. *Hopper and Wilson fetch a star*
Van Wright, Cornelius. *When an alien meets a swamp monster*
Verde, Susan. *You and me*
Wall, Laura. *Goose*

Wallace, Nancy Elizabeth. *Water! water! water!*
Webb, Holly. *Little puppy lost*
Wells, Rosemary. *Felix stands tall*
    Stella's Starliner
Yaccarino, Dan. *Billy and Goat at the state fair*

Frogs & toads

Angleberger, Tom. *McToad mows Tiny Island*
Brenning, Juli. *Maggi and Milo*
Feeney, Tatyana. *Little Frog's tadpole trouble*
FitzSimmons, David. *Curious critters, vol. 2*
Freedman, Deborah. *By Mouse and Frog*
Gray, Kes. *Frog on a log?*
Kimura, Ken. *999 frogs and a little brother*
Levy, Janice. *Thomas the toadilly terrible bully*
London, Jonathan. *Froggy gets a doggy*
    Froggy's birthday wish
Markle, Sandra. *Toad weather*
Petty, Dev. *I don't want to be a frog*
Pinkwater, Daniel. *Bear and Bunny*
Shea, Bob. *Kid Sheriff and the terrible Toads*
Stein, David Ezra. *Tad and Dad*

Frontier life *see* U.S. history – frontier &
    pioneer life

Furniture – beds

Samuels, Barbara. *Fred's beds*

Games

Barrett, Mary Brigid. *All fall down*
    Pat-a-cake
Joosse, Barbara. *Evermore dragon*
Surplice, Holly. *Peek-a-boo Bunny*
Walsh, Ellen Stoll. *Where is Jumper?*
Yoon, Salina. *Tap to play!*

Gangs *see* Clubs, gangs

Garage sales, rummage sales

Bunting, Eve. *Yard sale*

Garbage collectors *see* Careers – sanitation
    workers

Gardens, gardening

Best, Cari. *A perfect day for digging*
Colandro, Lucille. *There was an old lady who
    swallowed a frog!*
Corderoy, Tracey. *The magical snow garden*
Deak, Erzsi. *Pumpkin time!*

Gibbons, Gail. *The fruits we eat*
Lendroth, Susan. *Old Manhattan has some farms*
McQuinn, Anna. *Lola plants a garden*
Messner, Kate. *Up in the garden and down in the dirt*
Mora, Pat. *The remembering day / El día de los
    muertos*
Muller, Gerda. *How does my garden grow?*
Nelson, Kadir. *If you plant a seed*
Nolen, Jerdine. *Irene's wish*
Peppa Pig and the vegetable garden
Pryor, Katherine. *Zora's zucchini*
Schoonmaker, Elizabeth. *Square cat ABC*
Sierra, Judy. *E-I-E-I-O*
Wunderli, Stephen. *Little Boo*

Gender roles

Baldacchino, Christine. *Morris Micklewhite and the
    tangerine dress*
Engle, Margarita. *Drum dream girl*
Herthel, Jessica. *I am Jazz*
Hoffman, Sarah. *Jacob's new dress*
Krull, Kathleen. *Hillary Rodham Clinton*
McCully, Emily Arnold. *Queen of the diamond*
MacGregor, Roy. *The highest number in the world*
Nordling, Lee. *Shehewe*
Poletti, Frances. *Miss Todd and her wonderful flying
    machine*
Pomranz, Craig. *Made by Raffi*
Raczka, Bob. *Joy in Mudville*
Russell-Brown, Katheryn. *Little Melba and her big
    trombone*
Slade, Suzanne. *Friends for freedom*
Stone, Tanya Lee. *The house that Jane built*
Trent, Tereai. *The girl who buried her dreams in a can*
Wallmark, Laurie. *Ada Byron Lovelace and the
    thinking machine*

Generosity *see* Character traits – generosity

Ghosts

Baguley, Elizabeth. *Ready, steady, ghost!*
Bailey, Ella. *No such thing*
Barnett, Mac. *Leo: a ghost story*
Côté, Geneviève. *Bob's hungry ghost*
Goldie, Sonia. *Ghosts*
Ketteman, Helen. *The ghosts go haunting*
Newgarden, Mark. *Bow-Wow's nightmare neighbors*

Giants

Christopher, Neil. *On the shoulder of a giant*
Joyce, William. *A bean, a stalk, and a boy named Jack*

Gifts

Bright, Rachel. *Love Monster and the perfect present*
Cocca-Leffler, Maryann. *A homemade together
    Christmas*
Deedman, Heidi. *Too many toys!*
Diesen, Deborah. *The not very merry pout-pout fish*
Freeman, Tor. *Olive and the embarrassing gift*
The gingerbread boy. *The Gingerbread Man loose at
    Christmas*
Keane, Claire. *Once upon a cloud*
Lodding, Linda Ravin. *A gift for Mama*
McGhee, Alison. *Star bright*
Underwood, Deborah. *Here comes Santa Cat*

Weninger, Brigitte. *Happy Easter, Davy!*
Willis, Jeanne. *Boa's bad birthday*

Glasses

Berne, Jennifer. *Calvin, look out!*
Dean, James. *Pete the Cat and his magic sunglasses*

Gossip *see* Behavior – gossip, rumors

Grammar *see* Language

Graphic novels *see* Format, unusual – graphic
    novels

Greed *see* Behavior – greed

Grocery stores *see* Stores

Growing up *see* Behavior – growing up

Habits *see* Thumb sucking

Hair

Cohen, Jeff. *Eva and Sadie and the worst haircut ever!*
Lemke, Donald. *Book-o-beards*
Onyefulu, Ifeoma. *Ife's first haircut*
Rim, Sujean. *Birdie's big-girl hair*

Handicaps *see* Disabilities

Hares *see* Animals – rabbits

Health & fitness

Harris, Robie H. *What's so yummy?*
International Center for Assault Prevention. *My
    body belongs to me from my head to my toes*
Krall, Dan. *Sick Simon*
Martin, Jacqueline Briggs. *Alice Waters and the trip
    to delicious*
Starishevsky, Jill. *My body belongs to me*
Stewart, Whitney. *Meditation is an open sky*

Health & fitness – exercise

Beliveau, Kathy. *The yoga game by the sea*
Pajalunga, Lorena V. *Yoga for kids*

Hearing *see* Anatomy – ears

Heat *see* Concepts – cold & heat

Heavy equipment *see* Machines

Helpfulness *see* Character traits – helpfulness

Hens *see* Birds – chickens, roosters

Hibernation

Berger, Carin. *Finding spring*
Blecha, Aaron. *Goodnight, Grizzle Grump!*
Carnesi, Monica. *Sleepover with Beatrice and Bear*
Chaud, Benjamin. *The bear's sea escape*
McFarland, Clive. *A bed for Bear*

Hiccups

Bentley, Tadgh. *Little Penguin gets the hiccups*

Hiding *see* Behavior – hiding

Hiding things *see* Behavior – hiding things

Hogs *see* Animals – pigs

Holidays

Newman, Lesléa. *Here is the world*

Holidays – Chanukah *see* Holidays –
    Hanukkah

Holidays – Chinese New Year

Yim, Natasha. *Goldy Luck and the three pandas*

Holidays – Christmas

Biedrzycki, David. *Me and my dragon: Christmas
    spirit*
Brenner, Tom. *And then comes Christmas*
Brett, Jan. *The animals' Santa*
Buehner, Caralyn. *Merry Christmas, Mr. Mouse*
Chaconas, Dori. *Cork and Fuzz: merry merry holly
    holly*
Cocca-Leffler, Maryann. *A homemade together
    Christmas*
Cousins, Lucy. *Maisy's Christmas tree*
Cronin, Doreen. *Click, clack, ho! ho! ho!*
Czajak, Paul. *Monster needs a Christmas tree*
Diesen, Deborah. *The not very merry pout-pout fish*
The gingerbread boy. *The Gingerbread Man loose at
    Christmas*
Grün, Anselm. *The legend of Saint Nicholas*
Hennessy, B. G. *A Christmas wish for Corduroy*
Jane, Pamela. *Little elfie one*
Krensky, Stephen. *The last Christmas tree*
Luzzati, Emanuele. *Three little owls*
McGhee, Alison. *Star bright*
Manzano, Sonia. *Miracle on 133rd Street*
May, Robert L. *Rudolph shines again*
Metzger, Steve. *Waiting for Santa*

Moore, Clement Clarke. *The night before Christmas*, ill. by David Ercolini
  The night before Christmas, ill. by Barbara Reid
  'Twas the night before Christmas
Murguia, Bethanie Deeney. *The best parts of Christmas*
Paul, Ellis. *The night the lights went out on Christmas*
Peet, Amanda. *Dear Santa, Love Rachel Rosenstein*
Pingk, Rubin. *Samurai Santa*
Plourde, Lynn. *Merry Moosey Christmas*
Raczka, Bob. *Santa Clauses*
Reagan, Jean. *How to catch Santa*
Rose, Nancy. *Merry Christmas, squirrels!*
Sattler, Jennifer. *A Chick 'n' Pug Christmas*
Shaw, Stephanie. *A cookie for Santa*
Thong, Roseanne Greenfield. *'Twas nochebuena*
The twelve days of Christmas. English folk song..
  The twelve days of Christmas
Underwood, Deborah. *Here comes Santa Cat*
Walton, Rick. *Frankenstein's fright before Christmas*
Wick, Walter. *Can you see what I see? Christmas*

Holidays – Day of the Dead

Mora, Pat. *The remembering day / El día de los muertos*
Thong, Roseanne Greenfield. *Día de los muertos*

Holidays – Easter

Kaplan, Michael B. *Betty Bunny loves Easter*
Patricelli, Leslie. *Hop! hop!*
Underwood, Deborah. *Here comes the Easter Cat*
Weninger, Brigitte. *Happy Easter, Davy!*

Holidays – Groundhog Day

Pearlman, Robb. *Groundhog's day off*

Holidays – Halloween

Andrews, Julie. *The very fairy princess: a spooky, sparkly Halloween*
Bailey, Ella. *No such thing*
Brendler, Carol. *Not very scary*
Colby, Rebecca. *It's raining bats and frogs*
Day, Alexandra. *Carl's Halloween*
Garton, Sam. *Otter loves Halloween*
Graves, Keith. *The monsterator*
Ketteman, Helen. *At the old haunted house*
  The ghosts go haunting
Kimmelman, Leslie. *Trick ARRR treat*
Lester, Helen. *Tacky and the haunted igloo*
Little old lady who swallowed a fly. *There was an old mummy who swallowed a spider*
Long, Ethan. *Fright club*
McGhee, Alison. *The sweetest witch around*
Patricelli, Leslie. *Boo!*
Savage, Stephen. *Seven orange pumpkins*
Scotton, Rob. *Scaredy-cat, Splat!*
Seeger, Laura Vaccaro. *Dog and Bear: tricks and treats*
Siddals, Mary McKenna. *Shivery shades of Halloween*
Soman, David. *Ladybug Girl and the dress-up dilemma*
Wunderli, Stephen. *Little Boo*

Holidays – Hanukkah

Barash, Chris. *Is it Hanukkah yet?*

Bridwell, Norman. *Clifford celebrates Hanukkah*
Fischer, Ellen. *Latke, the lucky dog*
Fisman, Karen. *Nonna's Hanukkah surprise*
Kimmel, Eric A. *Simon and the bear*
Pinkwater, Daniel. *Beautiful Yetta's Hanukkah kitten*
Simon, Richard. *Oskar and the eight blessings*
Singer, Isaac Bashevis. *The parakeet named Dreidel*

Holidays – Juneteenth

Cooper, Floyd. *Juneteenth for Mazie*

Holidays – Martin Luther King Day

Watkins, Angela Farris. *Love will see you through*

Holidays – Mother's Day

Schiffer, Miriam B. *Stella brings the family*
Weninger, Brigitte. *Davy loves his mommy*

Holidays – Passover

Adler, David A. *The story of Passover*
Edwards, Michelle. *Max makes a cake*
Glaser, Linda. *Stone soup with matzoh balls*

Holidays – Ramadan

Faruqi, Reem. *Lailah's lunchbox*

Holidays – Sukkot

Hyde, Heidi Smith. *Shanghai Sukkah*

Holidays – Thanksgiving

Ashman, Linda. *Over the river and through the wood*
Detlefsen, Lisl H. *Time for cranberries*
Fearing, Mark. *The great Thanksgiving escape*
Kenah, Katharine. *The very stuffed turkey*
Miller, Pat Zietlow. *Sharing the bread*

Holidays – Tu B'Shevat

Gellman, Ellie B. *Netta and her plant*

Holidays – Valentine's Day

Friedman, Laurie. *Ruby Valentine and the sweet surprise*
Underwood, Deborah. *Here comes Valentine Cat*

Holocaust

Simon, Richard. *Oskar and the eight blessings*

Homes, houses

Anholt, Laurence. *Two nests*
Arnold, Tedd. *Vincent paints his house*
Aston, Dianna Hutts. *A nest is noisy*
Bean, Jonathan. *This is my home, this is my school*
Bee, William. *Stanley the builder*
Buzzeo, Toni. *Whose tools?*
Chiew, Suzanne. *When you need a friend*
dePaola, Tomie. *Jack*
Ellis, Carson. *Home*
Gavin, Ciara. *Room for Bear*
Hakte, Ben. *Julia's house for lost creatures*

Han, Eun-sun. *The flying birds*
Ketteman, Helen. *At the old haunted house*
Lester, Helen. *Tacky and the haunted igloo*
Lloyd-Jones, Sally. *The house that's your home*
Na, Il Sung. *Welcome home, Bear*
Sheehy, Shawn. *Welcome to the neighborwood*
Stanton, Karen. *Monday, Wednesday, and every other weekend*
Van, Muon. *In a village by the sea*
Verburg, Bonnie. *The tree house that Jack built*
Ward, Jennifer. *Mama built a little nest*
Wells, Rosemary. *Stella's Starliner*

Homework

Cali, Davide. *I didn't do my homework because . . .*
Heder, Thyra. *The bear report*

Homosexuality

Newman, Lesléa. *Heather has two mommies*
Pitman, Gayle E. *This day in June*
Schiffer, Miriam B. *Stella brings the family*

Honey bees *see* Insects – bees

Hope *see* Character traits – hopefulness

Hopefulness *see* Character traits – hopefulness

Hot air balloons *see* Activities – ballooning

Houses *see* Homes, houses

Hugging

Barnett, Mac. *President Taft is stuck in the bath*
Campbell, Scott. *Hug machine*
Chapman, Jane. *No more cuddles!*
Mack, Jeff. *Who wants a hug?*
Tafuri, Nancy. *Daddy hugs*
Willis, Jeanne. *Slug needs a hug!*

Humorous stories

Arnold, Tedd. *A pet for Fly Guy*
Auch, Mary Jane. *The buk buk buk festival*
Barnett, Mac. *The skunk*
Biedrzycki, David. *Breaking news: bear alert*
Bingham, Kelly. *Circle, square, Moose*
Black, Michael Ian. *Naked!*
Byous, Shawn. *Because I stubbed my toe*
Cali, Davide. *I didn't do my homework because . . .*
Carle, Eric. *The nonsense show*
DiPucchio, Kelly. *Dog days of school*
  Zombie in love 2 + 1
Dolan, Elys. *Nuts in space*
  Weasels
Doodler, Todd H. *Veggies with wedgies*
Escoffier, Michael. *Where's the baboon?*
Fox, Diane. *The cat, the dog, Little Red, the exploding eggs, the wolf, and Grandma*
Gerstein, Mordicai. *You can't have too many friends!*
Himmelman, John. *Duck to the rescue*
Holt, Kimberly Willis. *Dinner with the Highbrows*

Isaacs, Anne. *Meanwhile, back at the ranch*
LaReau, Kara. *No slurping, no burping!*
Lehrhaupt, Adam. *Please, open this book!*
Lester, Helen. *The loch mess monster*
Litwin, Eric. *The Nuts*
Long, Ethan. *Ms. Spell*
McKenna, Martin. *The octopuppy*
Miyares, Daniel. *Pardon me!*
Morris, Richard T. *This is a moose*
Novak, B. J. *The book with no pictures*
Palatini, Margie. *Under a pig tree*
Pearlman, Robb. *Groundhog's day off*
Pennypacker, Sara. *Meet the Dullards*
Perret, Delphine. *Pedro and George*
Pilutti, Deb. *Ten rules of being a superhero*
Portis, Antoinette. *Froodle*
Raschka, Chris. *Cowy cow*
  Crabby crab
Reeve, Rosie. *Training Tallulah*
Robinson, Michelle. *How to wash a woolly mammoth*
  There's a lion in my cornflakes
Rubin, Adam. *Big bad bubble*
Seuss, Dr. *Horton and the Kwuggerbug and more lost stories*
Torrey, Richard. *My dog, Bob*
Underwood, Deborah. *Here comes the Easter Cat*

Hurrying *see* Behavior – hurrying

Hygiene *see also* Character traits – cleanliness; Health & fitness

Coats, Lucy. *Captain Beastlie's pirate party*
Spector, Todd. *How to pee*

Identity *see* Self-concept

Illness

Appelt, Kathi. *Mogie*
Carlson, Nancy. *Sometimes you barf*
Colón, Raúl. *Draw!*
Gaiman, Neil. *Chu's first day of school*
Lobel, Anita. *Taking care of Mama Rabbit*
Rockliff, Mara. *Chik chak Shabbat*
Ross, Tony. *I feel sick!*
Wells, Rosemary. *A visit to Dr. Duck*

Illness – allergies

Berger, Lou. *Dream dog*
Singleton, Linda Joy. *Snow dog, sand dog*

Illness – Alzheimer's

Van Laan, Nancy. *Forget me not*

Illness – cold (disease)

Krall, Dan. *Sick Simon*

Illness – mental illness

Sterling, Cheryl. *Some bunny to talk to*

Imagination

Bailey, Linda. *If kids ruled the world*
Barnett, Mac. *Sam and Dave dig a hole*
Becker, Aaron. *Quest*
Bentley, Jonathan. *Little big*
Berger, Lou. *Dream dog*
Browne, Anthony. *What if . . . ?*
    Willy's stories
Burningham, John. *The way to the zoo*
Cali, Davide. *A funny thing happened on the way to
    school . . .*
    I didn't do my homework because . . .
Carlin, Laura. *A world of your own*
Chast, Roz. *Around the clock!*
Chung, Arree. *Ninja!*
Colón, Raúl. *Draw!*
Enersen, Adele. *Vincent and the night*
Engler, Michael. *Elephantastic!*
Escoffier, Michael. *The day I lost my superpowers*
Fergus, Maureen. *Buddy and Earl*
Garton, Sam. *Otter in space*
Gay, Marie-Louise. *Any questions?*
Gigot, Jami. *Mae and the moon*
Gill, Deirdre. *Outside*
Hall, Michael. *It's an orange aardvark!*
Hanson, Faye. *The wonder*
Harper, Charise Mericle. *Superlove*
Hole, Stian. *Anna's heaven*
Hutchins, Hazel. *Snap!*
Joyce, William. *Billy's booger*
    Jack Frost
Keane, Claire. *Once upon a cloud*
Kenney, Sean. *Cool creations in 101 pieces*
Knapman, Timothy. *A monster moved in!*
Kuefler, Joseph. *Beyond the pond*
Lammle, Leslie. *Princess wannabe*
Landström, Lena. *Pom and Pim*
Leiter, Richard. *The flying hand of Marco B.*
Luján, Jorge. *Moví la mano / I moved my hand*
McClure, Nikki. *In*
Mackintosh, David. *Lucky*
McPhail, David. *Andrew draws*
Maloney, Brenna. *Ready Rabbit gets ready!*
Martin, Emily Winfield. *Day dreamers*
Murguia, Bethanie Deeney. *Zoe's jungle*
Myers, Christopher. *My pen*
Offill, Jenny. *While you were napping*
O'Leary, Sara. *This is Sadie*
Phelan, Matt. *Druthers*
Pilutti, Deb. *Ten rules of being a superhero*
Pinkney, Brian. *On the ball*
Potter, Giselle. *Tell me what to dream about*
Raschka, Chris. *Cowy cow*
Regan, Dian Curtis. *Space Boy and his dog*
Rosen, Michael. *Send for a superhero!*
Schaefer, Lola M. *One busy day*
Schmid, Paul. *Oliver and his egg*
Sohn, Tania. *Socks!*
Soman, David. *Ladybug Girl and the best ever
    playdate*
Stubbs, Lisa. *Lily and Bear*

Swenson, Jamie A. *If you were a dog*
Tullet, Hervé. *Mix it up!*
Tupper Ling, Nancy. *The story I'll tell*
Usher, Sam. *Snow*
Van Wright, Cornelius. *When an alien meets a
    swamp monster*
Wilson, N. D. *Ninja boy goes to school*
Yoon, Salina. *Tap to play!*
Young, Cybèle. *Some things I've lost*
Zagarenski, Pamela. *The whisper*

Imagination – imaginary friends

Colfer, Eoin. *Imaginary Fred*
Goodrich, Carter. *We forgot Brock!*
Santat, Dan. *The adventures of Beekle*

Immigrants

Aylesworth, Jim. *My grandfather's coat*
Buitrago, Jairo. *Two white rabbits*
Hyde, Heidi Smith. *Shanghai Sukkah*
Kobald, Irena. *My two blankets*
Mora, Pat. *I pledge allegiance*
O'Brien, Anne Sibley. *I'm new here*
Polacco, Patricia. *Fiona's lace*

Incentive *see* Character traits – ambition

Indecision *see* Behavior – indecision

Indians of North America – Inuit

Christopher, Neil. *On the shoulder of a giant*

Indians of North America – Pueblo

Ts'o, Pauline. *Whispers of the wolf*

Indians, American *see* Indians of North
    America

Individuality *see* Character traits – individuality

Insects

American Museum of Natural History. *ABC insects*
DiTerlizzi, Angela. *Some bugs*
Donaldson, Julia. *Superworm*
Latimer, Alex. *Pig and small*
Monroe, Chris. *Bug on a bike*
Smith, Matthew Clark. *Small wonders*
Watt, Mélanie. *Bug in a vacuum*

Insects – ants

Aesop. *The grasshopper and the ants*
Hall, Michael. *It's an orange aardvark!*
Little old lady who swallowed a fly. *There once was a
    cowpoke who swallowed an ant*

Insects – bees

Chrustowski, Rick. *Bee dance*
Ruzzier, Sergio. *Too busy*

Insects – butterflies, caterpillars

Burns, Loree Griffin. *Handle with care*
McKee, David. *Elmer and Butterfly*
Pallotta, Jerry. *Butterfly counting*
Pringle, Laurence. *The secret life of the woolly bear caterpillar*
Shingu, Susumu. *Traveling butterflies*

Insects – fleas

Cohen, Laurie. *The flea*

Insects – flies

Arnold, Tedd. *A pet for Fly Guy*
Edwards, Karl Newsom. *Fly!*
Horácek, Petr. *The fly*
Little old lady who swallowed a fly. *There was an old lady who swallowed a fly*

Insects – grasshoppers

Aesop. *The grasshopper and the ants*

Insects – moths

Pringle, Laurence. *The secret life of the woolly bear caterpillar*

Internet *see* Technology

Inventions

Davis, Kathryn Gibbs. *Mr. Ferris and his wheel*
Falkenstern, Lisa. *Professor Whiskerton presents Steampunk ABC*
Kraft, Betsy Harvey. *The fantastic Ferris wheel*
McCarthy, Meghan. *Earmuffs for everyone!*
Rash, Andy. *Archie the daredevil penguin*
Reynolds, Peter H. *Going places*

Islands

Brunhoff, Laurent de. *Babar on Paradise Island*
Sherry, Kevin. *Turtle Island*

Jackets *see* Clothing – coats

Jealousy *see* Emotions – envy, jealousy

Jesters *see* Clowns, jesters

Jewish culture

Adler, David A. *The story of Passover*
Aylesworth, Jim. *My grandfather's coat*
Edwards, Michelle. *Max makes a cake*
Elvgren, Jennifer. *The whispering town*
Fields, Terri. *One good deed*
Gellman, Ellie B. *Netta and her plant*
Glaser, Linda. *Stone soup with matzoh balls*
Hyde, Heidi Smith. *Shanghai Sukkah*
Kimmel, Eric A. *Simon and the bear*
Newman, Lesléa. *Here is the world*
Peet, Amanda. *Dear Santa, Love Rachel Rosenstein*
Rockliff, Mara. *Chik chak Shabbat*
Simon, Richard. *Oskar and the eight blessings*
Singer, Isaac Bashevis. *The parakeet named Dreidel*

Jobs *see* Careers

Jokes *see* Riddles & jokes

Jungle

Duke, Kate. *In the rainforest*
Messner, Kate. *Tree of wonder*
Salerno, Steven. *Wild child*
Smallman, Steve. *Hiccupotamus*

Kindness *see* Character traits – kindness

Kindness to animals *see* Character traits – kindness to animals

Kissing

Fredrickson, Lane. *Monster trouble!*

Kites

Biddulph, Rob. *Blown away*
Oskarsson, Bardur. *The flat rabbit*

Knights

Klostermann, Penny Parker. *There was an old dragon who swallowed a knight*
Lewin, Betsy. *Good night, Knight*
Sabuda, Robert. *The dragon and the knight*
Sturm, James. *Sleepless knight*

Lakes, ponds

Kuefler, Joseph. *Beyond the pond*

Lambs *see* Animals – babies; Animals – sheep

Language

Barnett, Mac. *Telephone*
Bell, Cece. *I yam a donkey!*
Bryant, Jen. *The right word*
Delaunois, Angèle. *Magic little words*
Escoffier, Michael. *Take away the A*
    Where's the baboon?
Fern, Tracey. *W is for Webster*
Grant, Jacob. *Little Bird's bad word*
Holland, Loretta. *Fall leaves*
Long, Ethan. *In, over, and on (the farm)*
    Ms. Spell
Roberton, Fiona. *Cuckoo!*
Rosenthal, Betsy R. *An ambush of tigers*
Schwartz, Amy. *100 things that make me happy*
Viva, Frank. *Outstanding in the rain*
Ward, Lindsay. *Henry finds his word*
Wells, Rosemary. *Use your words, Sophie!*

Language – sign language *see* Sign language

Languages, foreign *see* Foreign languages

Law *see* Crime

Legends *see* Folk & fairy tales

Letters, cards

Cullen, Lynn. *Dear Mr. Washington*
Daywalt, Drew. *The day the crayons came home*
Kirk, Daniel. *Ten thank-you letters*
Kwan, James. *Dear Yeti*
Latimer, Alex. *Stay! a top dog story*
Latimer, Miriam. *Dear Panda*
Orloff, Karen Kaufman. *I wanna go home*
Peet, Amanda. *Dear Santa, Love Rachel Rosenstein*
Percival, Tom. *Herman's letter*
Ruzzier, Sergio. *A letter for Leo*
Sís, Peter. *Ice cream summer*

Libraries *see also* Books, reading

Becker, Bonny. *A library book for Bear*

Bottner, Barbara. *Miss Brooks' Story Nook (where*
    tales are told and ogres are welcome)
Browne, Anthony. *Willy's stories*
Fliess, Sue. *Books for me!*
Hopkins, Lee Bennett. *Jumping off library shelves*
Kohara, Kazuno. *The Midnight Library*
McQuinn, Anna. *Leo loves baby time*
Morrison, Toni. *Please, Louise*
Stoop, Naoko. *Red Knit Cap Girl and the reading tree*
Sutton, Sally. *Construction*

Light, lights

Boyd, Lizi. *Flashlight*
Heine, Theresa. *Chandra's magic light*
Paul, Ellis. *The night the lights went out on Christmas*
Pfeffer, Wendy. *Light is all around us*

Littleness *see* Character traits – smallness

Lost *see* Behavior – lost

Lost & found possessions *see* Behavior – lost
    & found possessions

Loyalty *see* Character traits – loyalty

Luck *see* Character traits – luck

Lullabies

Brown, Margaret Wise. *Goodnight songs*
Heidbreder, Robert. *Song for a summer night*
Zoboli, Giovanna. *The big book of slumber*

Lying *see* Behavior – lying

Machines

Angleberger, Tom. *McToad mows Tiny Island*
Bee, William. *Digger Dog*
    Stanley the builder
Burleigh, Robert. *Zoom! zoom!*
Davis, Kathryn Gibbs. *Mr. Ferris and his wheel*
Fleming, Candace. *Bulldozer's big day*
Green, Rod. *Giant vehicles*
Harper, Charise Mericle. *Go! go! go! stop!*
Holub, Joan. *Mighty dads*
Koehler, Lora. *The little snowplow*
Kraft, Betsy Harvey. *The fantastic Ferris wheel*
Macaulay, David. *How machines work: zoo break!*

McMullan, Kate. *I'm cool!*
Savage, Stephen. *Supertruck*
Steggall, Susan. *Colors*
Stein, Peter. *Little Red's riding 'hood*
Sutton, Sally. *Construction*

Magic

Berry, Lynne. *Squid Kid the Magnificent*
Jones, Ursula. *Beauty and the beast*
Joyce, William. *A bean, a stalk, and a boy named Jack*
Lee, H. Chuku. *Beauty and the beast*
Luján, Jorge. *Moví la mano / I moved my hand*
Rubin, Adam. *Robo-Sauce*
Sperring, Mark. *Max and the won't go to bed show*
Tegen, Katherine. *Pink cupcake magic*
Zagarenski, Pamela. *The whisper*

Mail *see* Careers – postal workers; Letters, cards

Mail carriers *see* Careers – postal workers; Letters, cards

Manners *see* Etiquette

Maps

Becker, Aaron. *Quest*

Markets *see* Stores

Marriages *see* Weddings

Masks

Lemke, Donald. *Book-o-beards*

Math *see* Counting, numbers

Mazes

Munro, Roxie. *Market maze*

Meanness *see* Character traits – meanness

Mechanical men *see* Robots

Memories, memory

Bar-el, Dan. *A fish named Glub*
Luxbacher, Irene. *Mr. Frank*
Mathers, Petra. *When Aunt Mattie got her wings*
Mora, Pat. *The remembering day / El día de los muertos*
Sheehan, Kevin. *The dandelion's tale*
Van Laan, Nancy. *Forget me not*
Winter, Jeanette. *Mr. Cornell's dream boxes*
Young, Cybèle. *Nancy knows*

Messy *see* Behavior – messy

Metamorphosis

Shingu, Susumu. *Traveling butterflies*

Middle Ages

Klostermann, Penny Parker. *There was an old dragon who swallowed a knight*

Migration

DePalma, Mary Newell. *Two little birds*
Marino, Gianna. *Following Papa's song*
Markle, Sandra. *Toad weather*
Shingu, Susumu. *Traveling butterflies*

Mimes *see* Clowns, jesters

Ministers *see* Careers – clergy

Minorities *see* Ethnic groups in the U.S.

Misbehavior *see* Behavior – misbehavior

Mistakes *see* Behavior – mistakes

Misunderstanding *see* Behavior – misunderstanding

Money

Borden, Louise. *Kindergarten luck*
Heine, Theresa. *Chandra's magic light*
Isabella, Jude. *The red bicycle*
Paul, Miranda. *One plastic bag*

Monsters

Anderson, Brian. *Monster chefs*
Anstee, Ashlyn. *Are we there, Yeti?*
Atteberry, Kevan. *Bunnies!!!*
Bach, Annie. *Monster party!*
Balmes, Santi. *I will fight monsters for you*
Bee, William. *Worst in show*
Brendler, Carol. *Not very scary*
Bright, Rachel. *Love Monster and the perfect present*
Brown, Peter. *My teacher is a monster! (no, I am not)*
Chapman, Jane. *No more cuddles!*
Czajak, Paul. *Monster needs a Christmas tree*
    Monster needs your vote
DiPucchio, Kelly. *Zombie in love 2 + 1*
Fraser, Mary Ann. *No Yeti yet*
Fredrickson, Lane. *Monster trouble!*
Freedman, Claire. *Spider sandwiches*
Graves, Keith. *The monsterator*
Imai, Ayano. *Puss and boots*
John, Jory. *I will chomp you!*
Ketteman, Helen. *The ghosts go haunting*
Knapman, Timothy. *A monster moved in!*
Knudsen, Michelle. *Marilyn's monster*
Kwan, James. *Dear Yeti*
Lester, Helen. *The loch mess monster*
Lewis, J. Patrick. *M is for monster*
Light, Steve. *Have you seen my monster?*

Long, Ethan. *Fright club*
McGee, Joe. *Peanut butter and brains*
McKee, David. *Elmer and the monster*
Manceau, Edouard. *Tickle monster*
Reynolds, Aaron. *Here comes Destructosaurus!*
Richards, Dan. *The problem with not being scared of monsters*
Rubin, Adam. *Big bad bubble*
Smith, A. J. *Even monsters*
Stine, R. L. *The Little Shop of Monsters*
Vogel, Vin. *The thing about yetis*
Walton, Rick. *Frankenstein's fright before Christmas*
Wohnoutka, Mike. *Little puppy and the big green monster*

Months of the year *see* Days of the week, months of the year

Moon

Agee, Jon. *It's only Stanley*
Bolden, Tonya. *Beautiful moon*
Brown-Wood, JaNay. *Imani's moon*
Dale, Penny. *Dinosaur rocket!*
Gigot, Jami. *Mae and the moon*
Horácek, Petr. *The mouse who ate the moon*
Pfister, Marcus. *The little moon raven*
Simon, Francesca. *Hello, Moon!*
Yankey, Lindsey. *Sun and Moon*

Morning

Gerstein, Mordicai. *The night world*
Judge, Lita. *Good morning to me!*

Mother Goose *see* Nursery rhymes

Motion pictures *see* Theater

Mountains

Berkes, Marianne. *Over on a mountain*

Moving

Border, Terry. *Peanut Butter and Cupcake!*
Bunting, Eve. *Yard sale*
Faruqi, Reem. *Lailah's lunchbox*
Pennypacker, Sara. *Meet the Dullards*
Percival, Tom. *Herman's letter*, ill. by Tom Percival *Herman's letter*, ill. by Tom Percival
Scanlon, Elizabeth Garton. *The good-pie party*
Stead, Philip C. *Lenny and Lucy*
Underwood, Deborah. *Bad bye, good bye*

Multi-ethnic *see* Ethnic groups in the U.S.

Multiple births – twins

Atinuke. *Double trouble for Anna Hibiscus!*
Winthrop, Elizabeth. *Lucy and Henry are twins*
Yum, Hyewon. *The twins' little sister*

Mummies

Ewert, Marcus. *Mummy cat*

Little old lady who swallowed a fly. *There was an old mummy who swallowed a spider*

Museums

Garton, Sam. *Otter in space*
Menchin, Scott. *Grandma in blue with red hat*

Music

Ajmera, Maya. *Music everywhere!*
Engle, Margarita. *Drum dream girl*
Golio, Gary. *Bird and Diz*
Lies, Brian. *Bats in the band*
McGowan, Jayme. *One bear extraordinaire*
Mayhew, James. *Ella Bella ballerina and A Midsummer Night's Dream*
Newman, Leslèa. *Ketzel, the cat who composed*
Nolan, Nina. *Mahalia Jackson*
Old MacDonald had a farm. *Pete the Cat: Old MacDonald had a farm*
Raschka, Chris. *The cosmobiography of Sun Ra*
Russell-Brown, Katheryn. *Little Melba and her big trombone*
Shields, Carol Diggory. *Baby's got the blues*
Smallman, Steve. *Hiccupotamus*
The twelve days of Christmas. English folk song.. *The twelve days of Christmas*
Weatherford, Carole Boston. *Leontyne Price*
Weinstone, David. *Music class today!*
Winter, Jonah. *How Jelly Roll Morton invented jazz*

Musical instruments

Ajmera, Maya. *Music everywhere!*
Saaf, Donald. *The ABC animal orchestra*
Weinstone, David. *Music class today!*

Musical instruments – bands

McGowan, Jayme. *One bear extraordinaire*

Musical instruments – drums

Engle, Margarita. *Drum dream girl*

Musical instruments – Fiddles *see* Musical instruments – violins

Musical instruments – guitars

Richards, Keith. *Gus and me*

Musical instruments – orchestras

Saaf, Donald. *The ABC animal orchestra*
Wright, Johana. *The orchestra pit*

Musical instruments – pianos

Newman, Leslèa. *Ketzel, the cat who composed*
Winter, Jonah. *How Jelly Roll Morton invented jazz*

Musical instruments – trombones

Andrews, Troy. *Trombone Shorty*
Russell-Brown, Katheryn. *Little Melba and her big trombone*

Musical instruments – violins

Ray, Mary Lyn. *A violin for Elva*
Uegaki, Chieri. *Hana Hashimoto, sixth violin*

Mystery stories

Olien, Jessica. *Shark Detective!*
Snicket, Lemony. *29 myths on the Swinster Pharmacy*

Mythical creatures

Hakte, Ben. *Julia's house for lost creatures*
Martin, Emily Winfield. *Day dreamers*

Mythical creatures – aliens *see* Aliens

Mythical creatures – mermaids, mermen

Campbell, K.G. *The mermaid and the shoe*
Turnbull, Victoria. *The sea tiger*

Mythical creatures – trolls

Hodgkinson, Leigh. *Troll swap*

Mythical creatures – unicorns

Clayton, Dallas. *Lily the unicorn*
Rosenthal, Amy Krouse. *Uni the unicorn*

Napping *see* Sleep

Native Americans *see* Indians of North America

Nature

Aregui, Matthias. *Before after*
Atteberry, Kevan. *Bunnies!!!*
Bissonette, Aimée. *North woods girl*
Day, Nancy Raines. *What in the world?*
dePaola, Tomie. *Look and be grateful*
Engle, Margarita. *The sky painter*
FitzSimmons, David. *Curious critters, vol. 2*
Frost, Helen. *Sweep up the sun*
Gifford, Peggy. *The great big green*
Gray, Rita. *Have you heard the nesting bird?*
Hurley, Jorey. *Nest*
Jenkins, Steve. *How to swallow a pig*
Johnston, Tony. *Sequoia*
Kuefler, Joseph. *Beyond the pond*
London, Jonathan. *Ollie's first year*
    The seasons of Little Wolf
Low, William. *Daytime nighttime*
Lyon, George Ella. *What forest knows*
McPhail, David. *Beatrix Potter and her paint box*

Messner, Kate. *Tree of wonder*
Nichols, Lori. *Maple and Willow together*
Posada, Mia. *Who was here?*
Root, Phyllis. *Plant a pocket of prairie*
Sayre, April Pulley. *Woodpecker wham!*
Sidman, Joyce. *Winter bees and other poems of the cold*
Smith, Matthew Clark. *Small wonders*
Viano, Hannah. *B is for bear*
Wahl, Phoebe. *Sonya's chickens*
Ward, Jennifer. *Mama built a little nest*
Weiss, George. *What a wonderful world*
Wigger, J. Bradley. *Thank you, God*
Yee, Wong Herbert. *My autumn book*

Naughty *see* Behavior – misbehavior

Needing someone *see* Behavior – needing someone

Negotiation *see* Activities – trading

Neighborhoods *see* Communities, neighborhoods

Night

Borando, Silvia. *Black cat, white cat*
Boyd, Lizi. *Flashlight*
Enersen, Adele. *Vincent and the night*
Gerstein, Mordicai. *The night world*
Heidbreder, Robert. *Song for a summer night*
Low, William. *Daytime nighttime*
Marino, Gianna. *Night animals*
Matheson, Christie. *Touch the brightest star*
Minor, Wendell. *Daylight starlight wildlife*
Roscoe, Lily. *The night parade*

Ninja *see* Sports – martial arts

No text *see* Wordless

Noise, sounds

Agee, Jon. *It's only Stanley*
Arndt, Michael. *Cat says meow and other animalopoeia*
Burleigh, Robert. *Zoom! zoom!*
Gude, Paul. *When Elephant met Giraffe*
Hannigan, Katherine. *Gwendolyn Grace*
Himmelman, John. *Noisy bird sing-along*
Husband, Amy. *The noisy foxes*
Judge, Lita. *Good morning to me!*
Kennedy, Anne Vittur. *The farmer's away! baa! neigh!*
Murphy, Mary. *Say hello like this!*
Naberhaus, Sarvinder. *Boom boom*
Portis, Antoinette. *Froodle*
Roques, Dominique. *Sleep tight, Anna Banana!*
Schofield-Morrison, Connie. *I got the rhythm*
Sims, Nat. *Peekaboo barn*
Smallman, Steve. *Hiccupotamus*
Van Biesen, Koen. *Roger is reading a book*
Wilson, Karma. *Duddle Puck*
Yuly, Toni. *Night owl*

North Pole *see* Foreign lands – Arctic

Noses *see* Senses – smell

Numbers *see* Counting, numbers

Nursery rhymes

Brown, Margaret Wise. *The find it book*
Cabrera, Jane. *Baa, baa, black sheep*
Dean, James. *Pete the Cat: twinkle, twinkle, little star*
Jackson, Alison. *When the wind blew*
Krumwiede, Lana. *Just Itzy*
Smith, Danna. *Mother Goose's pajama party*
Trapani, Iza. *Old King Cole*
Verburg, Bonnie. *The tree house that Jack built*

Nursery school *see* School – nursery

Nutrition *see* Food; *see* Health & fitness

Occupations *see* Careers

Oceans *see* Sea & seashore

Octopuses

Estes, Allison. *Izzy and Oscar*
Farrell, Darren. *Thank you, Octopus*
McKenna, Martin. *The octopuppy*

Odors *see* Senses – smell

Old age

Orloff, Karen Kaufman. *I wanna go home*
Ray, Mary Lyn. *A violin for Elva*
Shepherd, Jessica. *Grandma*
Van Laan, Nancy. *Forget me not*

Olympics *see* Sports – Olympics

Opossums *see* Animals – possums

Optimism *see* Character traits – optimism

Orderliness *see* Character traits – orderliness

Outer space *see* Space & space ships

Pageants *see* Theater

Painters *see* Activities – painting; Careers – artists

Panthers *see* Animals – leopards

Parades

Colby, Rebecca. *It's raining bats and frogs*
Pitman, Gayle E. *This day in June*
Roscoe, Lily. *The night parade*
Waldron, Kevin. *Panda-monium at Peek Zoo*

Parks

Nordling, Lee. *Shehewe*

Parks – amusement

Davis, Kathryn Gibbs. *Mr. Ferris and his wheel*
Kraft, Betsy Harvey. *The fantastic Ferris wheel*
Viva, Frank. *Outstanding in the rain*

Parrots *see* Birds – parakeets, parrots

Participation

Harrington, Tim. *Nose to toes, you are yummy!*
Jones, Christianne C. *The Santa shimmy*
Matheson, Christie. *Touch the brightest star*
Ramadier, Cédric. *Help! the wolf is coming!*
Tullet, Hervé. *Mix it up!*
Yoon, Salina. *Tap to play!*

Parties

Bach, Annie. *Monster party!*
Brendler, Carol. *Not very scary*
Browne, Anthony. *What if . . . ?*
Carlson, Nancy. *Armond goes to a party*
Chapin, Tom. *The backwards birthday party*
Desbordes, Astrid. *Edmond, the moonlit party*
Dodd, Emma. *The entertainer*
Fleming, Candace. *Bulldozer's big day*
Godin, Thelma Lynne. *The hula-hoopin' queen*
Harrison, Hannah E. *Bernice gets carried away*
London, Jonathan. *Froggy's birthday wish*
Mack, Jeff. *Who needs a bath?*
Mann, Jennifer K. *Two speckled eggs*
Miyakoshi, Akiko. *The tea party in the woods*
O'Connell, Rebecca. *Baby party*
Reagan, Jean. *How to surprise a dad*

Saltzberg, Barney. *Tea with Grandpa*
Samuels, Barbara. *Fred's beds*
Scanlon, Elizabeth Garton. *The good-pie party*

Patience *see* Character traits – patience

Peace *see* Violence, nonviolence

Peahens *see* Birds – peacocks, peahens

Pen pals

Percival, Tom. *Herman's letter*

Perfectionism *see* Character traits – perfectionism

Perseverance *see* Character traits – perseverance

Persistence *see* Character traits – persistence

Pets

Adderson, Caroline. *Norman, speak!*
Arnold, Tedd. *A pet for Fly Guy*
Barton, Byron. *My bus*
Biedrzycki, David. *Me and my dragon: Christmas spirit*
Côté, Geneviève. *Bob's hungry ghost*
Elliott, David. *This Orq. (He say "ugh!")*
    This Orq. (He cave boy.)
Estes, Allison. *Izzy and Oscar*
Friedman, Laurie. *Ruby Valentine and the sweet surprise*
Gorbachev, Valeri. *Cats are cats*
Gravett, Emily. *Matilda's cat*
Huneck, Stephen. *Sally goes to heaven*
Long, Ethan. *Me and my big mouse*
McDonald, Megan. *Shoe dog*
McKenna, Martin. *The octopuppy*
Mantchev, Lisa. *Strictly no elephants*
O'Connor, George. *If I had a raptor*
    If I had a triceratops
Offill, Jenny. *Sparky!*
Pett, Mark. *Lizard from the park*
Pinkwater, Daniel. *Bear and Bunny*
Ross, Tony. *Rita's rhino*
Rudy, Maggie. *I wish I had a pet*
Seuss, Dr. *What pet should I get?*
Shyba, Jessica. *Naptime with Theo and Beau*
Staake, Bob. *My pet book*
Stein, David Ezra. *I'm my own dog*
Stine, R. L. *The Little Shop of Monsters*
Stower, Adam. *Naughty kitty!*
Torrey, Richard. *My dog, Bob*
Trukhan, Ekaterina. *Patrick wants a dog!*
Van Allsburg, Chris. *The misadventures of Sweetie Pie*

Physicians *see* Careers – doctors

Picture puzzles

Brown, Margaret Wise. *The find it book*
Fairgray, Richard. *Gorillas in our midst*
Ljungkvist, Laura. *Search and spot: animals!*
Munro, Roxie. *Market maze*
Roderick, Stacey. *Dinosaurs from head to tail*
Tallec, Olivier. *Who done it?*
Teckentrup, Britta. *The odd one out*
    Where's the pair?
Wick, Walter. *Can you see what I see? Christmas*
    Hey, Seymour!

Pilgrims

Greenwood, Mark. *The Mayflower*

Pioneer life *see* U.S. history – frontier & pioneer life

Pirates

Bunting, Eve. *P is for pirate*
Chapman, Jared. *Pirate, Viking, and Scientist*
Coats, Lucy. *Captain Beastlie's pirate party*
Crowe, Caroline. *Pirates in pajamas*
Estes, Allison. *Izzy and Oscar*
Griswell, Kim T. *Rufus goes to sea*
Kimmelman, Leslie. *Trick ARRR treat*
Powell-Tuck, Maudie. *Pirates aren't afraid of the dark!*
Sattler, Jennifer. *Pig kahuna pirates!*
Winters, Kari-Lynn. *Bad pirate*

Planes *see* Airplanes, airports

Planets

Sanders, Rob. *Outer space bedtime race*

Plants

Brett, Jan. *The turnip*
Chapman, Jared. *Vegetables in underwear*
Duke, Kate. *In the rainforest*
Gellman, Ellie B. *Netta and her plant*
Hood, Susan. *Rooting for you*
Joyce, William. *A bean, a stalk, and a boy named Jack*
Rockwell, Lizzy. *Plants feed me*
Root, Phyllis. *Plant a pocket of prairie*
Sheehan, Kevin. *The dandelion's tale*
Wunderli, Stephen. *Little Boo*

Plays *see* Theater

Pockets *see* Clothing

Poetry

Argueta, Jorge. *Salsa*
Blanco, Richard. *One today*
Cleary, Brian P. *If it rains pancakes*
Elliott, David. *On the wing*

Engle, Margarita. *Orangutanka*
   The sky painter
Franco, Betsy. *A spectacular selection of sea critters*
Frost, Helen. *Sweep up the sun*
Graham, Joan Bransfield. *The poem that will not end*
Hopkins, Lee Bennett. *Jumping off library shelves*
   Manger
Hughes, Langston. *Sail away*
Janeczko, Paul B. *Firefly July*
Johnston, Tony. *Sequoia*
Latham, Irene. *Dear Wandering Wildebeest*
Luján, Jorge. *Moví la mano / I moved my hand*
McNamara, Margaret. *A poem in your pocket*
Moore, Clement Clarke. *The night before Christmas*,
   ill. by David Ercolini
   The night before Christmas, ill. by Barbara Reid
   'Twas the night before Christmas
Mora, Pat. *Water rolls, water rises / el agua ruda, el
   agua sube*
Muth, Jon J. *Hi, Koo!*
Oliver, Lin. *Little poems for tiny ears*
Raczka, Bob. *Santa Clauses*
Raschka, Chris. *Alphabetabum*
Ruddell, Deborah. *The popcorn astronauts*
Salas, Laura Purdie. *Water can be . . .*
Sidman, Joyce. *Winter bees and other poems of the cold*
Smith, Charles R. *28 days*
Wardlaw, Lee. *Won Ton and Chopstick*
Weatherford, Carole Boston. *Voice of freedom*

Pollution *see* Ecology

Poltergeists *see* Ghosts

Ponds *see* Lakes, ponds

Ponies *see* Animals – horses, ponies

Poor *see* Poverty

Pop-up books *see* Format, unusual – toy &
   movable books

Potty training *see* Toilet training

Poverty

Brandt, Lois. *Maddi's fridge*
Javaherbin, Mina. *Soccer star*
Stone, Tanya Lee. *The house that Jane built*

Prairie wolves *see* Animals – coyotes

Prayers *see* Religion

Preachers *see* Careers – clergy

Pregnancy *see* Birth

Prehistoric man *see* Cave dwellers

Prejudice

Bandy, Michael S. *Granddaddy's turn*
Bass, Hester. *Seeds of freedom*
Bildner, Phil. *The soccer fence*
Cooper, Floyd. *Juneteenth for Mazie*
Dempsey, Kristy. *A dance like starlight*
Meltzer, Brad. *I am Rosa Parks*
Meyer, Susan Lynn. *New shoes*
Slade, Suzanne. *With books and bricks*
Thompson, Laurie Ann. *Emmanuel's dream*
Tonatiuh, Duncan. *Separate is never equal*
Watkins, Angela Farris. *Love will see you through*
Weatherford, Carole Boston. *Gordon Parks*
   Voice of freedom
Winter, Jonah. *Lillian's right to vote*

Preschool *see* School – nursery

Pretending *see* Imagination

Priests *see* Careers – clergy

Problem solving

Brett, Jan. *The turnip*
Chase, Kit. *Oliver's tree*
Deedman, Heidi. *Too many toys!*
Driscoll, Amanda. *Duncan the story dragon*
Flory, Neil. *The short giraffe*
Kishira, Mayuko. *Who's next door?*
Krosoczka, Jarrett J. *It's tough to lose your balloon*
Pett, Mark. *The girl and the bicycle*
Raschka, Chris. *Give and take*

Promptness, tardiness *see* Behavior –
   promptness, tardiness

Punctuality *see* Behavior – promptness,
   tardiness

Questioning *see* Character traits – questioning

Quilts

Herkert, Barbara. *Sewing stories*

Rabbis *see* Careers – clergy

Race relations *see* Prejudice

Racially mixed *see* Ethnic groups in the U.S.

Railroads *see* Trains

Reading *see* Books, reading

Recycling *see* Ecology

Religion

Bible. Old Testament. Genesis. *Let there be light*
Bolden, Tonya. *Beautiful moon*
dePaola, Tomie. *Look and be grateful*
Grün, Anselm. *Jesus*
    The legend of Saint Nicholas
Hole, Stian. *Anna's heaven*
Lumbard, Alexis York. *Everyone prays*
Wigger, J. Bradley. *Thank you, God*

Religion – Islam

Faruqi, Reem. *Lailah's lunchbox*

Religion – Nativity

Hopkins, Lee Bennett. *Manger*
McGhee, Alison. *Star bright*

Religion – Noah

Sassi, Laura. *Goodnight, Ark*

Remembering *see* Memories, memory

Repetitive stories *see* Cumulative tales

Reptiles

FitzSimmons, David. *Curious critters, vol. 2*

Reptiles – alligators, crocodiles

Bedford, David. *Two tough crocs*
Dillard, Sarah. *First day at Zoo School*

Hannigan, Katherine. *Gwendolyn Grace*
Merino, Gemma. *The crocodile who didn't like water*
Miller, John. *Winston and George*
Miyares, Daniel. *Pardon me!*
O'Neill, Gemma. *Monty's magnificent mane*
Ormerod, Jan. *The baby swap*
Parsley, Elise. *If you ever want to bring an alligator to school, don't!*
Perret, Delphine. *Pedro and George*
Schubert, Ingrid. *There is a crocodile under my bed*
Van Wright, Cornelius. *When an alien meets a swamp monster*

Reptiles – lizards

Antony, Steve. *Green lizards vs. red rectangles*

Reptiles – snakes

Davies, Nicola. *I (don't) like snakes*
Shuttlewood, Craig. *Through the town*
Willis, Jeanne. *Boa's bad birthday*
Wright, Johana. *The orchestra pit*

Reptiles – turtles, tortoises

George, Jean Craighead. *Galápagos George*
Harris, Robie H. *Turtle and me*
Sherry, Kevin. *Turtle Island*

Resourcefulness *see* Behavior – resourcefulness

Responsibility *see* Character traits – responsibility

Rest *see* Sleep

Restaurants

Bee, William. *Stanley's diner*
Slegers, Liesbet. *Chefs and what they do*

Rhyming text

Agee, Jon. *It's only Stanley*
Allen, Kathryn Madeline. *Show me happy*
Allenby, Victoria. *Nat the cat can sleep like that*
Anderson, Derek. *Ten pigs*
Anholt, Laurence. *Two nests*
Appelt, Kathi. *Counting crows*
Bach, Annie. *Monster party!*
Bailey, Ella. *No such thing*
Bar-el, Dan. *A fish named Glub*
Barash, Chris. *Is it Hanukkah yet?*
Bardhan-Quallen, Sudipta. *Snoring Beauty*
    Tyrannosaurus wrecks!
Beaumont, Karen. *Crybaby*
    Wild about us!
Bently, Peter. *Meet the parents*
    Those magnificent sheep in their flying machine
Berger, Samantha. *Snoozefest at the Nuzzledome*
Berkes, Marianne. *Over on a mountain*
Biddulph, Rob. *Blown away*
Blackstone, Stella. *Bear's school day*
Blatt, Jane. *Books always everywhere*
Bluemle, Elizabeth. *Tap tap boom boom*

Bramsen, Carin. *Just a duck?*
Bright, Rachel. *Side by side*
Brisson, Pat. *Before we eat*
Buehner, Caralyn. *Merry Christmas, Mr. Mouse*
Bunting, Eve. *Whose shoe?*
Burfoot, Ella. *How to bake a book*
Burleigh, Robert. *Zoom! zoom!*
Byous, Shawn. *Because I stubbed my toe*
Cabrera, Jane. *Baa, baa, black sheep*
    Row, row, row your boat
Carle, Eric. *The nonsense show*
Caswell, Deanna. *Beach house*
Chast, Roz. *Around the clock!*
Chernesky, Felicia Sanzari. *Cheers for a dozen ears*
    From apple trees to cider, please!
    Sugar white snow and evergreens
    Sun above and blooms below
Clarkson, Stephanie. *Sleeping Cinderella and other*
    princess mix-ups
Coat, Janik. *Rhymoceros*
Colandro, Lucille. *There was an old lady who*
    swallowed a frog!
Coyle, Carmela LaVigna. *Do princesses make happy*
    campers?
Crowe, Caroline. *Pirates in pajamas*
Cuyler, Margery. *The little school bus*
Cyrus, Kurt. *Motor Dog*
Czajak, Paul. *Monster needs a Christmas tree*
    Monster needs your vote
Dahl, Michael. *Goodnight football*
Day, Nancy Raines. *What in the world?*
Dean, James. *Pete the Cat and the new guy*
Denise, Anika. *Baking day at Grandma's*
Dewdney, Anna. *Nelly Gnu and Daddy too*
Diesen, Deborah. *The not very merry pout-pout fish*
    The pout-pout fish goes to school
Diggs, Taye. *Mixed me!*
DiTerlizzi, Angela. *Baby love*
    Some bugs
Dodd, Emma. *Always*
    The entertainer
    Everything
    Happy
    More and more
    When I grow up
Donaldson, Julia. *Superworm*
Dotlich, Rebecca Kai. *All aboard!*
    Race car count
Duddle, Johnny. *Gigantosaurus*
Dunbar, Joyce. *Pat-a-cake baby*
Duval, Kathy. *A bear's year*
Elya, Susan Middleton. *Little Roja Riding Hood*
Emberley, Rebecca. *Spare parts*
Esbaum, Jill. *I am cow, hear me moo!*
    I hatched!
Ewert, Marcus. *Mummy cat*
Ferry, Beth. *Stick and Stone*
Fliess, Sue. *Books for me!*
Florian, Douglas. *How to draw a dragon*
    I love my hat
Fox, Mem. *Nellie Belle*
Freedman, Claire. *Spider sandwiches*
Friedman, Laurie. *Ruby Valentine and the sweet*
    surprise
Garland, Sally Anne. *Share*
Gehl, Laura. *One big pair of underwear*
Gershator, Phillis. *Time for a bath*
Gibson, Amy. *By day, by night*
Graham, Joan Bransfield. *The poem that will not end*

Graves, Keith. *The monsterator*
Gray, Kes. *Frog on a log?*
Gray, Rita. *Have you heard the nesting bird?*
Gutman, Dan. *Rappy the raptor*
Halpern, Shari. *Dinosaur parade*
Hamburg, Jennifer. *Monkey and Duck quack up!*
Harrington, Tim. *Nose to toes, you are yummy!*
Heidbreder, Robert. *Song for a summer night*
Hodgkinson, Jo. *A big day for Migs*
Holub, Joan. *Mighty dads*
Hood, Susan. *Tickly toes*
Horacek, Judy. *Yellow is my color star*
Horvath, James. *Work, dogs, work*
Houran, Lori Haskins. *A dozen cousins*
Howatt, Sandra J. *Sleepyheads*
Jackson, Alison. *When the wind blew*
Jackson, Ellen. *Beastly babies*
Jacobs, Paul DuBois. *Count on the subway*
Jane, Pamela. *Little elfie one*
Jantzen, Doug. *Henry Hyena, why won't you laugh?*
Jones, Christianne C. *The Santa shimmy*
Katz, Susan B. *ABC school's for me!*
Kennedy, Anne Vittur. *The farmer's away! baa!*
    neigh!
Ketteman, Helen. *At the old haunted house*
Kimmelman, Leslie. *Trick ARRR treat*
Krensky, Stephen. *I am so brave!*
Kyle, Tracey. *Gazpacho for Nacho*
Lang, Suzanne. *Families, families, families!*
Lawler, Janet. *Love is real*
Leiter, Richard. *The flying hand of Marco B.*
Lemke, Donald. *Book-o-beards*
Lies, Brian. *Bats in the band*
Litton, Jonthan. *Snip snap*
Litwin, Eric. *The Nuts*
    The Nuts: sing and dance in your polka-dot pants
Lord, Cynthia. *Hot Rod Hamster: monster truck*
    mania!
Lurie, Susan. *Swim, duck, swim!*
Luzzati, Emanuele. *Three little owls*
Lynch, Jane. *Marlene, Marlene, Queen of Mean*
Lyon, George Ella. *Boats float!*
McGrath, Barbara Barbieri. *Teddy bear addition*
McPike, Elizabeth. *Little sleepyhead*
Manushkin, Fran. *Happy in our skin*
Martin, David. *Peep and Ducky: rainy day*
Martin, Emily Winfield. *Day dreamers*
    The wonderful things you will be
Massini, Sarah. *Love always everywhere*
May, Robert L. *Rudolph shines again*
Miller, Pat Zietlow. *Sharing the bread*
    Wherever you go
Mitton, Tony. *Snowy Bear*
Molk, Laurel. *Eeny, Meeny, Miney, Mo and Flo!*
Monroe, Chris. *Bug on a bike*
Morrison, Toni. *Please, Louise*
Murray, Alison. *Hickory dickory dog*
Naberhaus, Sarvinder. *Boom boom*
Palatini, Margie. *No nap! yes nap!*
Parenteau, Shirley. *Bears and a birthday*
    Bears in the bath
Paul, Ellis. *The night the lights went out on Christmas*
Pearce, Clemency. *Three little words*
Pierce, Christa. *Did you know that I love you?*
Pitman, Gayle E. *This day in June*
Posada, Mia. *Who was here?*
Prasadam-Halls, Smriti. *I love you night and day*
Previn, Stacey. *Find spot!*
Price, Ben Joel. *Earth space moon base*

Raczka, Bob. *Joy in Mudville*
Ray, Mary Lyn. *Go to sleep, little farm*
Riehle, Mary Ann McCabe. *The little kids' table*
Roberts, Justin. *The smallest girl in the smallest grade*
Roscoe, Lily. *The night parade*
Rosen, Michael. *The bus is for us!*
Rosenthal, Amy Krouse. *Little Miss, big sis*
Rosenthal, Betsy R. *An ambush of tigers*
Sadler, Marilyn. *Tony Baroni loves macaroni*
Saltzberg, Barney. *Tea with Grandpa*
Salzano, Tammi. *I love you just the way you are*
Sanders, Rob. *Outer space bedtime race*
Sanderson, Ruth. *A castle full of cats*
Sassi, Laura. *Goodnight, Ark*
Sayres, Brianna Caplan. *Tiara Saurus Rex*
Scheffler, Axel. *Axel Scheffler's Flip flap safari*
Schneider, Josh. *Everybody sleeps (but not Fred)*
Schwartz, Amy. *100 things that make me happy*
Schwartz, Corey Rosen. *Ninja Red Riding Hood*
Seuss, Dr. *Horton and the Kwuggerbug and more lost*
    stories
    What pet should I get?
Shannon, George. *Hands say love*
Shaw, Stephanie. *A cookie for Santa*
Shields, Carol Diggory. *Baby's got the blues*
Shuttlewood, Craig. *Who's in the tree?*
Siddals, Mary McKenna. *Shivery shades of Halloween*
Sierra, Judy. *E-I-E-I-O*
Singer, Marilyn. *I'm gonna climb a mountain in my*
    patent leather shoes
Smallman, Steve. *Hiccupotamus*
Spinelli, Eileen. *Thankful*
Staake, Bob. *My pet book*
Stainton, Sue. *I love dogs!*
Stockdale, Susan. *Spectacular spots*
Surplice, Holly. *Peek-a-boo Bunny*
Sweeney, Linda Booth. *When the wind blows*
Tarpley, Todd. *Beep! beep! go to sleep!*
Thong, Roseanne Greenfield. *Green is a chile pepper*
    'Twas nochebuena
Tillman, Nancy. *You're here for a reason*
Todd, Mark. *Food trucks!*
Tougas, Chris. *Dojo Daycare*
Tuell, Todd. *Ninja, ninja, never stop!*
Underwood, Deborah. *Bad bye, good bye*
    Interstellar Cinderella
Vamos, Samantha R. *Alphabet trains*
Verde, Susan. *You and me*
Virján, Emma J. *What this story needs is a pig in a*
    wig
Viva, Frank. *Outstanding in the rain*
Walsh, Joanna. *I love Mom*
Walton, Rick. *Frankenstein's fright before Christmas*
Ward, Helen. *Spots in a box*
Ward, Jennifer. *Mama built a little nest*
Weatherford, Carole Boston. *Sugar Hill*
Weingarten, Gene. *Me and dog*
Weinstone, David. *Music class today!*
Wheeler, Lisa. *Dino-boarding*
    Dino-swimming
Whelan, Gloria. *Queen Victoria's bathing machine*
White, Dianne. *Blue on blue*
Wick, Walter. *Can you see what I see? Christmas*
    Hey, Seymour!
Willis, Jeanne. *Slug needs a hug!*
Wilson, Karma. *Bear counts*
    Bear sees colors
    Duddle Puck
Winthrop, Elizabeth. *Lucy and Henry are twins*

Yee, Wong Herbert. *My autumn book*
Yolen, Jane. *How do dinosaurs stay safe?*
    Sing a season song
    You nest here with me
Zoboli, Giovanna. *The big book of slumber*

Riddles & jokes

Gill, Timothy. *Flip and Fin: we rule the school!*

Riots *see* Violence, nonviolence

Roads

Horvath, James. *Work, dogs, work*

Robbers *see* Crime

Robots

Austin, Mike. *Junkyard*
Cyrus, Kurt. *Motor Dog*
Emberley, Rebecca. *Spare parts*
Houran, Lori Haskins. *How to spy on a shark*
Judge, Chris. *Tin*
Price, Ben Joel. *Earth space moon base*
Rosenthal, Marc. *Big bot, small bot*
Rubin, Adam. *Robo-Sauce*
Staniszewski, Anna. *Power down, Little Robot*
Tarpley, Todd. *Beep! beep! go to sleep!*
Watkins, Adam F. *R is for robot*
Yaccarino, Dan. *Doug unplugs on the farm*

Rockets *see* Space & space ships

Rocks

Ferry, Beth. *Stick and Stone*
Formento, Alison. *These rocks count!*

Roosters *see* Birds – chickens, roosters

Royalty

Sanderson, Ruth. *A castle full of cats*

Royalty – kings

Anderson, Brian. *Monster chefs*
Gerstein, Mordicai. *You can't have too many friends!*
Niemann, Christoph. *The potato king*

Royalty – princes

Brett, Jan. *Cinders*
Carey, Lorraine. *Cinderella's stepsister and the big*
    bad wolf
Grimm, Jacob and Wilhelm. *Sleeping beauty*
Underwood, Deborah. *Interstellar Cinderella*

Royalty – princesses

Andrews, Julie. *The very fairy princess: a spooky,*
    sparkly Halloween
    The very fairy princess: graduation girl!
Bardhan-Quallen, Sudipta. *Snoring Beauty*
Beaton, Kate. *The princess and the pony*

Clarkson, Stephanie. *Sleeping Cinderella and other princess mix-ups*
Coyle, Carmela LaVigna. *Do princesses make happy campers?*
French, Vivian. *The most wonderful thing in the world*
Grimm, Jacob and Wilhelm. *Sleeping beauty*
Jones, Ursula. *The princess who had no kingdom*
Lammle, Leslie. *Princess wannabe*
Lum, Kate. *Princesses are not just pretty*
Miura, Taro. *The big princess*
Ross, Tony. *I feel sick!*

Royalty – queens

Antony, Steve. *The Queen's hat*
Whelan, Gloria. *Queen Victoria's bathing machine*

Rummage sales *see* Garage sales, rummage sales

Rumors *see* Behavior – gossip, rumors

Running *see* Activities – running; Sports – racing

Running away *see* Behavior – running away

Safety

Braun, Sebastien. *Whoosh and Chug!*
Heos, Bridget. *Be safe around fire*
International Center for Assault Prevention. *My body belongs to me from my head to my toes*
Starishevsky, Jill. *My body belongs to me*
Yolen, Jane. *How do dinosaurs stay safe?*

Santa Claus

Bailey, Linda. *When Santa was a baby*
Brett, Jan. *The animals' Santa*
Cronin, Doreen. *Click, clack, ho! ho! ho!*
Grün, Anselm. *The legend of Saint Nicholas*
Hennessy, B. G. *A Christmas wish for Corduroy*
Jones, Christianne C. *The Santa shimmy*
Metzger, Steve. *Waiting for Santa*
Moore, Clement Clarke. *The night before Christmas*, ill. by David Ercolini
  The night before Christmas, ill. by Barbara Reid
  'Twas the night before Christmas
Peet, Amanda. *Dear Santa, Love Rachel Rosenstein*
Pingk, Rubin. *Samurai Santa*
Plourde, Lynn. *Merry Moosey Christmas*
Raczka, Bob. *Santa Clauses*
Reagan, Jean. *How to catch Santa*
Shaw, Stephanie. *A cookie for Santa*
Underwood, Deborah. *Here comes Santa Cat*

Scarecrows

Long, Loren. *Otis and the scarecrow*

School

Andrews, Julie. *The very fairy princess: a spooky, sparkly Halloween*
  The very fairy princess: graduation girl!
Bean, Jonathan. *This is my home, this is my school*
Best, Cari. *My three best friends and me, Zulay*
Blackstone, Stella. *Bear's school day*
Borden, Louise. *Kindergarten luck*
Brown, Peter. *My teacher is a monster! (no, I am not)*
Cali, Davide. *A funny thing happened on the way to school . . .*
Cline-Ransome, Lesa. *Freedom's school*
Cuyler, Margery. *The little school bus*
Davies, Matt. *Ben draws trouble*
De Kinder, Jan. *Red*
Durand, Hallie. *Catch that cookie!*
Faruqi, Reem. *Lailah's lunchbox*
Frankel, Erin. *Nobody!*
Gill, Timothy. *Flip and Fin: we rule the school!*
Johnson, Stephen T. *Alphabet school*
Joyce, William. *Billy's booger*
Katz, Susan B. *ABC school's for me!*
Ketteman, Helen. *The ghosts go haunting*
McNamara, Margaret. *A poem in your pocket*
Mann, Jennifer K. *I will never get a star on Mrs. Benson's blackboard*
Murray, Alison. *Hickory dickory dog*
Nichols, Lori. *Maple and Willow apart*
Noble, Trinka Hakes. *Lizzie and the last day of school*
O'Brien, Anne Sibley. *I'm new here*
Parsley, Elise. *If you ever want to bring an alligator to school, don't!*
Polacco, Patricia. *An A from Miss Keller*
  Mr. Wayne's masterpiece
Saab, Julie. *Little Lola*
Sauer, Tammi. *Ginny Louise and the school showdown*
Slade, Suzanne. *With books and bricks*
Tonatiuh, Duncan. *Separate is never equal*
Trent, Tereai. *The girl who buried her dreams in a can*
Van Slyke, Rebecca. *Mom school*
Vernick, Audrey. *First grade dropout*
Wall, Laura. *Goose goes to school*
Wilson, N. D. *Ninja boy goes to school*

School – field trips

Anstee, Ashlyn. *Are we there, Yeti?*
Chernesky, Felicia Sanzari. *Sun above and blooms below*
Formento, Alison. *These rocks count!*
Tougas, Chris. *Dojo daytrip*

School – first day

Ashdown, Rebecca. *Bob and Flo*
Auerbach, Adam. *Edda*
Brown, Marc. *Monkey*
Capucilli, Alyssa Satin. *Not this bear*
Chapman, Jared. *Steve, raised by wolves*
Cohen, Jeff. *Eva and Sadie and the best classroom ever!*
Diesen, Deborah. *The pout-pout fish goes to school*
Dillard, Sarah. *First day at Zoo School*
Gaiman, Neil. *Chu's first day of school*
Hodgkinson, Jo. *A big day for Migs*

Johnston, Tony. *First grade, here I come!*
Krumwiede, Lana. *Just Itzy*
Latimer, Miriam. *Dear Panda*
Livingston, A. A. *B. Bear and Lolly: off to school*
Puttock, Simon. *Mouse's first night at Moonlight School*
Rim, Sujean. *Birdie's first day of school*
Torrey, Richard. *Ally-Saurus and the first day of school*
Wohnoutka, Mike. *Dad's first day*

School – nursery

Ashdown, Rebecca. *Bob and Flo*
Katz, Karen. *Rosie goes to preschool*
Shea, Bob. *Dinosaur vs. school*
Tougas, Chris. *Dojo Daycare*

School teachers *see* Careers – teachers

Science

Bang, Molly. *Buried sunlight*
Chapman, Jared. *Pirate, Viking, and Scientist*
Chin, Jason. *Gravity*
Davies, Nicola. *Tiny creatures*
Gibbons, Gail. *It's raining!*
Kudlinski, Kathleen V. *Boy, were we wrong about the human body!*
Meltzer, Brad. *I am Albert Einstein*
Paul, Miranda. *Water is water*
Pfeffer, Wendy. *Light is all around us*

Sea & seashore

Barner, Bob. *Sea bones*
Beliveau, Kathy. *The yoga game by the sea*
Catrow, David. *Fun in the sun*
Franco, Betsy. *A spectacular selection of sea critters*
Hughes, Langston. *Sail away*
Preston-Gannon, Frann. *Deep deep sea*
Turnbull, Victoria. *The sea tiger*

Sea & seashore – beaches

Bottner, Barbara. *Feet go to sleep*
Caswell, Deanna. *Beach house*
Crum, Shutta. *Uh-oh!*
Fleming, Candace. *Tippy-tippy-tippy, splash!*
Gaiman, Neil. *Chu's day at the beach*
Gall, Chris. *Dinotrux dig the beach*
Hills, Tad. *Duck and Goose go to the beach*
Hurley, Jorey. *Fetch*
Idle, Molly. *Sea Rex*
Jay, Alison. *Out of the blue*
Larsen, Andrew. *See you next year*
Napoli, Donna Jo. *Hands and hearts*
Sattler, Jennifer. *Pig kahuna: who's that pig?*
  Pig kahuna pirates!

Sea serpents *see* Monsters; Mythical creatures

Seashore *see* Sea & seashore – beaches

Seasons

Bissonette, Aimée. *North woods girl*

Brown, Margaret Wise. *Goodnight songs*
Bruel, Nick. *A wonderful year*
Clement, Nathan. *Big tractor*
Duval, Kathy. *A bear's year*
Horáček, Petr. *A surprise for Tiny Mouse*
Hurley, Jorey. *Nest*
Janeczko, Paul B. *Firefly July*
Johnston, Tony. *Sequoia*
Kirk, Daniel. *The thing about spring*
Leduc, Emilie. *All year round*
Long, Loren. *Little tree*
Lyon, George Ella. *What forest knows*
Messner, Kate. *Up in the garden and down in the dirt*
Muth, Jon J. *Hi, Koo!*
Naberhaus, Sarvinder. *Boom boom*
Paul, Miranda. *Water is water*
Ruddell, Deborah. *The popcorn astronauts*
Schertle, Alice. *Such a little mouse*
Singleton, Linda Joy. *Snow dog, sand dog*
White, Teagan. *Adventures with barefoot critters*
Yolen, Jane. *Sing a season song*
Zoehfeld, Kathleen Weidner. *Secrets of the seasons*

Seasons – fall

Chernesky, Felicia Sanzari. *From apple trees to cider, please!*
Detlefsen, Lisl H. *Time for cranberries*
Holland, Loretta. *Fall leaves*
Johnston, Tony. *Winter is coming*
Wellington, Monica. *My leaf book*
Yee, Wong Herbert. *My autumn book*
Yoon, Salina. *Penguin and Pumpkin*

Seasons – spring

Berger, Carin. *Finding spring*
Chernesky, Felicia Sanzari. *Sun above and blooms below*
Colandro, Lucille. *There was an old lady who swallowed a frog!*
Kirk, Daniel. *The thing about spring*
Lloyd-Jones, Sally. *Bunny's first spring*
Rockwell, Anne. *My spring robin*

Seasons – summer

Chernesky, Felicia Sanzari. *Cheers for a dozen ears*
Heidbreder, Robert. *Song for a summer night*
Sís, Peter. *Ice cream summer*
Vogel, Vin. *The thing about yetis*

Seasons – winter

Aesop. *The grasshopper and the ants*
Berger, Carin. *Finding spring*
Boiger, Alexandra. *Max and Marla*
Brenner, Tom. *And then comes Christmas*
Carnesi, Monica. *Sleepover with Beatrice and Bear*
Chernesky, Felicia Sanzari. *Sugar white snow and evergreens*
Hillenbrand, Will. *Snowman's story*
Jenkins, Emily. *Toys meet snow*
McCarty, Peter. *First snow*
Mitton, Tony. *Snowy Bear*
Sidman, Joyce. *Winter bees and other poems of the cold*
Thornhill, Jan. *Winter's coming*
Trasler, Janee. *Mimi and Bear in the snow*
Vogel, Vin. *The thing about yetis*

Secrets *see* Behavior – secrets

Seeds

Hood, Susan. *Rooting for you*
Nelson, Kadir. *If you plant a seed*
Wunderli, Stephen. *Little Boo*

Seeing *see* Anatomy – eyes; Glasses; Disabilities – blindness; Senses – sight

Seeing eye dogs *see* Animals – service animals

Seeking better things *see* Behavior – seeking better things

Self-concept

Baldacchino, Christine. *Morris Micklewhite and the tangerine dress*
Beaumont, Karen. *Wild about us!*
Beck, Robert. *A bunny in the ballet*
Bradley, Sandra. *Henry Holton takes the ice*
Brown-Wood, JaNay. *Imani's moon*
Carlson, Nancy. *Armond goes to a party*
Cocca-Leffler, Maryann. *Janine*
Diesen, Deborah. *The pout-pout fish goes to school*
Diggs, Taye. *Mixed me!*
DiPucchio, Kelly. *Gaston*
Dumont, Jean-François. *The geese march in step*
Edwards, Karl Newsom. *Fly!*
Engle, Margarita. *Tiny rabbit's big wish*
Fisher, Valorie. *I can do it myself*
Frankel, Erin. *Nobody!*
Gutman, Dan. *Rappy the raptor*
Hall, Michael. *Red: a crayon's story*
Harrison, Hannah E. *Extraordinary Jane*
Hoffman, Sarah. *Jacob's new dress*
Hudson, Katy. *Bear and Duck*
International Center for Assault Prevention. *My body belongs to me from my head to my toes*
Jeffers, Oliver. *The Hueys in It wasn't me*
McLellan, Stephanie Simpson. *Tweezle into everything*
McNamara, Margaret. *A poem in your pocket*
Manushkin, Fran. *Happy in our skin*
Otoshi, Kathryn. *Two*
Parr, Todd. *It's okay to make mistakes*
Petty, Dev. *I don't want to be a frog*
Pfister, Marcus. *The little moon raven*
Polacco, Patricia. *An A from Miss Keller*
Rudolph, Shaina. *All my stripes*
Singer, Marilyn. *I'm gonna climb a mountain in my patent leather shoes*
Stanton, Elizabeth Rose. *Henny*
Starishevsky, Jill. *My body belongs to me*
Stewart, Whitney. *Meditation is an open sky*
Tillman, Nancy. *You're here for a reason*
Urban, Linda. *Little Red Henry*
Viorst, Judith. *And two boys booed*
Yankey, Lindsey. *Sun and Moon*

Self-esteem *see* Self-concept

Self-image *see* Self-concept

Self-reliance *see* Character traits – confidence

Selfishness *see* Character traits – selfishness

Senses

Brocket, Jane. *Cold, crunchy, colorful*
Waters, John F. *Sharks have six senses*

Senses – sight

Hawkes, Kevin. *Remy and Lulu*

Senses – smell

Mack, Jeff. *Who needs a bath?*

Senses – touch

International Center for Assault Prevention. *My body belongs to me from my head to my toes*
Starishevsky, Jill. *My body belongs to me*

Sex instruction

Blackall, Sophie. *The baby tree*
Roberts, Jillian. *Where do babies come from? our first talk about birth*

Sex roles *see* Gender roles

Shaped books *see* Format, unusual

Sharing *see* Behavior – sharing

Shells *see* Sea & seashore

Ships *see* Boats, ships

Shops *see* Stores

Showing off *see* Behavior – boasting, showing off

Shows *see* Theater

Shyness *see* Character traits – shyness

Sibling rivalry

Atinuke. *Double trouble for Anna Hibiscus!*
Child, Lauren. *The new small person*
Feeney, Tatyana. *Little Frog's tadpole trouble*
Kaplan, Bruce Eric. *Meaniehead*
Kornell, Max. *Me first*
Regan, Dian Curtis. *Space Boy and his dog*

Siblings *see* Family life – brothers; Family life – brothers & sisters; Family life – sisters; Family life – stepfamilies; Sibling rivalry

Sickness see Health & fitness; Illness

Sight see Anatomy – eyes; Glasses; Disabilities – blindness; Senses – sight

Sign language

Napoli, Donna Jo. *Hands and hearts*

Singers see Careers – singers

Sisters see Family life – brothers & sisters; Family life – sisters; Sibling rivalry

Skating see Sports – ice skating; Sports – hockey

Sky

Dean, James. *Pete the Cat: twinkle, twinkle, little star*

Slavery

Cooper, Floyd. *Juneteenth for Mazie*
Herkert, Barbara. *Sewing stories*
Johnson, Angela. *All different now*
Rappaport, Doreen. *Frederick's journey*
Woelfle, Gretchen. *Mumbet's Declaration of Independence*

Sleep

Allenby, Victoria. *Nat the cat can sleep like that*
Berger, Samantha. *Snoozefest at the Nuzzledome*
Bottner, Barbara. *Feet go to sleep*
Choldenko, Gennifer. *Putting the monkeys to bed*
Cronin, Doreen. *Click, clack, peep!*
Grimm, Jacob and Wilhelm. *Sleeping beauty*
Howatt, Sandra J. *Sleepyheads*
Moüy, Iris de. *Naptime*
Offill, Jenny. *While you were napping*
Palatini, Margie. *No nap! yes nap!*
Saltzberg, Barney. *Chengdu could not, would not, fall asleep*
Samuels, Barbara. *Fred's beds*
Shaw, Nancy. *Sheep go to sleep*
Shyba, Jessica. *Naptime with Theo and Beau*
Wood, Audrey. *The full moon at the napping house*

Sleep – snoring

Bardhan-Quallen, Sudipta. *Snoring Beauty*
Blecha, Aaron. *Goodnight, Grizzle Grump!*

Sleepovers

Dean, James. *Pete the Cat and the bedtime blues*
Dewdney, Anna. *Llama Llama Gram and Grandpa*
McDonnell, Patrick. *Thank you and good night*
Manning, Jane. *Millie Fierce sleeps out*
Russo, Marisabina. *Sophie sleeps over*
Smith, Danna. *Mother Goose's pajama party*

Sleight-of-hand see Magic

Smallness see Character traits – smallness

Smell see Senses – smell

Snoring see Noise, sounds; Sleep – snoring

Snow see Weather – blizzards; Weather – snow

Snow plows see Machines

Snowmen

Hillenbrand, Will. *Snowman's story*

Soldiers see Careers – military

Solitude see Behavior – solitude

Songs

Brown, Margaret Wise. *Goodnight songs*
Cabrera, Jane. *Row, row, row your boat*
Chapin, Tom. *The backwards birthday party*
Dean, James. *Pete the Cat: twinkle, twinkle, little star*
Ketteman, Helen. *The ghosts go haunting*
Lendroth, Susan. *Old Manhattan has some farms*
Little old lady who swallowed a fly. *There once was a cowpoke who swallowed an ant*
There was an old lady who swallowed a fly
There was an old mummy who swallowed a spider
Old MacDonald had a farm. *Pete the Cat: Old MacDonald had a farm*
Portis, Antoinette. *Froodle*
Sehgal, Kabir. *The wheels on the tuk tuk*
The twelve days of Christmas. English folk song.. *The twelve days of Christmas*
Weiss, George. *What a wonderful world*
Williams, Brenda. *Outdoor opposites*
Williams, Pharrell. *Happy!*

Sounds see Noise, sounds

Space & space ships

Dale, Penny. *Dinosaur rocket!*
Deneux, Xavier. *Vehicles*
Dolan, Elys. *Nuts in space*
Garton, Sam. *Otter in space*
Green, Rod. *Giant vehicles*
Grey, Mini. *Space Dog*
Houran, Lori Haskins. *A trip into space*
Price, Ben Joel. *Earth space moon base*
Regan, Dian Curtis. *Space Boy and his dog*
Underwood, Deborah. *Interstellar Cinderella*

Spectacles see Glasses

Speech see Disabilities – stuttering; Language

Spiders

Barton, Bethany. *I'm trying to love spiders*
Krumwiede, Lana. *Just Itzy*

Split page books *see* Format, unusual

Spooks *see* Ghosts

Sports

Stockdale, Sean. *Max the champion*
Wheeler, Lisa. *Dino-boarding*

Sports – baseball

Borden, Louise. *Baseball is . . .*
Hyman, Zachary. *The Bambino and me*
McCully, Emily Arnold. *Queen of the diamond*
Raczka, Bob. *Joy in Mudville*
Rosenstock, Barb. *The streak*
Tavares, Matt. *Growing up Pedro*
Winter, Jonah. *Joltin' Joe DiMaggio*

Sports – bicycling

Barton, Byron. *My bike*
Isabella, Jude. *The red bicycle*
Liu, Cynthea. *Bike on, Bear!*
Monroe, Chris. *Bug on a bike*
Pett, Mark. *The girl and the bicycle*
Thompson, Laurie Ann. *Emmanuel's dream*

Sports – camping *see* Camps, camping

Sports – fishing

Gravett, Emily. *Bear and Hare go fishing*

Sports – football

Dahl, Michael. *Goodnight football*

Sports – gymnastics

Isadora, Rachel. *Jake at gymnastics*

Sports – hiking

Bissonette, Aimée. *North woods girl*
Oldland, Nicholas. *Walk on the wild side*

Sports – hockey

Bradley, Sandra. *Henry Holton takes the ice*
MacGregor, Roy. *The highest number in the world*
McMullan, Kate. *I'm cool!*

Sports – hunting

Fraser, Mary Ann. *No Yeti yet*
Haughton, Chris. *Shh! we have a plan*
Nolan, Dennis. *Hunters of the great forest*

Sports – ice skating

Bradley, Sandra. *Henry Holton takes the ice*
Idle, Molly. *Flora and the penguin*

Lazar, Tara. *Little Red Gliding Hood*

Sports – martial arts

Chung, Arree. *Ninja!*
Ishida, Sanae. *Little Kunoichi, the ninja girl*
Olson, Jennifer Gray. *Ninja bunny*
Pingk, Rubin. *Samurai Santa*
Schwartz, Corey Rosen. *Ninja Red Riding Hood*
Tarpley, Todd. *My grandma's a ninja*
Tougas, Chris. *Dojo Daycare*
    Dojo daytrip
Tuell, Todd. *Ninja, ninja, never stop!*
Wilson, N. D. *Ninja boy goes to school*
Zeltser, David. *Ninja baby*

Sports – Olympics

Boiger, Alexandra. *Max and Marla*

Sports – racing

Dotlich, Rebecca Kai. *Race car count*
Pizzoli, Greg. *Number one Sam*
Reynolds, Peter H. *Going places*
Scieszka, Jon. *Race from A to Z*
Shulevitz, Uri. *Troto and the trucks*

Sports – sledding

Boiger, Alexandra. *Max and Marla*

Sports – soccer

Bildner, Phil. *The soccer fence*
Cousins, Lucy. *Maisy plays soccer*
Javaherbin, Mina. *Soccer star*
Kaplan, Michael B. *Betty Bunny wants a goal*
Pinkney, Brian. *On the ball*

Sports – swimming

Lurie, Susan. *Swim, duck, swim!*
Wheeler, Lisa. *Dino-swimming*
Whelan, Gloria. *Queen Victoria's bathing machine*

Squid

Berry, Lynne. *Squid Kid the Magnificent*

Stage *see* Theater

Stars

Dean, James. *Pete the Cat: twinkle, twinkle, little star*
McGhee, Alison. *Star bright*
van Lieshout, Maria. *Hopper and Wilson fetch a star*

Stealing *see* Behavior – stealing; Crime

Steam shovels *see* Machines

Steamrollers *see* Machines

Stepchildren *see* Divorce; Family life –
    stepfamilies

Stepfamilies *see* Divorce; Family life –
   stepfamilies

Stepparents *see* Divorce; Family life –
   stepfamilies

Stones *see* Rocks

Stores

Hillenbrand, Will. *All for a dime! a Bear and Mole
   story*
Munro, Roxie. *Market maze*
Nelson, Vaunda Micheaux. *The book itch*
Ormerod, Jan. *The baby swap*

Stories in rhyme *see* Rhyming text

Strangers *see* Behavior – talking to strangers

Streets *see* Roads

Submarines *see* Boats, ships

Subway *see* Trains

Sun

Bang, Molly. *Buried sunlight*
Gerstein, Mordicai. *The night world*
Graham, Bob. *How the sun got to Coco's house*
Stewart, Melissa. *Beneath the sun*
Yankey, Lindsey. *Sun and Moon*
Zoehfeld, Kathleen Weidner. *Secrets of the seasons*

Swamps

Rose, Caroline Starr. *Over in the wetlands*
Stewart, Whitney. *A catfish tale*

Swapping *see* Activities – trading

Talent shows *see* Theater

Talking to strangers *see* Behavior – talking to
   strangers

Tall tales

Isaacs, Anne. *Meanwhile, back at the ranch*
Myers, Anna. *Tumbleweed Baby*
Rozier, Lucy Margaret. *Jackrabbit McCabe and the
   electric telegraph*

Tardiness *see* Behavior – promptness, tardiness

Taxis

Sehgal, Kabir. *The wheels on the tuk tuk*

Teasing *see* Behavior – bullying, teasing

Technology

Saltzberg, Barney. *Tea with Grandpa*

Teddy bears *see* Toys – bears

Teeth

Coombs, Kate. *The tooth fairy wars*
Underwood, Deborah. *Here comes the Tooth Fairy
   Cat*

Television

Biedrzycki, David. *Breaking news: bear alert*

Telling stories *see* Activities – storytelling

Telling time *see* Clocks, watches; Time

Temper tantrums *see* Emotions – anger

Texas

Johnson, Angela. *All different now*
Myers, Anna. *Tumbleweed Baby*

Textless *see* Wordless

Theater

Boldt, Mike. *Colors versus shapes*
Brownlee, Sophia Grace. *Show time with Sophia
   Grace and Rosie*
Cousins, Lucy. *Maisy goes to the movies*
Gianferrari, Maria. *Penny and Jelly*
Mayhew, James. *Ella Bella ballerina and A
   Midsummer Night's Dream*
Polacco, Patricia. *Mr. Wayne's masterpiece*
Uegaki, Chieri. *Hana Hashimoto, sixth violin*
Viorst, Judith. *And two boys booed*
Wells, Rosemary. *Felix stands tall*

Thieves *see* Crime

Thumb sucking

Stille, Ljuba. *Mia's thumb*

Thunder *see* Weather – lightning, thunder;
Weather – storms

Time

Chast, Roz. *Around the clock!*
Perrin, Clotilde. *At the same moment, around the world*

Toads *see* Frogs & toads

Toddlers *see* Babies, toddlers

Toilet training

Oud, Pauline. *Sarah on the potty*
Spector, Todd. *How to pee*

Tools

Buzzeo, Toni. *Whose tools?*
Meshon, Aaron. *Tools rule!*
Riggs, Kate. *Time to build*

Tooth fairy *see* Fairies; Teeth

Tortoises *see* Reptiles – turtles, tortoises

Towns *see* Cities, towns

Toy & movable books *see* Format, unusual –
toy & movable books

Toys

Abbot, Judi. *Train!*
Beaumont, Karen. *Crybaby*
Castillo, Lauren. *The troublemaker*
Deedman, Heidi. *Too many toys!*
Engler, Michael. *Elephantastic!*
Ferrell, Sean. *I don't like Koala*
Harper, Charise Mericle. *Superlove*
Harris, Robie H. *Turtle and me*
Heap, Sue. *Mine!*
Henkes, Kevin. *Waiting*
Hissey, Jane. *Jolly snow*
Jenkins, Emily. *Toys meet snow*
Kenney, Sean. *Cool creations in 101 pieces*
Kirk, Daniel. *You are not my friend, but I miss you*
Landström, Lena. *Where is Pim?*
Miyares, Daniel. *Float*
Perkins, Maripat. *Rodeo Red*
Pilutti, Deb. *Ten rules of being a superhero*
Roques, Dominique. *Sleep tight, Anna Banana!*
Rowand, Phyllis. *It is night*
Scheffler, Axel. *Pip and Posy: the bedtime frog*
Soman, David. *Ladybug Girl and the best ever playdate*

Toys – balloons

Harrison, Hannah E. *Bernice gets carried away*
Judge, Chris. *Tin*

Toys – bears

Garton, Sam. *I am Otter*
Otter loves Halloween
Hennessy, B. G. *A Christmas wish for Corduroy*
Hissey, Jane. *Jolly snow*
McGrath, Barbara Barbieri. *Teddy bear addition*
Seeger, Laura Vaccaro. *Dog and Bear: tricks and treats*
Trasler, Janee. *Mimi and Bear in the snow*

Toys – blocks

Barrett, Mary Brigid. *All fall down*

Toys – dolls

Schneider, Josh. *Princess Sparkle-Heart gets a makeover*

Toys – teddy bears *see* Toys – bears

Tractors

Angleberger, Tom. *McToad mows Tiny Island*
Clement, Nathan. *Big tractor*
Hillenbrand, Will. *Down by the barn*
Long, Loren. *Otis and the scarecrow*
Swenson, Jamie A. *Big rig*

Traffic, traffic signs

Harper, Charise Mericle. *Go! go! go! stop!*

Trains

Abbot, Judi. *Train!*
Bluemle, Elizabeth. *Tap tap boom boom*
Braun, Sebastien. *Whoosh and Chug!*
Dotlich, Rebecca Kai. *All aboard!*
Jacobs, Paul DuBois. *Count on the subway*
Vamos, Samantha R. *Alphabet trains*

Transportation

Angleberger, Tom. *McToad mows Tiny Island*
Barton, Byron. *My bus*
Rosen, Michael. *The bus is for us!*

Trees

Chernesky, Felicia Sanzari. *Sugar white snow and evergreens*
Cousins, Lucy. *Maisy's Christmas tree*
Johnston, Tony. *Sequoia*
Karas, G. Brian. *As an oak tree grows*
Krensky, Stephen. *The last Christmas tree*
Long, Loren. *Little tree*
Lyon, George Ella. *What forest knows*
Messner, Kate. *Tree of wonder*
Murguia, Bethanie Deeney. *The best parts of Christmas*
Nichols, Lori. *Maple*
Prevot, Franck. *Wangari Maathai*
Wellington, Monica. *My leaf book*

Trickery *see* Behavior – trickery

Tricks *see* Magic

Trucks

Austin, Mike. *Fire Engine No. 9*
Davis, Sarah. *My first trucks*
Deneux, Xavier. *Vehicles*
Floca, Brian. *Five trucks*
Gall, Chris. *Dinotrux dig the beach*
Green, Rod. *Giant vehicles*
Harper, Charise Mericle. *Go! go! go! stop!*
Holub, Joan. *Mighty dads*
Koehler, Lora. *The little snowplow*
Lord, Cynthia. *Hot Rod Hamster: monster truck mania!*
McMullan, Kate. *I'm brave!*
Savage, Stephen. *Supertruck*
Scieszka, Jon. *Race from A to Z*
Shulevitz, Uri. *Troto and the trucks*
Steggall, Susan. *Colors*
Stein, Peter. *Little Red's riding 'hood*
Swenson, Jamie A. *Big rig*
Todd, Mark. *Food trucks!*

TV *see* Television

Twins *see* Multiple births – twins

U.S. history

Bandy, Michael S.. *Granddaddy's turn*
Barnett, Mac. *President Taft is stuck in the bath*
Bass, Hester. *Seeds of freedom*
Blanco, Richard. *One today*
Cooper, Floyd. *Juneteenth for Mazie*
Cullen, Lynn. *Dear Mr. Washington*
Greenwood, Mark. *The Mayflower*
Jenkins, Emily. *A fine dessert*
Johnson, Angela. *All different now*
Kalman, Maira. *Thomas Jefferson*
Kerley, Barbara. *A home for Mr. Emerson*
Krull, Kathleen. *Hillary Rodham Clinton*
Meltzer, Brad. *I am Rosa Parks*
Meyer, Susan Lynn. *New shoes*
Miller, Pat Zietlow. *Sharing the bread*
Mora, Pat. *I pledge allegiance*
Polacco, Patricia. *Clara and Davie*
Rappaport, Doreen. *Frederick's journey*
Rhodes-Pitts, Sharifa. *Jake makes a world*
Ringgold, Faith. *Harlem Renaissance party*
Slade, Suzanne. *Friends for freedom*
Smith, Charles R. *28 days*
Tonatiuh, Duncan. *Separate is never equal*
Watkins, Angela Farris. *Love will see you through*
Weatherford, Carole Boston. *Gordon Parks Sugar Hill*

Winter, Jonah. *Lillian's right to vote*
Woelfle, Gretchen. *Mumbet's Declaration of Independence*

U.S. history – frontier & pioneer life

Bunting, Eve. *Washday*
Isaacs, Anne. *Meanwhile, back at the ranch*
Shea, Bob. *Kid Sheriff and the terrible Toads*

Unhappiness *see* Emotions – happiness; Emotions – sadness

Unnoticed, unseen *see* Behavior – unnoticed, unseen

Unseen *see* Behavior – unnoticed, unseen

Unusual format *see* Format, unusual

Vanity *see* Character traits – vanity

Vikings

Chapman, Jared. *Pirate, Viking, and Scientist*

Violence, nonviolence

Antony, Steve. *Green lizards vs. red rectangles*
Bass, Hester. *Seeds of freedom*
Kimmel, Elizabeth Cody. *A taste of freedom*
Meltzer, Brad. *I am Rosa Parks*
Rappaport, Doreen. *Frederick's journey*
Smith, Charles R. *28 days*
Watkins, Angela Farris. *Love will see you through*
Weatherford, Carole Boston. *Voice of freedom*
Winter, Jeanette. *Malala, a brave girl from Pakistan / Iqbal, a brave boy from Pakistan*

War

Antony, Steve. *Green lizards vs. red rectangles*
Elvgren, Jennifer. *The whispering town*

Word games *see* Language

Wordless

Becker, Aaron. *Quest*
Boyd, Lizi. *Flashlight*
Camcam, Princesse. *Fox's garden*
Colón, Raúl. *Draw!*
Frazee, Marla. *The farmer and the clown*
Gordon, Domenica More. *Archie's vacation*
Gutierrez, Elisa. *Letter lunch*
Hillenbrand, Will. *Snowman's story*
Idle, Molly. *Flora and the penguin*
Jay, Alison. *Out of the blue*
Lawson, Jonarno. *Sidewalk flowers*
Miyares, Daniel. *Float*
Newgarden, Mark. *Bow-Wow's nightmare neighbors*
Nolan, Dennis. *Hunters of the great forest*
Pett, Mark. *The girl and the bicycle*
Savage, Stephen. *Where's Walrus? and Penguin?*

Working *see* Activities – working; Careers

World

Ajmera, Maya. *Global baby boys*
    Global baby girls
Ajmera, Maya. *Music everywhere!*
Dillon, Leo. *If kids ran the world*
Gibson, Amy. *By day, by night*
Graham, Bob. *How the sun got to Coco's house*
Kerley, Barbara. *With a friend by your side*
Perrin, Clotilde. *At the same moment, around the
    world*
Weiss, George. *What a wonderful world*

Worrying *see* Behavior – worrying

Wrecking machines *see* Machines

Writers *see* Careers – writers; Children as authors

Writing letters *see* Letters, cards

Yeti *see* Monsters

Yoga *see* Health & fitness – exercise

Zodiac

Chin, Oliver. *The year of the sheep*

Zombies *see* Monsters

Zoos

Beaumont, Karen. *Wild about us!*
Bleiman, Andrew. *1-2-3 zooborns!*
Burningham, John. *The way to the zoo*
Faulconer, Maria. *A mom for Umande*
Jantzen, Doug. *Henry Hyena, why won't you laugh?*
Johnson, Mariana Ruiz. *I know a bear*
Krull, Kathleen. *What's new? the zoo!*
Macaulay, David. *How machines work: zoo break!*
Mattick, Lindsay. *Finding Winnie*
Plant, David J. *Hungry Roscoe*
Savage, Stephen. *Where's Walrus? and Penguin?*
Waldron, Kevin. *Panda-monium at Peek Zoo*
Walker, Sally M. *Winnie*

Bibliographic Guide

Arranged alphabetically by author's name in boldface (or by title, if author is unknown), each entry includes title, illustrator, publisher, publication date, and subjects. Joint authors appear as short entries, with the main author name (in parentheses after the title) citing where the complete entry will be found. Where only an author and title are given, complete information is listed under the title as the main entry.

Abbot, Judi. *Train!* ill. by author. Tiger Tales, 2014. ISBN 978-158925163-2 Subj: Activities – playing. Animals – elephants. Toys. Trains.

Adderson, Caroline. *Norman, speak!* ill. by Qin Leng. Groundwood, 2014. ISBN 978-155498322-3 Subj: Animals – dogs. Character traits – kindness to animals. Foreign languages. Pets.

Adler, David A. *The story of Passover* ill. by Jill Weber. Holiday House, 2014. ISBN 978-082342902-8 Subj: Holidays – Passover. Jewish culture.

Triangles ill. by Edward Miller. Holiday House, 2014. ISBN 978-082342378-1 Subj: Concepts – shape. Counting, numbers.

Aesop. *The grasshopper and the ants* retold by Jerry Pinkney; ill. by reteller. Little, Brown, 2015. ISBN 978-031640081-7 Subj: Activities – working. Folk & fairy tales. Insects – ants. Insects – grasshoppers. Seasons – winter.

Agee, Jon. *It's only Stanley* ill. by author. Dial, 2015. ISBN 978-080373907-9 Subj: Animals – dogs. Moon. Noise, sounds. Rhyming text.

Ajmera, Maya. *Global baby boys* ill. with photos. Charlesbridge, 2014. ISBN 978-158089440-1 Subj: Babies, toddlers. Format, unusual – board books. World.

Global baby girls ill. with photos. Charlesbridge, 2013. ISBN 978-158089439-5 Subj: Babies, toddlers. Format, unusual – board books. World.

Music everywhere! ill. with photos. Charlesbridge, 2014. ISBN 978-157091936-7 Subj: Music. Musical instruments. World.

Alakija, Polly. *Counting chickens* ill. by author. Frances Lincoln, 2014. ISBN 978-184780437-2 Subj: Birds – chickens, roosters. Character traits – patience. Counting, numbers. Days of the week, months of the year. Foreign lands – Africa.

Alexander, Claire. *Monkey and the little one* ill. by author. Sterling, 2015. ISBN 978-145491580-5 Subj: Animals – mice. Animals – monkeys. Friendship.

Allen, Kathryn Madeline. *Show me happy* photos by Eric Futran. Albert Whitman, 2015. ISBN 978-080757349-5 Subj: Communication. Emotions. Rhyming text.

Allenby, Victoria. *Nat the cat can sleep like that* ill. by Tara Anderson. Pajama, 2014. ISBN 978-192748552-1 Subj: Animals – cats. Bedtime. Rhyming text. Sleep.

American Museum of Natural History. *ABC insects.* Sterling, 2014. ISBN 978-145491194-4 Subj: ABC books. Format, unusual – board books. Insects.

Anderson, Brian. *Monster chefs* by Brian Anderson and Liam Anderson ill. by Brian Anderson. Roaring Brook, 2014. ISBN 978-159643808-8 Subj: Activities – baking, cooking. Careers – chefs, cooks. Monsters. Royalty – kings.

Anderson, Derek. *Ten pigs: an epic bath adventure* ill. by author. Orchard, 2015. ISBN 978-054516846-5 Subj: Activities – bathing. Animals – pigs. Animals – wolves. Counting, numbers. Rhyming text.

Anderson, Liam. *Monster chefs* (Anderson, Brian)

Andrews, Julie. *The very fairy princess: a spooky, sparkly Halloween* by Julie Andrews and Emma Walton Hamilton ill. by Christine Davenier. Little, Brown, 2015. ISBN 978-031628304-5 Subj: Clothing – costumes. Holidays – Halloween. Royalty – princesses. School.

The very fairy princess: graduation girl! by Julie Andrews and Emma Walton Hamilton ill. by Christine Davenier. Little, Brown, 2014. ISBN 978-031621960-0 Subj: Behavior – worrying. Royalty – princesses. School.

Andrews, Troy. *Trombone Shorty* ill. by Bryan Collier. Abrams, 2015. ISBN 978-141971465-8 Subj: Caldecott award honor books. Careers – musicians. Ethnic groups in the U.S. – African Americans. Musical instruments – trombones.

Angleberger, Tom. *McToad mows Tiny Island* ill. by John Hendrix. Abrams, 2015. ISBN 978-141971650-8 Subj: Frogs & toads. Machines. Tractors. Transportation.

Anholt, Laurence. *Two nests* ill. by James Coplestone. Frances Lincoln, 2014. ISBN 978-184780323-8 Subj: Birds. Homes, houses. Rhyming text.

Anstee, Ashlyn. *Are we there, Yeti?* ill. by author. Simon & Schuster, 2015. ISBN 978-148143089-0 Subj: Careers – bus drivers. Monsters. School – field trips.

Antony, Steve. *Betty goes bananas* ill. by author. Random/Schwartz & Wade, 2014. ISBN 978-055350761-4 Subj: Animals – gorillas. Birds – toucans. Emotions – anger. Food.

Green lizards vs. red rectangles ill. by author. Scholastic, 2015. ISBN 978-054584902-9 Subj: Concepts – shape. Reptiles – lizards. Violence, nonviolence. War.

Please, Mr. Panda ill. by author. Scholastic, 2015. ISBN 978-054578892-2 Subj: Animals – pandas. Behavior – sharing. Etiquette.

The Queen's hat ill. by author. Scholastic, 2015. ISBN 978-054583556-5 Subj: Behavior – lost & found possessions. Clothing – hats. Foreign lands – England. Royalty – queens.

Appelt, Kathi. *Counting crows* ill. by Rob Dunlavey. Atheneum, 2015. ISBN 978-144242327-5 Subj: Birds – crows. Counting, numbers. Rhyming text.

Mogie: the heart of the house ill. by Marc Rosenthal. Atheneum, 2014. ISBN 978-144248054-4 Subj: Animals – dogs. Animals – service animals. Illness.

When Otis courted Mama ill. by Jill McElmurry. Houghton, 2015. ISBN 978-015216688-5 Subj: Animals – coyotes. Divorce. Family life – mothers. Family life – stepparents.

Applegate, Katherine. *Ivan: the remarkable true story of the shopping mall gorilla* ill. by G. Brian Karas.

Clarion, 2014. ISBN 978-054425230-1 Subj: Animals – gorillas. Character traits – kindness to animals.

Aregui, Matthias. *Before after* ill. by Anne-Margot Ramstein. Candlewick, 2014. ISBN 978-076367621-6 Subj: Concepts – change. Nature.

Argueta, Jorge. *Salsa: un poema para cocinar / a cooking poem* ill. by Duncan Tonatiuh. Groundwood, 2015. ISBN 978-155498442-8 Subj: Activities – baking, cooking. Foreign lands – Latin America. Foreign languages. Poetry.

Arndt, Michael. *Cat says meow and other animalopoeia* ill. by author. Chronicle, 2014. ISBN 978-145211234-3 Subj: Animals. Noise, sounds.

Arnold, Marsha Diane. *Lost. found* ill. by Matthew Cordell. Roaring Brook/Neal Porter, 2015. ISBN 978-162672017-6 Subj: Animals. Animals – bears. Behavior – lost & found possessions. Clothing – scarves.

Arnold, Tedd. *A pet for Fly Guy* ill. by author. Scholastic/Orchard, 2014. ISBN 978-054531615-6 Subj: Humorous stories. Insects – flies. Pets.

Vincent paints his house ill. by author. Holiday House, 2015. ISBN 978-082343210-3 Subj: Activities – painting. Animals. Careers – artists. Concepts – color. Homes, houses.

Asch, Frank. *Pizza* ill. by author. Simon & Schuster, 2015. ISBN 978-144246675-3 Subj: Animals – bears. Food.

Ashdown, Rebecca. *Bob and Flo* ill. by author. Houghton Mifflin Harcourt, 2015. ISBN 978-054444430-0 Subj: Birds – penguins. Friendship. School – first day. School – nursery.

Ashman, Linda. *Over the river and through the wood* ill. by Kim Smith. Sterling, 2015. ISBN 978-145491024-4 Subj: Activities – traveling. Family life. Holidays – Thanksgiving.

Aston, Dianna Hutts. *A nest is noisy* ill. by Sylvia Long. Chronicle, 2015. ISBN 978-145212713-2 Subj: Animals. Birds. Homes, houses.

Atinuke. *Double trouble for Anna Hibiscus!* ill. by Lauren Tobia. Kane/Miller, 2015. ISBN 978-161067367-9 Subj: Foreign lands – Africa. Multiple births – twins. Sibling rivalry.

Atteberry, Kevan. *Bunnies!!!* ill. by author. HarperCollins/Katherine Tegen, 2015. ISBN 978-006230783-5 Subj: Activities – playing. Animals – rabbits. Monsters. Nature.

Auch, Mary Jane. *The buk buk buk festival* ill. by author. Holiday House, 2015. ISBN 978-082343201-1 Subj: Activities – writing. Birds – chickens, roosters. Books, reading. Humorous stories.

Auerbach, Adam. *Edda: a little Valkyrie's first day of school* ill. by author. Holt, 2014. ISBN 978-080509703-0 Subj: Character traits – individuality. Folk & fairy tales. School – first day.

Austin, Mike. *Fire Engine No. 9* ill. by author. Random House, 2015. ISBN 978-055351095-9 Subj: Careers – firefighters. Trucks.

Junkyard ill. by author. Simon & Schuster/Beach Lane, 2014. ISBN 978-144245961-8 Subj: Ecology. Robots.

Averbeck, Jim. *One word from Sophia* ill. by Yasmeen Ismail. Atheneum, 2015. ISBN 978-148140514-0 Subj: Animals – giraffes. Birthdays. Ethnic groups in the U.S. Family life.

Aylesworth, Jim. *My grandfather's coat* ill. by Barbara McClintock. Scholastic, 2014. ISBN 978-043992545-7 Subj: Careers – tailors. Clothing – coats. Family life – grandfathers. Immigrants. Jewish culture.

Bach, Annie. *Monster party!* ill. by author. Sterling, 2014. ISBN 978-145491051-0 Subj: Birthdays. Monsters. Parties. Rhyming text.

Bagley, Jessixa. *Boats for Papa* ill. by author. Roaring Brook/Neal Porter, 2015. ISBN 978-162672039-8 Subj: Animals – beavers. Boats, ships. Death. Emotions – grief. Family life – mothers.

Baguley, Elizabeth. *Ready, steady, ghost!* ill. by Marion Lindsay. Disney/Hyperion, 2014. ISBN 978-142318039-5 Subj: Character traits – smallness. Emotions – fear. Ghosts.

Bailey, Ella. *No such thing* ill. by author. Flying Eye Books, 2014. ISBN 978-190926348-2 Subj: Ghosts. Holidays – Halloween. Rhyming text.

Bailey, Linda. *If kids ruled the world* ill. by David Huyck. Kids Can, 2014. ISBN 978-155453591-0 Subj: Imagination.

If you happen to have a dinosaur ill. by Colin Jack. Tundra, 2014. ISBN 978-177049568-5 Subj: Dinosaurs.

When Santa was a baby ill. by Geneviève Godbout. Tundra, 2015. ISBN 978-177049556-2 Subj: Behavior – growing up. Santa Claus.

Baker, Keith. *Little green peas: a big book of colors* ill. by author. Simon & Schuster/Beach Lane, 2014. ISBN 978-144247660-8 Subj: Concepts – color. Food.

Baldacchino, Christine. *Morris Micklewhite and the tangerine dress* ill. by Isabelle Malenfant. Groundwood, 2014. ISBN 978-155498347-6 Subj: Clothing – dresses. Gender roles. Self-concept.

Balmes, Santi. *I will fight monsters for you* ill. by Lyona. Albert Whitman, 2015. ISBN 978-080759056-0 Subj: Bedtime. Emotions – fear. Monsters.

Bandy, Michael S. *Granddaddy's turn: a journey to the ballot box* by Michael S. Bandy and Eric Stein ill. by James Ransome. Candlewick, 2015. ISBN 978-076366593-7 Subj: Character traits – persistence. Ethnic groups in the U.S. – African Americans. Family life – grandfathers. Prejudice. U.S. history.

Bang, Molly. *Buried sunlight: how fossil fuels have changed the earth* by Molly Bang and Penny Chisholm ill. by Molly Bang. Scholastic/Blue Sky, 2014. ISBN 978-054557785-4 Subj: Earth. Science. Sun.

When Sophie's feelings are really, really hurt ill. by author. Scholastic/Blue Sky, 2015. ISBN 978-054578831-1 Subj: Activities – painting. Art. Emotions. Emotions – sadness.

Banks, Kate. *Max's math* ill. by Boris Kulikov. Farrar/Frances Foster, 2015. ISBN 978-037434875-5 Subj: Concepts – shape. Counting, numbers.

Bar-el, Dan. *A fish named Glub* ill. by Josée Bisaillon. Kids Can, 2014. ISBN 978-155453812-6 Subj: Dreams. Fish. Memories, memory. Rhyming text.

Barash, Chris. *Is it Hanukkah yet?* ill. by Alessandra Psacharopulo. Albert Whitman, 2015. ISBN 978-080753384-0 Subj: Family life. Holidays – Hanukkah. Rhyming text.

Barclay, Eric. *Counting dogs* ill. by author. Scholastic, 2015. ISBN 978-054578392-7 Subj: Animals – dogs. Counting, numbers. Format, unusual – board books.

Bardhan-Quallen, Sudipta. *Snoring Beauty* ill. by Jane Manning. Harper, 2014. ISBN 978-

006087403-2 Subj: Animals – mice. Rhyming text. Royalty – princesses. Sleep – snoring.

Tyrannosaurus wrecks! ill. by Zachariah OHora. Abrams, 2014. ISBN 978-141971035-3 Subj: Behavior – misbehavior. Dinosaurs. Rhyming text.

Barner, Bob. *Sea bones* ill. by author. Chronicle, 2015. ISBN 978-145212500-8 Subj: Animals. Sea & seashore.

Barnett, Mac. *Leo: a ghost story* ill. by Christian Robinson. Chronicle, 2015. ISBN 978-145213156-6 Subj: Emotions – loneliness. Friendship. Ghosts.

President Taft is stuck in the bath ill. by Chris Van Dusen. Candlewick, 2014. ISBN 978-076366317-9 Subj: Activities – bathing. Hugging. U.S. history.

Sam and Dave dig a hole ill. by Jon Klassen. Candlewick, 2014. ISBN 978-076366229-5 Subj: Activities – digging. Caldecott award honor books. Imagination.

The skunk ill. by Patrick McDonnell. Roaring Brook, 2015. ISBN 978-159643966-5 Subj: Animals – skunks. Humorous stories.

Telephone ill. by Jen Corace. Chronicle, 2014. ISBN 978-145211023-3 Subj: Birds. Communication. Language.

Barrett, Mary Brigid. *All fall down* ill. by LeUyen Pham. Candlewick, 2014. ISBN 978-076364430-7 Subj: Format, unusual – board books. Games. Toys – blocks.

Pat-a-cake ill. by LeUyen Pham. Candlewick, 2014. ISBN 978-076364358-4 Subj: Format, unusual – board books. Games.

Barrett, Ron. *Cats got talent* ill. by author. Simon & Schuster/Paula Wiseman, 2014. ISBN 978-144249451-0 Subj: Activities – singing. Animals – cats. Friendship.

Barton, Bethany. *I'm trying to love spiders: (it isn't easy)* ill. by author. Viking, 2015. ISBN 978-067001693-8 Subj: Spiders.

Barton, Byron. *My bike* ill. by author. Greenwillow, 2015. ISBN 978-006233699-6 Subj: Circus. Clowns, jesters. Sports – bicycling.

My bus ill. by author. Greenwillow, 2014. ISBN 978-006228736-6 Subj: Animals. Buses. Counting, numbers. Pets. Transportation.

Bass, Hester. *Seeds of freedom: the peaceful integration of Huntsville, Alabama* ill. by E. B. Lewis. Candlewick, 2015. ISBN 978-076366919-5 Subj: Ethnic groups in the U.S. – African Americans. Prejudice. U.S. history. Violence, nonviolence.

Bass, Jennifer Vogel. *Edible colors* photos by author. Roaring Brook, 2014. ISBN 978-162672002-2 Subj: Concepts – color. Food.

Edible numbers photos by author. Roaring Brook, 2015. ISBN 978-162672003-9 Subj: Counting, numbers. Food.

Bateman, Teresa. *Job wanted* ill. by Chris Sheban. Holiday House, 2015. ISBN 978-082343391-9 Subj: Animals – dogs. Farms.

Baumgarten, Bret. *Beautiful hands* (Otoshi, Kathryn)

Bean, Jonathan. *This is my home, this is my school* ill. by author. Farrar, 2015. ISBN 978-037438020-5 Subj: Family life. Homes, houses. School.

Beaton, Kate. *The princess and the pony* ill. by author. Scholastic, 2015. ISBN 978-054563708-4 Subj: Animals – horses, ponies. Royalty – princesses.

Beaumont, Karen. *Crybaby* ill. by Eugene Yelchin. Holt, 2015. ISBN 978-080508974-5 Subj: Animals – dogs. Babies, toddlers. Bedtime. Emotions. Rhyming text. Toys.

Wild about us! ill. by Janet Stevens. Houghton Mifflin Harcourt, 2015. ISBN 978-015206294-1 Subj: Animals. Character traits – appearance. Character traits – individuality. Rhyming text. Self-concept. Zoos.

Beck, Robert. *A bunny in the ballet* ill. by author. Scholastic/Orchard, 2014. ISBN 978-054542930-6 Subj: Animals – rabbits. Ballet. Character traits – perseverance. Self-concept.

Becker, Aaron. *Quest* ill. by author. Candlewick, 2014. ISBN 978-076366595-1 Subj: Activities – drawing. Imagination. Maps. Wordless.

Becker, Bonny. *A library book for Bear* ill. by Kady MacDonald Denton. Candlewick, 2014. ISBN 978-076364924-1 Subj: Animals – bears. Animals – mice. Books, reading. Friendship. Libraries.

Bedford, David. *Two tough crocs* ill. by Tom Jellett. Holiday House, 2014. ISBN 978-082343048-2 Subj: Behavior – fighting, arguing. Reptiles – alligators, crocodiles.

Bee, William. *Digger Dog* ill. by Cecilia Johansson. Candlewick/Nosy Crow, 2014. ISBN 978-076366162-5 Subj: Animals – dogs. Machines.

Stanley the builder ill. by author. Peachtree, 2014. ISBN 978-156145801-1 Subj: Animals – hamsters. Careers – construction workers. Homes, houses. Machines.

Stanley the farmer ill. by author. Peachtree, 2015. ISBN 978-156145803-5 Subj: Animals – hamsters. Animals – moles. Careers – farmers. Farms.

Stanley's diner ill. by author. Peachtree, 2015. ISBN 978-156145802-8 Subj: Activities – baking, cooking. Animals – hamsters. Restaurants.

Stanley's garage ill. by author. Peachtree, 2014. ISBN 978-156145804-2 Subj: Animals – hamsters. Automobiles. Careers – mechanics.

Worst in show ill. by Kate Hindley. Candlewick, 2015. ISBN 978-076367318-5 Subj: Contests. Monsters.

Beebe, Katy. *Brother Hugo and the bear* ill. by S. D. Schindler. Eerdmans, 2014. ISBN 978-080285407-0 Subj: Animals – bears. Books, reading. Careers – clergy.

Beliveau, Kathy. *The yoga game by the sea* ill. by Denis Holmes. Simply Read, 2014. ISBN 978-192701849-1 Subj: Health & fitness – exercise. Sea & seashore.

Bell, Cece. *I yam a donkey!* ill. by author. Clarion, 2015. ISBN 978-054408720-0 Subj: Animals – donkeys. Language.

Bender, Rebecca. *Giraffe meets Bird* ill. by author. Pajama, 2015. ISBN 978-192748535-4 Subj: Animals – giraffes. Birds. Character traits – compromising. Character traits – cooperation. Friendship.

Bentley, Jonathan. *Little big* ill. by author. Eerdmans, 2015. ISBN 978-080285462-9 Subj: Character traits – smallness. Concepts – size. Family life – brothers. Imagination.

Bentley, Tadgh. *Little Penguin gets the hiccups* ill. by author. HarperCollins/Balzer & Bray, 2015. ISBN 978-006233536-4 Subj: Birds – penguins. Hiccups.

Bently, Peter. *Meet the parents* ill. by Sara Ogilvie. Simon & Schuster/Paula Wiseman, 2014. ISBN 978-148141483-8 Subj: Family life – parents. Rhyming text.

Those magnificent sheep in their flying machine ill. by David Roberts. Andersen, 2014. ISBN 978-146774935-0 Subj: Activities – flying. Airplanes, airports. Animals – sheep. Rhyming text.

Benton, Jim. *The end (almost)* ill. by author. Scholastic, 2014. ISBN 978-054517731-3 Subj: Activities – storytelling. Animals – bears. Books, reading.

Berger, Carin. *Finding spring* ill. by author. Greenwillow, 2015. ISBN 978-006225019-3 Subj: Animals – bears. Hibernation. Seasons – spring. Seasons – winter.

Berger, Lou. *Dream dog* ill. by David Catrow. Random/Schwartz & Wade, 2014. ISBN 978-037586655-5 Subj: Animals – dogs. Illness – allergies. Imagination.

Berger, Samantha. *Snoozefest at the Nuzzledome* ill. by Kristyna Litten. Dial, 2015. ISBN 978-080374046-4 Subj: Animals – sloths. Fairs, festivals. Rhyming text. Sleep.

Berkes, Marianne. *Over on a mountain: somewhere in the world* ill. by Jill Dubin. Dawn, 2015. ISBN 978-158469518-9 Subj: Animals. Counting, numbers. Mountains. Rhyming text.

Bernardo, Susan Schaefer. *The rhino who swallowed a storm* (Burton, LeVar)

Berne, Jennifer. *Calvin, look out! a bookworm birdie gets glasses* ill. by Keith Bendis. Sterling, 2014. ISBN 978-145490910-1 Subj: Birds. Books, reading. Glasses.

Berry, Lynne. *Pig and Pug* ill. by Gemma Correll. Simon & Schuster, 2015. ISBN 978-148142131-7 Subj: Animals – dogs. Animals – pigs.

Squid Kid the Magnificent ill. by Luke LaMarca. Disney/Hyperion, 2015. ISBN 978-142316119-6 Subj: Family life – brothers & sisters. Magic. Squid.

Bertier, Anne. *Wednesday* ill. by author. Enchanted Lion, 2014. ISBN 978-159270152-0 Subj: Activities – playing. Behavior – boasting, showing off. Character traits – cooperation. Concepts – shape. Friendship.

Best, Cari. *My three best friends and me, Zulay* ill. by Vanessa Brantley-Newton. Farrar/Margaret Ferguson, 2015. ISBN 978-037438819-5 Subj: Activities – running. Disabilities – blindness. Ethnic groups in the U.S. – African Americans. School.

A perfect day for digging ill. by Christine Davenier. Amazon/Two Lions, 2014. ISBN 978-147784706-0 Subj: Activities – playing. Character traits – cleanliness. Gardens, gardening.

Bible. Old Testament. Genesis. *Let there be light* by Archbishop Desmond Tutu; ill. by Nancy Tillman. Zonderkidz, 2014. ISBN 978-031072785-9 Subj: Creation. Religion.

Biddulph, Rob. *Blown away* ill. by author. Harper, 2015. ISBN 978-006236724-2 Subj: Activities – flying. Animals. Birds – penguins. Kites. Rhyming text.

Biedrzycki, David. *Breaking news: bear alert* ill. by author. Charlesbridge, 2014. ISBN 978-158089663-4 Subj: Animals – bears. Humorous stories. Television.

Me and my dragon: Christmas spirit ill. by author. Charlesbridge, 2015. ISBN 978-158089622-1 Subj: Character traits – generosity. Dragons. Holidays – Christmas. Pets.

Bijsterbosch, Anita. *Whose hat is that?* ill. by author. Clavis, 2014. ISBN 978-160537185-6 Subj: Animals. Clothing – hats. Weather – wind.

Bildner, Phil. *The soccer fence: a story of friendship, hope, and apartheid in South Africa* ill. by Jesse Joshua Watson. Putnam, 2014. ISBN 978-039924790-3 Subj: Foreign lands – South Africa. Prejudice. Sports – soccer.

Bingham, Kelly. *Circle, square, Moose* ill. by Paul O. Zelinsky. Greenwillow, 2014. ISBN 978-006229003-8 Subj: Animals – moose. Animals – zebras. Behavior – misbehavior. Concepts – shape. Humorous stories.

Bissonette, Aimée. *North woods girl* ill. by Claudia McGehee. Minnesota Historical Society, 2015. ISBN 978-087351966-3 Subj: Family life – grandmothers. Forest, woods. Nature. Seasons. Sports – hiking.

Black, Michael Ian. *Naked!* ill. by Debbie Ridpath Ohi. Simon & Schuster, 2014. ISBN 978-144246738-5 Subj: Clothing. Humorous stories.

Blackall, Sophie. *The baby tree* ill. by author. Penguin/Nancy Paulsen, 2014. ISBN 978-039925718-6 Subj: Babies, toddlers. Character traits – questioning. Sex instruction.

Blackstone, Stella. *Bear's school day* ill. by Debbie Harter. Barefoot, 2014. ISBN 978-178285085-4 Subj: Animals – bears. Rhyming text. School.

Blanco, Richard. *One today* ill. by Dav Pilkey. Little, Brown, 2015. ISBN 978-031637144-5 Subj: Poetry. U.S. history.

Blatt, Jane. *Books always everywhere* ill. by Sarah Massini. Random House, 2014. ISBN 978-038537506-1 Subj: Books, reading. Rhyming text.

Blecha, Aaron. *Goodnight, Grizzle Grump!* ill. by author. Harper, 2015. ISBN 978-006229746-4 Subj: Animals – bears. Hibernation. Sleep – snoring.

Bleiman, Andrew. *1-2-3 zooborns!* by Andrew Bleiman and Chris Eastland ill. with photos. Simon & Schuster, 2015. ISBN 978-148143103-3 Subj: Animals. Counting, numbers. Zoos.

Bloom, C. P. *The Monkey goes bananas* ill. by Peter Raymundo. Abrams, 2014. ISBN 978-141970885-5 Subj: Animals – monkeys. Character traits – persistence. Fish – sharks.

Bloom, Suzanne. *Alone together* ill. by author. Boyds Mills, 2014. ISBN 978-162091736-7 Subj: Animals – bears. Animals – foxes. Behavior – solitude. Birds – geese. Character traits – Individuality. Friendship.

Bear can dance! ill. by author. Boyds Mills, 2015. ISBN 978-162979442-6 Subj: Activities – dancing. Activities – flying. Animals – bears. Animals – foxes. Birds – geese. Character traits – helpfulness.

Bluemle, Elizabeth. *Tap tap boom boom* ill. by G. Brian Karas. Candlewick, 2014. ISBN 978-076365696-6 Subj: Cities, towns. Rhyming text. Trains. Weather – lightning, thunder. Weather – rain.

Bogan, Paulette. *Virgil and Owen* ill. by author. Bloomsbury, 2015. ISBN 978-161963372-8 Subj: Animals – polar bears. Behavior – bossy. Birds – penguins. Friendship.

Boiger, Alexandra. *Max and Marla* ill. by author. Putnam, 2015. ISBN 978-039917504-6 Subj: Birds – owls. Character traits – persistence. Seasons – winter. Sports – Olympics. Sports – sledding.

Bolden, Tonya. *Beautiful moon: a child's prayer* ill. by Eric Velasquez. Abrams, 2014. ISBN 978-141970792-6 Subj: Bedtime. Ethnic groups in the U.S. – African Americans. Moon. Religion.

Boldt, Mike. *Colors versus shapes* ill. by author. HarperCollins, 2014. ISBN 978-006210303-1 Subj: Concepts – color. Concepts – shape. Theater.

Borando, Silvia. *Black cat, white cat* ill. by author. Candlewick, 2015. ISBN 978-076368106-7 Subj: Animals – cats. Day. Friendship. Night.

Borden, Louise. *Baseball is . . .* ill. by Raúl Colón. Simon & Schuster, 2014. ISBN 978-141695502-3 Subj: Sports – baseball.

Kindergarten luck ill. by Genevieve Godbout. Chronicle, 2015. ISBN 978-145211394-4 Subj: Character traits – luck. Money. School.

Border, Terry. *Peanut Butter and Cupcake!* photos by author. Philomel, 2014. ISBN 978-039916773-7 Subj: Activities – playing. Food. Friendship. Moving.

Bottner, Barbara. *Feet go to sleep* ill. by Maggie Smith. Knopf, 2015. ISBN 978-044981325-6 Subj: Anatomy. Bedtime. Sea & seashore – beaches. Sleep.

Miss Brooks' Story Nook (where tales are told and ogres are welcome) ill. by Michael Emberley. Knopf, 2014. ISBN 978-044981328-7 Subj: Activities – storytelling. Careers – librarians. Libraries.

Bowles, Paula. *Messy Jesse* ill. by author. Tiger Tales, 2015. ISBN 978-158925133-5 Subj: Animals – dogs. Behavior – messy.

Boyd, Lizi. *Big bear little chair* ill. by author. Chronicle, 2015. ISBN 978-145214447-4 Subj: Animals. Concepts – opposites. Concepts – size.

Flashlight ill. by author. Chronicle, 2014. ISBN 978-145211894-9 Subj: Light, lights. Night. Wordless.

Bradley, Sandra. *Henry Holton takes the ice* ill. by Sara Palacios. Dial, 2015. ISBN 978-080373856-0 Subj: Character traits – Individuality. Self-concept. Sports – hockey. Sports – ice skating.

Bram, Elizabeth. *Rufus the writer* ill. by Chuck Groenink. Random/Schwartz & Wade, 2015. ISBN 978-038537853-6 Subj: Activities – trading. Activities – writing. Careers – writers.

Bramsen, Carin. *Just a duck?* ill. by author. Random House, 2015. ISBN 978-038538415-5 Subj: Animals – cats. Birds – ducks. Friendship. Rhyming text.

Brandt, Lois. *Maddi's fridge* ill. by Vin Vogel. IPG, 2014. ISBN 978-193626129-1 Subj: Behavior – secrets. Character traits – helpfulness. Character traits – kindness. Food. Poverty.

Braun, Sebastien. *Whoosh and Chug!* ill. by author. Harper, 2014. ISBN 978-006207754-7 Subj: Character traits – perseverance. Concepts – speed. Safety. Trains.

Brendler, Carol. *Not very scary* ill. by Greg Pizzoli. Farrar, 2014. ISBN 978-037435547-0 Subj: Cumulative tales. Emotions – fear. Holidays – Halloween. Monsters. Parties.

Brenner, Tom. *And then comes Christmas* ill. by Jana Christy. Candlewick, 2014. ISBN 978-076365342-2 Subj: Holidays – Christmas. Seasons – winter.

Brenning, Juli. *Maggi and Milo* ill. by Priscilla Burris. Dial, 2014. ISBN 978-080373795-2 Subj: Animals – dogs. Frogs & toads.

Brett, Jan. *The animals' Santa* ill. by author. Putnam, 2014. ISBN 978-039925784-1 Subj: Animals. Animals – rabbits. Holidays – Christmas. Santa Claus.

Cinders: a chicken Cinderella ill. by author. Putnam, 2013. ISBN 978-039925783-4 Subj: Birds – chickens, roosters. Folk & fairy tales. Royalty – princes.

The turnip ill. by author. Putnam, 2015. ISBN 978-039917070-6 Subj: Animals. Character traits – cooperation. Cumulative tales. Farms. Folk & fairy tales. Foreign lands – Russia. Plants. Problem solving.

Brett, Jeannie. *Wild about bears* ill. by author. Charlesbridge, 2014. ISBN 978-158089418-0 Subj: Animals – bears.

Bridwell, Norman. *Clifford celebrates Hanukkah* ill. by author. Scholastic, 2015. ISBN 978-054582334-0 Subj: Animals – dogs. Holidays – Hanukkah.

Bright, Rachel. *Love Monster and the perfect present* ill. by author. Farrar, 2014. ISBN 978-037434648-5 Subj: Activities – making things. Friendship. Gifts. Monsters.

Side by side ill. by Debi Gliori. Scholastic, 2015. ISBN 978-054581326-6 Subj: Animals – mice. Animals – voles. Friendship. Rhyming text.

Brisson, Pat. *Before we eat: from farm to table* ill. by Mary Azarian. Tilbury House, 2014. ISBN 978-088448352-6 Subj: Character traits – helpfulness. Food. Rhyming text.

Brocket, Jane. *Cold, crunchy, colorful: using our senses* ill. with photos. Lerner/Millbrook, 2014. ISBN 978-146770233-1 Subj: Senses.

Brown, Alison. *Eddie and Dog* ill. by author. Capstone, 2014. ISBN 978-162370114-7 Subj: Animals – dogs. Friendship.

Brown, Marc. *In New York* ill. by author. Knopf, 2014. ISBN 978-037586454-4 Subj: Cities, towns.

Monkey: not ready for kindergarten ill. by author. Knopf, 2015. ISBN 978-055349658-1 Subj: Animals – monkeys. Behavior – worrying. School – first day.

Brown, Margaret Wise. *The find it book* ill. by Lisa Sheehan. Paragon, 2015. ISBN 978-147237818-7 Subj: Nursery rhymes. Picture puzzles.

Goodnight songs. illustrated. Sterling, 2014. ISBN 978-145490446-5 Subj: Lullabies. Seasons. Songs.

Brown, Monica. *Maya's blanket* ill. by David Diaz. Lee & Low, 2015. ISBN 978-089239292-6 Subj: Activities – sewing. Behavior – resourcefulness. Books, reading. Foreign languages.

Brown, Peter. *My teacher is a monster! (no, I am not)* ill. by author. Little, Brown, 2014. ISBN 978-031607029-4 Subj: Behavior – misunderstanding. Careers – teachers. Monsters. School.

Brown-Wood, JaNay. *Imani's moon* ill. by Hazel Mitchell. Charlesbridge, 2014. ISBN 978-193413357-6 Subj: Behavior – bullying, teasing. Character traits – persistence. Character traits – smallness. Foreign lands – Africa. Moon. Self-concept.

Browne, Anthony. *The little Bear book* ill. by author. Candlewick, 2014. ISBN 978-076367007-8 Subj: Activities – drawing. Animals – bears.

What if . . . ? ill. by author. Candlewick, 2014. ISBN 978-076367419-9 Subj: Behavior – worrying. Imagination. Parties.

Willy's stories ill. by author. Candlewick, 2015. ISBN 978-076367761-9 Subj: Animals – chimpanzees. Books, reading. Imagination. Libraries.

Brownlee, Sophia Grace. *Show time with Sophia Grace and Rosie* by Sophia Grace Brownlee and Rosie McClelland ill. by Shelagh McNicholas. Orchard, 2014. ISBN 978-054563135-8 Subj: Family life – cousins. Theater.

Bruel, Nick. *A wonderful year* ill. by author. Roaring Brook, 2015. ISBN 978-159643611-4 Subj: Seasons.

Brunhoff, Laurent de. *Babar on Paradise Island* ill. by author. Abrams, 2014. ISBN 978-141971038-4 Subj: Animals – elephants. Boats, ships. Dragons. Islands.

Bryant, Jen. *The right word: Roget and his thesaurus* ill. by Melissa Sweet. Eerdmans, 2014. ISBN 978-080285385-1 Subj: Books, reading. Caldecott award honor books. Language.

Buehner, Caralyn. *Merry Christmas, Mr. Mouse* ill. by Mark Buehner. Dial, 2015. ISBN 978-080374010-5 Subj: Animals – mice. Holidays – Christmas. Rhyming text.

Buitrago, Jairo. *Two white rabbits* ill. by Rafael Yockteng. Groundwood, 2015. ISBN 978-155498741-2 Subj: Activities – traveling. Behavior – seeking better things. Counting, numbers. Family life – daughters. Family life – fathers. Immigrants.

Bunting, Eve. *P is for pirate: a pirate alphabet* ill. by John Manders. Sleeping Bear, 2014. ISBN 978-158536815-0 Subj: ABC books. Pirates.

Washday ill. by Brad Sneed. Holiday House, 2014. ISBN 978-082342868-7 Subj: Character traits – cleanliness. Family life – grandmothers. U.S. history – frontier & pioneer life.

Whose shoe? ill. by Sergio Ruzzier. Clarion, 2015. ISBN 978-054430210-5 Subj: Animals. Animals – mice. Behavior – lost & found possessions. Clothing – shoes. Rhyming text.

Yard sale ill. by Lauren Castillo. Candlewick, 2015. ISBN 978-076366542-5 Subj: Behavior – worrying. Garage sales, rummage sales. Moving.

Burfoot, Ella. *How to bake a book* ill. by author. Sourcebooks/Jabberwocky, 2014. ISBN 978-149260651-2 Subj: Activities – baking, cooking. Books, reading. Rhyming text.

Burleigh, Robert. *Edward Hopper paints his world* ill. by Wendell Minor. Holt, 2014. ISBN 978-080508752-9 Subj: Art. Careers – artists.

Trapped! a whale's rescue ill. by Wendell Minor. Charlesbridge, 2015. ISBN 978-158089558-3 Subj: Animals – whales. Character traits – kindness to animals.

Zoom! zoom! sounds of things that go in the city ill. by Tad Carpenter. Simon & Schuster/Paula Wiseman, 2014. ISBN 978-144248315-6 Subj: Automobiles. Cities, towns. Machines. Noise, sounds. Rhyming text.

Burningham, John. *Picnic* ill. by author. Candlewick, 2014. ISBN 978-076366945-4 Subj: Activities – picnicking. Friendship.

The way to the zoo ill. by author. Candlewick, 2014. ISBN 978-076367317-8 Subj: Animals. Imagination. Zoos.

Burns, Loree Griffin. *Handle with care: an unusual butterfly journey* ill. with photos. Millbrook, 2014. ISBN 978-076139342-9 Subj: Foreign lands – Costa Rica. Insects – butterflies, caterpillars.

Burton, LeVar. *The rhino who swallowed a storm* by LeVar Burton and Susan Schaefer Bernardo ill. by Courtenay Fletcher. Reading Rainbow, 2014. ISBN 978-099053950-6 Subj: Animals – mice. Animals – rhinoceros. Weather – storms.

Busch, Miriam. *Lion, lion* ill. by Larry Day. HarperCollins/Balzer & Bray, 2014. ISBN 978-006227104-4 Subj: Animals – cats. Animals – lions. Behavior – lost & found possessions. Ethnic groups in the U.S. – African Americans.

Buzzeo, Toni. *My Bibi always remembers* ill. by Mike Wohnoutka. Disney/Hyperion, 2014. ISBN 978-142318385-3 Subj: Animals – elephants. Character traits – curiosity. Family life – grandmothers. Foreign lands – Africa.

A passion for elephants: the real life adventure of field scientist Cynthia Moss ill. by Holly Berry. Dial, 2015. ISBN 978-080374090-7 Subj: Animals – elephants. Careers – scientists.

Whose tools? ill. by Jim Datz. Abrams/Appleseed, 2015. ISBN 978-141971431-3 Subj: Careers – construction workers. Format, unusual – toy & movable books. Homes, houses. Tools.

Byous, Shawn. *Because I stubbed my toe* ill. by author. Capstone, 2014. ISBN 978-162370088-1 Subj: Accidents. Anatomy – toes. Humorous stories. Rhyming text.

Byrd, Robert. *Brave Chicken Little* (Chicken Little)

Byrne, Richard. *This book just ate my dog!* ill. by author. Holt, 2014. ISBN 978-162779071-0 Subj: Animals – dogs. Books, reading.

Cabrera, Jane. *Baa, baa, black sheep* ill. by author. Holiday House, 2015. ISBN 978-082343388-9 Subj: Animals – sheep. Books, reading. Nursery rhymes. Rhyming text.

Row, row, row your boat ill. by author. Holiday House, 2014. ISBN 978-082343050-5 Subj: Animals. Boats, ships. Rhyming text. Songs.

Cali, Davide. *A funny thing happened on the way to school . . .* ill. by Benjamin Chaud. Chronicle, 2015. ISBN 978-145213168-9 Subj: Behavior – promptness, tardiness. Imagination. School.

I didn't do my homework because . . . ill. by Benjamin Chaud. Chronicle, 2014. ISBN 978-145212551-0 Subj: Behavior – resourcefulness. Homework. Humorous stories. Imagination.

Camcam, Princesse. *Fox's garden* ill. by author. Enchanted Lion, 2014. ISBN 978-159270167-4 Subj: Animals – foxes. Character traits – kindness to animals. Wordless.

Campbell, K. G. *The mermaid and the shoe* ill. by author. Kids Can, 2014. ISBN 978-155453771-6 Subj: Character traits – curiosity. Character traits – questioning. Clothing – shoes. Mythical creatures – mermaids, mermen.

Campbell, Scott. *Hug machine* ill. by author. Atheneum, 2014. ISBN 978-144245935-9 Subj: Hugging.

Capucilli, Alyssa Satin. *Not this bear* ill. by Lorna Hussey. Holt, 2015. ISBN 978-080509896-9 Subj: Animals – bears. School – first day.

Tulip loves Rex ill. by Sarah Massini. HarperCollins/Katherine Tegen, 2014. ISBN 978-006209413-1 Subj: Activities – dancing. Animals – dogs. Character traits – kindness to animals.

Carey, Lorraine. *Cinderella's stepsister and the big bad wolf* ill. by Migy Blanco. Nosy Crow, 2015. ISBN 978-076368005-3 Subj: Animals – wolves. Family life – stepfamilies. Folk & fairy tales. Royalty – princes.

Carle, Eric. *The nonsense show* ill. by author. Philomel, 2015. ISBN 978-039917687-6 Subj: Humorous stories. Rhyming text.

Carle, Eric, et al. *What's your favorite animal?* ill. by author. Holt, 2014. ISBN 978-080509641-5 Subj: Animals. Art.

Carlin, Laura. *A world of your own* ill. by author. Phaidon, 2014. ISBN 978-071486362-7 Subj: Activities – drawing. Art. Imagination.

Carlson, Nancy. *Armond goes to a party: a book about Asperger's and friendship* by Nancy Carlson and Armond Isaak ill. by Nancy Carlson. Free Spirit, 2014. ISBN 978-157542466-8 Subj: Character traits – being different. Disabilities – Asperger's. Disabilities – autism. Parties. Self-concept.

Sometimes you barf ill. by author. Carolrhoda, 2014. ISBN 978-146771412-9 Subj: Emotions – embarrassment. Illness.

Carnesi, Monica. *Sleepover with Beatrice and Bear* ill. by author. Penguin/Nancy Paulsen, 2014. ISBN 978-039925667-7 Subj: Animals – bears. Animals – rabbits. Friendship. Hibernation. Seasons – winter.

Carroll, James Christopher. *Papa's backpack* ill. by author. Sleeping Bear, 2015. ISBN 978-158536613-2 Subj: Animals – bears. Careers – military. Emotions – sadness. Family life – fathers.

Cash, Megan Montague. *Bow-Wow's nightmare neighbors* (Newgarden, Mark)

Castillo, Lauren. *Nana in the city* ill. by author. Houghton, 2014. ISBN 978-054410443-3 Subj: Caldecott award honor books. Cities, towns. Emotions – fear. Family life – grandmothers.

The troublemaker ill. by author. Clarion, 2014. ISBN 978-054772991-6 Subj: Animals – raccoons. Behavior – lost & found possessions. Behavior – misbehavior. Toys.

Caswell, Deanna. *Beach house* ill. by Amy June Bates. Chronicle, 2015. ISBN 978-145212408-7 Subj: Rhyming text. Sea & seashore – beaches.

Catrow, David. *Fun in the sun* ill. by author. Holiday House, 2015. ISBN 978-082342945-5 Subj: Animals – rabbits. Sea & seashore.

Chaconas, Dori. *Cork and Fuzz: merry merry holly holly* ill. by Lisa McCue. Viking, 2015. ISBN 978-045147501-5 Subj: Animals – muskrats. Animals – possums. Friendship. Holidays – Christmas.

Chang, Victoria. *Is Mommy?* ill. by Marla Frazee. Simon & Schuster/Beach Lane, 2015. ISBN 978-148140292-7 Subj: Character traits – questioning. Family life – mothers.

Chapin, Tom. *The backwards birthday party* by Tom Chapin and John Forster ill. by Chuck Groenink.

Simon & Schuster, 2015. ISBN 978-144246798-9 Subj: Birthdays. Parties. Songs.

Chapman, Jane. *No more cuddles!* ill. by author. Tiger Tales, 2015. ISBN 978-158925195-3 Subj: Animals. Hugging. Monsters.

Chapman, Jared. *Pirate, Viking, and Scientist* ill. by author. Little, Brown, 2014. ISBN 978-031625389-5 Subj: Behavior – resourcefulness. Careers – scientists. Friendship. Pirates. Science. Vikings.

Steve, raised by wolves ill. by author. Little, Brown, 2015. ISBN 978-031625390-1 Subj: Animals – wolves. Character traits – being different. Character traits – Individuality. School – first day.

Vegetables in underwear ill. by author. Abrams/Appleseed, 2015. ISBN 978-141971464-1 Subj: Clothing – underwear. Food. Plants.

Chase, Kit. *Oliver's tree* ill. by author. Putnam, 2014. ISBN 978-039925700-1 Subj: Animals – elephants. Animals – rabbits. Behavior – resourcefulness. Birds – owls. Friendship. Problem solving.

Chast, Roz. *Around the clock!* ill. by author. Simon & Schuster, 2015. ISBN 978-141698476-4 Subj: Clocks, watches. Day. Imagination. Rhyming text. Time.

Chaud, Benjamin. *The bear's sea escape* ill. by author. Chronicle, 2014. ISBN 978-145212743-9 Subj: Animals – bears. Family life – fathers. Hibernation.

The bear's surprise ill. by author. Chronicle, 2015. ISBN 978-145214028-5 Subj: Animals – bears. Circus. Family life. Family life – new sibling.

Chernesky, Felicia Sanzari. *Cheers for a dozen ears: a summer crop of counting* ill. by Susan Swan. Albert Whitman, 2014. ISBN 978-080751130-5 Subj: Counting, numbers. Farms. Food. Rhyming text. Seasons – summer.

From apple trees to cider, please! ill. by Julia Patton. Albert Whitman, 2015. ISBN 978-080756513-1 Subj: Farms. Food. Rhyming text. Seasons – fall.

Sugar white snow and evergreens: a winter wonderland of color ill. by Susan Swan. Albert Whitman, 2014. ISBN 978-080757234-4 Subj: Concepts – color. Rhyming text. Seasons – winter. Trees.

Sun above and blooms below: a springtime of opposites ill. by Susan Swan. Albert Whitman, 2015. ISBN 978-080753632-2 Subj: Concepts – opposites. Farms. Rhyming text. School – field trips. Seasons – spring.

Chichester Clark, Emma. *Love is my favorite thing* ill. by author. Penguin/Nancy Paulsen, 2015. ISBN 978-039917503-9 Subj: Animals – dogs. Emotions – love.

Chicken Little. *Brave Chicken Little* by Robert Byrd; ill. by author. Viking, 2014. ISBN 978-067078616-9 Subj: Animals. Behavior – gossip, rumors. Behavior – trickery. Birds – chickens, roosters. Cumulative tales. Folk & fairy tales.

Chiew, Suzanne. *When you need a friend* ill. by Caroline Pedler. Tiger Tales, 2015. ISBN 978-158925173-1 Subj: Animals. Animals – badgers. Character traits – helpfulness. Friendship. Homes, houses. Weather – storms.

Child, Lauren. *The new small person* ill. by author. Candlewick, 2015. ISBN 978-076367810-4 Subj: Emotions – envy, jealousy. Ethnic groups in the U.S. – African Americans. Family life – brothers. Sibling rivalry.

Chin, Jason. *Gravity* ill. by author. Roaring Brook, 2014. ISBN 978-159643717-3 Subj: Science.

Chin, Oliver. *The year of the sheep: tales from the Chinese zodiac* ill. by Alina Chau. Immedium, 2015. ISBN 978-159702104-3 Subj: Animals – sheep. Character traits – cooperation. Zodiac.

Chisholm, Penny. *Buried sunlight: how fossil fuels have changed the earth* (Bang, Molly)

Choldenko, Gennifer. *Putting the monkeys to bed* ill. by Jack E. Davis. Putnam, 2015. ISBN 978-039924623-4 Subj: Animals – monkeys. Bedtime. Sleep.

Christie, R. Gregory. *Mousetropolis* ill. by author. Holiday House, 2015. ISBN 978-082342319-4 Subj: Animals – mice. Cities, towns. Country. Folk & fairy tales.

Christopher, Neil. *On the shoulder of a giant: an Inuit folktale* ill. by Jim Nelson. Inhabit, 2015. ISBN 978-177227002-0 Subj: Folk & fairy tales. Giants. Indians of North America – Inuit.

Chrustowski, Rick. *Bee dance* ill. by author. Holt, 2015. ISBN 978-080509919-5 Subj: Communication. Insects – bees.

Chung, Arree. *Ninja!* ill. by author. Holt, 2014. ISBN 978-080509911-9 Subj: Activities – playing. Imagination. Sports – martial arts.

Clanton, Ben. *Rex wrecks it!* ill. by author. Candlewick, 2014. ISBN 978-076366501-2 Subj: Activities – playing. Behavior – misbehavior. Character traits – cooperation. Dinosaurs.

Clarkson, Stephanie. *Sleeping Cinderella and other princess mix-ups* ill. by Brigette Barrager. Orchard, 2015. ISBN 978-054556564-6 Subj: Behavior – dissatisfaction. Folk & fairy tales. Rhyming text. Royalty – princesses.

Clayton, Dallas. *A is for awesome* ill. by author. Candlewick, 2014. ISBN 978-076365745-1 Subj: ABC books.

Lily the unicorn ill. by author. Harper, 2014. ISBN 978-006211668-0 Subj: Birds – penguins. Emotions – fear. Friendship. Mythical creatures – unicorns.

Cleary, Brian P. *If it rains pancakes: haiku and lantern poems* ill. by Andy Rowland. Millbrook, 2014. ISBN 978-146771609-3 Subj: Poetry.

Clement, Nathan. *Big tractor* ill. by author. Boyds Mills, 2015. ISBN 978-162091790-9 Subj: Farms. Seasons. Tractors.

Climo, Liz. *Rory the dinosaur: me and my dad* ill. by author. Little, Brown, 2015. ISBN 978-031627728-0 Subj: Dinosaurs. Family life – fathers.

Cline-Ransome, Lesa. *Freedom's school* ill. by James Ransome. Disney/Jump at the Sun, 2015. ISBN 978-142316103-5 Subj: Ethnic groups in the U.S. – African Americans. School.

Whale trails, before and now ill. by G. Brian Karas. Holt, 2015. ISBN 978-080509642-2 Subj: Animals – endangered animals. Animals – whales.

Coat, Janik. *Rhymoceros* ill. by author. Abrams/Appleseed, 2015. ISBN 978-141971514-3 Subj: Animals – rhinoceros. Format, unusual – board books. Rhyming text.

Coats, Lucy. *Captain Beastlie's pirate party* ill. by Chris Mould. Candlewick/Nosy Crow, 2014. ISBN 978-076367399-4 Subj: Behavior – messy. Birthdays. Hygiene. Pirates.

Cocca-Leffler, Maryann. *A homemade together Christmas* ill. by author. Albert Whitman, 2015. ISBN 978-080753366-6 Subj: Activities – making things. Animals – pigs. Gifts. Holidays – Christmas.

Janine ill. by author. Albert Whitman, 2015. ISBN 978-080753754-1 Subj: Behavior – bullying, teasing. Character traits – individuality. Self-concept.

Cohen, Jeff. *Eva and Sadie and the best classroom ever!* ill. by Elanna Allen. Harper, 2015. ISBN 978-006224938-8 Subj: Family life – sisters. School – first day.

Eva and Sadie and the worst haircut ever! ill. by Elanna Allen. Harper, 2014. ISBN 978-006224906-7 Subj: Character traits – appearance. Family life – sisters. Hair.

Cohen, Laurie. *The flea* ill. by Marjorie Béal. Owlkids, 2014. ISBN 978-177147056-8 Subj: Character traits – smallness. Concepts – size. Insects – fleas.

Colandro, Lucille. *There was an old lady who swallowed a frog!* ill. by Jared Lee. Scholastic, 2014. ISBN 978-054569138-3 Subj: Cumulative tales. Gardens, gardening. Rhyming text. Seasons – spring.

Colby, Rebecca. *It's raining bats and frogs* ill. by Steven Henry. Feiwel and Friends, 2015. ISBN 978-125004992-6 Subj: Holidays – Halloween. Parades. Weather – rain. Witches.

Cole, Henry. *Big bug* ill. by author. Simon & Schuster, 2014. ISBN 978-144249897-6 Subj: Concepts – size. Farms.

Colfer, Eoin. *Imaginary Fred* ill. by Oliver Jeffers. Harper, 2015. ISBN 978-000812614-8 Subj: Emotions – loneliness. Friendship. Imagination – imaginary friends.

Colón, Raúl. *Draw!* ill. by author. Simon & Schuster/Paula Wiseman, 2014. ISBN 978-144249493-0 Subj: Activities – drawing. Animals. Illness. Imagination. Wordless.

Coombs, Kate. *The tooth fairy wars* ill. by Jake Parker. Atheneum, 2014. ISBN 978-141697915-9 Subj: Fairies. Teeth.

Cooper, Elisha. *8, an animal alphabet* ill. by author. Scholastic/Orchard, 2015. ISBN 978-054547083-4 Subj: ABC books. Animals. Counting, numbers.

Cooper, Floyd. *Juneteenth for Mazie* ill. by author. Capstone, 2015. ISBN 978-162370170-3 Subj: Character traits – freedom. Ethnic groups in the U.S. – African Americans. Holidays – Juneteenth. Prejudice. Slavery. U.S. history.

Copeland, Misty. *Firebird* ill. by Christopher Myers. Putnam, 2014. ISBN 978-039916615-0 Subj: Ballet. Careers – dancers. Ethnic groups in the U.S. – African Americans.

Cordell, Matthew. *Wish* ill. by author. Disney/Hyperion, 2015. ISBN 978-148470875-0 Subj: Animals – elephants. Babies, toddlers. Behavior – wishing. Character traits – hopefulness. Family life.

Corderoy, Tracey. *I want my daddy* ill. by Alison Edgson. Tiger Tales, 2015. ISBN 978-158925177-9 Subj: Animals – mice. Family life – fathers.

Just right for two ill. by Rosalind Beardshaw. Nosy Crow, 2014. ISBN 978-076367344-4 Subj: Animals – dogs. Animals – mice. Behavior – collecting things. Emotions – loneliness. Friendship. Weather – snow.

The magical snow garden ill. by Jane Chapman. Tiger Tales, 2014. ISBN 978-158925162-5 Subj: Birds – penguins. Character traits – perseverance. Gardens, gardening.

Côté, Geneviève. *Bob's hungry ghost* ill. by author. Tundra, 2014. ISBN 978-177049713-9 Subj: Friendship. Ghosts. Pets.

Goodnight, you ill. by author. Kids Can, 2014. ISBN 978-177138050-8 Subj: Animals – pigs. Animals – rabbits. Camps, camping. Emotions – fear.

Starring me and you ill. by author. Kids Can, 2014. ISBN 978-189478639-3 Subj: Animals – pigs. Animals – rabbits. Character traits – compromising. Emotions. Friendship.

Cotton, Katie. *Counting lions: portraits from the wild* ill. by Stephen Walton. Candlewick, 2015. ISBN 978-076368207-1 Subj: Animals – endangered animals. Counting, numbers.

Cousins, Lucy. *Count with Maisy, cheep, cheep, cheep!* ill. by author. Candlewick, 2015. ISBN 978-076367643-8 Subj: Animals – mice. Birds – chickens, roosters. Counting, numbers. Format, unusual – toy & movable books.

Maisy goes on a plane ill. by author. Candlewick, 2015. ISBN 978-076367825-8 Subj: Activities – traveling. Airplanes, airports. Animals – mice.

Maisy goes to the movies ill. by author. Candlewick, 2014. ISBN 978-076366950-8 Subj: Animals – mice. Theater.

Maisy plays soccer ill. by author. Candlewick, 2014. ISBN 978-076367228-7 Subj: Animals – mice. Friendship. Sports – soccer.

Maisy's Christmas tree ill. by author. Candlewick, 2014. ISBN 978-076367457-1 Subj: Animals – mice. Format, unusual – board books. Holidays – Christmas. Trees.

Cox, Lynne. *Elizabeth, queen of the seas* ill. by Brian Floca. Random/Schwartz & Wade, 2014. ISBN 978-037585888-8 Subj: Animals – seals. Character traits – kindness to animals.

Coyle, Carmela LaVigna. *Do princesses make happy campers?* ill. by Mike Gordon. Taylor Trade, 2015. ISBN 978-163076054-0 Subj: Camps, camping. Character traits – questioning. Rhyming text. Royalty – princesses.

Cronin, Doreen. *Boom Snot Twitty* ill. by Renata Liwska. Viking, 2014. ISBN 978-067078575-9 Subj: Animals. Friendship.

Boom, Snot, Twitty, this way that way ill. by Renata Liwska. Viking, 2015. ISBN 978-067078577-3 Subj: Animals. Friendship.

Click, clack, ho! ho! ho! ill. by Betsy Lewin. Atheneum, 2015. ISBN 978-144249673-6 Subj: Animals. Birds – ducks. Holidays – Christmas. Santa Claus.

Click, clack, peep! ill. by Betsy Lewin. Atheneum, 2015. ISBN 978-148142411-0 Subj: Animals – babies. Birds – ducks. Farms. Sleep.

Smick! ill. by Juana Medina. Viking, 2015. ISBN 978-067078578-0 Subj: Animals – dogs. Birds – chickens, roosters. Friendship.

Crowe, Caroline. *Pirates in pajamas* ill. by Tom Knight. Tiger Tales, 2015. ISBN 978-158925190-8 Subj: Bedtime. Pirates. Rhyming text.

Crowther, Robert. *Robert Crowther's pop-up dinosaur ABC* ill. by author. Candlewick, 2015. ISBN 978-076367296-6 Subj: ABC books. Dinosaurs. Format, unusual – toy & movable books.

Crum, Shutta. *Uh-oh!* ill. by Patrice Barton. Knopf, 2015. ISBN 978-038575268-8 Subj: Activities – playing. Babies, toddlers. Sea & seashore – beaches.

Cullen, Lynn. *Dear Mr. Washington* ill. by Nancy Carpenter. Dial, 2015. ISBN 978-080373038-0 Subj: Behavior – misbehavior. Etiquette. Family life – brothers & sisters. Letters, cards. U.S. history.

Curato, Mike. *Little Elliot, big city* ill. by author. Holt, 2014. ISBN 978-080509825-9 Subj: Animals – elephants. Animals – mice. Character traits – helpfulness. Character traits – smallness. Cities, towns. Friendship.

Little Elliot, big family ill. by author. Holt, 2015. ISBN 978-080509826-6 Subj: Animals – elephants. Animals – mice. Emotions – loneliness. Family life.

Cuyler, Margery. *The little school bus* ill. by Bob Kolar. Holt/Christy Ottaviano, 2014. ISBN 978-080509435-0 Subj: Buses. Rhyming text. School.

Cyrus, Kurt. *Motor Dog* ill. by David Gordon. Disney/Hyperion, 2014. ISBN 978-142316822-5 Subj: Animals – dogs. Rhyming text. Robots.

Czajak, Paul. *Monster needs a Christmas tree* ill. by Wendy Grieb. Scarletta, 2014. ISBN 978-193806346-6 Subj: Holidays – Christmas. Monsters. Rhyming text.

Monster needs your vote ill. by Wendy Grieb. Mighty Media, 2015. ISBN 978-193806363-3 Subj: Character traits – ambition. Character traits – assertiveness. Monsters. Rhyming text.

Dahl, Michael. *Goodnight football* ill. by Christina Forshay. Capstone, 2014. ISBN 978-162370106-2 Subj: Bedtime. Rhyming text. Sports – football.

Dale, Penny. *Dinosaur rocket!* ill. by author. Candlewick, 2015. ISBN 978-076367999-6 Subj: Dinosaurs. Moon. Space & space ships.

Daly, Cathleen. *Emily's blue period* ill. by Lisa Brown. Roaring Brook, 2014. ISBN 978-159643469-1 Subj: Art. Divorce. Emotions.

Daly, Niki. *Thank you, Jackson* ill. by Jude Daly. Frances Lincoln/Janetta Otter-Barry, 2015. ISBN 978-184780484-6 Subj: Animals – donkeys. Character traits – kindness to animals. Etiquette. Foreign lands – South Africa.

Davies, Matt. *Ben draws trouble* ill. by author. Roaring Brook, 2015. ISBN 978-159643795-1 Subj: Activities – drawing. Behavior – lost & found possessions. School.

Davies, Nicola. *I (don't) like snakes* ill. by Luciano Lozano. Candlewick, 2015. ISBN 978-076367831-9 Subj: Emotions – fear. Reptiles – snakes.

The promise ill. by Laura Carlin. Candlewick, 2014. ISBN 978-076366633-0 Subj: Behavior – stealing. Character traits – hopefulness.

Tiny creatures: the world of microbes ill. by Emily Sutton. Candlewick, 2014. ISBN 978-076367315-4 Subj: Science.

Davis, Jacky. *Ladybug Girl and the best ever playdate* (Soman, David)

Ladybug Girl and the dress-up dilemma (Soman, David)

Davis, Jon. *Small Blue and the deep dark night* ill. by author. Houghton, 2014. ISBN 978-054416466-6 Subj: Animals – bears. Animals – rabbits. Emotions – fear.

Davis, Kathryn Gibbs. *Mr. Ferris and his wheel* ill. by Gilbert Ford. Houghton, 2014. ISBN 978-054795922-1 Subj: Careers – engineers. Careers – inventors. Fairs, festivals. Inventions. Machines. Parks – amusement.

Davis, Sarah. *My first trucks* ill. with photos. DK, 2015. ISBN 978-146542904-9 Subj: Format, unusual – board books. Trucks.

Day, Alexandra. *Carl's Halloween* ill. by author. Farrar, 2015. ISBN 978-037431082-0 Subj: Animals – dogs. Clothing – costumes. Holidays – Halloween.

Day, Nancy Raines. *What in the world? numbers in nature* ill. by Kurt Cyrus. Simon & Schuster, 2015. ISBN 978-148140060-2 Subj: Counting, numbers. Nature. Rhyming text.

Daywalt, Drew. *The day the crayons came home* ill. by Oliver Jeffers. Philomel, 2015. ISBN 978-039917275-5 Subj: Behavior – lost & found possessions. Concepts – color. Letters, cards.

Deak, Erzsi. *Pumpkin time!* ill. by Doug Cushman. Sourcebooks/Jabberwocky, 2014. ISBN 978-140229526-3 Subj: Animals. Farms. Gardens, gardening.

Dean, James. *Pete the Cat: twinkle, twinkle, little star* ill. by author. Harper, 2014. ISBN 978-006230416-2 Subj: Animals – cats. Nursery rhymes. Sky. Songs. Stars.

Pete the Cat and his magic sunglasses by James Dean and Kim Dean ill. by James Dean. HarperCollins, 2013. ISBN 978-006227556-1 Subj: Animals – cats. Behavior – bad day, bad mood. Glasses.

Pete the Cat and the bedtime blues by James Dean and Kim Dean ill. by James Dean. HarperCollins, 2015. ISBN 978-006230430-8 Subj: Animals – cats. Bedtime. Sleepovers.

Pete the Cat and the new guy by James Dean and Kim Dean ill. by James Dean. Harper, 2014. ISBN 978-006227560-8 Subj: Animals – cats. Animals – platypuses. Character traits – being different. Rhyming text.

Dean, Kim. *Pete the Cat and his magic sunglasses* (Dean, James)

Pete the Cat and the bedtime blues (Dean, James)

Pete the Cat and the new guy (Dean, James)

Deedman, Heidi. *Too many toys!* ill. by author. Candlewick, 2015. ISBN 978-076367861-6 Subj: Behavior – sharing. Gifts. Problem solving. Toys.

De Kinder, Jan. *Red* ill. by author. Eerdmans, 2015. ISBN 978-080285446-9 Subj: Behavior – bullying, teasing. Character traits – being different. School.

de la Peña, Matt. *Last stop on Market Street* ill. by Christian Robinson. Putnam, 2015. ISBN 978-039925774-2 Subj: Buses. Caldecott award honor books. Character traits – helpfulness. Character traits – kindness. Cities, towns. Ethnic groups in the U.S. Family life – grandmothers.

Delacroix, Sibylle. *Prickly Jenny* ill. by author. Owlkids, 2015. ISBN 978-177147129-9 Subj: Behavior – bad day.

DeLaporte, Bérengère. *Superfab saves the day* by Bérengère DeLaporte and Jean Leroy ill. by Bérengère DeLaporte. Owlkids, 2014. ISBN 978-177147076-6 Subj: Animals – rabbits. Character traits – vanity. Clothing – costumes.

Delaunois, Angèle. *Magic little words* ill. by Manon Gauthier. Owlkids, 2015. ISBN 978-177147106-0 Subj: Etiquette. Language.

Demi. *Florence Nightingale* ill. by author. Holt, 2014. ISBN 978-080509729-0 Subj: Careers – nurses.

Dempsey, Kristy. *A dance like starlight: one ballerina's dream* ill. by Floyd Cooper. Philomel, 2014. ISBN 978-039925284-6 Subj: Ballet. Careers – dancers. Ethnic groups in the U.S. – African Americans. Prejudice.

Deneux, Xavier. *Vehicles* ill. by author. Chronicle, 2015. ISBN 978-145214516-7 Subj: Automobiles. Buses. Format, unusual – toy & movable books. Space & space ships. Trucks.

Denise, Anika. *Baking day at Grandma's* ill. by Christopher Denise. Philomel, 2014. ISBN 978-039924244-1 Subj: Activities – baking, cooking. Animals – bears. Emotions – love. Family life – grandmothers. Rhyming text.

DePalma, Mary Newell. *Two little birds* ill. by author. Eerdmans, 2014. ISBN 978-080285421-6 Subj: Birds. Migration.

dePaola, Tomie. *Jack* ill. by author. Penguin/Nancy Paulsen, 2014. ISBN 978-039916154-4 Subj: Animals. Cumulative tales. Homes, houses.

Look and be grateful ill. by author. Holiday House, 2015. ISBN 978-082343443-5 Subj: Behavior – sharing. Character traits – kindness. Character traits – wisdom. Nature. Religion.

Strega Nona does it again ill. by author. Penguin/Nancy Paulsen, 2013. ISBN 978-039925781-0 Subj: Behavior – bossy. Character traits – vanity. Witches.

Desbordes, Astrid. *Edmond, the moonlit party* ill. by Marc Boutavant. Enchanted Lion, 2015. ISBN 978-159270174-2 Subj: Animals – bears. Animals – squirrels. Birds – owls. Character traits – individuality. Character traits – shyness. Parties.

Detlefsen, Lisl H. *Time for cranberries* ill. by Jed Henry. Roaring Brook, 2015. ISBN 978-162672098-5 Subj: Farms. Food. Holidays – Thanksgiving. Seasons – fall.

Dewdney, Anna. *Llama Llama Gram and Grandpa* ill. by author. Viking, 2015. ISBN 978-067001396-8 Subj: Animals – llamas. Family life – grandparents. Sleepovers.

Nelly Gnu and Daddy too ill. by author. Viking, 2014. ISBN 978-067001227-5 Subj: Activities – playing. Animals – gnus. Family life – fathers. Rhyming text.

Diesen, Deborah. *The not very merry pout-pout fish* ill. by Dan Hanna. Farrar, 2015. ISBN 978-037435549-4 Subj: Fish. Gifts. Holidays – Christmas. Rhyming text.

The pout-pout fish goes to school ill. by Dan Hanna. Farrar, 2014. ISBN 978-037436095-5 Subj: Behavior – worrying. Character traits – confidence. Fish. Rhyming text. School – first day. Self-concept.

Diggs, Taye. *Mixed me!* ill. by Shane W Evans. Feiwel and Friends, 2015. ISBN 978-125004719-9 Subj: Ethnic groups in the U.S. Rhyming text. Self-concept.

Dillard, Sarah. *First day at Zoo School* ill. by author. Sleeping Bear, 2014. ISBN 978-158536890-7 Subj: Animals – pandas. Reptiles – alligators, crocodiles. School – first day.

Dillon, Diane. *If kids ran the world* (Dillon, Leo)

Dillon, Leo. *If kids ran the world* by Leo Dillon and Diane Dillon ill. by Leo Dillon. Scholastic/Blue Sky, 2014. ISBN 978-054544196-4 Subj: Behavior. Character traits – helpfulness. World.

DiPucchio, Kelly. *Dog days of school* ill. by Brian Biggs. Disney/Hyperion, 2014. ISBN 978-078685493-6 Subj: Animals – dogs. Behavior – dissatisfaction. Behavior – wishing. Humorous stories.

Everyone loves bacon ill. by Eric Wight. Farrar, 2015. ISBN 978-037430052-4 Subj: Character traits – vanity. Food.

Gaston ill. by Christian Robinson. Atheneum, 2014. ISBN 978-144245102-5 Subj: Animals – dogs. Character traits – being different. Character traits – individuality. Self-concept.

Zombie in love 2 + 1 ill. by Scott Campbell. Atheneum, 2015. ISBN 978-144245937-3 Subj: Babies, toddlers. Humorous stories. Monsters.

DiSiena, Laura Lyn. *Dinosaurs live on! and other fun facts* by Laura Lyn DiSiena and Hannah Eliot ill. by Aaron Spurgeon. Simon & Schuster, 2015. ISBN 978-148142425-7 Subj: Dinosaurs. Fossils.

DiTerlizzi, Angela. *Baby love* ill. by Brooke Boynton Hughes. Simon & Schuster/Beach Lane, 2015. ISBN 978-144243392-2 Subj: Babies, toddlers. Emotions – love. Family life – parents. Rhyming text.

Some bugs ill. by Brendan Wenzel. Simon & Schuster/Beach Lane, 2014. ISBN 978-144245880-2 Subj: Insects. Rhyming text.

Dodd, Emma. *Always* ill. by author. Candlewick/Templar, 2014. ISBN 978-076367544-8 Subj: Animals – elephants. Emotions – love. Rhyming text.

The entertainer ill. by author. Little Bee, 2015. ISBN 978-149980078-4 Subj: Animals – bears. Birthdays. Parties. Rhyming text.

Everything ill. by author. Candlewick/Templar, 2015. ISBN 978-076367128-0 Subj: Animals – koalas. Emotions – love. Family life – mothers. Rhyming text.

Happy ill. by author. Candlewick/Nosy Crow, 2015. ISBN 978-076368008-4 Subj: Birds – owls. Emotions – love. Family life – mothers. Rhyming text.

More and more ill. by author. Candlewick/Templar, 2014. ISBN 978-076367543-1 Subj: Animals – monkeys. Emotions – love. Rhyming text.

When I grow up ill. by author. Candlewick/Templar, 2015. ISBN 978-076367985-9 Subj: Animals – bears. Behavior – growing up. Rhyming text.

Dolan, Elys. *Nuts in space* ill. by author. Candlewick, 2015. ISBN 978-076367609-4 Subj: Aliens. Food. Humorous stories. Space & space ships.

Weasels ill. by author. Candlewick, 2014. ISBN 978-076367100-6 Subj: Animals – weasels. Humorous stories.

Dominguez, Angela. *Knit together* ill. by author. Dial, 2015. ISBN 978-080374099-0 Subj: Activities – drawing. Activities – knitting. Character traits – cooperation. Family life – daughters. Family life – mothers.

Donaldson, Julia. *Superworm* ill. by Axel Scheffler. Scholastic, 2014. ISBN 978-054559176-8 Subj: Animals – worms. Character traits – helpfulness. Insects. Rhyming text.

Donofrio, Beverly. *Where's Mommy?* ill. by Barbara McClintock. Random/Schwartz & Wade, 2014. ISBN 978-037584423-2 Subj: Animals – mice. Friendship.

Doodler, Todd H. *Veggies with wedgies* ill. by author. Simon & Schuster, 2014. ISBN 978-144249340-7 Subj: Clothing – underwear. Farms. Food. Humorous stories.

Dorros, Arthur. *Abuelo* ill. by Raúl Colón. Harper, 2014. ISBN 978-006168627-6 Subj: Family life – grandfathers. Foreign lands – Argentina. Foreign languages.

Dotlich, Rebecca Kai. *All aboard!* ill. by Mike Lowery. Knopf, 2014. ISBN 978-038575420-0 Subj: Rhyming text. Trains.

One day, the end: short, very short, shorter-than-ever stories ill. by Fred Koehler. Boyds Mills, 2015. ISBN 978-162091451-9 Subj: Activities – storytelling. Activities – writing. Books, reading.

Race car count ill. by Michael Slack. Holt, 2015. ISBN 978-162779009-3 Subj: Automobiles. Counting, numbers. Rhyming text. Sports – racing.

Driscoll, Amanda. *Duncan the story dragon* ill. by author. Knopf, 2015. ISBN 978-038575507-8 Subj: Books, reading. Dragons. Problem solving.

Drummond, Ree. *Charlie and the new baby* ill. by Diane deGroat. Harper, 2014. ISBN 978-006229750-1 Subj: Animals – bulls, cows. Animals – dogs. Careers – ranchers. Emotions – envy, jealousy.

Dubuc, Marianne. *The lion and the bird* ill. by author. Enchanted Lion, 2014. ISBN 978-159270151-3 Subj: Animals – lions. Birds. Character traits – kindness to animals. Friendship.

Mr. Postmouse's rounds ill. by author. Kids Can, 2015. ISBN 978-177138572-5 Subj: Animals – mice. Careers – postal workers.

Duddle, Johnny. *Gigantosaurus* ill. by author. Candlewick, 2014. ISBN 978-076367131-0 Subj: Behavior – lying. Dinosaurs. Rhyming text.

Dudley, Rebecca. *Hank has a dream* ill. by author. Peter Pauper, 2014. ISBN 978-144131572-4 Subj: Activities – flying. Dreams.

Duke, Kate. *In the rainforest* ill. by author. Harper, 2014. ISBN 978-006028259-2 Subj: Animals. Jungle. Plants.

Dumont, Jean-François. *The geese march in step* ill. by author. Eerdmans, 2014. ISBN 978-080285443-8 Subj: Birds – geese. Character traits – being different. Character traits – individuality. Self-concept.

The sheep go on strike ill. by author. Eerdmans, 2014. ISBN 978-080285470-4 Subj: Animals – sheep. Character traits – compromising. Farms.

Dunbar, Joyce. *Pat-a-cake baby* ill. by Polly Dunbar. Candlewick, 2015. ISBN 978-076367577-6 Subj: Activities – baking, cooking. Babies, toddlers. Rhyming text.

Dunrea, Olivier. *Gemma and Gus* ill. by author. Houghton Mifflin Harcourt, 2015. ISBN 978-054786851-6 Subj: Birds – geese. Family life – brothers & sisters.

Durand, Hallie. *Catch that cookie!* ill. by David Small. Dial, 2014. ISBN 978-052542835-0 Subj: Behavior – running away. Folk & fairy tales. School.

Duval, Kathy. *A bear's year* ill. by Gerry Turley. Random House, 2015. ISBN 978-038537011-0 Subj: Animals – bears. Rhyming text. Seasons.

Dyckman, Ame. *Wolfie the bunny* ill. by Zachariah OHora. Little, Brown, 2015. ISBN 978-031622614-1 Subj: Adoption. Animals – rabbits. Animals – wolves.

Eastland, Chris. *1-2-3 zooborns!* (Bleiman, Andrew)

Edwards, Karl Newsom. *Fly!* ill. by author. Knopf, 2015. ISBN 978-038539283-9 Subj: Insects – flies. Self-concept.

Edwards, Michelle. *Max makes a cake* ill. by Charles Santoso. Random House, 2014. ISBN 978-044981431-4 Subj: Activities – baking, cooking. Food. Holidays – Passover. Jewish culture.

Ehlert, Lois. *The scraps book: notes from a colorful life* ill. by author. Simon & Schuster/Beach Lane, 2014. ISBN 978-144243571-1 Subj: Art. Books, reading. Careers – artists.

Einhorn, Edward. *Fractions in disguise: A math adventure* ill. by David Clark. Charlesbridge, 2014. ISBN 978-157091773-8 Subj: Counting, numbers.

Eliot, Hannah. *Dinosaurs live on! and other fun facts* (DiSiena, Laura Lyn)

Elliott, David. *Nobody's perfect* ill. by Sam Zuppardi. Candlewick, 2015. ISBN 978-076366699-6 Subj: Character traits – patience. Character traits – perfectionism. Family life.

On the wing ill. by Becca Stadtlander. Candlewick, 2014. ISBN 978-076365324-8 Subj: Birds. Poetry.

This Orq. (He say "ugh!") ill. by Lori Nichols. Boyds Mills, 2015. ISBN 978-162091789-3 Subj: Animals – woolly mammoths. Behavior – bullying, teasing. Cave dwellers. Pets.

This Orq. (He cave boy.) ill. by Lori Nichols. Boyds Mills, 2014. ISBN 978-162091521-9 Subj: Animals – woolly mammoths. Cave dwellers. Pets.

Elliott, Devlin. *Naughty Mabel* (Lane, Nathan)

Ellis, Carson. *Home* ill. by author. Candlewick, 2015. ISBN 978-076366529-6 Subj: Homes, houses.

Elvgren, Jennifer. *The whispering town* ill. by Fabio Santomauro. Lerner/Kar-Ben, 2014. ISBN 978-146771194-4 Subj: Character traits – bravery. Character traits – freedom. Foreign lands – Denmark. Jewish culture. War.

Elya, Susan Middleton. *Little Roja Riding Hood* ill. by Susan Guevara. Putnam, 2014. ISBN 978-039924767-5 Subj: Animals – wolves. Family life – grandmothers. Folk & fairy tales. Foreign languages. Rhyming text.

Emberley, Rebecca. *Spare parts* ill. by Ed Emberley. Roaring Brook/Neal Porter, 2015. ISBN 978-159643723-4 Subj: Emotions – loneliness. Friendship. Rhyming text. Robots.

Enersen, Adele. *Vincent and the night* ill. by author. Dial, 2015. ISBN 978-080374106-5 Subj: Babies, toddlers. Bedtime. Behavior – misbehavior. Imagination. Night.

Engle, Margarita. *Drum dream girl: how one girl's courage changed music* ill. by Rafael López. Houghton Mifflin Harcourt, 2015. ISBN 978-054410229-3 Subj: Foreign lands – Cuba. Gender roles. Music. Musical instruments – drums.

Orangutanka ill. by Renee Kurilla. Holt, 2015. ISBN 978-080509839-6 Subj: Animals – orangutans. Poetry.

The sky painter ill. by Aliona Bereghici. Amazon/Two Lions, 2015. ISBN 978-147782633-1 Subj: Activities – painting. Art. Birds. Careers – artists. Nature. Poetry.

Tiny rabbit's big wish ill. by David Walker. Houghton, 2014. ISBN 978-054785286-7 Subj: Animals – rabbits. Character traits – smallness. Concepts – size. Self-concept.

Engler, Michael. *Elephantastic!* ill. by Joelle Tourlonias. Peter Pauper, 2015. ISBN 978-144130841-2 Subj: Animals – elephants. Friendship. Imagination. Toys.

Esbaum, Jill. *I am cow, hear me moo!* ill. by Gus Gordon. Dial, 2014. ISBN 978-080373524-8 Subj: Animals – bulls, cows. Character traits – bravery. Emotions – fear. Rhyming text.

I hatched! ill. by Jen Corace. Dial, 2014. ISBN 978-080373688-7 Subj: Birds. Rhyming text.

Escoffier, Michael. *The day I lost my superpowers* ill. by Kris DiGiacomo. Enchanted Lion, 2014. ISBN 978-159270144-5 Subj: Activities – playing. Imagination.

Take away the A ill. by Kris DiGiacomo. Enchanted Lion, 2014. ISBN 978-159270156-8 Subj: ABC books. Language.

Where's the baboon? ill. by Kris DiGiacomo. Enchanted Lion, 2015. ISBN 978-159270189-6 Subj: Humorous stories. Language.

Estes, Allison. *Izzy and Oscar* by Allison Estes and Dan Stark ill. by Tracy Dockray. Sourcebooks/Jabberwocky, 2015. ISBN 978-149260150-0 Subj: Octopuses. Pets. Pirates.

Ewert, Marcus. *Mummy cat* ill. by Lisa Brown. Clarion, 2015. ISBN 978-054434082-4 Subj: Animals – cats. Foreign lands – Egypt. Mummies. Rhyming text.

Fairgray, Richard. *Gorillas in our midst* by Richard Fairgray and Terry Jones ill. by Richard Fairgray. Sky Pony, 2015. ISBN 978-163220607-7 Subj: Animals – gorillas. Disguises. Picture puzzles.

Falkenstern, Lisa. *Professor Whiskerton presents Steampunk ABC* ill. by author. Amazon/Two Lions, 2014. ISBN 978-147784722-0 Subj: ABC books. Animals – mice. Inventions.

Farrell, Darren. *Thank you, Octopus* ill. by author. Dial, 2014. ISBN 978-080373438-8 Subj: Bedtime. Octopuses.

Faruqi, Reem. *Lailah's lunchbox* ill. by Lea Lyon. Tilbury, 2015. ISBN 978-088448431-8 Subj: Ethnic groups in the U.S. Holidays – Ramadan. Moving. Religion – Islam. School.

Faulconer, Maria. *A mom for Umande* ill. by Susan Kathleen Hartung. Dial, 2014. ISBN 978-080373762-4 Subj: Animals – babies. Animals – gorillas. Character traits – kindness to animals. Zoos.

Fearing, Mark. *The great Thanksgiving escape* ill. by author. Candlewick, 2014. ISBN 978-076366306-3 Subj: Family life. Holidays – Thanksgiving.

Federle, Tim. *Tommy can't stop!* ill. by Mark Fearing. Disney/Hyperion, 2015. ISBN 978-142316917-8 Subj: Activities – dancing. Family life.

Feeney, Tatyana. *Little Frog's tadpole trouble* ill. by author. Knopf, 2014. ISBN 978-038575372-2 Subj: Family life – brothers & sisters. Family life – new sibling. Frogs & toads. Sibling rivalry.

Small Elephant's bathtime ill. by author. Knopf, 2015. ISBN 978-055349721-2 Subj: Activities – bathing. Animals – elephants. Behavior – misbehavior.

Feiffer, Jules. *Rupert can dance* ill. by author. Farrar, 2014. ISBN 978-037436363-5 Subj: Activities – dancing. Animals – cats.

Fergus, Maureen. *Buddy and Earl* ill. by Carey Sookocheff. Groundwood, 2015. ISBN 978-155498712-2 Subj: Animals – dogs. Animals – hedgehogs. Behavior – boredom. Friendship. Imagination.

Fern, Tracey. *W is for Webster: Noah Webster and his American dictionary* ill. by Boris Kulikov. Farrar/Margaret Ferguson, 2015. ISBN 978-037438240-7 Subj: Dictionaries. Language.

Ferrell, Sean. *I don't like Koala* ill. by Charles Santoso. Atheneum, 2015. ISBN 978-148140068-8 Subj: Animals – koalas. Toys.

Ferri, Giuliano. *Peekaboo* ill. by author. Minedition, 2015. ISBN 978-988824093-7 Subj: Animals. Format, unusual – board books. Format, unusual – toy & movable books.

Ferry, Beth. *Stick and Stone* ill. by Tom Lichtenheld. Harcourt, 2015. ISBN 978-054403256-9 Subj: Emotions – loneliness. Friendship. Rhyming text. Rocks.

Fields, Terri. *One good deed* ill. by Deborah Melmon. Kar-Ben, 2015. ISBN 978-146773478-3 Subj: Character traits – kindness. Jewish culture.

Fischer, Ellen. *Latke, the lucky dog* ill. by Tiphanie Beeke. Kar-Ben, 2014. ISBN 978-076139038-1 Subj: Animals – dogs. Character traits – kindness to animals. Holidays – Hanukkah.

Fisher, Valorie. *I can do it myself* ill. by author. Random/Schwartz & Wade, 2014. ISBN 978-044981593-9 Subj: Concepts. Counting, numbers. Self-concept.

Fisman, Karen. *Nonna's Hanukkah surprise* ill. by Martha Avilés. Kar-Ben, 2015. ISBN 978-146773476-9 Subj: Behavior – lost & found possessions. Family life – grandmothers. Holidays – Hanukkah.

FitzSimmons, David. *Curious critters, vol. 2* photos by author. Wild Iris, 2014. ISBN 978-193660770-9 Subj: Animals. Frogs & toads. Nature. Reptiles.

Fleming, Candace. *Bulldozer's big day* ill. by Eric Rohmann. Atheneum, 2015. ISBN 978-148140097-8 Subj: Birthdays. Machines. Parties.

Tippy-tippy-tippy, splash! ill. by G. Brian Karas. Atheneum, 2014. ISBN 978-141695403-3 Subj: Animals – rabbits. Sea & seashore – beaches.

Fleming, Denise. *Go, shapes, go!* ill. by author. Simon & Schuster/Beach Lane, 2014. ISBN 978-144248240-1 Subj: Animals – mice. Concepts – shape.

Fliess, Sue. *Books for me!* ill. by Mike Laughead. Amazon/Two Lions, 2015. ISBN 978-147782036-0 Subj: Animals – hippopotamuses. Books, reading. Libraries. Rhyming text.

Floca, Brian. *Five trucks* ill. by author. Simon & Schuster, 2014. ISBN 978-148140593-5 Subj: Airplanes, airports. Trucks.

Florian, Douglas. *How to draw a dragon* ill. by author. Simon & Schuster/Beach Lane, 2015. ISBN 978-144247399-7 Subj: Activities – drawing. Dragons. Rhyming text.

I love my hat ill. by Paige Keiser. Amazon/Two Lions, 2014. ISBN 978-147784780-0 Subj: Animals. Careers – farmers. Clothing. Rhyming text.

Flory, Neil. *The short giraffe* ill. by Mark Cleary. Albert Whitman, 2014. ISBN 978-080757346-4 Subj: Animals – giraffes. Character traits – cooperation. Character traits – smallness. Problem solving.

Foreman, Michael. *I love you, too!* ill. by author. Andersen, 2014. ISBN 978-146773451-6 Subj: Animals – bears. Bedtime. Emotions – love. Family life – fathers.

Formento, Alison. *These rocks count!* ill. by Sarah Snow. Albert Whitman, 2014. ISBN 978-080757870-4 Subj: Counting, numbers. Rocks. School – field trips.

Forster, John. *The backwards birthday party* (Chapin, Tom)

Fox, Diane. *The cat, the dog, Little Red, the exploding eggs, the wolf, and Grandma* ill. by Christyan Fox. Scholastic, 2014. ISBN 978-054569481-0 Subj: Animals – cats. Animals – dogs. Books, reading. Folk & fairy tales. Humorous stories.

Fox, Mem. *Baby bedtime* ill. by Emma Quay. Simon & Schuster/Beach Lane, 2014. ISBN 978-148142097-6 Subj: Animals – elephants. Babies, toddlers. Bedtime.

Nellie Belle ill. by Mike Austin. Simon & Schuster/Beach Lane, 2015. ISBN 978-141699005-5 Subj: Animals – dogs. Character traits – willfulness. Rhyming text.

Franceschelli, Christopher. *Countablock* ill. by Peskimo. Abrams/Appleseed, 2014. ISBN 978-141971374-3 Subj: Counting, numbers. Format, unusual – toy & movable books.

Dinoblock ill. by Peskimo. Abrams/Appleseed, 2015. ISBN 978-141971674-4 Subj: Dinosaurs. Format, unusual – board books.

Franco, Betsy. *A spectacular selection of sea critters: concrete poems* ill. by Michael Wertz. Millbrook, 2015. ISBN 978-146772152-3 Subj: Animals. Poetry. Sea & seashore.

Frankel, Erin. *Nobody! a story about overcoming bullying in schools* ill. by Paula Heaphy. Free Spirit, 2015. ISBN 978-157542495-8 Subj: Behavior – bullying, teasing. School. Self-concept.

Fraser, Mary Ann. *No Yeti yet* ill. by author. Peter Pauper, 2015. ISBN 978-144130855-9 Subj: Family life – brothers. Monsters. Sports – hunting.

Frazee, Marla. *The farmer and the clown* ill. by author. Simon & Schuster/Beach Lane, 2014. ISBN 978-144249744-3 Subj: Behavior – lost. Careers – farmers. Circus. Clowns, jesters. Wordless.

Fredrickson, Lane. *Monster trouble!* ill. by Michael Robertson. Sterling, 2015. ISBN 978-145491345-0 Subj: Bedtime. Ethnic groups in the U.S. – African Americans. Kissing. Monsters.

Freedman, Claire. *Spider sandwiches* ill. by Sue Hendra and Paul Linnet. Bloomsbury, 2014. ISBN 978-161963364-3 Subj: Food. Monsters. Rhyming text.

Freedman, Deborah. *By Mouse and Frog* ill. by author. Viking, 2015. ISBN 978-067078490-5 Subj: Animals – mice. Careers – writers. Character traits – compromising. Character traits – cooperation. Frogs & toads.

Freeman, Tor. *Olive and the embarrassing gift* ill. by author. Candlewick/Templar, 2014. ISBN 978-076367406-9 Subj: Animals. Clothing – hats. Emotions – embarrassment. Friendship. Gifts.

French, Vivian. *The most wonderful thing in the world* ill. by Angela Barrett. Candlewick, 2015. ISBN 978-076367501-1 Subj: Character traits – wisdom. Folk & fairy tales. Royalty – princesses.

Friedman, Laurie. *Ruby Valentine and the sweet surprise* ill. by Lynne Avril. Carolrhoda, 2014. ISBN 978-076138873-9 Subj: Animals – cats. Birds – parakeets, parrots. Holidays – Valentine's Day. Pets. Rhyming text.

Frost, Helen. *Sweep up the sun* photos by Rick Lieder. Candlewick, 2015. ISBN 978-076366904-1 Subj: Birds. Nature. Poetry.

Gaiman, Neil. *Chu's day at the beach* ill. by Adam Rex. Harper, 2015. ISBN 978-006222399-9 Subj: Animals – pandas. Sea & seashore – beaches.

Chu's first day of school ill. by Adam Rex. Harper, 2014. ISBN 978-006222397-5 Subj: Animals – pandas. Behavior – worrying. Illness. School – first day.

Galbraith, Kathryn O. *Two bunny buddies* ill. by Joe Cepeda. Houghton, 2014. ISBN 978-054417652-2 Subj: Animals – rabbits. Behavior – fighting, arguing. Friendship.

Gall, Chris. *Dinotrux dig the beach* ill. by author. Little, Brown, 2015. ISBN 978-031637553-5 Subj: Dinosaurs. Sea & seashore – beaches. Trucks.

Dog vs. Cat ill. by author. Little, Brown, 2014. ISBN 978-031623801-4 Subj: Animals – cats. Animals – dogs. Character traits – being different. Friendship.

Garland, Michael. *Tugboat* ill. by author. Holiday House, 2014. ISBN 978-082342866-3 Subj: Boats, ships.

Garland, Sally Anne. *Share* ill. by author. Owlkids, 2014. ISBN 978-177147005-6 Subj: Activities – playing. Animals – rabbits. Behavior – sharing. Family life – cousins. Rhyming text.

Garton, Sam. *I am Otter* ill. by author. HarperCollins/Balzer & Bray, 2014. ISBN 978-006224775-9 Subj: Animals – otters. Behavior – lost & found possessions. Behavior – messy. Friendship. Toys – bears.

Otter in space ill. by author. HarperCollins/Balzer & Bray, 2015. ISBN 978-006224776-6 Subj: Animals – otters. Imagination. Museums. Space & space ships.

Otter loves Halloween ill. by author. HarperCollins/Balzer & Bray, 2015. ISBN 978-006236666-5 Subj: Animals – otters. Emotions – fear. Holidays – Halloween. Toys – bears.

Gavin, Ciara. *Room for Bear* ill. by author. Knopf, 2015. ISBN 978-038575473-6 Subj: Animals – bears. Birds – ducks. Concepts – size. Homes, houses.

Gay, Marie-Louise. *Any questions?* ill. by author. Groundwood, 2014. ISBN 978-155498382-7 Subj: Activities – storytelling. Books, reading. Careers – writers. Character traits – questioning. Imagination.

Gehl, Laura. *One big pair of underwear* ill. by Tom Lichtenheld. Simon & Schuster/Beach Lane, 2014. ISBN 978-144245336-4 Subj: Animals. Behavior – sharing. Counting, numbers. Rhyming text.

Gehrmann, Katja. *Goose the bear* ill. by author. Sky Pony, 2014. ISBN 978-162636384-7 Subj: Animals – bears. Birds – geese. Character traits – being different.

Gellman, Ellie B. *Netta and her plant* ill. by Natascia Ugliano. Lerner/Kar-Ben, 2014. ISBN 978-146770422-9 Subj: Holidays – Tu B'Shevat. Jewish culture. Plants.

George, Jean Craighead. *Galápagos George* ill. by Wendell Minor. Harper, 2014. ISBN 978-006028793-1 Subj: Foreign lands – Galapagos Islands. Reptiles – turtles, tortoises.

Gerber, Carole. *Tuck-in time* ill. by Tracey Campbell Pearson. Farrar, 2014. ISBN 978-037437860-8 Subj: Babies, toddlers. Bedtime. Family life – parents.

Gershator, Phillis. *Time for a bath* ill. by David Walker. Sterling, 2014. ISBN 978-145491032-9 Subj: Activities – bathing. Animals – rabbits. Behavior – messy. Rhyming text.

Gerstein, Mordicai. *The night world* ill. by author. Little, Brown, 2015. ISBN 978-031618822-7 Subj: Animals – cats. Morning. Night. Sun.

You can't have too many friends! ill. by author. Holiday House, 2014. ISBN 978-082342393-4 Subj: Birds – ducks. Friendship. Humorous stories. Royalty – kings.

Gianferrari, Maria. *Penny and Jelly: the school show* ill. by Thyra Heder. Houghton Mifflin Harcourt, 2015. ISBN 978-054423014-9 Subj: Animals – dogs. Friendship. Theater.

Gibbons, Gail. *The fruits we eat* ill. by author. Holiday House, 2015. ISBN 978-082343204-2 Subj: Food. Gardens, gardening.

It's raining! ill. by author. Holiday House, 2014. ISBN 978-082342924-0 Subj: Science. Water. Weather – rain.

Gibson, Amy. *By day, by night* ill. by Meilo So. Boyds Mills, 2014. ISBN 978-159078991-9 Subj: Activities. Rhyming text. World.

Gifford, Peggy. *The great big green* ill. by Lisa Desimini. Boyds Mills, 2014. ISBN 978-162091629-2 Subj: Earth. Nature.

Gigot, Jami. *Mae and the moon* ill. by author. Ripple Grove, 2015. ISBN 978-099138662-8 Subj: Imagination. Moon.

Gill, Deirdre. *Outside* ill. by author. Houghton, 2014. ISBN 978-054791065-9 Subj: Activities – playing. Imagination. Weather – snow.

Gill, Timothy. *Flip and Fin: we rule the school!* ill. by Neil Numberman. HarperCollins/Greenwillow, 2014. ISBN 978-006224300-3 Subj: Family life – brothers & sisters. Fish – sharks. Riddles & jokes. School.

The gingerbread boy. *The Gingerbread Man loose at Christmas* by Laura Murray; ill. by Mike Lowery. Putnam, 2015. ISBN 978-039916866-6 Subj: Behavior – sharing. Folk & fairy tales. Food. Gifts. Holidays – Christmas.

Glaser, Linda. *Stone soup with matzoh balls: a Passover tale in Chelm* ill. by Maryam Tabatabaei. Albert Whitman, 2014. ISBN 978-080757620-5 Subj: Character traits – cleverness. Folk & fairy tales. Food. Holidays – Passover. Jewish culture.

Gliori, Debi. *Dragon's extraordinary egg* ill. by author. Walker, 2014. ISBN 978-080273759-5 Subj: Adoption. Birds – penguins. Character traits – being different. Dragons.

Godin, Thelma Lynne. *The hula-hoopin' queen* ill. by Vanessa Brantley-Newton. Lee & Low, 2014. ISBN 978-160060846-9 Subj: Birthdays. Character traits – responsibility. Contests. Ethnic groups in the U.S. – African Americans. Parties.

Goldie, Sonia. *Ghosts* ill. by Marc Boutavant. Enchanted Lion, 2013. ISBN 978-159270142-1 Subj: Ghosts.

Goldstone, Bruce. *I see a pattern here* ill. by author. Holt, 2015. ISBN 978-080509209-7 Subj: Concepts – patterns.

Golio, Gary. *Bird and Diz* ill. by Ed Young. Candlewick, 2015. ISBN 978-076366660-6 Subj: Careers – musicians. Ethnic groups in the U.S. – African Americans. Music.

Gomi, Taro. *The great day* ill. by author. Chronicle, 2014. ISBN 978-145211125-4 Subj: Activities – playing. Day.

Good, Jason. *Must. push. buttons!* ill. by Jarrett J. Krosoczka. Bloomsbury, 2015. ISBN 978-161963095-6 Subj: Babies, toddlers. Behavior.

Goodrich, Carter. *Mister Bud wears the cone* ill. by author. Simon & Schuster, 2014. ISBN 978-144248088-9 Subj: Animals – dogs. Behavior – misbehavior.

We forgot Brock! ill. by author. Simon & Schuster, 2015. ISBN 978-144248090-2 Subj: Behavior – lost. Friendship. Imagination – imaginary friends.

Gorbachev, Valeri. *Cats are cats* ill. by author. Holiday House, 2014. ISBN 978-082343052-9 Subj: Animals – cats. Animals – tigers. Pets.

Gordon, Domenica More. *Archie's vacation* ill. by author. Bloomsbury, 2014. ISBN 978-161963190-8 Subj: Animals – dogs. Behavior – worrying. Wordless.

Gore, Emily. *And Nick* ill. by author. Atheneum, 2015. ISBN 978-141695506-1 Subj: Animals – mice. Character traits – individuality. Character traits – smallness. Family life – brothers.

Graham, Bob. *How the sun got to Coco's house* ill. by author. Candlewick, 2015. ISBN 978-076368109-8 Subj: Day. Sun. World.

Graham, Joan Bransfield. *The poem that will not end* ill. by Kyrsten Brooker. Amazon/Two Lions, 2014. ISBN 978-147784715-2 Subj: Activities – writing. Poetry. Rhyming text.

Grant, Jacob. *Little Bird's bad word* ill. by author. Feiwel and Friends, 2015. ISBN 978-125005149-3 Subj: Behavior – misbehavior. Birds. Family life – fathers. Language.

Graves, Keith. *The monsterator* ill. by author. Roaring Brook, 2014. ISBN 978-159643855-2 Subj: Format, unusual – toy & movable books. Holidays – Halloween. Monsters. Rhyming text.

Second banana ill. by author. Roaring Brook, 2015. ISBN 978-159643883-5 Subj: Animals – gorillas. Animals – monkeys. Circus.

Gravett, Emily. *Bear and Hare: snow!* ill. by author. Simon & Schuster, 2015. ISBN 978-148144514-6 Subj: Animals – bears. Animals – rabbits. Friendship. Weather – snow.

Bear and Hare go fishing ill. by author. Simon & Schuster, 2015. ISBN 978-148142289-5 Subj: Animals – bears. Animals – rabbits. Sports – fishing.

Matilda's cat ill. by author. Simon & Schuster, 2014. ISBN 978-144247527-4 Subj: Animals – cats. Pets.

Gray, Kes. *Frog on a log?* ill. by Jim Field. Scholastic, 2015. ISBN 978-054568791-1 Subj: Animals – cats. Frogs & toads. Rhyming text.

Gray, Rita. *Have you heard the nesting bird?* ill. by Kenard Pak. Houghton, 2014. ISBN 978-054410580-5 Subj: Birds. Nature. Rhyming text.

Green, Rod. *Giant vehicles* ill. by Stephen Biesty. Candlewick/Templar, 2014. ISBN 978-076367404-5 Subj: Airplanes, airports. Format, unusual – toy & movable books. Machines. Space & space ships. Trucks.

Greenwood, Mark. *The Mayflower* ill. by Frané Lessac. Holiday House, 2014. ISBN 978-082342943-1 Subj: Boats, ships. Pilgrims. U.S. history.

Grey, Mini. *Hermelin the detective mouse* ill. by author. Knopf, 2014. ISBN 978-038575433-0 Subj: Animals – mice. Behavior – lost & found possessions. Careers – detectives. Communities, neighborhoods.

Space Dog ill. by author. Knopf, 2015. ISBN 978-055351058-4 Subj: Animals – cats. Animals – dogs. Animals – mice. Careers – astronauts. Friendship. Space & space ships.

Grimm, Jacob and Wilhelm. *Hansel and Gretel* retold by Holly Hobbie; ill. by reteller. Little, Brown, 2015. ISBN 978-031607017-1 Subj: Behavior – lost. Folk & fairy tales. Forest, woods. Witches.

Sleeping beauty retold by Sarah Gibb; ill. by reteller. Albert Whitman, 2015. ISBN 978-080757351-8 Subj: Fairies. Folk & fairy tales. Royalty – princes. Royalty – princesses. Sleep. Witches.

Griswell, Kim T. *Rufus goes to sea* ill. by Valeri Gorbachev. Sterling, 2015. ISBN 978-145491052-7 Subj: Animals – pigs. Books, reading. Pirates.

Grün, Anselm. *Jesus* ill. by Giuliano Ferri. Eerdmans, 2014. ISBN 978-080285438-4 Subj: Religion.

The legend of Saint Nicholas ill. by Giuliano Ferri. Eerdmans, 2014. ISBN 978-080285434-6 Subj: Holidays – Christmas. Religion. Santa Claus.

Gude, Paul. *When Elephant met Giraffe* ill. by author. Disney/Hyperion, 2014. ISBN 978-142316303-9 Subj: Animals – elephants. Animals – giraffes. Character traits – compromising. Friendship. Noise, sounds.

Guion, Melissa. *Baby penguins love their Mama* ill. by author. Philomel, 2014. ISBN 978-039916365-4 Subj: Birds – penguins. Days of the week, months of the year. Family life – mothers.

Gutierrez, Elisa. *Letter lunch* ill. by author. Owlkids, 2014. ISBN 978-177147000-1 Subj: ABC books. Food. Wordless.

Gutman, Dan. *Rappy the raptor* ill. by Tim Bowers. HarperCollins, 2015. ISBN 978-006229180-6 Subj: Character traits – individuality. Dinosaurs. Rhyming text. Self-concept.

Hacohen, Dean. *Who's hungry?* ill. by Sherry Scharschmidt. Candlewick, 2015. ISBN 978-076366586-9 Subj: Animals. Food. Format, unusual – toy & movable books.

Hakte, Ben. *Julia's house for lost creatures* ill. by author. First Second, 2014. ISBN 978-159643866-8 Subj: Behavior – lost. Behavior – resourcefulness. Character traits – responsibility. Homes, houses. Mythical creatures.

Hale, Bruce. *Big Bad Baby* ill. by Steve Breen. Dial, 2014. ISBN 978-080373585-9 Subj: Babies, toddlers. Behavior – misbehavior.

Hall, Kirsten. *The jacket* ill. by Dasha Tolstikova. Enchanted Lion, 2014. ISBN 978-159270168-1 Subj: Activities – making things. Animals – dogs. Books, reading.

Hall, Michael. *It's an orange aardvark!* ill. by author. Greenwillow, 2014. ISBN 978-006225206-7 Subj: Concepts – color. Format, unusual – toy & movable books. Imagination. Insects – ants.

Red: a crayon's story ill. by author. Greenwillow, 2015. ISBN 978-006225207-4 Subj: Character traits – appearance. Character traits – being different. Concepts – color. Self-concept.

Hall, Pamela. *Miss you like crazy* ill. by Jennifer A. Bell. Tanglewood, 2014. ISBN 978-193371891-0 Subj: Animals – squirrels. Family life – mothers.

Halpern, Shari. *Dinosaur parade* ill. by author. Holt, 2014. ISBN 978-080509242-4 Subj: Dinosaurs. Rhyming text.

Hamburg, Jennifer. *Monkey and Duck quack up!* ill. by Edwin Fotheringham. Scholastic, 2015. ISBN 978-054564514-0 Subj: Animals – monkeys. Birds – ducks. Contests. Rhyming text.

Hamilton, Emma Walton. *The very fairy princess: a spooky, sparkly Halloween* (Andrews, Julie)

The very fairy princess: graduation girl! (Andrews, Julie)

Han, Eun-sun. *The flying birds* ill. by Ju-kyoung Kim. IPG/TanTan, 2015. ISBN 978-193924805-3 Subj: Birds. Counting, numbers. Homes, houses.

Hancocks, Helen. *Penguin in peril* ill. by author. Candlewick/Templar, 2014. ISBN 978-076367159-

4 Subj: Animals – cats. Behavior – stealing. Birds – penguins. Crime.

Hannigan, Katherine. *Gwendolyn Grace* ill. by author. HarperCollins/Greenwillow, 2015. ISBN 978-006234519-6 Subj: Activities – playing. Character traits – patience. Family life. Noise, sounds. Reptiles – alligators, crocodiles.

Hanson, Faye. *The wonder* ill. by author. Candlewick/Templar, 2015. ISBN 978-076367957-6 Subj: Careers – artists. Dreams. Imagination.

Harper, Charise Mericle. *Go! go! go! stop!* ill. by author. Knopf, 2014. ISBN 978-037586924-2 Subj: Machines. Traffic, traffic signs. Trucks.

Superlove ill. by Mark Chambers. Knopf, 2014. ISBN 978-037586923-5 Subj: Animals – cats. Imagination. Toys. Weddings.

Harrington, Tim. *Nose to toes, you are yummy!* ill. by author. HarperCollins/Balzer & Bray, 2015. ISBN 978-006232816-8 Subj: Anatomy. Animals. Participation. Rhyming text.

Harris, Robie H. *Turtle and me* ill. by Tor Freeman. Little Bee, 2015. ISBN 978-149980046-3 Subj: Friendship. Reptiles – turtles, tortoises. Toys.

What's so yummy? all about eating well and feeling good ill. by Nadine Bernard Westcott. Candlewick, 2014. ISBN 978-076363632-6 Subj: Food. Health & fitness.

Harrison, Hannah E. *Bernice gets carried away* ill. by author. Dial, 2015. ISBN 978-080373916-1 Subj: Animals – cats. Behavior – bad day, bad mood. Birthdays. Parties. Toys – balloons.

Extraordinary Jane ill. by author. Dial, 2014. ISBN 978-080373914-7 Subj: Animals – dogs. Circus. Self-concept.

Hatanaka, Kellen. *Drive: a look at roadside opposites* ill. by author. Groundwood, 2015. ISBN 978-155498731-3 Subj: Activities – driving. Concepts – opposites.

Work: an occupational ABC ill. by author. Groundwood, 2014. ISBN 978-155498409-1 Subj: ABC books. Careers.

Haughton, Chris. *Shh! we have a plan* ill. by author. Candlewick, 2014. ISBN 978-076367293-5 Subj: Birds. Sports – hunting.

Hawkes, Kevin. *Remy and Lulu* ill. by author and Hannah E. Harrison. Knopf, 2014. ISBN 978-044981085-9 Subj: Activities – painting. Animals – dogs. Careers – artists. Foreign lands – France. Senses – sight.

Heap, Sue. *Mine!* ill. by author. Candlewick, 2014. ISBN 978-076366888-4 Subj: Behavior – sharing. Toys.

Heapy, Teresa. *Very little Red Riding Hood* ill. by Sue Heap. Houghton, 2014. ISBN 978-054428000-7 Subj: Animals – wolves. Behavior – talking to strangers. Character traits – smallness. Family life – grandmothers. Folk & fairy tales.

Heder, Thyra. *The bear report* ill. by author. Abrams, 2015. ISBN 978-141970783-4 Subj: Animals – polar bears. Foreign lands – Arctic. Homework.

Heidbreder, Robert. *Song for a summer night: a lullaby* ill. by Qin Leng. Groundwood, 2015. ISBN 978-155498493-0 Subj: Lullabies. Night. Rhyming text. Seasons – summer.

Heine, Theresa. *Chandra's magic light: a story in Nepal* ill. by Judith Gueyfier. Barefoot, 2014. ISBN 978-184686493-3 Subj: Behavior – resourcefulness. Family life – sisters. Foreign lands – Nepal. Light, lights. Money.

Heinz, Brian. *Mocha Dick: the legend and fury* ill. by Randall Enos. Creative Company, 2014. ISBN 978-156846242-4 Subj: Animals – whales.

Helakoski, Leslie. *Big pigs* ill. by author. Boyds Mills, 2014. ISBN 978-162091023-8 Subj: Animals – pigs. Behavior – messy. Concepts – size.

Henkes, Kevin. *Waiting* ill. by author. Greenwillow, 2015. ISBN 978-006236843-0 Subj: Animals. Caldecott award honor books. Character traits – patience. Toys. Weather.

Henn, Sophy. *Pom Pom Panda gets the grumps* ill. by author. Philomel, 2015. ISBN 978-039917159-8 Subj: Animals – pandas. Behavior – bad day, bad mood. Emotions – anger.

Hennessy, B. G. *A Christmas wish for Corduroy* ill. by Jody Wheeler. Viking, 2014. ISBN 978-067078550-6 Subj: Clothing. Holidays – Christmas. Santa Claus. Toys – bears.

Heos, Bridget. *Be safe around fire* ill. by Silvia Baroncelli. Amicus, 2014. ISBN 978-160753444-0 Subj: Fire. Safety.

Mustache Baby meets his match ill. by Joy Ang. Clarion, 2015. ISBN 978-054436375-5 Subj: Babies, toddlers. Character traits – appearance. Contests.

Herkert, Barbara. *Sewing stories: Harriet Powers' journey from slave to artist* ill. by Vanessa Brantley-Newton. Knopf, 2015. ISBN 978-038575462-0 Subj: Activities – sewing. Art. Ethnic groups in the U.S. – African Americans. Quilts. Slavery.

Hernandez, Leeza. *Cat napped* ill. by author. Putnam, 2014. ISBN 978-039916438-5 Subj: Animals – cats. Behavior – lost & found possessions. Character traits – kindness to animals.

Herthel, Jessica. *I am Jazz* by Jessica Herthel and Jazz Jennings ill. by Shelagh McNicholas. Dial, 2014. ISBN 978-080374107-2 Subj: Character traits – being different. Gender roles.

Higgins, Ryan T. *Mother Bruce* ill. by author. Disney/Hyperion, 2015. ISBN 978-148473088-1 Subj: Animals – bears. Behavior – bad day, bad mood. Birds – geese. Eggs.

Hillenbrand, Will. *All for a dime! a Bear and Mole story* ill. by author. Holiday House, 2015. ISBN 978-082342946-2 Subj: Animals – bears. Animals – moles. Animals – skunks. Stores.

Down by the barn ill. by author. Amazon/Two Lions, 2014. ISBN 978-147784731-2 Subj: Animals. Farms. Tractors.

Snowman's story ill. by author. Amazon/Two Lions, 2014. ISBN 978-147784787-9 Subj: Animals – rabbits. Clothing – hats. Seasons – winter. Snowmen. Wordless.

Hills, Tad. *Duck and Goose go to the beach* ill. by author. Random/Schwartz & Wade, 2014. ISBN 978-038537235-0 Subj: Birds – ducks. Birds – geese. Friendship. Sea & seashore – beaches.

R is for Rocket ill. by author. Random Schwartz & Wade, 2015. ISBN 978-055352228-0 Subj: ABC books. Animals – dogs.

Himmelman, John. *Duck to the rescue* ill. by author. Holt, 2014. ISBN 978-080509485-5 Subj: Birds – ducks. Humorous stories.

Noisy bird sing-along ill. by author. Dawn, 2015. ISBN 978-158469513-4 Subj: Birds. Noise, sounds.

Hissey, Jane. *Jolly snow.* Book House Scribblers, 2014. ISBN 978-190897302-3 Subj: Animals. Toys. Toys – bears. Weather – snow.

Hoban, Russell. *Ace Dragon Ltd* ill. by Quentin Blake. Candlewick, 2015. ISBN 978-076367482-3 Subj: Dragons.

Hodgkinson, Jo. *A big day for Migs* ill. by author. Andersen, 2014. ISBN 978-146775014-1 Subj: Animals – mice. Behavior – misbehavior. Character traits – shyness. Rhyming text. School – first day.

Hodgkinson, Leigh. *Troll swap* ill. by author. Candlewick/Nosy Crow, 2014. ISBN 978-076367101-3 Subj: Behavior – messy. Character traits – individuality. Character traits – orderliness. Mythical creatures – trolls.

Hoffman, Ian. *Jacob's new dress* (Hoffman, Sarah)

Hoffman, Sarah. *Jacob's new dress* by Sarah Hoffman and Ian Hoffman ill. by Chris Case. Albert Whitman, 2014. ISBN 978-080756373-1 Subj: Behavior – bullying, teasing. Clothing – dresses. Gender roles. Self-concept.

Holabird, Katharine. *Angelina's big city ballet* ill. by Helen Craig. Viking, 2014. ISBN 978-067001560-3 Subj: Animals – mice. Ballet. Family life – cousins.

Angelina's Cinderella ill. by Helen Craig. Viking, 2015. ISBN 978-045147359-2 Subj: Activities – traveling. Animals – mice. Ballet.

Hole, Stian. *Anna's heaven* ill. by author. Eerdmans, 2014. ISBN 978-080285441-4 Subj: Death. Emotions – grief. Family life – fathers. Imagination. Religion.

Holland, Loretta. *Fall leaves* ill. by Elly MacKay. Houghton, 2014. ISBN 978-054410664-2 Subj: Language. Seasons – fall.

Holt, Kimberly Willis. *Dinner with the Highbrows* ill. by Kyrsten Brooker. Holt, 2014. ISBN 978-080508088-9 Subj: Etiquette. Food. Humorous stories.

Holub, Joan. *Mighty dads* ill. by James Dean. Scholastic, 2014. ISBN 978-054560968-5 Subj: Family life – fathers. Machines. Rhyming text. Trucks.

Hood, Susan. *Mission: new baby* ill. by Mary Lundquist. Random House, 2015. ISBN 978-038537672-3 Subj: Babies, toddlers. Family life – brothers & sisters.

Rooting for you ill. by Matthew Cordell. Disney/Hyperion, 2014. ISBN 978-142315230-9 Subj: Plants. Seeds.

Tickly toes ill. by Barroux. Kids Can, 2014. ISBN 978-189478652-2 Subj: Anatomy – toes. Babies, toddlers. Format, unusual – board books. Rhyming text.

Hopkins, Lee Bennett, editor. *Jumping off library shelves: a book of poems* ill. by Jane Manning. Boyds Mills, 2015. ISBN 978-159078924-7 Subj: Books, reading. Libraries. Poetry.

Manger ill. by Helen Cann. Eerdmans, 2014. ISBN 978-080285419-3 Subj: Poetry. Religion – Nativity.

Horacek, Judy. *Yellow is my color star* ill. by author. Simon & Schuster, 2014. ISBN 978-144249299-8 Subj: Concepts – color. Rhyming text.

Horácek, Petr. *The fly* ill. by author. Candlewick, 2015. ISBN 978-076367480-9 Subj: Insects – flies.

The mouse who ate the moon ill. by author. Candlewick, 2014. ISBN 978-076367059-7 Subj: Animals

– mice. Format, unusual – toy & movable books. Moon.

A surprise for Tiny Mouse ill. by author. Candlewick, 2015. ISBN 978-076367967-5 Subj: Animals – mice. Format, unusual – board books. Format, unusual – toy & movable books. Seasons. Weather – rainbows.

Time for bed ill. by author. Candlewick, 2014. ISBN 978-076366779-5 Subj: Babies, toddlers. Bedtime. Format, unusual – board books.

Horvath, James. *Work, dogs, work: a highway tail* ill. by author. Harper, 2014. ISBN 978-006218970-7 Subj: Animals – dogs. Careers – construction workers. Rhyming text. Roads.

Houran, Lori Haskins. *A dozen cousins* ill. by Sam Usher. Sterling, 2015. ISBN 978-145491062-6 Subj: Behavior – misbehavior. Family life – cousins. Rhyming text.

How to spy on a shark ill. by Francisca Marquez. Albert Whitman, 2015. ISBN 978-080753402-1 Subj: Careers – scientists. Fish – sharks. Robots.

A trip into space: an adventure to the International Space Station ill. by Francisca Marquez. Albert Whitman, 2014. ISBN 978-080758091-2 Subj: Careers – astronauts. Space & space ships.

Howatt, Sandra J. *Sleepyheads* ill. by Joyce Wan. Simon & Schuster/Beach Lane, 2014. ISBN 978-144242266-7 Subj: Animals – babies. Bedtime. Rhyming text. Sleep.

Hudson, Katy. *Bear and Duck* ill. by author. Harper, 2015. ISBN 978-006232051-3 Subj: Animals – bears. Birds – ducks. Friendship. Self-concept.

Hughes, Langston. *Sail away* ill. by Ashley Bryan. Atheneum, 2015. ISBN 978-148143085-2 Subj: Poetry. Sea & seashore.

Huneck, Stephen. *Sally goes to heaven* ill. by author. Abrams, 2014. ISBN 978-141970969-2 Subj: Animals – dogs. Death. Pets.

Hurley, Jorey. *Fetch!* ill. by author. Simon & Schuster/Paula Wiseman, 2015. ISBN 978-144248969-1 Subj: Animals – dogs. Sea & seashore – beaches.

Nest ill. by author. Simon & Schuster/Paula Wiseman, 2014. ISBN 978-144248971-4 Subj: Birds – robins. Nature. Seasons.

Husband, Amy. *The noisy foxes* ill. by author. Little Bee, 2015. ISBN 978-149980154-5 Subj: Animals – foxes. Noise, sounds.

Hutchins, Hazel. *Snap!* ill. by Dusan Petricic. Annick, 2015. ISBN 978-155451770-1 Subj: Art. Concepts – color. Imagination.

Hyde, Heidi Smith. *Shanghai Sukkah* ill. by Jing Jing Tsong. Kar-Ben, 2015. ISBN 978-146773474-5 Subj: Foreign lands – China. Friendship. Holidays – Sukkot. Immigrants. Jewish culture.

Hyman, Zachary. *The Bambino and me* ill. by Zachary Pullen. Tundra, 2014. ISBN 978-177049627-9 Subj: Sports – baseball.

Idle, Molly. *Camp Rex* ill. by author. Viking, 2014. ISBN 978-067078573-5 Subj: Camps, camping. Dinosaurs.

Flora and the penguin ill. by author. Chronicle, 2014. ISBN 978-145212891-7 Subj: Birds – penguins. Character traits – kindness. Format, unusual – toy & movable books. Sports – ice skating. Wordless.

Sea Rex ill. by author. Viking, 2015. ISBN 978-067078574-2 Subj: Dinosaurs. Sea & seashore – beaches.

Imai, Ayano. *Mr. Brown's fantastic hat* ill. by author. Minedition, 2014. ISBN 978-988824084-5 Subj: Animals – bears. Birds. Clothing – hats. Emotions – loneliness. Friendship.

Puss and boots ill. by author. Minedition, 2014. ISBN 978-988824071-5 Subj: Animals – cats. Behavior – resourcefulness. Careers – shoemakers. Character traits – cleverness. Folk & fairy tales. Monsters.

International Center for Assault Prevention. *My body belongs to me from my head to my toes* ill. by Dagmar Geisler. Sky Pony, 2014. ISBN 978-162636345-8 Subj: Child abuse. Health & fitness. Safety. Self-concept. Senses – touch.

Isaacs, Anne. *Meanwhile, back at the ranch* ill. by Kevin Hawkes. Random/Schwartz & Wade, 2014. ISBN 978-037586745-3 Subj: Humorous stories. Tall tales. U.S. history – frontier & pioneer life.

Isaak, Armond. *Armond goes to a party: a book about Asperger's and friendship* (Carlson, Nancy)

Isabella, Jude. *The red bicycle: the extraordinary story of one ordinary bicycle* ill. by Simone Shin. Kids Can, 2015. ISBN 978-177138023-2 Subj: Character traits – helpfulness. Ecology. Foreign lands – Burkina Faso. Money. Sports – bicycling.

Isadora, Rachel. *Bea in The Nutcracker* ill. by author. Penguin/Nancy Paulsen, 2015. ISBN 978-039925231-0 Subj: Activities – dancing. Babies, toddlers. Ballet.

Jake at gymnastics ill. by author. Penguin/Nancy Paulsen, 2014. ISBN 978-039916048-6 Subj: Sports – gymnastics.

Ishida, Sanae. *Little Kunoichi, the ninja girl* ill. by author. Sasquatch, 2015. ISBN 978-157061954-0 Subj: Character traits – cooperation. Character traits – persistence. Contests. Sports – martial arts.

Ismail, Yasmeen. *Time for bed, Fred!* ill. by author. Bloomsbury, 2014. ISBN 978-080273597-3 Subj: Animals – dogs. Bedtime. Behavior – misbehavior.

Jackson, Alison. *When the wind blew* ill. by Doris Barrette. Holt, 2014. ISBN 978-080508688-1 Subj: Behavior – lost & found possessions. Nursery rhymes. Rhyming text. Weather – wind.

Jackson, Ellen. *Beastly babies* ill. by Brendan Wenzel. Simon & Schuster/Beach Lane, 2015. ISBN 978-144240834-0 Subj: Animals – babies. Rhyming text.

Jacobs, Paul DuBois. *Count on the subway* by Paul DuBois Jacobs and Jennifer Swender ill. by Dan Yaccarino. Knopf, 2014. ISBN 978-030797923-0 Subj: Counting, numbers. Rhyming text. Trains.

James, Ann. *Bird and Bear* ill. by author. Little Bee, 2015. ISBN 978-149980037-1 Subj: Animals – bears. Birds. Friendship.

Jane, Pamela. *Little elfie one* ill. by Jane Manning. HarperCollins/Balzer & Bray, 2015. ISBN 978-006220673-2 Subj: Counting, numbers. Holidays – Christmas. Rhyming text.

Janeczko, Paul B. *Firefly July: a year of very short poems* ill. by Melissa Sweet. Candlewick, 2014. ISBN 978-076364842-8 Subj: Poetry. Seasons.

Jantzen, Doug. *Henry Hyena, why won't you laugh?* ill. by Jean Claude. Aladdin, 2015. ISBN 978-148142822-4 Subj: Animals – hyenas. Behavior – bullying, teasing. Character traits – kindness. Rhyming text. Zoos.

Javaherbin, Mina. *Elephant in the dark* ill. by Eugene Yelchin. Scholastic, 2015. ISBN 978-054563670-4 Subj: Animals – elephants. Folk & fairy tales. Foreign lands – India.

Soccer star ill. by Renato Alarcao. Candlewick, 2014. ISBN 978-076366056-7 Subj: Family life – brothers & sisters. Foreign lands – Brazil. Poverty. Sports – soccer.

Jay, Alison. *Out of the blue* ill. by author. Barefoot, 2014. ISBN 978-178285042-7 Subj: Character traits – kindness to animals. Sea & seashore – beaches. Wordless.

Jeffers, Oliver. *The Hueys in It wasn't me* ill. by author. Philomel, 2014. ISBN 978-000742067-4 Subj: Behavior – fighting, arguing. Character traits – individuality. Self-concept.

The Hueys in None the number: a counting adventure ill. by author. Philomel, 2014. ISBN 978-039925769-8 Subj: Counting, numbers.

Jenkins, Emily. *A fine dessert: four centuries, four families, one delicious treat* ill. by Sophie Blackall. Random/Schwartz & Wade, 2015. ISBN 978-037586832-0 Subj: Activities – baking, cooking. Food. U.S. history.

The fun book of scary stuff ill. by Hyewon Yum. Farrar/Frances Foster, 2015. ISBN 978-037430000-5 Subj: Animals – dogs. Emotions – fear.

Toys meet snow: being the wintertime adventures of a curious stuffed buffalo, a sensitive plush stingray, and a book-loving rubber ball ill. by Paul O. Zelinsky. Random/Schwartz & Wade, 2015. ISBN 978-038537330-2 Subj: Activities – playing. Seasons – winter. Toys. Weather – snow.

Jenkins, Steve. *Creature features: 25 animals explain why they look the way they do* by Steve Jenkins and Robin Page ill. by Steve Jenkins. Houghton, 2014. ISBN 978-054423351-5 Subj: Anatomy. Animals. Character traits – appearance.

Eye to eye: how animals see the world ill. by author. Houghton, 2014. ISBN 978-054795907-8 Subj: Anatomy – eyes. Animals.

How to swallow a pig: step-by-step advice from the animal kingdom by Steve Jenkins and Robin Page ill. by Steve Jenkins. Houghton Mifflin Harcourt, 2015. ISBN 978-054431365-1 Subj: Animals. Character traits – questioning. Nature.

Jennings, Jazz. *I am Jazz* (Herthel, Jessica)

John, Jory. *Goodnight already!* ill. by Benji Davies. Harper, 2014. ISBN 978-006228620-8 Subj: Animals – bears. Bedtime. Birds – ducks.

I love you already! ill. by Benji Davies. HarperCollins, 2015. ISBN 978-006237095-2 Subj: Animals

– bears. Birds – ducks. Character traits – individuality. Friendship.

I will chomp you! ill. by Bob Shea. Random House, 2015. ISBN 978-038538986-0 Subj: Books, reading. Food. Monsters.

Johnson, Angela. *All different now: Juneteenth, the first day of freedom* ill. by E. B. Lewis. Simon & Schuster, 2014. ISBN 978-068987376-8 Subj: Ethnic groups in the U.S. – African Americans. Slavery. Texas. U.S. history.

Johnson, Mariana Ruiz. *I know a bear* ill. by author. Random/Schwartz & Wade, 2014. ISBN 978-038538614-2 Subj: Animals – bears. Character traits – kindness to animals. Zoos.

Johnson, Stephen T. *Alphabet school* ill. by author. Simon & Schuster Books for Young Readers, 2015. ISBN 978-141692521-7 Subj: ABC books. School.

Johnston, Tony. *First grade, here I come!* ill. by David Walker. Scholastic, 2015. ISBN 978-054520143-8 Subj: Animals – mice. School – first day.

Sequoia ill. by Wendell Minor. Roaring Brook, 2014. ISBN 978-159643727-2 Subj: Nature. Poetry. Seasons. Trees.

Winter is coming ill. by Jim LaMarche. Simon & Schuster, 2014. ISBN 978-144247251-8 Subj: Animals. Forest, woods. Seasons – fall.

Jones, Christianne C. *The Santa shimmy* ill. by Emma Randall. Picture Window, 2015. ISBN 978-147956494-1 Subj: Format, unusual – board books. Participation. Rhyming text. Santa Claus.

Jones, Terry. *Gorillas in our midst* (Fairgray, Richard)

Jones, Ursula. *Beauty and the beast* ill. by Sarah Gibb. Albert Whitman, 2014. ISBN 978-080750600-4 Subj: Character traits – appearance. Character traits – loyalty. Emotions – love. Folk & fairy tales. Magic.

The princess who had no kingdom ill. by Sarah Gibb. Albert Whitman, 2014. ISBN 978-080756630-5 Subj: Clowns, jesters. Folk & fairy tales. Royalty – princesses.

Joosse, Barbara. *Evermore dragon* ill. by Randy Cecil. Candlewick, 2015. ISBN 978-076366882-2 Subj: Behavior – hiding. Dragons. Friendship. Games.

Joyce, William. *A bean, a stalk, and a boy named Jack* ill. by author and Kenny Callicutt. Atheneum, 2014. ISBN 978-144247350-8 Subj: Folk & fairy tales. Giants. Magic. Plants.

Billy's booger ill. by author. Atheneum, 2015. ISBN 978-144247351-5 Subj: Activities – writing.

Books, reading. Careers – writers. Careers – writers. Contests. Imagination. School.

Jack Frost ill. by author. Atheneum, 2015. ISBN 978-144243043-3 Subj: Character traits – bravery. Imagination.

The Numberlys ill. by author and Christina Ellis. Atheneum, 2014. ISBN 978-144247343-0 Subj: ABC books. Counting, numbers. Format, unusual.

Judge, Chris. *Tin* ill. by author. Andersen, 2014. ISBN 978-146775013-4 Subj: Family life – brothers & sisters. Robots. Toys – balloons.

Judge, Lita. *Born in the wild: baby mammals and their parents* ill. by author. Roaring Brook, 2014. ISBN 978-159643925-2 Subj: Animals – babies.

Flight school ill. by author. Atheneum, 2014. ISBN 978-144248177-0 Subj: Activities – flying. Birds – penguins. Character traits – perseverance.

Good morning to me! ill. by author. Simon & Schuster, 2015. ISBN 978-148140369-6 Subj: Birds – parakeets, parrots. Morning. Noise, sounds.

Kalman, Maira. *Thomas Jefferson: life, liberty, and the pursuit of everything* ill. by author. Penguin/Nancy Paulsen, 2014. ISBN 978-039924040-9 Subj: U.S. history.

Kang, Anna. *That's not mine* ill. by Christopher Weyant. Amazon/Two Lions, 2015. ISBN 978-147782639-3 Subj: Animals. Behavior – fighting, arguing. Behavior – sharing.

You are (not) small ill. by Christopher Weyant. Amazon/Two Lions, 2014. ISBN 978-147784772-5 Subj: Behavior – fighting, arguing. Character traits – smallness. Concepts – size.

Kaplan, Bruce Eric. *Meaniehead* ill. by author. Simon & Schuster, 2014. ISBN 978-144248542-6 Subj: Behavior – fighting, arguing. Family life – brothers & sisters. Sibling rivalry.

Kaplan, Michael B. *Betty Bunny loves Easter* ill. by Stéphane Jorisch. Dial, 2015. ISBN 978-080374061-7 Subj: Animals – rabbits. Eggs. Holidays – Easter.

Betty Bunny wants a goal ill. by Stéphane Jorisch. Dial, 2014. ISBN 978-080373859-1 Subj: Animals

– rabbits. Character traits – perseverance. Family life. Sports – soccer.

Karas, G. Brian. *As an oak tree grows* ill. by author. Penguin/Nancy Paulsen, 2014. ISBN 978-039925233-4 Subj: Ecology. Trees.

Kasza, Keiko. *Finders keepers* ill. by author. Putnam, 2015. ISBN 978-039916898-7 Subj: Animals. Animals – squirrels. Behavior – lost & found possessions. Clothing – hats.

Katz, Karen. *Rosie goes to preschool* ill. by author. Random/Schwartz & Wade, 2015. ISBN 978-038537917-5 Subj: School – nursery.

Katz, Susan B. *ABC school's for me!* ill. by Lynn Munsinger. Scholastic, 2015. ISBN 978-054553092-7 Subj: ABC books. Animals – bears. Rhyming text. School.

Keane, Claire. *Once upon a cloud* ill. by author. Dial, 2015. ISBN 978-080373911-6 Subj: Gifts. Imagination.

Kellogg, Steven. *Pinkerton, behave!* ill. by author. Dial, 2014. ISBN 978-080374130-0 Subj: Animals – dogs. Behavior – misbehavior.

Kelly, Sheila M. *Families* (Rotner, Shelley)

Kenah, Katharine. *Ferry tail* ill. by Nicole Wong. Sleeping Bear, 2014. ISBN 978-158536829-7 Subj: Animals – dogs. Behavior – running away. Boats, ships.

The very stuffed turkey ill. by Binny Talib. Scholastic, 2015. ISBN 978-054576109-3 Subj: Birds – turkeys. Food. Friendship. Holidays – Thanksgiving.

Kennedy, Anne Vittur. *The farmer's away! baa! neigh!* ill. by Anne Kennedy. Candlewick, 2014. ISBN 978-076366679-8 Subj: Animals. Farms. Noise, sounds. Rhyming text.

Ragweed's farm dog handbook ill. by Anne Kennedy. Candlewick, 2015. ISBN 978-076367417-5 Subj: Animals – dogs. Farms.

Kenney, Sean. *Cool creations in 101 pieces* ill. with photos. Holt/Christy Ottaviano, 2014. ISBN 978-162779017-8 Subj: Activities – making things. Imagination. Toys.

Kerley, Barbara. *A home for Mr. Emerson* ill. by Edwin Fotheringham. Scholastic, 2014. ISBN 978-054535088-4 Subj: Books, reading. Careers – writers. U.S. history.

With a friend by your side ill. with photos. National Geographic, 2015. ISBN 978-142631905-1 Subj: Friendship. World.

Ketteman, Helen. *At the old haunted house* ill. by Nate Wragg. Two Lions, 2014. ISBN 978-

147784769-5 Subj: Counting, numbers. Holidays – Halloween. Homes, houses. Rhyming text.

The ghosts go haunting ill. by Adam Record. Albert Whitman, 2014. ISBN 978-080752852-5 Subj: Ghosts. Holidays – Halloween. Monsters. School. Songs. Witches.

There once was a cowpoke who swallowed an ant (Little old lady who swallowed a fly)

Kheiriyeh, Rashin. *There was an old lady who swallowed a fly* (Little old lady who swallowed a fly)

Kimmel, Elizabeth Cody. *A taste of freedom: Gandhi and the Great Salt March* ill. by Giuliano Ferri. Bloomsbury, 2014. ISBN 978-080279467-3 Subj: Behavior – seeking better things. Character traits – perseverance. Foreign lands – India. Violence, nonviolence.

Kimmel, Eric A. *Simon and the bear: a Hanukkah tale* ill. by Matthew Trueman. Hyperion, 2014. ISBN 978-142314355-0 Subj: Animals – polar bears. Holidays – Hanukkah. Jewish culture.

Kimmelman, Leslie. *Trick ARRR treat: a pirate Halloween* ill. by Jorge Monlongo. Albert Whitman, 2015. ISBN 978-080758061-5 Subj: Holidays – Halloween. Pirates. Rhyming text.

Kimura, Ken. *999 frogs and a little brother* ill. by Yasunari Murakami. NorthSouth, 2015. ISBN 978-073584202-1 Subj: Character traits – smallness. Concepts – size. Friendship. Frogs & toads.

Kirk, Daniel. *Ten thank-you letters* ill. by author. Penguin/Nancy Paulsen, 2014. ISBN 978-039916937-3 Subj: Animals – pigs. Animals – rabbits. Character traits. Character traits – kindness. Letters, cards.

The thing about spring ill. by author. Abrams, 2015. ISBN 978-141971492-4 Subj: Animals. Concepts – change. Seasons. Seasons – spring.

You are not my friend, but I miss you ill. by author. Abrams, 2014. ISBN 978-141971236-4 Subj: Behavior – sharing. Friendship. Toys.

Kirk, David. *Oh so brave dragon* ill. by author. Feiwel and Friends, 2014. ISBN 978-125001689-8 Subj: Character traits – bravery. Dragons. Emotions – fear. Friendship.

Kirwan, Wednesday. *Baby loves to boogie!* ill. by author. Simon & Schuster, 2014. ISBN 978-148140383-2 Subj: Activities – dancing. Animals – babies. Babies, toddlers. Format, unusual – board books.

Kishira, Mayuko. *Who's next door?* ill. by Jun Takabatake. Owlkids, 2014. ISBN 978-177147071-1 Subj: Birds – chickens, roosters. Birds – owls. Problem solving.

Klostermann, Penny Parker. *There was an old dragon who swallowed a knight* ill. by Ben Mantle. Random House, 2015. ISBN 978-038539080-4 Subj: Cumulative tales. Dragons. Knights. Middle Ages.

Knapman, Timothy. *A monster moved in!* ill. by Loretta Schauer. Tiger Tales, 2015. ISBN 978-158925176-2 Subj: Behavior – boredom. Imagination. Monsters.

Soon ill. by Patrick Benson. Candlewick, 2015. ISBN 978-076367478-6 Subj: Animals – elephants. Family life – mothers.

Knudsen, Michelle. *Marilyn's monster* ill. by Matt Phelan. Candlewick, 2015. ISBN 978-076366011-6 Subj: Friendship. Monsters.

Ko, Sangmi. *A dog wearing shoes* ill. by author. Random/Schwartz & Wade, 2015. ISBN 978-038538396-7 Subj: Animals – dogs. Behavior – lost & found possessions. Character traits – kindness to animals. Clothing – shoes.

Kobald, Irena. *My two blankets* ill. by Freya Blackwood. Houghton Mifflin Harcourt, 2015. ISBN 978-054443228-4 Subj: Emotions – sadness. Immigrants. War.

Koehler, Fred. *How to cheer up Dad* ill. by author. Dial, 2014. ISBN 978-080373922-2 Subj: Animals – elephants. Behavior – bad day, bad mood. Behavior – misbehavior. Family life – fathers.

Koehler, Lora. *The little snowplow* ill. by Jake Parker. Candlewick, 2015. ISBN 978-076367074-0 Subj: Character traits – persistence. Character traits – smallness. Machines. Trucks. Weather – snow.

Kohara, Kazuno. *The Midnight Library* ill. by author. Roaring Brook, 2014. ISBN 978-159643985-6 Subj: Animals. Books, reading. Libraries.

Könnecke, Ole. *You can do it, Bert!* ill. by author. Gecko, 2015. ISBN 978-192727103-2 Subj: Birds. Character traits – confidence.

Kornell, Max. *Me first* ill. by author. Penguin/Nancy Paulsen, 2014. ISBN 978-039915997-8 Subj: Animals – donkeys. Behavior – fighting, arguing. Family life – brothers & sisters. Sibling rivalry.

Kraft, Betsy Harvey. *The fantastic Ferris wheel: the story of inventor George Ferris* ill. by Steven Salerno. Holt/Christy Ottaviano, 2015. ISBN 978-162779072-7 Subj: Careers – engineers. Careers – inventors. Fairs, festivals. Inventions. Machines. Parks – amusement.

Krall, Dan. *Sick Simon* ill. by author. Simon & Schuster, 2015. ISBN 978-144249097-0 Subj: Character traits – cleanliness. Health & fitness. Illness – cold (disease).

Krensky, Stephen. *I am so brave!* ill. by Sara Gillingham. Abrams/Appleseed, 2014. ISBN 978-141970937-1 Subj: Babies, toddlers. Behavior – growing up. Ethnic groups in the U.S. – African Americans. Format, unusual – board books. Rhyming text.

The last Christmas tree ill. by Pascal Campion. Dial, 2014. ISBN 978-080373757-0 Subj: Character traits – hopefulness. Holidays – Christmas. Trees.

Krosoczka, Jarrett J. *It's tough to lose your balloon* ill. by author. Knopf, 2015. ISBN 978-038575479-8 Subj: Character traits – optimism. Emotions. Problem solving.

Krull, Kathleen. *Hillary Rodham Clinton: dreams taking flight* ill. by Amy June Bates. Simon & Schuster, 2015. ISBN 978-148145113-0 Subj: Character traits – persistence. Gender roles. U.S. history.

What's new? the zoo! a zippy history of zoos ill. by Marcellus Hall. Scholastic, 2014. ISBN 978-054513571-9 Subj: Zoos.

Krumwiede, Lana. *Just Itzy* ill. by Greg Pizzoli. Candlewick, 2015. ISBN 978-076365811-3 Subj: Character traits – confidence. Character traits – perseverance. Nursery rhymes. School – first day. Spiders.

Kudlinski, Kathleen V. *Boy, were we wrong about the human body!* ill. by Debbie Tilley. Dial, 2015. ISBN 978-080373792-1 Subj: Anatomy. Science.

Boy, were we wrong about the weather! ill. by Sebastià Serra. Dial, 2015. ISBN 978-080373793-8 Subj: Careers – meteorologists. Careers – scientists. Weather.

Kuefler, Joseph. *Beyond the pond* ill. by author. HarperCollins/Balzer & Bray, 2015. ISBN 978-006236427-2 Subj: Imagination. Lakes, ponds. Nature.

Kuhlmann, Torben. *Moletown* ill. by author. NorthSouth, 2015. ISBN 978-073584208-3 Subj: Animals – moles. Cities, towns. Ecology.

Kwan, James. *Dear Yeti* ill. by author. Farrar, 2015. ISBN 978-037430045-6 Subj: Activities – hiking. Character traits – helpfulness. Letters, cards. Monsters.

Kyle, Tracey. *Gazpacho for Nacho* ill. by Carolina Farias. Amazon/Two Lions, 2014. ISBN 978-147781727-8 Subj: Activities – baking, cooking. Ethnic groups in the U.S. – Hispanic Americans. Food. Foreign languages. Rhyming text.

Lammle, Leslie. *Princess wannabe* ill. by author. Harper, 2014. ISBN 978-006125197-9 Subj: Books, reading. Imagination. Royalty – princesses.

Landau, Orna. *Leopardpox!* ill. by Omer Hoffmann. Clarion, 2015. ISBN 978-054429001-3 Subj: Animals – leopards. Character traits – appearance. Character traits – being different. Family life – mothers.

Landström, Lena. *Pom and Pim* ill. by Olof Landström. Gecko, 2014. ISBN 978-187757966-0 Subj: Activities – playing. Character traits – luck. Friendship. Imagination.

Where is Pim? ill. by Olof Landström. Gecko, 2015. ISBN 978-192727173-5 Subj: Activities – playing. Behavior – lost & found possessions. Friendship. Toys.

Lane, Nathan. *Naughty Mabel* by Nathan Lane and Devlin Elliott ill. by Dan Krall. Simon & Schuster, 2015. ISBN 978-148143022-7 Subj: Animals – dogs. Behavior – misbehavior. Etiquette.

Lang, Suzanne. *Families, families, families!* ill. by Max Lang. Random House, 2015. ISBN 978-055349938-4 Subj: Animals. Family life. Rhyming text.

LaReau, Kara. *No slurping, no burping! a tale of table manners* ill. by Lorelay Bove. Disney/Hyperion, 2014. ISBN 978-142315733-5 Subj: Behavior – misbehavior. Etiquette. Family life – fathers. Food. Humorous stories.

Larsen, Andrew. *See you next year* ill. by Todd Stewart. Owlkids, 2015. ISBN 978-192697399-9 Subj: Activities – vacationing. Sea & seashore – beaches.

Latham, Irene. *Dear Wandering Wildebeest: and other poems from the Water Hole* ill. by Anna Wadham. Lerner/Millbrook, 2014. ISBN 978-146771232-3 Subj: Animals. Foreign lands – Africa. Poetry.

Latimer, Alex. *Pig and small* ill. by author. Peachtree, 2014. ISBN 978-156145797-7 Subj: Animals – pigs. Character traits – smallness. Concepts – size. Friendship. Insects.

Stay! a top dog story ill. by author. Peachtree, 2015. ISBN 978-156145884-4 Subj: Activities – vacationing. Animals – dogs. Family life – grandfathers. Letters, cards.

Latimer, Miriam. *Dear Panda* ill. by author. Owlkids, 2014. ISBN 978-177147078-0 Subj: Animals – pandas. Behavior – worrying. Friendship. Letters, cards. School – first day.

Lawler, Janet. *Love is real* ill. by Anna Brown. Harper, 2014. ISBN 978-006224170-2 Subj: Animals. Emotions – love. Rhyming text.

Lawson, Jonarno. *Sidewalk flowers* ill. by Sydney Smith. Groundwood, 2015. ISBN 978-155498431-2 Subj: Activities – walking. Family life – fathers. Flowers. Wordless.

Lazar, Tara. *Little Red Gliding Hood* ill. by Troy Cummings. Random House, 2015. ISBN 978-038537006-6 Subj: Animals – wolves. Contests. Folk & fairy tales. Sports – ice skating.

Leathers, Philippa. *How to catch a mouse* ill. by author. Candlewick, 2015. ISBN 978-076366912-6 Subj: Animals – cats. Animals – mice.

Leduc, Emilie. *All year round* ill. by Shelley Tanaka. Groundwood, 2015. ISBN 978-155498411-4 Subj: Days of the week, months of the year. Seasons.

Lee, H. Chuku. *Beauty and the beast: a retelling* ill. by Pat Cummings. Amistad, 2014. ISBN 978-068814819-5 Subj: Character traits – appearance. Character traits – loyalty. Emotions – love. Folk & fairy tales. Foreign lands – Africa. Magic.

Lehrhaupt, Adam. *Please, open this book!* ill. by Matthew Forsythe. Simon & Schuster/Paula Wiseman, 2015. ISBN 978-144245071-4 Subj: Animals. Books, reading. Humorous stories.

Leiter, Richard. *The flying hand of Marco B.* ill. by Shahar Kober. Sleeping Bear, 2015. ISBN 978-158536888-4 Subj: Activities – flying. Automobiles. Imagination. Rhyming text.

Lemke, Donald. *Book-o-beards: a wearable book* ill. by Bob Lentz. Capstone, 2015. ISBN 978-162370183-3 Subj: Format, unusual – board books. Format, unusual – toy & movable books. Hair. Masks. Rhyming text.

Lendroth, Susan. *Old Manhattan has some farms: e-i-e-i-grow!* ill. by Kate Endle. Charlesbridge, 2014. ISBN 978-158089572-9 Subj: Cities, towns. Cumulative tales. Farms. Gardens, gardening. Songs.

Leroy, Jean. *Superfab saves the day* (DeLaporte, Bérengère)

Lester, Helen. *The loch mess monster* ill. by Lynn Munsinger. Houghton, 2014. ISBN 978-054409990-6 Subj: Behavior – messy. Foreign lands – Scotland. Humorous stories. Monsters.

Tacky and the haunted igloo ill. by Lynn Munsinger. Houghton Mifflin Harcourt, 2015. ISBN 978-054433994-1 Subj: Birds – penguins. Clothing – costumes. Emotions – fear. Holidays – Halloween. Homes, houses.

Levy, Janice. *Thomas the toadilly terrible bully* ill. by Bill Slavin. Eerdmans, 2014. ISBN 978-080285373-8 Subj: Behavior – bullying, teasing. Friendship. Frogs & toads.

Lewin, Betsy. *Good night, Knight* ill. by author. Holiday House, 2015. ISBN 978-082343206-6 Subj: Animals – horses, ponies. Food. Knights.

Lewis, J. Patrick. *M is for monster: a fantastic creatures alphabet* ill. by Gerald Kelley. Sleeping Bear, 2014. ISBN 978-158536818-1 Subj: ABC books. Monsters.

Lies, Brian. *Bats in the band* ill. by author. Houghton Mifflin Harcourt, 2014. ISBN 978-054410569-0 Subj: Animals – bats. Music. Rhyming text.

Light, Kelly. *Louise loves art* ill. by author. HarperCollins/Balzer & Bray, 2014. ISBN 978-006224817-6 Subj: Activities – drawing. Art. Family life – brothers & sisters.

Light, Steve. *Have you seen my dragon?* ill. by author. Candlewick, 2014. ISBN 978-076366648-4 Subj: Cities, towns. Counting, numbers. Dragons.

Have you seen my monster? ill. by author. Candlewick, 2015. ISBN 978-076367513-4 Subj: Behavior – lost & found possessions. Concepts – shape. Fairs, festivals. Monsters.

Planes go ill. by author. Chronicle, 2014. ISBN 978-145212899-3 Subj: Airplanes, airports. Format, unusual – board books.

Liniers. *What there is before there is anything there: a scary story* ill. by author. House of Anansi Groundwood, 2014. ISBN 978-155498385-8 Subj: Emotions – fear.

Little old lady who swallowed a fly. *There once was a cowpoke who swallowed an ant* by Helen Ketteman; ill. by Will Terry. Albert Whitman, 2014. ISBN 978-080757850-6 Subj: Cowboys, cowgirls. Cumulative tales. Folk & fairy tales. Insects – ants. Songs.

There was an old lady who swallowed a fly by Rashin Kheiriyeh; ill. by author. NorthSouth, 2014. ISBN 978-073584183-3 Subj: Cumulative tales. Folk & fairy tales. Insects – flies. Songs.

There was an old mummy who swallowed a spider by Jennifer Ward; ill. by Steve Gray. Two Lions, 2015. ISBN 978-147782637-9 Subj: Cumulative tales. Holidays – Halloween. Mummies. Songs.

Litton, Jonthan. *Snip snap: pop-up fun* ill. by Kasia Nowowiejska. Tiger Tales, 2015. ISBN 978-158925548-7 Subj: Animals. Format, unusual – toy & movable books. Rhyming text.

Litwin, Eric. *The Nuts: bedtime at the Nut house* ill. by Scott Magoon. Little, Brown, 2014. ISBN 978-031632244-7 Subj: Activities – playing. Bedtime. Humorous stories. Rhyming text.

The Nuts: sing and dance in your polka-dot pants ill. by Scott Magoon. Little, Brown, 2015. ISBN 978-031632250-8 Subj: Activities – dancing. Activities – playing. Activities – singing. Rhyming text.

Liu, Cynthea. *Bike on, Bear!* ill. by Kristyna Litten. Aladdin, 2015. ISBN 978-148140507-2 Subj: Animals – bears. Character traits – persistence. Sports – bicycling.

Livingston, A. A. *B. Bear and Lolly: off to school* ill. by Joey Chou. Harper, 2014. ISBN 978-00621978-8-7 Subj: Animals – bears. Folk & fairy tales. Friendship. School – first day.

B. Bear and Lolly: catch that cookie! ill. by Joey Chou. HarperCollins, 2015. ISBN 978-006219791-7 Subj: Activities – baking, cooking. Animals – bears. Folk & fairy tales. Food.

Ljungkvist, Laura. *Search and spot: animals!* ill. by author. Houghton Mifflin Harcourt, 2015. ISBN 978-054454005-7 Subj: Animals. Picture puzzles.

Lloyd-Jones, Sally. *Bunny's first spring* ill. by David McPhail. Zonderkidz, 2015. ISBN 978-031073386-7 Subj: Animals – rabbits. Seasons – spring.

The house that's your home ill. by Jane Dyer. Random/Schwartz & Wade, 2015. ISBN 978-037585884-0 Subj: Family life. Homes, houses.

Poor Doreen: a fishy tale ill. by Alexandra Boiger. Random/Schwartz & Wade, 2014. ISBN 978-037586918-1 Subj: Activities – traveling. Character traits – optimism. Fish.

Lobe, Mira. *Hoppelpopp and the best bunny* ill. by Angelika Kaufmann. Holiday House, 2015. ISBN 978-082343287-5 Subj: Animals – rabbits. Character traits – cooperation. Contests. Family life – brothers & sisters.

Lobel, Anita. *Playful pigs from A to Z* ill. by author. Knopf, 2015. ISBN 978-055350832-1 Subj: ABC books. Activities – playing. Animals – pigs.

Taking care of Mama Rabbit ill. by author. Knopf, 2014. ISBN 978-038575368-5 Subj: Animals – rabbits. Family life. Family life – mothers. Illness.

Lodding, Linda Ravin. *A gift for Mama* ill. by Alison Jay. Knopf, 2014. ISBN 978-038575331-9 Subj: Activities – trading. Circular tales. Foreign lands – Austria. Gifts.

London, Jonathan. *Froggy gets a doggy* ill. by Frank Remkiewicz. Viking, 2014. ISBN 978-067001428-6 Subj: Animals – dogs. Frogs & toads.

Froggy's birthday wish ill. by Frank Remkiewicz. Viking, 2015. ISBN 978-067001572-6 Subj: Birthdays. Frogs & toads. Parties.

Hippos are huge! ill. by Matthew Trueman. Candlewick, 2015. ISBN 978-076366592-0 Subj: Animals – hippopotamuses. Foreign lands – Africa.

Little Puffin's first flight ill. by Jon Van Zyle. Alaska Northwest, 2015. ISBN 978-194182140-4 Subj: Alaska. Birds – puffins.

Ollie's first year ill. by Jon Van Zyle. Univ. of Alaska/Snowy Owl, 2014. ISBN 978-160223229-7 Subj: Animals – otters. Nature.

The seasons of Little Wolf ill. by Jon Van Zyle. WestWinds, 2014. ISBN 978-194182106-0 Subj: Animals – wolves. Nature.

Long, Ethan. *Fright club* ill. by author. Bloomsbury, 2015. ISBN 978-161963337-7 Subj: Clubs, gangs. Holidays – Halloween. Monsters.

In, over, and on (the farm) ill. by author. Putnam, 2015. ISBN 978-039916907-6 Subj: Animals. Farms. Language.

Me and my big mouse ill. by author. Amazon/Two Lions, 2014. ISBN 978-147784728-2 Subj: Animals – mice. Concepts – size. Pets.

Ms. Spell ill. by author. Holiday House, 2015. ISBN 978-082343292-9 Subj: Humorous stories. Language.

The Wing Wing brothers geometry palooza! ill. by author. Holiday House, 2014. ISBN 978-082342951-6 Subj: Birds – ducks. Counting, numbers. Family life – brothers.

Long, Loren. *Little tree* ill. by author. Philomel, 2015. ISBN 978-039916397-5 Subj: Animals. Concepts – change. Seasons. Trees.

Otis and the scarecrow ill. by author. Philomel, 2014. ISBN 978-039916396-8 Subj: Farms. Scarecrows. Tractors.

Lord, Cynthia. *Hot Rod Hamster: monster truck mania!* ill. by Derek Anderson. Scholastic, 2014. ISBN 978-054546261-7 Subj: Animals – hamsters. Fairs, festivals. Rhyming text. Trucks.

Low, William. *Daytime nighttime* ill. by author. Holt, 2014. ISBN 978-080509751-1 Subj: Animals. Day. Nature. Night.

Luján, Jorge. *Moví la mano / I moved my hand* ill. by Mandana Sadat. Groundwood, 2014. ISBN 978-155498485-5 Subj: Activities – storytelling. Foreign languages. Imagination. Magic. Poetry.

Lum, Kate. *Princesses are not just pretty* ill. by Sue Hellard. Bloomsbury, 2014. ISBN 978-159990778-9 Subj: Character traits – helpfulness. Character traits – vanity. Contests. Royalty – princesses.

Lumbard, Alexis York. *Everyone prays: celebrating faith around the world* ill. by Alireza Sadeghian. Wisdom Tales, 2014. ISBN 978-193778619-9 Subj: Religion.

Lundquist, Mary. *Cat and Bunny* ill. by author. HarperCollins/Balzer & Bray, 2015. ISBN 978-006228780-9 Subj: Activities – playing. Animals – cats. Animals – rabbits. Friendship.

Lurie, Susan. *Swim, duck, swim!* ill. by Murray Head. Feiwel and Friends, 2014. ISBN 978-125004642-0 Subj: Birds – ducks. Rhyming text. Sports – swimming.

Luxbacher, Irene. *Mr. Frank* ill. by author. Groundwood, 2014. ISBN 978-155498435-0 Subj: Activities – sewing. Careers – tailors. Clothing. Family life. Memories, memory.

Luzzati, Emanuele. *Three little owls* by Emanuele Luzzati and John Yeoman ill. by Quentin Blake. Tate, 2014. ISBN 978-184976080-5 Subj: Activities – traveling. Birds – owls. Holidays – Christmas. Rhyming text.

Lynch, Jane. *Marlene, Marlene, Queen of Mean* ill. by Tricia Tusa. Random House, 2014. ISBN 978-038537908-3 Subj: Behavior – bullying, teasing. Rhyming text.

Lyon, Benn. *Boats float!* (Lyon, George Ella)

Lyon, George Ella. *Boats float!* by George Ella Lyon and Benn Lyon ill. by Mick Wiggins. Atheneum, 2015. ISBN 978-148140380-1 Subj: Boats, ships. Rhyming text.

What forest knows ill. by August Hall. Atheneum, 2014. ISBN 978-144246775-0 Subj: Forest, woods. Nature. Seasons. Trees.

Macaulay, David. *How machines work: zoo break!* ill. by author. DK, 2015. ISBN 978-146544012-9 Subj: Animals – shrews. Animals – sloths. Behavior – resourcefulness. Format, unusual – toy & movable books. Machines. Zoos.

Maccarone, Grace. *The three little pigs count to 100* ill. by Pistacchio. Albert Whitman, 2015. ISBN 978-080757901-5 Subj: Animals – pigs. Concepts – shape. Counting, numbers. Folk & fairy tales.

McCarthy, Meghan. *Earmuffs for everyone! how Chester Greenwood became known as the inventor of earmuffs* ill. by author. Simon & Schuster/Paula Wiseman, 2015. ISBN 978-148140637-6 Subj: Anatomy – ears. Careers – inventors. Inventions.

McCarty, Peter. *First snow* ill. by author. HarperCollins/Balzer & Bray, 2015. ISBN 978-006218996-7 Subj: Activities – playing. Animals – dogs. Family life – cousins. Seasons – winter. Weather – snow.

McClelland, Rosie. *Show time with Sophia Grace and Rosie* (Brownlee, Sophia Grace)

McClure, Nikki. *In* ill. by author. Abrams/Appleseed, 2015. ISBN 978-141971486-3 Subj: Activities – playing. Birds – owls. Imagination.

McClurkan, Rob. *Aw, nuts!* ill. by author. HarperCollins, 2014. ISBN 978-006231729-2 Subj: Animals – squirrels. Behavior – greed.

McCully, Emily Arnold. *Queen of the diamond: the Lizzie Murphy story* ill. by author. Farrar, 2015. ISBN 978-037430007-4 Subj: Gender roles. Sports – baseball.

Strongheart: the world's first movie star dog ill. by author. Holt, 2014. ISBN 978-080509448-0 Subj: Animals – dogs. Careers – actors.

McDonald, Megan. *Shoe dog* ill. by Katherine Tillotson. Atheneum/Richard Jackson, 2014. ISBN 978-141697932-6 Subj: Animals – dogs. Character traits – kindness to animals. Clothing – shoes. Pets.

McDonnell, Patrick. *A perfectly messed-up story* ill. by author. Little, Brown, 2014. ISBN 978-031622258-7 Subj: Behavior – messy. Books, reading. Character traits – orderliness. Emotions – anger.

Thank you and good night ill. by author. Little, Brown, 2015. ISBN 978-031633801-1 Subj: Bedtime. Character traits – kindness. Friendship. Sleepovers.

McFarland, Clive. *A bed for Bear* ill. by author. Harper, 2014. ISBN 978-006223705-7 Subj: Animals. Animals – bears. Bedtime. Forest, woods. Hibernation.

McGee, Joe. *Peanut butter and brains: a zombie culinary tale* ill. by Charles Santoso. Abrams/Appleseed, 2015. ISBN 978-141971247-0 Subj: Food. Monsters.

McGhee, Alison. *Star bright: a Christmas story* ill. by Peter H. Reynolds. Atheneum, 2014. ISBN 978-141695858-1 Subj: Angels. Gifts. Holidays – Christmas. Religion – Nativity. Stars.

The sweetest witch around ill. by Harry Bliss. Simon & Schuster/Paula Wiseman, 2014. ISBN 978-144247833-6 Subj: Character traits – bravery. Character traits – curiosity. Family life – sisters. Holidays – Halloween. Witches.

McGowan, Jayme. *One bear extraordinaire* ill. by author. Abrams, 2015. ISBN 978-141971654-6 Subj: Animals. Animals – bears. Music. Musical instruments – bands.

McGrath, Barbara Barbieri. *Teddy bear addition* ill. by Tim Nihoff. Charlesbridge, 2014. ISBN 978-158089424-1 Subj: Counting, numbers. Rhyming text. Toys – bears.

MacGregor, Roy. *The highest number in the world* ill. by Geneviève Després. Tundra, 2014. ISBN 978-177049575-3 Subj: Family life – grandmothers. Foreign lands – Canada. Gender roles. Sports – hockey.

Mack, Jeff. *Duck in the fridge* ill. by author. Amazon/Two Lions, 2014. ISBN 978-147784776-3 Subj: Animals. Bedtime. Behavior – misbehavior. Birds – ducks. Books, reading. Family life – fathers.

Look! ill. by author. Philomel, 2015. ISBN 978-039916205-3 Subj: Animals – gorillas. Books, reading.

Who needs a bath? ill. by author. Harper, 2015. ISBN 978-006222028-8 Subj: Activities – bathing. Animals – bears. Animals – skunks. Parties. Senses – smell.

Who wants a hug? ill. by author. Harper, 2015. ISBN 978-006222026-4 Subj: Animals – bears. Animals – skunks. Hugging.

McKee, David. *Elmer and Butterfly* ill. by author. Andersen, 2015. ISBN 978-146776326-4 Subj: Animals – elephants. Character traits – helpfulness. Insects – butterflies, caterpillars.

Elmer and the flood ill. by author. Andersen, 2015. ISBN 978-146779312-4 Subj: Animals – elephants. Behavior – resourcefulness. Behavior – solitude. Weather – floods. Weather – rain.

Elmer and the monster ill. by author. Andersen, 2014. ISBN 978-146774200-9 Subj: Animals – elephants. Emotions – fear. Monsters.

Elmer and the whales ill. by author. Andersen, 2014. ISBN 978-146773453-0 Subj: Animals – elephants. Animals – whales. Family life – cousins.

McKenna, Martin. *The octopuppy* ill. by author. Scholastic, 2015. ɪsʙɴ 978-054575140-7 Subj: Humorous stories. Octopuses. Pets.

Mackintosh, David. *Lucky* ill. by author. Abrams, 2014. ɪsʙɴ 978-141970809-1 Subj: Family life. Imagination.

MacLachlan, Patricia. *The iridescence of birds: a book about Henri Matisse* ill. by Hadley Hooper. Roaring Brook/Neal Porter, 2014. ɪsʙɴ 978-159643948-1 Subj: Art. Careers – artists.

McLellan, Stephanie Simpson. *Tweezle into everything* ill. by Dean Griffiths. Pajama, 2014. ɪsʙɴ 978-192748547-7 Subj: Character traits – helpfulness. Family life. Self-concept.

McMullan, Kate. *I'm brave!* ill. by Jim McMullan. HarperCollins/Balzer & Bray, 2014. ɪsʙɴ 978-006220318-2 Subj: Careers – firefighters. Character traits – bravery. Trucks.

I'm cool! ill. by Jim McMullan. HarperCollins/ Balzer & Bray, 2015. ɪsʙɴ 978-006230629-6 Subj: Machines. Sports – hockey.

McNamara, Margaret. *A poem in your pocket* ill. by G. Brian Karas. Random/Schwartz & Wade, 2015. ɪsʙɴ 978-030797947-6 Subj: Activities – writing. Careers – writers. Poetry. School. Self-concept.

McPhail, David. *Andrew draws* ill. by author. Holiday House, 2014. ɪsʙɴ 978-082343063-5 Subj: Activities – drawing. Imagination.

Baby Pig Pig talks ill. by author. Charlesbridge, 2014. ɪsʙɴ 978-158089597-2 Subj: Animals – babies. Animals – pigs. Format, unusual – board books.

Bad dog ill. by author. Holiday House, 2014. ɪsʙɴ 978-082342852-6 Subj: Animals – dogs. Behavior – misbehavior.

Beatrix Potter and her paint box ill. by author. Holt, 2015. ɪsʙɴ 978-080509170-0 Subj: Activities – drawing. Activities – painting. Art. Careers – artists. Careers – writers. Nature.

Brothers ill. by author. Harcourt, 2014. ɪsʙɴ 978-054430200-6 Subj: Character traits – individuality. Emotions – love. Family life – brothers.

McPike, Elizabeth. *Little sleepyhead* ill. by Patrice Barton. Putnam, 2015. ɪsʙɴ 978-039916240-4 Subj: Babies, toddlers. Bedtime. Rhyming text.

McQuinn, Anna. *Leo loves baby time* ill. by Ruth Hearson. Charlesbridge, 2014. ɪsʙɴ 978-158089665-8 Subj: Activities – playing. Activities – storytelling. Babies, toddlers. Ethnic groups in the U.S. – African Americans. Libraries.

Lola plants a garden ill. by Rosalind Beardshaw. Charlesbridge, 2014. ɪsʙɴ 978-158089694-8 Subj: Ethnic groups in the U.S. – African Americans. Flowers. Gardens, gardening.

Mader, C. Roger. *Tiptop cat* ill. by author. Houghton, 2014. ɪsʙɴ 978-054414799-7 Subj: Animals – cats. Character traits – bravery. Emotions – fear. Foreign lands – France.

Magoon, Scott. *Breathe* ill. by author. Simon & Schuster/Paula Wiseman, 2014. ɪsʙɴ 978-144241258-3 Subj: Animals – babies. Animals – whales.

Maloney, Brenna. *Ready Rabbit gets ready!* photos by Chuck Kennedy. Viking, 2015. ɪsʙɴ 978-067001549-8 Subj: Animals – rabbits. Character traits – willfulness. Imagination.

Manceau, Edouard. *Tickle monster* ill. by author. Abrams/Appleseed, 2015. ɪsʙɴ 978-141971731-4 Subj: Bedtime. Emotions – fear. Monsters.

Mann, Jennifer K. *I will never get a star on Mrs. Benson's blackboard* ill. by author. Candlewick/ Nosy Crow, 2015. ɪsʙɴ 978-076366514-2 Subj: Careers – teachers. Character traits – individuality. School.

Two speckled eggs ill. by author. Candlewick, 2014. ɪsʙɴ 978-076366168-7 Subj: Birthdays. Character traits – being different. Friendship. Parties.

Manning, Jane. *Millie Fierce sleeps out* ill. by author. Philomel, 2014. ɪsʙɴ 978-039916093-6 Subj: Camps, camping. Character traits – assertiveness. Sleepovers.

Mantchev, Lisa. *Strictly no elephants* ill. by Taeeun Yoo. Simon & Schuster/Paula Wiseman, 2015. ɪsʙɴ 978-148141647-4 Subj: Animals – elephants. Character traits – being different. Pets.

Manushkin, Fran. *Happy in our skin* ill. by Lauren Tobia. Candlewick, 2015. ɪsʙɴ 978-076367002-3 Subj: Anatomy – skin. Ethnic groups in the U.S. Family life. Rhyming text. Self-concept.

Manzano, Sonia. *Miracle on 133rd Street* ill. by Marjorie Priceman. Atheneum, 2015. ɪsʙɴ 978-068987887-9 Subj: Activities – baking, cooking. Character traits – cooperation. Communities, neighborhoods. Ethnic groups in the U.S. – Puerto Rican Americans. Holidays – Christmas.

Marino, Gianna. *Following Papa's song* ill. by author. Viking, 2014. ɪsʙɴ 978-067001315-9 Subj: Animals – whales. Behavior – worrying. Family life – fathers. Migration.

Night animals ill. by author. Viking, 2015. ɪsʙɴ 978-045146954-0 Subj: Animals. Animals – possums. Emotions – fear. Night.

Markle, Sandra. *Toad weather* ill. by Thomas Gonzalez. Peachtree, 2015. ISBN 978-156145818-9 Subj: Frogs & toads. Migration. Weather – rain.

Martin, David. *Peep and Ducky: rainy day* ill. by David Walker. Candlewick, 2015. ISBN 978-076366884-6 Subj: Activities – playing. Birds – bluebirds. Birds – ducks. Friendship. Rhyming text. Weather – rain.

Martin, Emily Winfield. *Day dreamers: a journey of imagination* ill. by author. Random House, 2014. ISBN 978-038537670-9 Subj: Dreams. Imagination. Mythical creatures. Rhyming text.

The wonderful things you will be ill. by author. Random House, 2015. ISBN 978-038537671-6 Subj: Character traits. Family life – parents. Rhyming text.

Martin, Jacqueline Briggs. *Alice Waters and the trip to delicious* ill. by Hayelin Choi. Readers to Eaters, 2014. ISBN 978-098366156-6 Subj: Activities – baking, cooking. Careers – chefs, cooks. Food. Health & fitness.

Martinez, Libby. *I pledge allegiance* (Mora, Pat)

Massini, Sarah. *Love always everywhere* ill. by author. Random House, 2014. ISBN 978-038537552-8 Subj: Emotions – love. Rhyming text.

Mathers, Petra. *When Aunt Mattie got her wings* ill. by author. Simon & Schuster/Beach Lane, 2014. ISBN 978-148141044-1 Subj: Birds – chickens, roosters. Birds – ducks. Death. Memories, memory.

Matheson, Christie. *Touch the brightest star* ill. by author. Greenwillow, 2015. ISBN 978-006227447-2 Subj: Bedtime. Night. Participation.

Mattick, Lindsay. *Finding Winnie: the true story of the world's most famous bear* ill. by Sophie Blackall. Little, Brown, 2015. ISBN 978-031632490-8 Subj: Animals – bears. Books, reading. Caldecott award books. Zoos.

May, Eleanor. *Albert the muffin-maker* ill. by Deborah Melmon. Kane, 2014. ISBN 978-157565631-1 Subj: Activities – baking, cooking. Animals – mice. Counting, numbers.

May, Robert L. *Rudolph shines again* ill. by Antonio Caparo. Simon & Schuster, 2015. ISBN 978-144247498-7 Subj: Animals – rabbits. Animals – reindeer. Behavior – lost. Character traits – helpfulness. Holidays – Christmas. Rhyming text.

Mayhew, James. *Ella Bella ballerina and A Midsummer Night's Dream* ill. by author. Barron's, 2015. ISBN 978-076416797-3 Subj: Ballet. Music. Theater.

Medina, Meg. *Mango, Abuela, and me* ill. by Angela Dominguez. Candlewick, 2015. ISBN 978-076366900-3 Subj: Birds – parakeets, parrots. Family life – grandmothers. Foreign languages.

Meltzer, Brad. *I am Albert Einstein* ill. by Christopher Eliopoulos. Dial, 2014. ISBN 978-080374084-6 Subj: Careers – scientists. Character traits – curiosity. Character traits – individuality. Science.

I am Rosa Parks ill. by Christopher Eliopoulos. Dial, 2014. ISBN 978-080374085-3 Subj: Ethnic groups in the U.S. – African Americans. Prejudice. U.S. history. Violence, nonviolence.

Membrino, Anna. *I want to be a ballerina* ill. by Smiljana Coh. Random House, 2014. ISBN 978-037597330-7 Subj: Ballet. Careers – dancers. Family life – sisters.

Menchin, Scott. *Grandma in blue with red hat* ill. by Harry Bliss. Abrams, 2015. ISBN 978-141971484-9 Subj: Art. Family life – grandmothers. Museums.

Merino, Gemma. *The crocodile who didn't like water* ill. by author. NorthSouth, 2014. ISBN 978-073584163-5 Subj: Character traits – being different. Dragons. Reptiles – alligators, crocodiles.

Meshon, Aaron. *Tools rule!* ill. by author. Atheneum, 2014. ISBN 978-144249601-9 Subj: Activities – making things. Character traits – cooperation. Tools.

Messner, Kate. *How to read a story* ill. by Mark Siegel. Chronicle, 2015. ISBN 978-145211233-6 Subj: Behavior – sharing. Books, reading.

Tree of wonder: the many marvelous lives of a rainforest tree ill. by Simona Mulazzani. Chronicle, 2015. ISBN 978-145211248-0 Subj: Animals. Ecology. Jungle. Nature. Trees.

Up in the garden and down in the dirt ill. by Christopher Silas Neal. Chronicle, 2015. ISBN 978-145211936-6 Subj: Gardens, gardening. Seasons.

Metzger, Steve. *Waiting for Santa* ill. by Alison Edgson. Tiger Tales, 2015. ISBN 978-158925199-1 Subj: Animals. Holidays – Christmas. Santa Claus.

Meyer, Susan Lynn. *New shoes* ill. by Eric Velasquez. Holiday House, 2015. ISBN 978-082342528-0 Subj: Clothing – shoes. Ethnic groups in the U.S. – African Americans. Prejudice. U.S. history.

Migy. *And away we go!* ill. by author. Holt, 2014. ISBN 978-080509901-0 Subj: Activities – ballooning. Animals. Animals – foxes.

Milgrim, David. *Wild feelings* ill. by author. Holt, 2015. ISBN 978-080509587-6 Subj: Animals. Clothing – costumes. Emotions.

Miller, John. *Winston and George* ill. by Giuliano Cucco. Enchanted Lion, 2014. ISBN 978-159270145-2 Subj: Behavior – lying. Behavior – trickery. Birds – plovers. Reptiles – alligators, crocodiles.

Miller, Pat Zietlow. *Sharing the bread: an old-fashioned Thanksgiving story* ill. by Jill McElmurry. Random/Schwartz & Wade, 2015. ISBN 978-030798182-0 Subj: Activities – baking, cooking. Behavior – sharing. Family life. Food. Holidays – Thanksgiving. Rhyming text. U.S. history.

Wherever you go ill. by Eliza Wheeler. Little, Brown, 2015. ISBN 978-031640002-2 Subj: Activities – traveling. Animals – rabbits. Rhyming text.

Minor, Wendell. *Daylight starlight wildlife* ill. by author. Penguin/Nancy Paulsen, 2015. ISBN 978-039924662-3 Subj: Animals. Day. Night.

Mitton, Tony. *Snowy Bear* ill. by Alison Brown. Bloomsbury, 2015. ISBN 978-161963905-8 Subj: Animals – bears. Rhyming text. Seasons – winter. Weather – snow.

Miura, Taro. *The big princess* ill. by author. Candlewick, 2015. ISBN 978-076367459-5 Subj: Concepts – size. Royalty – princesses.

Miyakoshi, Akiko. *The tea party in the woods* ill. by author. Kids Can, 2015. ISBN 978-177138107-9 Subj: Animals. Forest, woods. Parties.

Miyares, Daniel. *Float* ill. by author. Simon & Schuster, 2015. ISBN 978-148141524-8 Subj: Behavior – lost & found possessions. Boats, ships. Toys. Weather – rain. Wordless.

Pardon me! ill. by author. Simon & Schuster, 2014. ISBN 978-144248997-4 Subj: Behavior – sharing. Birds. Humorous stories. Reptiles – alligators, crocodiles.

Molk, Laurel. *Eeny, Meeny, Miney, Mo and Flo!* ill. by author. Viking, 2015. ISBN 978-067001538-2 Subj: Animals – mice. Family life – brothers & sisters. Rhyming text.

Monfreid, Dorothée de. *The cake* ill. by author. Gecko, 2014. ISBN 978-187757945-5 Subj: Animals. Behavior – fighting, arguing. Food.

Monroe, Chris. *Bug on a bike* ill. by author. Carolrhoda, 2014. ISBN 978-146772154-7 Subj: Birthdays. Cumulative tales. Insects. Rhyming text. Sports – bicycling.

Montalván, Luis Carlos. *Tuesday tucks me in: the loyal bond between a soldier and his service dog* by Luis Carlos Montalván and Bret Witter ill. with photos. Roaring Brook, 2014. ISBN 978-159643891-0 Subj: Animals – dogs. Animals – service animals. Careers – military. Disabilities.

Moore, Clement Clarke. *The night before Christmas* ill. by David Ercolini. Scholastic/Orchard, 2015. ISBN 978-054539112-2 Subj: Holidays – Christmas. Poetry. Santa Claus.

The night before Christmas ill. by Barbara Reid. Albert Whitman, 2014. ISBN 978-080755625-2 Subj: Animals – mice. Holidays – Christmas. Poetry. Santa Claus.

'Twas the night before Christmas adapt. by Daniel Kirk; ill. by adapter. Abrams, 2015. ISBN 978-141971233-3 Subj: Animals – mice. Holidays – Christmas. Poetry. Santa Claus.

Mora, Pat. *I pledge allegiance* by Pat Mora and Libby Martinez ill. by Patrice Barton. Knopf, 2014. ISBN 978-030793181-8 Subj: Ethnic groups in the U.S. – Mexican Americans. Family life. Foreign languages. Immigrants. U.S. history.

The remembering day / El día de los muertos ill. by Robert Casilla. Arte Publico, 2015. ISBN 978-155885805-3 Subj: Death. Family life – grandmothers. Foreign lands – Mexico. Foreign languages. Gardens, gardening. Holidays – Day of the Dead. Memories, memory.

Water rolls, water rises / el agua ruda, el agua sube ill. by Meilo So. Lee & Low, 2014. ISBN 978-089239325-1 Subj: Foreign languages. Poetry. Water.

Morales, Yuyi. *Viva Frida* ill. by Tim O'Meara. Roaring Brook, 2014. ISBN 978-159643603-9 Subj: Art. Caldecott award honor books. Careers – artists. Foreign lands – Mexico. Foreign languages.

Morris, Richard T. *This is a moose* ill. by Tom Lichtenheld. Little, Brown, 2014. ISBN 978-031621360-8 Subj: Animals – moose. Humorous stories.

Morrison, Slade. *Please, Louise* (Morrison, Toni)

Morrison, Toni. *Please, Louise* by Toni Morrison and Slade Morrison ill. by Shadra Strickland. Simon & Schuster, 2014. ISBN 978-141698338-5 Subj: Books, reading. Emotions – fear. Libraries. Rhyming text.

Moüy, Iris de. *Naptime* ill. by author. House of Anansi Groundwood, 2014. ISBN 978-155498487-9 Subj: Animals. Behavior – fighting, arguing. Sleep.

Muller, Gerda. *How does my garden grow?* ill. by author. Floris, 2014. ISBN 978-178250037-7 Subj: Family life – grandfathers. Foreign lands – France. Gardens, gardening.

Muncaster, Harriet. *I am a witch's cat* ill. by author. Harper, 2014. ISBN 978-006222914-4 Subj: Animals – cats. Witches.

Muñoz Ryan, Pam. *Tony Baloney: buddy trouble* ill. by Edwin Fotheringham. Scholastic, 2014. ISBN 978-054548169-4 Subj: Birds – penguins. Character traits – responsibility. Family life – brothers & sisters.

Munro, Roxie. *Market maze* ill. by author. Holiday House, 2015. ISBN 978-082343092-5 Subj: Farms. Mazes. Picture puzzles. Stores.

Murguia, Bethanie Deeney. *The best parts of Christmas* ill. by author. Candlewick, 2015. ISBN 978-076367556-1 Subj: Holidays – Christmas. Trees.

I feel five! ill. by author. Candlewick, 2014. ISBN 978-076366291-2 Subj: Behavior – growing up. Birthdays.

Zoe's jungle ill. by author. Scholastic/Arthur A. Levine, 2014. ISBN 978-054555869-3 Subj: Activities – playing. Family life – sisters. Imagination.

Murphy, Mary. *Say hello like this!* ill. by author. Candlewick, 2014. ISBN 978-076366951-5 Subj: Animals. Format, unusual – toy & movable books. Noise, sounds.

Murray, Alison. *Hickory dickory dog* ill. by author. Candlewick, 2014. ISBN 978-076366826-6 Subj: Animals – dogs. Rhyming text. School.

Murray, Laura. *The Gingerbread Man loose at Christmas* (The gingerbread boy)

Muth, Jon J. *Hi, Koo! a year of seasons* ill. by author. Scholastic, 2014. ISBN 978-054516668-3 Subj: Animals – pandas. Poetry. Seasons.

Zen socks ill. by author. Scholastic, 2015. ISBN 978-054516669-0 Subj: Activities – storytelling. Animals – pandas. Behavior – greed. Behavior – sharing. Character traits – kindness. Character traits – patience. Family life – brothers & sisters.

Myers, Anna. *Tumbleweed Baby* ill. by Charles Vess. Abrams, 2014. ISBN 978-141971232-6 Subj: Babies, toddlers. Family life. Tall tales. Texas.

Myers, Christopher. *My pen* ill. by author. Disney/Hyperion, 2015. ISBN 978-142310371-4 Subj: Activities – drawing. Imagination.

Na, Il Sung. *Welcome home, Bear: a book of animal habitats* ill. by author. Knopf, 2015. ISBN 978-038575375-3 Subj: Activities – traveling. Animals – bears. Homes, houses.

Naberhaus, Sarvinder. *Boom boom* ill. by Margaret Chodos-Irvine. Simon & Schuster/Beach Lane, 2014. ISBN 978-144243412-7 Subj: Noise, sounds. Rhyming text. Seasons.

Napoli, Donna Jo. *Hands and hearts: with 15 words in American Sign Language* ill. by Amy June Bates. Abrams, 2014. ISBN 978-141971022-3 Subj: Family life – mothers. Sea & seashore – beaches. Sign language.

National Wildlife Federation. *My first book of baby animals* ill. with photos. Imagine, 2014. ISBN 978-162354028-9 Subj: Animals – babies. Format, unusual – board books.

Nelson, Kadir. *Baby Bear* ill. by author. HarperCollins/Balzer & Bray, 2014. ISBN 978-006224172-6 Subj: Animals. Animals – bears. Behavior – lost.

If you plant a seed ill. by author. HarperCollins/Balzer & Bray, 2015. ISBN 978-006229889-8 Subj: Animals. Character traits – cooperation. Character traits – kindness. Gardens, gardening. Seeds.

Nelson, Vaunda Micheaux. *The book itch: freedom, truth, and Harlem's greatest bookstore* ill. by R. Gregory Christie. Carolrhoda, 2015. ISBN 978-076133943-4 Subj: Books, reading. Ethnic groups in the U.S. – African Americans. Stores.

Newgarden, Mark. *Bow-Wow's nightmare neighbors* by Mark Newgarden and Megan Montague Cash ill. by Mark Newgarden. Roaring Brook, 2014. ISBN 978-159643640-4 Subj: Animals – cats. Animals – dogs. Character traits – bravery. Ghosts. Wordless.

Newman, Lesléa. *Heather has two mommies* ill. by Laura Cornell. Candlewick, 2015. ISBN 978-076366631-6 Subj: Family life – daughters. Family life – mothers. Family life – same-sex parents. LGBTQ issues.

Here is the world: a year of Jewish holidays ill. by Susan Gal. Abrams, 2014. ISBN 978-141971185-5 Subj: Holidays. Jewish culture.

Ketzel, the cat who composed ill. by Amy June Bates. Candlewick, 2015. ISBN 978-076366555-5 Subj: Animals – cats. Careers – composers. Character traits – kindness to animals. Friendship. Music. Musical instruments – pianos.

Nichols, Lori. *Maple* ill. by author. Penguin/Nancy Paulsen, 2014. ISBN 978-039916085-1 Subj: Family life – new sibling. Friendship. Trees.

Maple and Willow apart ill. by author. Penguin/Nancy Paulsen, 2015. ISBN 978-039916753-9 Subj: Emotions – loneliness. Family life – sisters. School.

Maple and Willow together ill. by author. Penguin/Nancy Paulsen, 2014. ISBN 978-039916283-1 Subj: Behavior – fighting, arguing. Family life – sisters. Friendship. Nature.

Niemann, Christoph. *The potato king* ill. by author. Owlkids, 2015. ISBN 978-177147139-8 Subj: Behavior – trickery. Food. Foreign lands. Royalty – kings.

Noble, Trinka Hakes. *Lizzie and the last day of school* ill. by Kris Aro McLeod. Sleeping Bear, 2015. ISBN 978-158536895-2 Subj: School.

Nolan, Dennis. *Hunters of the great forest* ill. by author. Roaring Brook, 2014. ISBN 978-159643896-5 Subj: Sports – hunting. Wordless.

Nolan, Nina. *Mahalia Jackson: walking with kings and queens* ill. by John Holyfield. Amistad, 2015. ISBN 978-006087944-0 Subj: Careers – singers. Ethnic groups in the U.S. – African Americans. Music.

Nolen, Jerdine. *Irene's wish* ill. by A. G. Ford. Simon & Schuster/Paula Wiseman, 2014. ISBN 978-068986300-4 Subj: Behavior – wishing. Ethnic groups in the U.S. – African Americans. Family life – fathers. Gardens, gardening.

Nordling, Lee. *Shehewe* ill. by Meritxell Bosch. Lerner/Graphic Universe, 2015. ISBN 978-146774574-1 Subj: Activities – playing. Format, unusual – graphic novels. Gender roles. Parks.

Norman, Kim. *Puddle pug* ill. by Keika Yamaguchi. Sterling, 2014. ISBN 978-145490436-6 Subj: Animals – dogs. Animals – pigs. Behavior – lost.

Novak, B. J. *The book with no pictures.* Dial, 2014. ISBN 978-080374171-3 Subj: Books, reading. Humorous stories.

O'Brien, Anne Sibley. *I'm new here* ill. by author. Charlesbridge, 2015. ISBN 978-158089612-2 Subj: Ethnic groups in the U.S. – Guatemalan Americans. Ethnic groups in the U.S. – Korean Americans. Ethnic groups in the U.S. – Somali Americans. Immigrants. School.

O'Connell, Rebecca. *Baby party* ill. by Susie Poole. Albert Whitman, 2015. ISBN 978-080750512-0 Subj: Babies, toddlers. Concepts – shape. Parties.

O'Connor, George. *If I had a raptor* ill. by author. Candlewick, 2014. ISBN 978-076366012-3 Subj: Dinosaurs. Ethnic groups in the U.S. – African Americans. Pets.

If I had a triceratops ill. by author. Candlewick, 2015. ISBN 978-076366013-0 Subj: Dinosaurs. Pets.

O'Connor, Jane. *Fancy Nancy and the wedding of the century* ill. by Robin Preiss Glasser. Harper, 2014. ISBN 978-006208319-7 Subj: Character traits – compromising. Weddings.

Offill, Jenny. *Sparky!* ill. by Chris Appelhans. Random House, 2014. ISBN 978-037587023-1 Subj: Animals – sloths. Pets.

While you were napping ill. by Barry Blitt. Random/Schwartz & Wade, 2014. ISBN 978-037586572-5 Subj: Family life – brothers & sisters. Imagination. Sleep.

Ohi, Debbie Ridpath. *Where are my books?* ill. by author. Simon & Schuster, 2015. ISBN 978-144246741-5 Subj: Animals – squirrels. Behavior – lost & found possessions. Books, reading.

OHora, Zachariah. *My cousin Momo* ill. by author. Dial, 2015. ISBN 978-080374011-2 Subj: Animals – squirrels. Character traits – being different. Character traits – individuality. Family life – cousins.

Old MacDonald had a farm. *Pete the Cat: Old MacDonald had a farm* ill. by James Dean. HarperCollins, 2014. ISBN 978-006219873-0 Subj: Animals. Careers – farmers. Cumulative tales. Farms. Music. Songs.

Oldland, Nicholas. *Walk on the wild side* ill. by author. Kids Can, 2015. ISBN 978-177138109-3 Subj: Animals – bears. Animals – beavers. Animals – moose. Contests. Friendship. Sports – hiking.

O'Leary, Sara. *This is Sadie* ill. by Julie Morstad. Tundra, 2015. ISBN 978-177049532-6 Subj: Activities – storytelling. Books, reading. Imagination.

Olien, Jessica. *Shark Detective!* ill. by author. HarperCollins/Balzer & Bray, 2015. ISBN 978-006235714-4 Subj: Animals – cats. Behavior – lost & found possessions. Careers – detectives. Fish – sharks. Mystery stories.

Oliver, Lin. *Little poems for tiny ears* ill. by Tomie dePaola. Penguin/Nancy Paulsen, 2014. ISBN 978-039916605-1 Subj: Babies, toddlers. Poetry.

Olivera, Ramon. *ABCs on wings* ill. by author. Simon & Schuster, 2015. ISBN 978-148143242-9 Subj: ABC books. Airplanes, airports.

Olson, Jennifer Gray. *Ninja bunny* ill. by author. Knopf, 2015. ISBN 978-038575493-4 Subj: Animals – rabbits. Friendship. Sports – martial arts.

O'Neill, Gemma. *Monty's magnificent mane* ill. by author. Candlewick, 2015. ISBN 978-076367593-6 Subj: Animals – lions. Animals – meerkats. Character traits – appearance. Friendship. Reptiles – alligators, crocodiles.

Oh dear, Geoffrey! ill. by author. Candlewick, 2014. ISBN 978-076366659-0 Subj: Animals – giraffes. Character traits – clumsiness. Foreign lands – Africa. Friendship.

Onyefulu, Ifeoma. *Ife's first haircut* photos by author. Frances Lincoln/Janetta Otter-Barry, 2014. ISBN 978-184780364-1 Subj: Foreign lands – Nigeria. Hair.

Orloff, Karen Kaufman. *I wanna go home* ill. by David Catrow. Putnam, 2014. ISBN 978-039925407-9 Subj: Family life – grandparents. Letters, cards. Old age.

Ormerod, Jan. *The baby swap* ill. by Andrew Joyner. Simon & Schuster, 2015. ISBN 978-148141914-7 Subj: Activities – trading. Emotions – envy, jealousy. Family life – brothers & sisters. Family life – new sibling. Reptiles – alligators, crocodiles. Stores.

Oskarsson, Bardur. *The flat rabbit* ill. by author. Owl, 2014. ISBN 978-177147059-9 Subj: Animals – rabbits. Death. Kites.

Otoshi, Kathryn. *Beautiful hands* by Kathryn Otoshi and Bret Baumgarten ill. by Kathryn Otoshi. Blue Dot, 2015. ISBN 978-099079930-6 Subj: Anatomy – hands. Art. Character traits – helpfulness. Character traits – optimism.

Two ill. by author. KO Kids, 2014. ISBN 978-097239466-6 Subj: Behavior – fighting, arguing. Counting, numbers. Friendship. Self-concept.

Oud, Pauline. *Sarah on the potty* ill. by author. Clavis, 2014. ISBN 978-160537175-7 Subj: Toilet training.

Page, Robin. *Creature features: 25 animals explain why they look the way they do* (Jenkins, Steve)

How to swallow a pig: step-by-step advice from the animal kingdom (Jenkins, Steve)

Pajalunga, Lorena V. *Yoga for kids* ill. by Anna Forlati. Albert Whitman, 2015. ISBN 978-080759172-7 Subj: Animals. Health & fitness – exercise.

Palatini, Margie. *No nap! yes nap!* ill. by Dan Yaccarino. Little, Brown, 2014. ISBN 978-031624821-1 Subj: Babies, toddlers. Behavior – misbehavior. Rhyming text. Sleep.

Under a pig tree: a history of the noble fruit ill. by Chuck Groenink. Abrams, 2015. ISBN 978-141971488-7 Subj: Activities – writing. Animals – pigs. Books, reading. Careers – writers. Food. Humorous stories.

Pallotta, Jerry. *Butterfly counting* ill. by Shennen Bersani. Charlesbridge, 2015. ISBN 978-157091414-0 Subj: Counting, numbers. Insects – butterflies, caterpillars.

Parenteau, Shirley. *Bears and a birthday* ill. by David Walker. Candlewick, 2015. ISBN 978-076367152-5 Subj: Activities – baking, cooking. Animals – bears. Birthdays. Rhyming text.

Bears in the bath ill. by David Walker. Candlewick, 2014. ISBN 978-076366418-3 Subj: Activities – bathing. Animals – bears. Rhyming text.

Parr, Todd. *The goodbye book* ill. by author. Little, Brown, 2015. ISBN 978-031640497-6 Subj: Emotions – grief. Emotions – sadness.

It's okay to make mistakes ill. by author. Little, Brown, 2014. ISBN 978-031623053-7 Subj: Behavior – mistakes. Self-concept.

Parsley, Elise. *If you ever want to bring an alligator to school, don't!* ill. by author. Little, Brown, 2015. ISBN 978-031637657-0 Subj: Behavior – misbehavior. Reptiles – alligators, crocodiles. School.

Paschkis, Julie. *P. Zonka lays an egg* ill. by author. Peachtree, 2015. ISBN 978-156145819-6 Subj: Birds – chickens, roosters. Character traits – being different. Concepts – color. Eggs.

Patricelli, Leslie. *Boo!* ill. by author. Candlewick, 2015. ISBN 978-076366320-9 Subj: Clothing – costumes. Format, unusual – board books. Holidays – Halloween.

Hop! hop! ill. by author. Candlewick, 2015. ISBN 978-076366319-3 Subj: Animals – rabbits. Concepts – color. Eggs. Format, unusual – board books. Holidays – Easter.

Paul, Alison. *The plan* ill. by Barbara Lehman. Houghton Mifflin Harcourt, 2015. ISBN 978-054428333-6 Subj: Activities – flying. Airplanes, airports. Behavior – resourcefulness. Emotions – sadness. Family life – daughters. Family life – fathers.

Paul, Ellis. *The night the lights went out on Christmas* ill. by Scott Brundage. Albert Whitman, 2015. ISBN 978-080754543-0 Subj: Contests. Holidays – Christmas. Light, lights. Rhyming text.

Paul, Miranda. *One plastic bag: Isatou Ceesay and the recycling women of the Gambia* ill. by Elizabeth Zunon. Lerner/Millbrook, 2015. ISBN 978-146771608-6 Subj: Behavior – seeking better things. Ecology. Foreign lands – Gambia. Money.

Water is water ill. by Jason Chin. Roaring Brook, 2015. ISBN 978-159643984-9 Subj: Science. Seasons. Water.

Paul, Ruth. *Bad dog, Flash* ill. by author. Sourcebooks/Jabberwocky, 2014. ISBN 978-149260153-1 Subj: Animals – dogs. Behavior – misbehavior.

Go home Flash ill. by author. Sourcebooks/Jabberwocky, 2015. ISBN 978-149261523-1 Subj: Animals – dogs. Behavior – misbehavior.

Pearce, Clemency. *Three little words* ill. by Rosalind Beardshaw. Doubleday, 2014. ISBN 978-038537001-1 Subj: Animals. Emotions – love. Rhyming text.

Pearlman, Robb. *Groundhog's day off* ill. by Brett Helquist. Bloomsbury, 2015. ISBN 978-161963289-9 Subj: Activities – vacationing. Animals – groundhogs. Behavior – dissatisfaction. Holidays – Groundhog Day. Humorous stories.

Peet, Amanda. *Dear Santa, Love Rachel Rosenstein* by Amanda Peet and Andrea Troyer ill. by Christine Davenier. Knopf, 2015. ISBN 978-055351061-4 Subj: Holidays – Christmas. Jewish culture. Letters, cards. Santa Claus.

Pennypacker, Sara. *Meet the Dullards* ill. by Daniel Salmieri. HarperCollins/Balzer & Bray, 2015. ISBN 978-006219856-3 Subj: Behavior – boredom. Family life. Humorous stories. Moving.

Peppa Pig and the vegetable garden. Candlewick, 2014. ISBN 978-076366987-4 Subj: Activities – baking, cooking. Animals – pigs. Gardens, gardening.

Percival, Tom. *Herman's letter* ill. by author. Bloomsbury, 2014. ISBN 978-161963423-7 Subj: Animals – bears. Animals – raccoons. Friendship. Letters, cards. Moving. Moving. Pen pals.

Perepeczko, Jenny. *Moses: the true story of an elephant baby* ill. by author. Atheneum, 2014. ISBN 978-144249603-3 Subj: Animals – elephants. Character traits – kindness to animals.

Perkins, Maripat. *Rodeo Red* ill. by Molly Idle. Peachtree, 2015. ISBN 978-156145816-5 Subj: Cowboys, cowgirls. Family life – brothers & sisters. Family life – new sibling. Toys.

Perl, Erica S. *Goatilocks and the three bears* (The three bears)

Totally tardy Marty ill. by Jarrett J. Krosoczka. Abrams, 2015. ISBN 978-141971661-4 Subj: Behavior – promptness, tardiness. Friendship.

Perret, Delphine. *Pedro and George* ill. by author. Atheneum, 2015. ISBN 978-148142925-2 Subj: Family life – cousins. Humorous stories. Reptiles – alligators, crocodiles.

Perrin, Clotilde. *At the same moment, around the world* ill. by author. Chronicle, 2014. ISBN 978-145212208-3 Subj: Time. World.

Petricic, Dusan. *My family tree and me* ill. by author. Kids Can, 2015. ISBN 978-177138049-2 Subj: Ethnic groups in the U.S. Ethnic groups in the U.S. – Chinese Americans. Family life.

Pett, Mark. *The girl and the bicycle* ill. by author. Simon & Schuster, 2014. ISBN 978-144248319-4 Subj: Problem solving. Sports – bicycling. Wordless.

Lizard from the park ill. by author. Simon & Schuster, 2015. ISBN 978-144248321-7 Subj: Dinosaurs. Friendship. Pets.

Petty, Dev. *I don't want to be a frog* ill. by Mike Boldt. Doubleday, 2015. ISBN 978-038537866-6 Subj: Animals. Behavior – dissatisfaction. Frogs & toads. Self-concept.

Pfeffer, Wendy. *Light is all around us* ill. by Paul Meisel. HarperCollins, 2014. ISBN 978-006029121-1 Subj: Light, lights. Science.

Pfister, Marcus. *The little moon raven* ill. by author. Minedition, 2014. ISBN 978-988824081-4 Subj: Behavior – bullying, teasing. Birds – ravens. Character traits – bravery. Moon. Self-concept.

Pham, LeUyen. *A piece of cake* ill. by author. HarperCollins/Balzer & Bray, 2014. ISBN 978-006199264-3 Subj: Activities – trading. Animals. Animals – mice. Birthdays. Character traits – cooperation. Food.

There's no such thing as little ill. by author. Knopf, 2015. ISBN 978-038539150-4 Subj: Character traits – smallness. Concepts. Format, unusual – toy & movable books.

Phelan, Matt. *Druthers* ill. by author. Candlewick, 2014. ISBN 978-076365955-4 Subj: Activities – playing. Behavior – boredom. Family life – fathers. Imagination. Weather – rain.

Phillipps, J. C. *The Simples love a picnic* ill. by author. Houghton, 2014. ISBN 978-054416667-7 Subj: Activities – picnicking. Family life.

Pierce, Christa. *Did you know that I love you?* ill. by author. HarperCollins, 2014. ISBN 978-006229744-0 Subj: Animals – foxes. Birds. Emotions – love. Rhyming text.

Pilcher, Steve. *Over there* ill. by author. Disney/Hyperion, 2014. ISBN 978-142314793-0 Subj: Animals – moles. Animals – shrews. Emotions – loneliness. Friendship.

Pilutti, Deb. *Bear and Squirrel are friends . . . yes, really!* ill. by author. Simon & Schuster/Paula Wiseman, 2015. ISBN 978-148142913-9 Subj: Animals – bears. Animals – squirrels. Friendship.

Ten rules of being a superhero ill. by author. Holt, 2014. ISBN 978-080509759-7 Subj: Activities – playing. Humorous stories. Imagination. Toys.

Pinder, Eric. *How to share with a bear* ill. by Stephanie Graegin. Farrar, 2015. ISBN 978-037430019-7 Subj: Animals – bears. Behavior – sharing. Clothing – costumes. Family life – brothers.

Pingk, Rubin. *Samurai Santa: a very Ninja Christmas* ill. by author. Simon & Schuster, 2015. ISBN 978-148143057-9 Subj: Holidays – Christmas. Santa Claus. Sports – martial arts.

Pinkney, Brian. *On the ball* ill. by author. Disney/Hyperion, 2015. ISBN 978-148472329-6 Subj: Imagination. Sports – soccer.

Pinkwater, Daniel. *Bear and Bunny* ill. by Will Hillenbrand. Candlewick, 2015. ISBN 978-076367153-2 Subj: Animals – bears. Animals – rabbits. Friendship. Frogs & toads. Pets.

Beautiful Yetta's Hanukkah kitten ill. by Jill Pinkwater. Feiwel and Friends, 2014. ISBN 978-031262134-6 Subj: Animals – cats. Birds – chickens, roosters. Foreign languages. Holidays – Hanukkah.

Pitman, Gayle E. *This day in June* ill. by Kristyna Litten. Magination, 2014. ISBN 978-143381658-1 Subj: LGBTQ issues. Parades. Rhyming text.

Pizzoli, Greg. *Number one Sam* ill. by author. Disney/Hyperion, 2014. ISBN 978-142317111-9 Subj: Animals – dogs. Automobiles. Contests. Sports – racing.

Templeton gets his wish ill. by author. Disney/Hyperion, 2015. ISBN 978-148471274-0 Subj: Animals – cats. Behavior – wishing. Emotions – loneliness. Family life.

Plant, David J. *Hungry Roscoe* ill. by David J. Plant. Flying Eye, 2015. ISBN 978-190926353-6 Subj: Animals – raccoons. Zoos.

Plourde, Lynn. *Merry Moosey Christmas* ill. by Russ Cox. Islandport Press, 2014. ISBN 978-193901738-3 Subj: Animals – moose. Animals – reindeer. Holidays – Christmas. Santa Claus.

Polacco, Patricia. *An A from Miss Keller* ill. by author. Putnam, 2015. ISBN 978-039916691-4 Subj: Activities – writing. Careers – teachers. Death. Emotions – grief. School. Self-concept.

Clara and Davie: the true story of young Clara Barton ill. by author. Scholastic, 2014. ISBN 978-054535477-6 Subj: Careers – nurses. U.S. history.

Fiona's lace ill. by author. Simon & Schuster/Paula Wiseman, 2014. ISBN 978-144248724-6 Subj: Character traits – perseverance. Ethnic groups in the U.S. – Irish Americans. Immigrants.

Mr. Wayne's masterpiece ill. by author. Putnam, 2014. ISBN 978-039916095-0 Subj: Careers – teachers. Character traits – shyness. Emotions – fear. School. Theater.

Poletti, Frances. *Miss Todd and her wonderful flying machine* by Frances Poletti and Kristina Yee ill. by Kristina Yee, et al. Compendium, 2015. ISBN 978-193829876-9 Subj: Airplanes, airports. Careers – airplane pilots. Gender roles.

Pomranz, Craig. *Made by Raffi* ill. by Margaret Chamberlain. Frances Lincoln, 2014. ISBN 978-184780433-4 Subj: Activities – knitting. Character traits – being different. Character traits – shyness. Gender roles.

Portis, Antoinette. *Froodle* ill. by author. Roaring Brook, 2014. ISBN 978-159643922-1 Subj: Birds. Character traits – individuality. Humorous stories. Noise, sounds. Songs.

Wait ill. by author. Roaring Brook/Neal Porter, 2015. ISBN 978-159643921-4 Subj: Behavior – hurrying. Character traits – patience. Family life – mothers.

Posada, Mia. *Who was here? discovering wild animal tracks* ill. by author. Millbrook, 2014. ISBN 978-146771871-4 Subj: Animals. Nature. Rhyming text.

Potter, Alicia. *Miss Hazeltine's Home for Shy and Fearful Cats* ill. by Birgitta Sif. Knopf, 2015. ISBN 978-038575334-0 Subj: Animals – cats. Character traits – shyness. Emotions – fear.

Potter, Giselle. *Tell me what to dream about* ill. by author. Random/Schwartz & Wade, 2015. ISBN 978-038537423-1 Subj: Bedtime. Dreams. Family life – sisters. Imagination.

Powell-Tuck, Maudie. *Pirates aren't afraid of the dark!* ill. by Alison Edgson. Tiger Tales, 2014. ISBN 978-158925165-6 Subj: Camps, camping.

Emotions – fear. Family life – brothers & sisters. Pirates.

Prasadam-Halls, Smriti. *I love you night and day* ill. by Alison Brown. Bloomsbury, 2014. ISBN 978-161963222-6 Subj: Animals – bears. Animals – rabbits. Emotions – love. Rhyming text.

Preston-Gannon, Frann. *Deep deep sea* ill. by author. IPG/Pavilion, 2015. ISBN 978-184365268-7 Subj: Counting, numbers. Format, unusual – board books. Sea & seashore.

Dinosaur farm ill. by author. Sterling, 2014. ISBN 978-145491132-6 Subj: Careers – farmers. Dinosaurs. Farms.

How to lose a lemur ill. by author. Sterling, 2014. ISBN 978-145491131-9 Subj: Animals – lemurs. Behavior – lost. Friendship.

Pepper and Poe ill. by author. Scholastic/Orchard, 2015. ISBN 978-054568357-9 Subj: Animals – cats. Days of the week, months of the year.

Previn, Stacey. *Find spot!* ill. by author. Little, Brown, 2014. ISBN 978-031621332-5 Subj: Concepts – patterns. Concepts – shape. Format, unusual – toy & movable books. Rhyming text.

Prevot, Franck. *Wangari Maathai: the woman who planted millions of trees* ill. by Aurelia Fronty. Charlesbridge, 2014. ISBN 978-158089626-9 Subj: Ecology. Foreign lands – Kenya. Trees.

Price, Ben Joel. *Earth space moon base* ill. by author. Random House, 2014. ISBN 978-038537311-1 Subj: Animals – monkeys. Careers – astronauts. Rhyming text. Robots. Space & space ships.

Pringle, Laurence. *The secret life of the woolly bear caterpillar* ill. by Joan Paley. Boyds Mills, 2014. ISBN 978-162091000-9 Subj: Insects – butterflies, caterpillars. Insects – moths.

Proimos, James. *Waddle! waddle!* ill. by author. Scholastic, 2015. ISBN 978-054541846-1 Subj: Activities – dancing. Birds – penguins. Friendship.

Provensen, Alice. *Murphy in the city* ill. by author. Simon & Schuster, 2015. ISBN 978-144241971-1 Subj: Animals – dogs. Cities, towns.

Pryor, Katherine. *Zora's zucchini* ill. by Anna Raff. Readers to Eaters, 2015. ISBN 978-098366157-3 Subj: Activities – trading. Behavior – resourcefulness. Food. Gardens, gardening.

Puttock, Simon. *Mouse's first night at Moonlight School* ill. by Ali Pye. Candlewick/Nosy Crow, 2015. ISBN 978-076367607-0 Subj: Animals – mice. Character traits – shyness. School – first day.

Rabinowitz, Alan. *A boy and a jaguar* ill. by Catia Chien. Houghton, 2014. ISBN 978-054787507-1 Subj: Animals – jaguars. Careers – scientists. Disabilities – stuttering. Ecology.

Raczka, Bob. *Joy in Mudville* ill. by Glin Dibley. Carolrhoda, 2014. ISBN 978-076136015-5 Subj: Gender roles. Rhyming text. Sports – baseball.

Santa Clauses: short poems from the North Pole ill. by Chuck Groenink. Carolrhoda, 2014. ISBN 978-146771805-9 Subj: Holidays – Christmas. Poetry. Santa Claus.

Radunsky, Vladimir. *Alphabetabum* (Raschka, Chris)

Ramadier, Cédric. *Help! the wolf is coming!* ill. by Vincent Bourgeau. Gecko, 2015. ISBN 978-192727184-1 Subj: Animals – wolves. Format, unusual – board books. Participation.

Rankin, Laura. *Ruthie and the (not so) very busy day* ill. by author. Bloomsbury, 2014. ISBN 978-159990052-0 Subj: Animals – foxes. Behavior – bad day, bad mood. Emotions – anger.

Rappaport, Doreen. *Frederick's journey: the life of Frederick Douglass* ill. by London Ladd. Disney/Jump at the Sun, 2015. ISBN 978-142311438-3 Subj: Ethnic groups in the U.S. – African Americans. Slavery. U.S. history. Violence, nonviolence.

Raschka, Chris. *Alphabetabum* by Chris Raschka and Vladimir Radunsky ill. with photos. New York Review, 2014. ISBN 978-159017817-1 Subj: ABC books. Poetry.

The cosmobiography of Sun Ra: the sound of joy is enlightening ill. by author. Candlewick, 2014. ISBN 978-076365806-9 Subj: Ethnic groups in the U.S. – African Americans. Music.

Cowy cow ill. by author. Abrams/Appleseed, 2014. ISBN 978-141971055-1 Subj: Animals – bulls, cows. Humorous stories. Imagination.

Crabby crab ill. by author. Abrams/Appleseed, 2014. ISBN 978-141971056-8 Subj: Character traits – appearance. Crustaceans – crabs. Humorous stories.

Give and take ill. by author. Atheneum, 2014. ISBN 978-144241655-0 Subj: Careers – farmers. Farms. Problem solving.

Rash, Andy. *Archie the daredevil penguin* ill. by author. Viking, 2015. ISBN 978-045147123-9 Subj: Birds – penguins. Emotions – fear. Inventions.

Ray, Mary Lyn. *Deer dancer* ill. by Lauren Stringer. Simon & Schuster/Beach Lane, 2014. ISBN 978-144243421-9 Subj: Activities – dancing. Animals – deer.

Go to sleep, little farm ill. by Christopher Silas Neal. Houghton, 2014. ISBN 978-054415014-0 Subj: Bedtime. Farms. Rhyming text.

Goodnight, good dog ill. by Rebecca Malone. Houghton, 2015. ISBN 978-054428612-2 Subj: Animals – dogs. Bedtime.

A lucky author has a dog ill. by Steven Henry. Scholastic, 2015. ISBN 978-054551876-5 Subj: Animals – dogs. Careers – writers.

A violin for Elva ill. by Tricia Tusa. Houghton, 2015. ISBN 978-015225483-4 Subj: Character traits – persistence. Musical instruments – violins. Old age.

Reagan, Jean. *How to babysit a grandma* ill. by Lee Wildish. Knopf, 2014. ISBN 978-038575384-5 Subj: Activities – babysitting. Family life – grandmothers.

How to catch Santa ill. by Lee Wildish. Knopf, 2015. ISBN 978-055349839-4 Subj: Holidays – Christmas. Santa Claus.

How to surprise a dad ill. by Lee Wildish. Knopf, 2015. ISBN 978-055349836-3 Subj: Family life – fathers. Parties.

Reeve, Rosie. *Training Tallulah* ill. by author. Walker, 2014. ISBN 978-080273590-4 Subj: Animals – cats. Humorous stories.

Regan, Dian Curtis. *Space Boy and his dog* ill. by Robert Neubecker. Boyds Mills, 2015. ISBN 978-159078955-1 Subj: Animals – dogs. Family life – brothers & sisters. Imagination. Sibling rivalry. Space & space ships.

Reynolds, Aaron. *Here comes Destructosaurus!* ill. by Jeremy Tankard. Chronicle, 2014. ISBN 978-145212454-4 Subj: Behavior – messy. Emotions – anger. Monsters.

Nerdy birdy ill. by Matt Davies. Roaring Brook/Neal Porter, 2015. ISBN 978-162672127-2 Subj: Birds. Character traits – kindness. Friendship.

Reynolds, Paul A. *Going places* (Reynolds, Peter H.)

Reynolds, Peter H. *Going places* by Peter H. Reynolds and Paul A. Reynolds ill. by Peter H. Reyn-olds. Atheneum, 2014. ISBN 978-144246608-1 Subj: Behavior – resourcefulness. Character traits – cleverness. Character traits – cooperation. Contests. Inventions. Sports – racing.

Rhodes-Pitts, Sharifa. *Jake makes a world: Jacob Lawrence, a young artist in Harlem* ill. by Christopher Myers. Museum of Modern Art, 2015. ISBN 978-087070965-4 Subj: Activities – painting. Art. Careers – artists. Ethnic groups in the U.S. – African Americans. U.S. history.

Richards, Dan. *The problem with not being scared of monsters* ill. by Robert Neubecker. Boyds Mills, 2014. ISBN 978-162091024-5 Subj: Behavior – misbehavior. Friendship. Monsters.

Richards, Keith. *Gus and me: the story of my grand-dad and my first guitar* ill. by Theodora Richards. Little, Brown, 2014. ISBN 978-031632065-8 Subj: Careers – musicians. Family life – grandfathers. Musical instruments – guitars.

Riecherter, Daryn. *The Cambodian dancer: Sophany's gift of hope* ill. by Christy Hale. Tuttle, 2015. ISBN 978-080484516-8 Subj: Activities – dancing. Ethnic groups in the U.S. – Cambodian Americans. Foreign lands – Cambodia.

Riehle, Mary Ann McCabe. *The little kids' table* ill. by Mary Reaves. Sleeping Bear, 2015. ISBN 978-158536913-3 Subj: Etiquette. Food. Rhyming text.

Riggs, Kate. *Time to build* ill. by Laszlo Kubinyi. Creative Editions, 2015. ISBN 978-156846271-4 Subj: Format, unusual – board books. Tools.

Rim, Sujean. *Birdie's big-girl hair* ill. by author. Little, Brown, 2014. ISBN 978-031622791-9 Subj: Character traits – individuality. Family life – mothers. Hair.

Birdie's first day of school ill. by author. Little, Brown, 2015. ISBN 978-031640745-8 Subj: Emotions – fear. School – first day.

Ringgold, Faith. *Harlem Renaissance party* ill. by author. Amistad, 2015. ISBN 978-006057911-1 Subj: Careers – musicians. Careers – writers. Ethnic groups in the U.S. – African Americans. U.S. history.

Ritchie, Scot. *Look where we live!* ill. by author. Kids Can, 2015. ISBN 978-177138102-4 Subj: Communities, neighborhoods.

Roberton, Fiona. *Cuckoo!* ill. by author. Putnam, 2014. ISBN 978-039916497-2 Subj: Birds – cuckoos. Communication. Language.

Roberts, Jillian. *Where do babies come from? our first talk about birth* ill. by Cindy Revell. Orca, 2015.

ISBN 978-145980942-0 Subj: Babies, toddlers. Birth. Sex instruction.

Roberts, Justin. *The smallest girl in the smallest grade* ill. by Christian Robinson. Putnam, 2014. ISBN 978-039925743-8 Subj: Behavior – bullying, teasing. Character traits – kindness. Character traits – smallness. Concepts – size. Rhyming text.

Robinson, Michelle. *How to wash a woolly mammoth* ill. by Kate Hindley. Holt, 2014. ISBN 978-080509966-9 Subj: Activities – bathing. Animals – woolly mammoths. Humorous stories.

There's a lion in my cornflakes ill. by Jim Field. Bloomsbury, 2015. ISBN 978-080273836-3 Subj: Animals. Food. Humorous stories.

Robinson, Sharon. *Under the same sun* ill. by A. G. Ford. Scholastic, 2014. ISBN 978-054516672-0 Subj: Birthdays. Family life. Family life – grandmothers. Foreign lands – Tanzania.

Rocco, John. *Blizzard* ill. by author. Hyperion, 2014. ISBN 978-142317865-1 Subj: Character traits – helpfulness. Weather – blizzards. Weather – snow.

Rockliff, Mara. *Chik chak Shabbat* ill. by Kyrsten Brooker. Candlewick, 2014. ISBN 978-076365528-0 Subj: Behavior – sharing. Communities, neighborhoods. Food. Illness. Jewish culture.

The Grudge Keeper ill. by Eliza Wheeler. Peachtree, 2014. ISBN 978-156145729-8 Subj: Behavior. Behavior – forgiving. Emotions.

Rockwell, Anne. *My spring robin* ill. by Harlow Rockwell and Lizzy Rockwell. Simon & Schuster, 2015. ISBN 978-148141137-0 Subj: Birds – robins. Flowers. Seasons – spring.

Rockwell, Lizzy. *Plants feed me* ill. by author. Holiday House, 2014. ISBN 978-082342526-6 Subj: Food. Plants.

Roderick, Stacey. *Dinosaurs from head to tail* ill. by Kwanchai Moriya. Kids Can, 2015. ISBN 978-177138044-7 Subj: Dinosaurs. Picture puzzles.

Rolli, Jennifer Hanson. *Just one more* ill. by author. Viking, 2014. ISBN 978-067001563-4 Subj: Behavior – greed. Character traits – selfishness.

Root, Phyllis. *Plant a pocket of prairie* ill. by Betsy Bowen. Univ. of Minnesota, 2014. ISBN 978-081667980-5 Subj: Nature. Plants.

Roques, Dominique. *Sleep tight, Anna Banana!* ill. by Alexis Dormal. First Second, 2014. ISBN 978-162672019-0 Subj: Bedtime. Noise, sounds. Toys.

Roscoe, Lily. *The night parade* ill. by David Walker. Orchard, 2014. ISBN 978-054539623-3 Subj: Bedtime. Night. Parades. Rhyming text.

Rose, Caroline Starr. *Over in the wetlands: a hurricane-on-the-bayou story* ill. by Rob Dunlavey. Random/Schwartz & Wade, 2015. ISBN 978-044981016-3 Subj: Animals. Birds. Swamps. Weather – hurricanes.

Rose, Nancy. *Merry Christmas, squirrels!* photos by author. Little, Brown, 2015. ISBN 978-031630257-9 Subj: Animals – squirrels. Family life – cousins. Holidays – Christmas.

The secret life of squirrels photos by author. Little, Brown, 2014. ISBN 978-031637027-1 Subj: Animals – squirrels. Family life – cousins.

Rosen, Michael. *The bus is for us!* ill. by Gillian Tyler. Candlewick, 2015. ISBN 978-076366983-6 Subj: Buses. Rhyming text. Transportation.

Send for a superhero! ill. by Katharine McEwen. Candlewick, 2014. ISBN 978-076366438-1 Subj: Bedtime. Books, reading. Imagination.

Rosenberg, Liz. *What James said* ill. by Matthew Myers. Roaring Brook, 2015. ISBN 978-159643908-5 Subj: Behavior – gossip, rumors. Behavior – misunderstanding. Friendship.

Rosenstock, Barb. *The noisy paint box: the color and sounds of Kandinsky's abstract art* ill. by Mary GrandPré. Knopf, 2014. ISBN 978-0307978-48-6 Subj: Art. Caldecott award honor books. Careers – artists.

The streak: how Joe DiMaggio became America's hero ill. by Terry Widener. Boyds Mills, 2014. ISBN 978-159078992-6 Subj: Sports – baseball.

Rosenthal, Amy Krouse. *Awake beautiful child* ill. by Gracia Lam. McSweeneys/McMullens, 2015. ISBN 978-193807392-2 Subj: ABC books. Day.

Friendshape ill. by Tom Lichtenheld. Scholastic, 2015. ISBN 978-054543682-3 Subj: Concepts – shape. Friendship.

I wish you more ill. by Tom Lichtenheld. Chronicle, 2015. ISBN 978-145212699-9 Subj: Behavior – wishing.

Little Miss, big sis ill. by Peter H. Reynolds. Harper, 2015. ISBN 978-006230203-8 Subj: Babies, toddlers. Family life – new sibling. Family life – sisters. Rhyming text.

Uni the unicorn ill. by Brigette Barrager. Random House, 2014. ISBN 978-038537555-9 Subj: Friendship. Mythical creatures – unicorns.

Rosenthal, Betsy R. *An ambush of tigers: a wild gathering of collective nouns* ill. by Jago. Lerner/Millbrook, 2015. ISBN 978-146771464-8 Subj: Animals. Language. Rhyming text.

Rosenthal, Marc. *Big bot, small bot: a book of robot opposites* ill. by author. POW!, 2015. ISBN 978-

157687750-0 Subj: Concepts – opposites. Format, unusual – toy & movable books. Robots.

Ross, Tony. *I feel sick!* ill. by author. Lerner, 2015. ISBN 978-146775797-3 Subj: Illness. Royalty – princesses.

Rita's rhino ill. by author. Lerner, 2015. ISBN 978-146776315-8 Subj: Animals – rhinoceros. Behavior – hiding things. Pets.

Rotner, Shelley. *Families* by Shelley Rotner and Sheila M. Kelly; photos by author. Holiday House, 2015. ISBN 978-082343053-6 Subj: Family life. Family life – same-sex parents. Family life – single-parent families. Family life – stepfamilies.

Roussen, Jean. *Beautiful birds* ill. by Emmanuelle Walker. Flying Eye, 2015. ISBN 978-190926329-1 Subj: ABC books. Birds.

Rowand, Phyllis. *It is night* ill. by Laura Dronzek. HarperCollins/Greenwillow, 2014. ISBN 978-006225024-7 Subj: Animals. Bedtime. Toys.

Royer, Danielle. *All my stripes: a story for children with autism* (Rudolph, Shaina)

Rozier, Lucy Margaret. *Jackrabbit McCabe and the electric telegraph* ill. by Leo Espinosa. Random/Schwartz & Wade, 2015. ISBN 978-038537843-7 Subj: Concepts – speed. Contests. Tall tales.

Rubin, Adam. *Big bad bubble* ill. by Daniel Salmieri. Clarion, 2014. ISBN 978-054404549-1 Subj: Bubbles. Emotions – fear. Humorous stories. Monsters.

Robo-Sauce ill. by Daniel Salmieri. Dial, 2015. ISBN 978-052542887-9 Subj: Format, unusual – toy & movable books. Magic. Robots.

Ruddell, Deborah. *The popcorn astronauts: and other biteable rhymes* ill. by Joan Rankin. Simon & Schuster/Margaret K. McElderry, 2015. ISBN 978-144246555-8 Subj: Food. Poetry. Seasons.

Rudge, Leila. *A perfect place for Ted* ill. by author. Candlewick, 2014. ISBN 978-076366781-8 Subj: Animals – dogs. Behavior – needing someone. Behavior – unnoticed, unseen. Character traits – individuality.

Rudolph, Shaina. *All my stripes: a story for children with autism* by Shaina Rudolph and Danielle Royer ill. by Jennifer Zivoin. Magination, 2015. ISBN 978-143381917-9 Subj: Animals – zebras. Disabilities – autism. Family life – mothers. Self-concept.

Rudy, Maggie. *I wish I had a pet* ill. by author. Simon & Schuster/Beach Lane, 2014. ISBN 978-144245332-6 Subj: Animals – mice. Character traits – responsibility. Pets.

Russell, Natalie. *Lost for words* ill. by author. Peachtree, 2014. ISBN 978-156145739-7 Subj: Activities – drawing. Animals – tapirs. Character traits – individuality.

Russell-Brown, Katheryn. *Little Melba and her big trombone* ill. by Frank Morrison. Lee & Low, 2014. ISBN 978-160060898-8 Subj: Ethnic groups in the U.S. – African Americans. Gender roles. Music. Musical instruments – trombones.

Russo, Marisabina. *Little Bird takes a bath* ill. by author. Random/Schwartz & Wade, 2015. ISBN 978-038537014-1 Subj: Activities – bathing. Birds. Cities, towns. Weather – rain.

Sophie sleeps over ill. by author. Roaring Brook, 2014. ISBN 978-159643933-7 Subj: Animals – rabbits. Friendship. Sleepovers.

Ruth, Greg. *Coming home* ill. by author. Feiwel and Friends, 2014. ISBN 978-125005547-7 Subj: Careers – military. Family life – mothers. War.

Ruzzier, Sergio. *A letter for Leo* ill. by author. Clarion, 2014. ISBN 978-054422360-8 Subj: Animals – weasels. Birds. Careers – postal workers. Emotions – loneliness. Friendship. Letters, cards.

Too busy ill. by author. Disney/Hyperion, 2014. ISBN 978-142315961-2 Subj: Animals – bears. Friendship. Insects – bees.

Two mice ill. by author. Clarion, 2015. ISBN 978-054430209-9 Subj: Animals – mice. Boats, ships.

Ryan, Candace. *Ewe and Aye* ill. by Stephanie Ruble. Hyperion, 2014. ISBN 978-142317591-9 Subj: Activities – flying. Animals – lemurs. Animals – sheep. Character traits – cooperation.

Saab, Julie. *Little Lola* ill. by David Gothard. Greenwillow, 2014. ISBN 978-006227457-1 Subj: Animals – cats. School.

Saaf, Donald. *The ABC animal orchestra* ill. by author. Holt/Christy Ottaviano, 2015. ISBN 978-080509072-7 Subj: ABC books. Animals. Musical instruments. Musical instruments – orchestras.

Sabuda, Robert. *The dragon and the knight: a pop-up misadventure* ill. by author. Simon & Schuster, 2014. ISBN 978-141696081-2 Subj: Dragons. Folk & fairy tales. Format, unusual – toy & movable books. Knights.

Sadler, Marilyn. *Alice from Dallas* ill. by Ard Hoyt. Abrams, 2014. ISBN 978-141970790-2 Subj: Cowboys, cowgirls. Friendship.

Tony Baroni loves macaroni ill. by Lucie Crovatto. Blue Apple, 2014. ISBN 978-160905293-5 Subj: Family life – grandmothers. Food. Rhyming text.

Salas, Laura Purdie. *Water can be . . .* ill. by Violeta Dabija. Millbrook, 2014. ISBN 978-146770591-2 Subj: Poetry. Water.

Salerno, Steven. *Wild child* ill. by author. Abrams, 2015. ISBN 978-141971662-1 Subj: Babies, toddlers. Jungle.

Saltzberg, Barney. *Chengdu could not, would not, fall asleep* ill. by author. Disney/Hyperion, 2014. ISBN 978-142316721-1 Subj: Animals – pandas. Bedtime. Sleep.

Inside this book (are three books) ill. by author. Abrams/Appleseed, 2015. ISBN 978-141971487-0 Subj: Activities – writing. Books, reading. Children as authors. Family life – brothers & sisters.

Tea with Grandpa ill. by author. Roaring Brook, 2014. ISBN 978-159643894-1 Subj: Computers. Family life – grandfathers. Parties. Rhyming text. Technology.

Salzano, Tammi. *I love you just the way you are* ill. by Ada Grey. Tiger Tales, 2014. ISBN 978-158925161-8 Subj: Emotions – love. Family life – mothers. Rhyming text.

Samuels, Barbara. *Fred's beds* ill. by author. Farrar, 2014. ISBN 978-037431813-0 Subj: Animals – dogs. Birthdays. Furniture – beds. Parties. Sleep.

Sanders, Rob. *Outer space bedtime race* ill. by Brian Won. Random House, 2015. ISBN 978-038538647-0 Subj: Aliens. Bedtime. Planets. Rhyming text.

Sanderson, Ruth. *A castle full of cats* ill. by author. Random House, 2015. ISBN 978-044981307-2 Subj: Animals – cats. Rhyming text. Royalty.

Sandu, Anca. *Churchill's tale of tails* ill. by author. Peachtree, 2014. ISBN 978-156145738-0 Subj: Anatomy – tails. Animals – pigs. Friendship.

Santat, Dan. *The adventures of Beekle: the unimaginary friend* ill. by author. Little, Brown, 2014. ISBN 978-031619998-8 Subj: Caldecott award books. Friendship. Imagination – imaginary friends.

Sarcone-Roach, Julia. *The bear ate your sandwich* ill. by author. Knopf, 2015. ISBN 978-037585860-4 Subj: Animals – bears. Animals – dogs. Cities, towns. Food.

Sassi, Laura. *Goodnight, Ark* ill. by Jane Chapman. Zondervan, 2014. ISBN 978-031073784-1 Subj: Animals. Bedtime. Religion – Noah. Rhyming text.

Sattler, Jennifer. *A Chick 'n' Pug Christmas* ill. by author. Bloomsbury, 2014. ISBN 978-159990602-7 Subj: Animals – dogs. Birds – chickens, roosters. Holidays – Christmas.

Pig kahuna: who's that pig? ill. by author. Bloomsbury, 2015. ISBN 978-161963632-3 Subj: Animals – pigs. Character traits – shyness. Sea & seashore – beaches.

Pig kahuna pirates! ill. by author. Bloomsbury, 2014. ISBN 978-161963200-4 Subj: Activities – playing. Animals – pigs. Behavior – bad day, bad mood. Family life – brothers. Pirates. Sea & seashore – beaches.

Sauer, Tammi. *Ginny Louise and the school showdown* ill. by Lynn Munsinger. Disney/Hyperion, 2015. ISBN 978-142316853-9 Subj: Animals. Animals – hedgehogs. Behavior – bullying, teasing. Character traits – kindness. Character traits – meanness. Character traits – optimism. School.

Your alien ill. by Goro Fujita. Sterling, 2015. ISBN 978-145491129-6 Subj: Aliens. Family life. Friendship.

Savage, Stephen. *Seven orange pumpkins* ill. by author. Dial, 2015. ISBN 978-080374138-6 Subj: Counting, numbers. Format, unusual – board books. Holidays – Halloween.

Supertruck ill. by author. Roaring Brook/Neal Porter, 2015. ISBN 978-159643821-7 Subj: Careers – sanitation workers. Machines. Trucks. Weather – snow.

Where's Walrus? and Penguin? ill. by author. Scholastic, 2015. ISBN 978-054540295-8 Subj: Animals – walruses. Behavior – running away. Birds – penguins. Careers – zookeepers. Wordless. Zoos.

Sayre, April Pulley. *Raindrops roll* ill. by author. Simon & Schuster/Beach Lane, 2015. ISBN 978-148142064-8 Subj: Water. Weather – rain.

Woodpecker wham! ill. by Steve Jenkins. Holt, 2015. ISBN 978-080508842-7 Subj: Birds – woodpeckers. Nature.

Sayres, Brianna Caplan. *Tiara Saurus Rex* ill. by Mike Boldt. Bloomsbury, 2015. ISBN 978-161963263-9 Subj: Contests. Dinosaurs. Rhyming text.

Scanlon, Elizabeth Garton. *The good-pie party* ill. by Kady MacDonald Denton. Scholastic, 2014. ISBN 978-054544870-3 Subj: Food. Friendship. Moving. Parties.

Schaefer, Lola M. *One busy day: a story for big brothers and sisters* ill. by Jessica Meserve. Disney/

Hyperion, 2014. ISBN 978-142317112-6 Subj: Activities – playing. Family life – brothers & sisters. Imagination.

Schatell, Brian. *Owl boy* ill. by author. Holiday House, 2015. ISBN 978-082343208-0 Subj: Birds – owls. Camps, camping.

Scheffler, Axel. *Axel Scheffler's Flip flap safari* ill. by author. Candlewick, 2015. ISBN 978-076367605-6 Subj: Animals. Format, unusual – toy & movable books. Rhyming text.

Pip and Posy: the bedtime frog ill. by author. Candlewick, 2014. ISBN 978-076367068-9 Subj: Animals – mice. Animals – rabbits. Bedtime. Toys.

Schertle, Alice. *Such a little mouse* ill. by Stephanie Yue. Scholastic/Orchard, 2015. ISBN 978-054564929-2 Subj: Animals – mice. Seasons.

Schiffer, Miriam B. *Stella brings the family* ill. by Holly Clifton-Brown. Chronicle, 2015. ISBN 978-145211190-2 Subj: Family life – same-sex parents. Holidays – Mother's Day. LGBTQ issues.

Schindel, John. *The babies and doggies book* by John Schindel and Molly Woodward ill. with photos. Houghton Mifflin Harcourt, 2015. ISBN 978-054444477-5 Subj: Animals – dogs. Babies, toddlers. Format, unusual – board books.

Schmid, Paul. *Oliver and his egg* ill. by author. Disney/Hyperion, 2014. ISBN 978-142317573-5 Subj: Eggs. Friendship. Imagination.

Schneider, Josh. *Everybody sleeps (but not Fred)* ill. by author. Clarion, 2015. ISBN 978-054433924-8 Subj: Animals. Bedtime. Behavior – misbehavior. Rhyming text.

Princess Sparkle-Heart gets a makeover ill. by author. Clarion, 2014. ISBN 978-054414228-2 Subj: Animals – dogs. Emotions – envy, jealousy. Friendship. Toys – dolls.

Schofield-Morrison, Connie. *I got the rhythm* ill. by Frank Morrison. Bloomsbury, 2014. ISBN 978-161963178-6 Subj: Activities – dancing. Ethnic groups in the U.S. – African Americans. Noise, sounds.

Schoonmaker, Elizabeth. *Square cat ABC* ill. by author. Aladdin, 2014. ISBN 978-144249895-2 Subj: ABC books. Animals – cats. Animals – mice. Gardens, gardening.

Schubert, Ingrid. *There is a crocodile under my bed* ill. by Dieter Schubert. Lemniscaat, 2015. ISBN 978-193595408-8 Subj: Bedtime. Reptiles – alligators, crocodiles.

Schwartz, Amy. *I can't wait!* ill. by author. Simon & Schuster/Beach Lane, 2015. ISBN 978-144248231-

9 Subj: Character traits – patience. Family life. Friendship.

100 things that make me happy ill. by author. Abrams/Appleseed, 2014. ISBN 978-141970518-2 Subj: Emotions – happiness. Language. Rhyming text.

Schwartz, Corey Rosen. *Ninja Red Riding Hood* ill. by Dan Santat. Putnam, 2014. ISBN 978-039916354-8 Subj: Animals – wolves. Behavior – talking to strangers. Folk & fairy tales. Rhyming text. Sports – martial arts.

Schwarz, Viviane. *Is there a dog in this book?* ill. by author. Candlewick, 2014. ISBN 978-076366991-1 Subj: Animals – cats. Animals – dogs. Format, unusual – toy & movable books.

Scieszka, Jon. *Race from A to Z* ill. by David Shannon and Loren Long, et al. Simon & Schuster, 2014. ISBN 978-141694136-1 Subj: ABC books. Sports – racing. Trucks.

Scotton, Rob. *Scaredy-cat, Splat!* ill. by author. Harper, 2015. ISBN 978-006236897-3 Subj: Animals – cats. Clothing – costumes. Holidays – Halloween.

Sebe, Masayuki. *100 hungry monkeys!* ill. by author. Kids Can, 2014. ISBN 978-177138045-4 Subj: Animals – monkeys. Counting, numbers. Food.

Seeger, Laura Vaccaro. *Dog and Bear: tricks and treats* ill. by author. Roaring Brook/Neal Porter, 2014. ISBN 978-159643632-9 Subj: Animals – dogs. Friendship. Holidays – Halloween. Toys – bears.

Sehgal, Kabir. *A bucket of blessings* by Kabir Sehgal and Surishtha Sehgal ill. by Jing Jing Tsong. Simon & Schuster/Beach Lane, 2014. ISBN 978-144245870-3 Subj: Animals – monkeys. Birds – peacocks, peahens. Folk & fairy tales. Foreign lands – India. Weather – rain.

The wheels on the tuk tuk by Kabir Sehgal and Surishtha Sehgal ill. by Jess Golden. Simon & Schuster/Beach Lane, 2015. ISBN 978-148144831-4 Subj: Automobiles. Foreign lands – India. Songs. Taxis.

Sehgal, Surishtha. *A bucket of blessings* (Sehgal, Kabir)

The wheels on the tuk tuk (Sehgal, Kabir)

Seuss, Dr. *Horton and the Kwuggerbug and more lost stories* ill. by Dr. Seuss. Random House, 2014. ISBN 978-038538298-4 Subj: Humorous stories. Rhyming text.

What pet should I get? ill. by Dr. Seuss. Random House, 2015. ISBN 978-055352426-0 Subj: Behavior – indecision. Pets. Rhyming text.

Shannon, George. *Hands say love* ill. by Taeeun Yoo. Little, Brown, 2014. ISBN 978-031608479-6 Subj: Anatomy – hands. Emotions – love. Rhyming text.

One family ill. by Blanca Gomez. Farrar, 2015. ISBN 978-037430003-6 Subj: Counting, numbers. Ethnic groups in the U.S. Family life.

Shaw, Nancy. *Sheep go to sleep* ill. by Margot Apple. Houghton Mifflin Harcourt, 2015. ISBN 978-054430989-0 Subj: Animals – dogs. Animals – sheep. Bedtime. Sleep.

Shaw, Stephanie. *A cookie for Santa* ill. by Bruno Robert. Sleeping Bear, 2014. ISBN 978-158536883-9 Subj: Food. Holidays – Christmas. Rhyming text. Santa Claus.

Shea, Bob. *Dinosaur vs. Mommy* ill. by author. Disney/Hyperion, 2015. ISBN 978-142316086-1 Subj: Behavior – misbehavior. Dinosaurs. Family life – mothers.

Dinosaur vs. school ill. by author. Disney/Hyperion, 2014. ISBN 978-142316087-8 Subj: Dinosaurs. School – nursery.

Kid Sheriff and the terrible Toads ill. by Lane Smith. Roaring Brook, 2014. ISBN 978-159643975-7 Subj: Careers – sheriffs. Crime. Dinosaurs. Frogs & toads. U.S. history – frontier & pioneer life.

Sheehan, Kevin. *The dandelion's tale* ill. by Rob Dunlavey. Random/Schwartz & Wade, 2014. ISBN 978-037587032-3 Subj: Birds – sparrows. Friendship. Memories, memory. Plants.

Sheehy, Shawn. *Welcome to the neighborwood* ill. by author. Candlewick, 2015. ISBN 978-076366594-4 Subj: Animals. Format, unusual – toy & movable books. Homes, houses.

Shepherd, Jessica. *Grandma* ill. by author. Child's Play, 2014. ISBN 978-184643602-4 Subj: Behavior – forgetfulness. Family life – grandmothers. Old age.

Sherry, Kevin. *Turtle Island* ill. by author. Dial, 2014. ISBN 978-080373391-6 Subj: Animals. Emotions – loneliness. Friendship. Islands. Reptiles – turtles, tortoises.

Shields, Carol Diggory. *Baby's got the blues* ill. by Lauren Tobia. Candlewick, 2014. ISBN 978-076363260-1 Subj: Babies, toddlers. Music. Rhyming text.

Shingu, Susumu. *Traveling butterflies* ill. by author. Owlkids, 2015. ISBN 978-177147148-0 Subj: Insects – butterflies, caterpillars. Metamorphosis. Migration.

Shulevitz, Uri. *Troto and the trucks* ill. by author. Farrar, 2015. ISBN 978-037430080-7 Subj: Auto-

mobiles. Behavior – bullying, teasing. Character traits – smallness. Contests. Sports – racing. Trucks.

Shuttlewood, Craig. *Through the town* ill. by author. Little Bee, 2015. ISBN 978-149980076-0 Subj: Cities, towns. Format, unusual – board books. Reptiles – snakes.

Who's in the tree? ill. by author. Sterling, 2014. ISBN 978-145491193-7 Subj: Animals. Format, unusual – toy & movable books. Rhyming text.

Shyba, Jessica. *Naptime with Theo and Beau* photos by author. Feiwel and Friends, 2015. ISBN 978-125005906-2 Subj: Animals – dogs. Pets. Sleep.

Siddals, Mary McKenna. *Shivery shades of Halloween: a spooky book of colors* ill. by Jimmy Pickering. Random House, 2014. ISBN 978-038536999-2 Subj: Concepts – color. Holidays – Halloween. Rhyming text.

Sidman, Joyce. *Winter bees and other poems of the cold* ill. by Rick Allen. Harcourt, 2014. ISBN 978-054790650-8 Subj: Animals. Nature. Poetry. Seasons – winter.

Sierra, Judy. *E-I-E-I-O: how Old MacDonald got his farm* ill. by Matthew Myers. Candlewick, 2014. ISBN 978-076366043-7 Subj: Animals. Farms. Gardens, gardening. Rhyming text.

Sif, Birgitta. *Frances Dean who loved to dance and dance* ill. by author. Candlewick, 2014. ISBN 978-076367306-2 Subj: Activities – dancing. Character traits – confidence.

Sill, Cathryn. *Forests* ill. by John Sill. Peachtree, 2014. ISBN 978-156145734-2 Subj: Animals. Ecology. Forest, woods.

Simon, Francesca. *Hello, Moon!* ill. by Ben Cort. Scholastic, 2014. ISBN 978-054564795-3 Subj: Bedtime. Moon.

Simon, Richard. *Oskar and the eight blessings* by Richard Simon and Tanya Simon ill. by Mark Siegel. Roaring Brook, 2015. ISBN 978-159643949-8 Subj: Character traits – kindness. Holidays – Hanukkah. Holocaust. Jewish culture.

Simon, Tanya. *Oskar and the eight blessings* (Simon, Richard)

Sims, Nat. *Peekaboo barn* ill. by Nathan Tabor. Candlewick, 2014. ISBN 978-076367557-8 Subj: Farms. Format, unusual – board books. Format, unusual – toy & movable books. Noise, sounds.

Singer, Isaac Bashevis. *The parakeet named Dreidel* ill. by Suzanne Raphael Berkson. Farrar, 2015. ISBN 978-037430094-4 Subj: Behavior –

lost & found possessions. Birds – parakeets, parrots. Holidays – Hanukkah. Jewish culture.

Singer, Marilyn. *I'm gonna climb a mountain in my patent leather shoes* ill. by Lynne Avril. Abrams, 2014. ISBN 978-141970336-2 Subj: Camps, camping. Family life – brothers & sisters. Rhyming text. Self-concept.

Tallulah's tap shoes ill. by Alexandra Boiger. Clarion, 2015. ISBN 978-054423687-5 Subj: Activities – dancing. Ballet. Character traits – cooperation. Character traits – perseverance.

Singleton, Linda Joy. *Snow dog, sand dog* ill. by Jess Golden. Albert Whitman, 2014. ISBN 978-080757536-9 Subj: Animals – dogs. Behavior – resourcefulness. Character traits – cleverness. Illness – allergies. Seasons.

Sirett, Dawn. *Happy birthday Sophie!* ill. by Polly Appleton. DK, 2015. ISBN 978-146543256-8 Subj: Animals – giraffes. Birthdays. Format, unusual – toy & movable books.

Sís, Peter. *Ice cream summer* ill. by author. Scholastic, 2015. ISBN 978-054573161-4 Subj: Activities – writing. Family life – grandfathers. Food. Letters, cards. Seasons – summer.

The pilot and the Little Prince: the life of Antoine de Saint-Exupery ill. by author. Farrar, 2014. ISBN 978-037438069-4 Subj: Careers – airplane pilots. Careers – writers. Foreign lands – France.

Sisson, Stephanie Roth. *Star stuff: Carl Sagan and the mysteries of the cosmos* ill. by author. Roaring Brook, 2014. ISBN 978-159643960-3 Subj: Astronomy. Careers – astronomers.

Skofield, James. *Bear and Bird* ill. by Jennifer Thermes. Sleeping Bear, 2014. ISBN 978-158536835-8 Subj: Animals – bears. Birds. Death. Emotions – grief.

Slack, Michael. *Wazdot?* ill. by author. Disney/Hyperion, 2014. ISBN 978-142318347-1 Subj: Aliens. Farms.

Slade, Suzanne. *Friends for freedom: the story of Susan B. Anthony and Frederick Douglass* ill. by Nicole Tadgell. Charlesbridge, 2014. ISBN 978-158089568-2 Subj: Ethnic groups in the U.S. – African Americans. Friendship. Gender roles. U.S. history.

With books and bricks: how Booker T. Washington built a school ill. by Nicole Tadgell. Albert Whitman, 2014. ISBN 978-080750897-8 Subj: Books, reading. Character traits – perseverance. Ethnic groups in the U.S. – African Americans. Prejudice. School.

Slegers, Liesbet. *Chefs and what they do* ill. by author. Clavis, 2014. ISBN 978-160537179-5 Subj: Careers – chefs, cooks. Restaurants.

Smallman, Steve. *Hiccupotamus* ill. by Ada Grey. Tiger Tales, 2015. ISBN 978-158925171-7 Subj: Animals. Animals – hippopotamuses. Jungle. Music. Noise, sounds. Rhyming text.

Scowl ill. by Richard Watson. Tiger Tales, 2014. ISBN 978-158925155-7 Subj: Behavior – bad day, bad mood. Birds – owls. Character traits – being different.

Smith, A. J. *Even monsters* ill. by A. J. Smith. Sourcebooks/Jabberwocky, 2014. ISBN 978-140228652-0 Subj: Emotions. Monsters.

Smith, Charles R. *28 days: moments in black history that changed the world* ill. by Shane W. Evans. Roaring Brook/Neal Porter, 2015. ISBN 978-159643820-0 Subj: Ethnic groups in the U.S. – African Americans. Poetry. U.S. history. Violence, nonviolence.

Smith, Danna. *Mother Goose's pajama party* ill. by Virginia Allyn. Doubleday, 2015. ISBN 978-055349756-4 Subj: Bedtime. Nursery rhymes. Sleepovers.

Smith, Matthew Clark. *Small wonders: Jean-Henri Fabre and his world of insects* ill. by Giuliano Ferri. Amazon/Two Lions, 2015. ISBN 978-147782632-4 Subj: Careers – naturalists. Foreign lands – France. Insects. Nature.

Snicket, Lemony. *29 myths on the Swinster Pharmacy* ill. by Lisa Brown. McSweeney's, 2014. ISBN 978-193807378-6 Subj: Family life – brothers & sisters. Mystery stories.

Soffer, Gilad. *Duck's vacation* ill. by author. Feiwel and Friends, 2015. ISBN 978-125005647-4 Subj: Activities – vacationing. Birds – ducks.

Sohn, Tania. *Socks!* ill. by author. Kane/Miller, 2014. ISBN 978-161067244-3 Subj: Clothing – socks. Imagination.

Soman, David. *Ladybug Girl and the best ever playdate* by David Soman and Jacky Davis ill. by David Soman. Dial, 2015. ISBN 978-080374030-3 Subj: Activities – playing. Friendship. Imagination. Toys.

Ladybug Girl and the dress-up dilemma by David Soman and Jacky Davis ill. by David Soman. Dial, 2014. ISBN 978-080373584-2 Subj: Clothing – costumes. Holidays – Halloween.

Three bears in a boat ill. by author. Dial, 2014. ISBN 978-080373993-2 Subj: Animals – bears. Behavior – misbehavior. Boats, ships.

Spector, Todd. *How to pee: potty training for boys* ill. by Arree Chung. Holt, 2015. ISBN 978-080509773-3 Subj: Hygiene. Toilet training.

Sperring, Mark. *Max and the won't go to bed show* ill. by Sarah Warburton. Scholastic, 2014. ISBN 978-054570822-7 Subj: Bedtime. Magic.

Spinelli, Eileen. *Thankful* ill. by Archie Preston. HarperCollins Zonderkidz, 2015. ISBN 978-031000088-4 Subj: Character traits – generosity. Character traits – kindness. Rhyming text.

Spinelli, Jerry. *Mama Seeton's whistle* ill. by LeUyen Pham. Little, Brown, 2015. ISBN 978-031612217-7 Subj: Activities – whistling. Family life. Family life – mothers.

Spires, Ashley. *The most magnificent thing* ill. by author. Kids Can, 2014. ISBN 978-155453704-4 Subj: Animals – dogs. Behavior – resourcefulness. Character traits – ambition. Character traits – persistence. Emotions – anger.

Srinivasan, Divya. *Little Owl's day* ill. by author. Viking, 2014. ISBN 978-067001650-1 Subj: Birds – owls. Day. Forest, woods.

Staake, Bob. *My pet book* ill. by author. Random House, 2014. ISBN 978-038537312-8 Subj: Books, reading. Pets. Rhyming text.

Stainton, Sue. *I love dogs!* ill. by Bob Staake. HarperCollins/Katherine Tegen, 2014. ISBN 978-006117057-7 Subj: Animals – dogs. Rhyming text.

Staniszewski, Anna. *Power down, Little Robot* ill. by Tim Zeltner. Holt, 2015. ISBN 978-162779125-0 Subj: Bedtime. Robots.

Stanton, Elizabeth Rose. *Henny* ill. by author. Simon & Schuster/Paula Wiseman, 2014. ISBN 978-144248436-8 Subj: Birds – chickens, roosters. Character traits – being different. Character traits – individuality. Self-concept.

Stanton, Karen. *Monday, Wednesday, and every other weekend* ill. by author. Feiwel and Friends, 2014. ISBN 978-125003489-2 Subj: Animals – dogs. Divorce. Homes, houses.

Starishevsky, Jill. *My body belongs to me* ill. by Angela Padron. Free Spirit, 2014. ISBN 978-157542461-3 Subj: Child abuse. Health & fitness. Safety. Self-concept. Senses – touch.

Stark, Dan. *Izzy and Oscar* (Estes, Allison)

Stead, Philip C. *Lenny and Lucy* ill. by Erin E Stead. Roaring Brook/Neal Porter, 2015. ISBN 978-159643932-0 Subj: Friendship. Moving.

Sebastian and the balloon ill. by author. Roaring Brook, 2014. ISBN 978-159643930-6 Subj: Activities – ballooning. Activities – traveling.

Special delivery ill. by Matthew Cordell. Roaring Brook, 2015. ISBN 978-159643931-3 Subj: Activities – traveling. Animals – elephants.

Steggall, Susan. *Colors* ill. by author. Frances Lincoln, 2015. ISBN 978-184780742-7 Subj: Concepts – color. Machines. Trucks.

Stein, David Ezra. *I'm my own dog* ill. by author. Candlewick, 2014. ISBN 978-076366139-7 Subj: Animals – dogs. Character traits – individuality. Pets.

Tad and Dad ill. by author. Penguin/Nancy Paulsen, 2015. ISBN 978-039925671-4 Subj: Bedtime. Family life – fathers. Frogs & toads.

Stein, Eric. *Granddaddy's turn: a journey to the ballot box* (Bandy, Michael S.)

Stein, Peter. *Little Red's riding 'hood* ill. by Chris Gall. Scholastic/Orchard, 2015. ISBN 978-054560969-2 Subj: Character traits – bravery. Folk & fairy tales. Machines. Trucks.

Stemple, Heidi E. Y. *You nest here with me* (Yolen, Jane)

Sterling, Cheryl. *Some bunny to talk to: a story about going to therapy* ill. by Tiphanie Beeke. Magination, 2014. ISBN 978-143381649-9 Subj: Animals – rabbits. Behavior – needing someone. Behavior – worrying. Emotions. Illness – mental illness.

Sternberg, Julie. *Bedtime at Bessie and Lil's* ill. by Adam Gudeon. Boyds Mills, 2015. ISBN 978-159078934-6 Subj: Animals – rabbits. Bedtime. Behavior – misbehavior.

Stewart, Melissa. *Beneath the sun* ill. by Constance R. Bergum. Peachtree, 2014. ISBN 978-156145733-5 Subj: Animals. Concepts – cold & heat. Sun.

Feathers: not just for flying ill. by Sarah S. Brannen. Charlesbridge, 2014. ISBN 978-158089430-2 Subj: Birds. Feathers.

Stewart, Whitney. *A catfish tale: a bayou story of the fisherman and his wife* ill. by Gerald Guerlais. Albert Whitman, 2014. ISBN 978-080751098-8 Subj: Behavior – greed. Folk & fairy tales. Swamps.

Meditation is an open sky: mindfulness for kids ill. by Sally Rippin. Albert Whitman, 2015. ISBN 978-080754908-7 Subj: Animals. Emotions. Health & fitness. Self-concept.

Stille, Ljuba. *Mia's thumb* ill. by author. Holiday House, 2014. ISBN 978-082343067-3 Subj: Family life. Thumb sucking.

Stills, Caroline. *Mice mischief: math facts in action* ill. by Judith Rossell. Holiday House, 2014. ISBN 978-082342947-9 Subj: Animals – mice. Circus. Counting, numbers.

Stine, R. L. *The Little Shop of Monsters* ill. by Marc Brown. Little, Brown, 2015. ISBN 978-031636983-1 Subj: Monsters. Pets.

Stockdale, Sean. *Max the champion* by Sean Stockdale and Alexandra Strick ill. by Ros Asquith. Frances Lincoln, 2014. ISBN 978-184780388-7 Subj: Disabilities. Sports.

Stockdale, Susan. *Spectacular spots* ill. by author. Peachtree, 2015. ISBN 978-156145817-2 Subj: Animals. Disguises. Rhyming text.

Stoeke, Janet Morgan. *Oh no! a fox!* ill. by author. Dial, 2014. ISBN 978-080373952-9 Subj: Animals – foxes. Birds – chickens, roosters.

Stone, Tanya Lee. *The house that Jane built: a story about Jane Addams* ill. by Kathryn Brown. Holt/Christy Ottaviano, 2015. ISBN 978-080509049-9 Subj: Behavior – seeking better things. Character traits – helpfulness. Gender roles. Poverty.

Stoop, Naoko. *Red Knit Cap Girl and the reading tree* ill. by author. Little, Brown, 2014. ISBN 978-031622886-2 Subj: Animals. Behavior – sharing. Books, reading. Libraries.

Stower, Adam. *Naughty kitty!* ill. by author. Scholastic/Orchard, 2014. ISBN 978-054557604-8 Subj: Animals – cats. Animals – tigers. Pets.

Slam! a tale of consequences ill. by author. Owlkids, 2014. ISBN 978-177147007-0 Subj: Accidents.

Strick, Alexandra. *Max the champion* (Stockdale, Sean)

Stubbs, Lisa. *Lily and Bear* ill. by author. Simon & Schuster, 2015. ISBN 978-148144416-3 Subj: Activities – drawing. Animals – bears. Imagination.

Sturm, James. *Sleepless knight* ill. by author. First Second, 2015. ISBN 978-159643651-0 Subj: Animals. Behavior – lost & found possessions. Camps, camping. Format, unusual – graphic novels. Knights.

Subramaniam, Manasi, reteller. *The fox and the crow* ill. by Culpeo Fox. Karadi Tales, 2014. ISBN 978-818190303-7 Subj: Animals – foxes. Behavior – trickery. Birds – crows. Folk & fairy tales.

Surplice, Holly. *Peek-a-boo Bunny* ill. by author. Harper, 2014. ISBN 978-006224265-5 Subj: Animals. Animals – rabbits. Behavior – hiding. Games. Rhyming text.

Sutton, Sally. *Construction* ill. by Brian Lovelock. Candlewick, 2014. ISBN 978-076367325-3 Subj: Careers – construction workers. Libraries. Machines.

Sweeney, Linda Booth. *When the wind blows* ill. by Jana Christy. Putnam, 2015. ISBN 978-039916015-8 Subj: Family life. Rhyming text. Weather – storms. Weather – wind.

Swender, Jennifer. *Count on the subway* (Jacobs, Paul DuBois)

Swenson, Jamie A. *Big rig* ill. by Ned Young. Hyperion/Disney, 2014. ISBN 978-142316330-5 Subj: Tractors. Trucks.

If you were a dog ill. by Chris Raschka. Farrar, 2014. ISBN 978-037433530-4 Subj: Animals. Imagination.

Tafuri, Nancy. *Daddy hugs* ill. by author. Little, Brown, 2014. ISBN 978-031622923-4 Subj: Animals. Family life – fathers. Hugging.

Tallec, Olivier. *Who done it?* ill. by author. Chronicle, 2015. ISBN 978-145214198-5 Subj: Picture puzzles.

Tamaki, Mariko. *This one summer* ill. by Jillian Tamaki. First Second, 2014. ISBN 978-162672094-7 Subj: Caldecott award honor books. Format, unusual – graphic novels.

Tarpley, Todd. *Beep! beep! go to sleep!* ill. by John Rocco. Little, Brown, 2015. ISBN 978-031625443-4 Subj: Bedtime. Rhyming text. Robots.

My grandma's a ninja ill. by Danny Chatzikonstantinou. NorthSouth, 2015. ISBN 978-073584199-4 Subj: Character traits – being different. Character traits – individuality. Family life – grandmothers. Sports – martial arts.

Tavares, Matt. *Growing up Pedro* ill. by author. Candlewick, 2015. ISBN 978-076366824-2 Subj: Foreign lands – Dominican Republic. Sports – baseball.

Taylor, Sean. *Hoot owl, master of disguise* ill. by Jean Jullien. Candlewick, 2015. ISBN 978-076367578-3 Subj: Birds – owls. Disguises.

Teague, Mark. *The sky is falling!* ill. by author. Scholastic/Orchard, 2015. ISBN 978-054563217-1 Subj: Activities – dancing. Animals. Behavior – trickery. Birds – chickens, roosters. Folk & fairy tales.

Teckentrup, Britta. *Busy bunny days: in the town, on the farm, and at the port* ill. by author. Chronicle, 2014. ISBN 978-145211700-3 Subj: Animals. Animals – rabbits. Cities, towns. Family life. Farms.

Get out of my bath! ill. by author. Candlewick/ Nosy Crow, 2015. ISBN 978-076368006-0 Subj: Activities – bathing. Animals. Animals – elephants. Format, unusual – toy & movable books.

The odd one out: a spotting book ill. by author. Candlewick/Big Picture, 2014. ISBN 978-076367127-3 Subj: Animals. Picture puzzles.

Where's the pair? ill. by author. Candlewick, 2015. ISBN 978-076367772-5 Subj: Animals. Picture puzzles.

Tegen, Katherine. *Pink cupcake magic* ill. by Kristin Varner. Holt, 2014. ISBN 978-080509611-8 Subj: Activities – baking, cooking. Food. Magic.

Thiele, Bob. *What a wonderful world* (Weiss, George)

Thomas, Shelley Moore. *No, no, kitten!* ill. by Lori Nichols. Boyds Mills, 2015. ISBN 978-162091631-5 Subj: Activities – playing. Animals – cats.

Thompson, Laurie Ann. *Emmanuel's dream: the true story of Emmanuel Ofosu Yeboah* ill. by Sean Qualls. Random House, 2015. ISBN 978-044981744-5 Subj: Disabilities – physical disabilities. Foreign lands – Ghana. Prejudice. Sports – bicycling.

My dog is the best ill. by Paul Schmid. Farrar, 2015. ISBN 978-037430051-7 Subj: Animals – dogs.

Thong, Roseanne Greenfield. *Día de los muertos* ill. by Carles Ballesteros. Albert Whitman, 2015. ISBN 978-080751566-2 Subj: Foreign lands – Latin America. Foreign languages. Holidays – Day of the Dead.

Green is a chile pepper: a book of colors ill. by John Parra. Chronicle, 2014. ISBN 978-145210203-0 Subj: Concepts – color. Ethnic groups in the U.S. – Hispanic Americans. Rhyming text.

'Twas nochebuena ill. by Sara Palacios. Viking, 2014. ISBN 978-067001634-1 Subj: Foreign lands – Latin America. Foreign languages. Holidays – Christmas. Rhyming text.

Thornhill, Jan. *Winter's coming: a story of seasonal change* ill. by Josée Bisaillon. Owlkids, 2014. ISBN 978-177147002-5 Subj: Animals. Animals – rabbits. Seasons – winter.

The three bears. *Goatilocks and the three bears* by Erica S. Perl; ill. by Arthur Howard. Simon & Schuster/Beach Lane, 2014. ISBN 978-144240168-6 Subj: Animals – bears. Animals – goats. Folk & fairy tales.

Tillman, Nancy. *You're here for a reason* ill. by author. Feiwel and Friends, 2015. ISBN 978-125005626-9 Subj: Character traits – individuality. Rhyming text. Self-concept.

Todd, Mark. *Food trucks!* ill. by author. Houghton, 2014. ISBN 978-054415784-2 Subj: Food. Rhyming text. Trucks.

Tonatiuh, Duncan. *Separate is never equal: Sylvia Mendez and her family's fight for desegregation* ill. by author. Abrams, 2014. ISBN 978-141971054-4 Subj: Character traits – bravery. Ethnic groups in the U.S. – Mexican Americans. Prejudice. School. U.S. history.

Torrey, Richard. *Ally-Saurus and the first day of school* ill. by author. Sterling, 2015. ISBN 978-145491179-1 Subj: Character traits – willfulness. School – first day.

My dog, Bob ill. by author. Holiday House, 2015. ISBN 978-082343386-5 Subj: Animals – dogs. Humorous stories. Pets.

Tougas, Chris. *Dojo Daycare* ill. by author. Owlkids, 2014. ISBN 978-177147057-5 Subj: Behavior – misbehavior. Rhyming text. School – nursery. Sports – martial arts.

Dojo daytrip ill. by author. Owlkids, 2015. ISBN 978-177147142-8 Subj: Farms. School – field trips. Sports – martial arts.

Trapani, Iza, reteller. *Old King Cole* ill. by reteller. Charlesbridge, 2015. ISBN 978-158089632-0 Subj: Nursery rhymes.

Trasler, Janee. *Mimi and Bear in the snow* ill. by author. Farrar, 2014. ISBN 978-037434971-4 Subj: Animals – rabbits. Behavior – lost & found possessions. Seasons – winter. Toys – bears. Weather – snow.

Trent, Tereai. *The girl who buried her dreams in a can* ill. by Jan Spivey Gilchrist. Viking, 2015. ISBN 978-067001654-9 Subj: Careers – teachers. Foreign lands – Zimbabwe. Gender roles. School.

Trimmer, Christian. *Simon's new bed* ill. by Melissa Van der Paardt. Atheneum, 2015. ISBN

978-148143019-7 Subj: Animals – cats. Animals – dogs. Behavior – sharing. Character traits – compromising.

Troyer, Andrea. *Dear Santa, Love Rachel Rosenstein* (Peet, Amanda)

Trukhan, Ekaterina. *Me and my cat* ill. by author. Sterling, 2015. ISBN 978-145491612-3 Subj: Animals – cats. Friendship.

Patrick wants a dog! ill. by author. Sterling, 2015. ISBN 978-145491613-0 Subj: Animals – dogs. Pets.

Ts'o, Pauline. *Whispers of the wolf* ill. by author. Wisdom Tales, 2015. ISBN 978-193778645-8 Subj: Animals – wolves. Character traits – kindness to animals. Friendship. Indians of North America – Pueblo.

Tuell, Todd. *Ninja, ninja, never stop!* ill. by Tad Carpenter. Abrams/Appleseed, 2014. ISBN 978-141971027-8 Subj: Family life. Rhyming text. Sports – martial arts.

Tullet, Hervé. *Help! we need a title!* ill. by author. Candlewick, 2014. ISBN 978-076367021-4 Subj: Activities – writing. Books, reading. Careers – writers.

Mix it up! ill. by author. Chronicle, 2014. ISBN 978-145213735-3 Subj: Concepts – color. Format, unusual. Imagination. Participation.

Tupera, Tupera. *Polar Bear's underwear* ill. by author. Chronicle, 2015. ISBN 978-145214199-2 Subj: Animals – mice. Animals – polar bears. Behavior – lost & found possessions. Clothing – underwear. Format, unusual – toy & movable books.

Tupper Ling, Nancy. *The story I'll tell* ill. by Jessica Lanan. Lee & Low, 2015. ISBN 978-162014160-1 Subj: Adoption. Emotions – love. Family life – mothers. Foreign lands. Imagination.

Turnbull, Victoria. *The sea tiger* ill. by author. Candlewick/Templar, 2015. ISBN 978-076367986-6 Subj: Animals – tigers. Character traits – shyness. Friendship. Mythical creatures – mermaids, mermen. Sea & seashore.

Tutu, Archbishop Desmond. *Let there be light* (Bible. Old Testament. Genesis)

The twelve days of Christmas. English folk song. *The twelve days of Christmas* ill. by Rachel Griffin. Barefoot, 2015. ISBN 978-178285221-6 Subj: Cumulative tales. Holidays – Christmas. Music. Songs.

Twohy, Mike. *Wake up, Rupert!* ill. by author. Simon & Schuster, 2014. ISBN 978-144245998-4 Subj: Animals – sheep. Birds – chickens, roosters. Character traits – responsibility. Farms.

Uegaki, Chieri. *Hana Hashimoto, sixth violin* ill. by Qin Leng. Kids Can, 2014. ISBN 978-189478633-1 Subj: Character traits – persistence. Ethnic groups in the U.S. – Japanese Americans. Family life – grandfathers. Musical instruments – violins. Theater.

Underwood, Deborah. *Bad bye, good bye* ill. by Jonathan Bean. Houghton, 2014. ISBN 978-054792852-4 Subj: Friendship. Moving. Rhyming text.

Here comes Santa Cat ill. by Claudia Rueda. Dial, 2014. ISBN 978-080374100-3 Subj: Animals – cats. Behavior – misbehavior. Character traits – generosity. Gifts. Holidays – Christmas. Santa Claus.

Here comes the Easter Cat ill. by Claudia Rueda. Dial, 2014. ISBN 978-080373939-0 Subj: Animals – cats. Holidays – Easter. Humorous stories.

Here comes the Tooth Fairy Cat ill. by Claudia Rueda. Dial, 2015. ISBN 978-052542774-2 Subj: Animals – cats. Animals – mice. Fairies. Teeth.

Here comes Valentine Cat ill. by Claudia Rueda. Dial, 2015. ISBN 978-052542915-9 Subj: Animals – cats. Animals – dogs. Holidays – Valentine's Day.

Interstellar Cinderella ill. by Meg Hunt. Chronicle, 2015. ISBN 978-145212532-9 Subj: Careers – engineers. Family life – stepfamilies. Folk & fairy tales. Rhyming text. Royalty – princes. Space & space ships.

Urban, Linda. *Little Red Henry* ill. by Madeline Valentine. Candlewick, 2015. ISBN 978-076366176-2 Subj: Behavior – growing up. Family life. Self-concept.

Usher, Sam. *Snow* ill. by author. Candlewick, 2015. ISBN 978-076367958-3 Subj: Character traits – patience. Family life – grandfathers. Imagination. Weather – snow.

Vamos, Samantha R. *Alphabet trains* ill. by Ryan O'Rourke. Charlesbridge, 2015. ISBN 978-158089592-7 Subj: ABC books. Rhyming text. Trains.

Van, Muon. *In a village by the sea* ill. by April Chu. Creston, 2015. ISBN 978-193954715-6 Subj: Careers – fishermen. Family life. Foreign lands – Vietnam. Homes, houses.

Van Allsburg, Chris. *The misadventures of Sweetie Pie* ill. by author. Harcourt, 2014. ISBN 978-054731582-9 Subj: Animals – hamsters. Character traits – kindness to animals. Pets.

Van Biesen, Koen. *Roger is reading a book* ill. by author. Eerdmans, 2015. ISBN 978-080285442-1 Subj: Books, reading. Noise, sounds.

Van Laan, Nancy. *Forget me not* ill. by Stephanie Graegin. Random/Schwartz & Wade, 2014. ISBN 978-044981543-4 Subj: Family life – grandmothers. Illness – Alzheimer's. Memories, memory. Old age.

van Lieshout, Maria. *Hopper and Wilson fetch a star* ill. by author. Philomel, 2014. ISBN 978-039925772-8 Subj: Animals – elephants. Animals – mice. Friendship. Stars.

Van Slyke, Rebecca. *Mom school* ill. by Priscilla Burris. Doubleday, 2015. ISBN 978-038538892-4 Subj: Family life – mothers. School.

Van Wright, Cornelius. *When an alien meets a swamp monster* ill. by author. Penguin/Nancy Paulsen, 2014. ISBN 978-039925623-3 Subj: Friendship. Imagination. Reptiles – alligators, crocodiles.

Verburg, Bonnie. *The tree house that Jack built* ill. by Mark Teague. Scholastic/Orchard, 2014. ISBN 978-043985338-5 Subj: Cumulative tales. Homes, houses. Nursery rhymes.

Verde, Susan. *You and me* ill. by Peter H. Reynolds. Abrams, 2015. ISBN 978-141971197-8 Subj: Animals – cats. Friendship. Rhyming text.

Vere, Ed. *Max the brave* ill. by author. Sourcebooks/Jabberwocky, 2015. ISBN 978-149261651-1 Subj: Animals – cats. Character traits – bravery.

Vernick, Audrey. *First grade dropout* ill. by Matthew Cordell. Clarion, 2015. ISBN 978-054412985-6 Subj: Emotions – embarrassment. School.

Viano, Hannah. *B is for bear: a natural alphabet* ill. by author. Sasquatch, 2015. ISBN 978-163217039-2 Subj: ABC books. Animals. Nature.

Viorst, Judith. *Alexander, who's trying his best to be the best boy ever* ill. by Isidre Monés. Atheneum, 2014. ISBN 978-148142353-3 Subj: Behavior – misbehavior. Family life.

And two boys booed ill. by Sophie Blackall. Farrar/Margaret Ferguson, 2014. ISBN 978-037430302-0 Subj: Character traits – confidence. Emotions – fear. Format, unusual – toy & movable books. Self-concept. Theater.

Virján, Emma J. *What this story needs is a pig in a wig* ill. by author. HarperCollins, 2015. ISBN 978-006232724-6 Subj: Activities – storytelling. Animals. Boats, ships. Circular tales. Rhyming text.

Viva, Frank. *Outstanding in the rain* ill. by author. Little, Brown, 2015. ISBN 978-031636627-4 Subj: Birthdays. Format, unusual – toy & movable books. Language. Parks – amusement. Rhyming text.

Vogel, Vin. *The thing about yetis* ill. by author. Dial, 2015. ISBN 978-080374170-6 Subj: Activities. Monsters. Seasons – summer. Seasons – winter.

Waber, Bernard. *Ask me* ill. by Suzy Lee. Houghton Mifflin Harcourt, 2015. ISBN 978-054773394-4 Subj: Character traits – questioning. Family life – daughters. Family life – fathers.

Wahl, Phoebe. *Sonya's chickens* ill. by author. Tundra, 2015. ISBN 978-17704978-9-4 Subj: Animals – foxes. Birds – chickens, roosters. Death. Farms. Nature.

Waldron, Kevin. *Panda-monium at Peek Zoo* ill. by author. Candlewick/Templar, 2014. ISBN 978-076366658-3 Subj: Animals. Careers – zookeepers. Parades. Zoos.

Walker, Anna. *Peggy: a brave chicken on a big adventure* ill. by author. Clarion, 2014. ISBN 978-

054425900-3 Subj: Birds – chickens, roosters. Cities, towns.

Walker, Sally M. *Winnie: the true story of the bear who inspired Winnie-the-Pooh* ill. by Jonathon D. Voss. Holt, 2015. ISBN 978-080509715-3 Subj: Animals – bears. Books, reading. Careers – military. Foreign lands – Canada. Zoos.

Wall, Laura. *Goose* ill. by author. HarperCollins, 2015. ISBN 978-006232435-1 Subj: Birds – geese. Emotions – loneliness. Friendship.

Goose goes to school ill. by author. Harper, 2015. ISBN 978-006232437-5 Subj: Birds – geese. School.

Wallace, Nancy Elizabeth. *Water! water! water!* ill. by author. Amazon/Two Lions, 2014. ISBN 978-147784730-5 Subj: Animals – warthogs. Ecology. Friendship. Water.

Wallmark, Laurie. *Ada Byron Lovelace and the thinking machine* ill. by April Chu. Creston, 2015. ISBN 978-193954720-0 Subj: Computers. Counting, numbers. Gender roles.

Walsh, Ellen Stoll. *Where is Jumper?* ill. by author. Beach Lane, 2015. ISBN 978-148144508-5 Subj: Animals – mice. Behavior – hiding. Games.

Walsh, Joanna. *I love Mom* ill. by Judi Abbot. Simon & Schuster/Paula Wiseman, 2014. ISBN 978-148142808-8 Subj: Animals. Family life – mothers. Rhyming text.

Walton, Rick. *Frankenstein's fright before Christmas* ill. by Nathan Hale. Feiwel and Friends, 2014. ISBN 978-031255367-8 Subj: Holidays – Christmas. Monsters. Rhyming text.

Ward, Helen. *Spots in a box* ill. by author. Candlewick, 2015. ISBN 978-076367597-4 Subj: Birds – guinea fowl. Character traits – being different. Character traits – individuality. Concepts. Rhyming text.

Ward, Jennifer. *Mama built a little nest* ill. by Steve Jenkins. Simon & Schuster/Beach Lane, 2014. ISBN 978-144242116-5 Subj: Birds. Homes, houses. Nature. Rhyming text.

There was an old mummy who swallowed a spider (Little old lady who swallowed a fly)

Ward, Lindsay. *Henry finds his word* ill. by author. Dial, 2015. ISBN 978-080373990-1 Subj: Babies, toddlers. Language.

Wardlaw, Lee. *Won Ton and Chopstick: a cat and dog tale told in haiku* ill. by Eugene Yelchin. Holt, 2015. ISBN 978-080509987-4 Subj: Animals – cats. Animals – dogs. Poetry.

Warnes, Tim. *The great cheese robbery* ill. by author. Tiger Tales, 2015. ISBN 978-158925174-8 Subj: Animals – elephants. Animals – mice. Crime. Emotions – fear.

Waters, John F. *Sharks have six senses* ill. by Bob Barner. Harper, 2015. ISBN 978-006028140-3 Subj: Fish – sharks. Senses.

Watkins, Adam F. *R is for robot: a noisy alphabet* ill. by Adam F. Watkins. Price Stern Sloan, 2014. ISBN 978-084317237-9 Subj: ABC books. Robots.

Watkins, Angela Farris. *Love will see you through: Martin Luther King Jr.'s six guiding beliefs* ill. by Sally Wern Comport. Simon & Schuster, 2015. ISBN 978-141698693-5 Subj: Ethnic groups in the U.S. – African Americans. Holidays – Martin Luther King Day. Prejudice. U.S. history. Violence, nonviolence.

Watkins, Rowboat. *Rude cakes* ill. by author. Chronicle, 2015. ISBN 978-145213851-0 Subj: Behavior – bossy. Character traits – kindness. Character traits – selfishness. Etiquette. Food.

Watt, Mélanie. *Bug in a vacuum* ill. by author. Tundra, 2015. ISBN 978-177049645-3 Subj: Character traits – cleanliness. Insects.

Watts, Bernadette. *The golden plate* ill. by author. NorthSouth, 2014. ISBN 978-073584175-8 Subj: Behavior – stealing. Character traits – responsibility. Emotions.

Weatherford, Carole Boston. *Gordon Parks: how the photographer captured black and white America* ill. by Jamey Christoph. Albert Whitman, 2015. ISBN 978-080753017-7 Subj: Careers – photographers. Ethnic groups in the U.S. – African Americans. Prejudice. U.S. history.

Leontyne Price: voice of a century ill. by Raúl Colón. Knopf, 2014. ISBN 978-037585606-8 Subj: Careers – singers. Ethnic groups in the U.S. – African Americans. Music.

Sugar Hill: Harlem's historic neighborhood ill. by R. Gregory Christie. Albert Whitman, 2014. ISBN 978-080757650-2 Subj: Ethnic groups in the U.S. – African Americans. Rhyming text. U.S. history.

Voice of freedom: Fannie Lou Hamer, spirit of the civil rights movement ill. by Ekua Holmes. Candlewick, 2015. ISBN 978-076366531-9 Subj: Caldecott award honor books. Ethnic groups in the U.S. – African Americans. Poetry. Prejudice. Violence, nonviolence.

Webb, Holly. *Little puppy lost* ill. by Rebecca Harry. Tiger Tales, 2015. ISBN 978-158925170-0 Subj: Animals – cats. Animals – dogs. Behavior – lost. Friendship.

Weeks, Sarah. *Glamourpuss* ill. by David Small. Scholastic, 2015. ISBN 978-054560954-8 Subj: Animals – cats. Animals – dogs. Character traits – vanity. Emotions – envy, jealousy.

Wegman, William. *Flo and Wendell explore* ill. by author. Dial, 2014. ISBN 978-080373930-7 Subj: Animals – dogs. Camps, camping. Family life – brothers & sisters.

Weinberg, Steven. *Rex finds an egg! egg! egg!* ill. by author. Simon & Schuster, 2015. ISBN 978-148140308-5 Subj: Dinosaurs. Eggs.

Weingarten, Gene. *Me and dog* ill. by Eric Shansby. Simon & Schuster, 2014. ISBN 978-144249413-8 Subj: Animals – dogs. Rhyming text.

Weinstone, David. *Music class today!* ill. by Vin Vogel. Farrar, 2015. ISBN 978-037435131-1 Subj: Babies, toddlers. Character traits – shyness. Music. Musical instruments. Rhyming text.

Weiss, George. *What a wonderful world* by George Weiss and Bob Thiele ill. by Tim Hopgood. Holt, 2015. ISBN 978-162779254-7 Subj: Nature. Songs. World.

Wellington, Monica. *My leaf book* ill. by author. Dial, 2015. ISBN 978-080374141-6 Subj: Behavior – collecting things. Seasons – fall. Trees.

Wells, Rosemary. *Felix stands tall* ill. by author. Candlewick, 2015. ISBN 978-076366111-3 Subj: Animals – guinea pigs. Behavior – bullying, teasing. Character traits – assertiveness. Friendship. Theater.

Max and Ruby at the Warthogs' wedding ill. by author. Viking, 2014. ISBN 978-067078461-5 Subj: Animals – rabbits. Behavior – lost & found possessions. Format, unusual – toy & movable books. Weddings.

Sophie's terrible twos ill. by author. Viking, 2014. ISBN 978-067078512-4 Subj: Animals – mice. Behavior – bad day, bad mood. Behavior – misbehavior. Birthdays. Family life.

Stella's Starliner ill. by author. Candlewick, 2014. ISBN 978-076361495-9 Subj: Animals. Behavior – bullying, teasing. Family life. Friendship. Homes, houses.

Use your words, Sophie! ill. by author. Viking, 2015. ISBN 978-067001663-1 Subj: Animals – mice. Communication. Family life – new sibling. Family life – sisters. Language.

A visit to Dr. Duck ill. by author. Candlewick, 2014. ISBN 978-076367229-4 Subj: Birds – ducks. Careers – doctors. Emotions – fear. Format, unusual – board books. Illness.

Weninger, Brigitte. *Davy loves his mommy* ill. by Eve Tharlet. NorthSouth, 2014. ISBN 978-073584164-

2 Subj: Animals – rabbits. Etiquette. Family life – mothers. Holidays – Mother's Day.

Happy Easter, Davy! ill. by Eve Tharlet. North-South, 2014. ISBN 978-073584161-1 Subj: Animals – rabbits. Gifts. Holidays – Easter.

Wheeler, Lisa. *Dino-boarding* ill. by Barry Gott. Carolrhoda, 2014. ISBN 978-146770213-3 Subj: Dinosaurs. Rhyming text. Sports.

Dino-swimming ill. by Barry Gott. Lerner, 2015. ISBN 978-146770214-0 Subj: Dinosaurs. Rhyming text. Sports – swimming.

Whelan, Gloria. *Queen Victoria's bathing machine* ill. by Nancy Carpenter. Simon & Schuster/Paula Wiseman, 2014. ISBN 978-141692753-2 Subj: Foreign lands – England. Rhyming text. Royalty – queens. Sports – swimming.

White, Dianne. *Blue on blue* ill. by Beth Krommes. Simon & Schuster/Beach Lane, 2014. ISBN 978-144241267-5 Subj: Rhyming text. Weather – rain. Weather – storms.

White, Teagan. *Adventures with barefoot critters* ill. by author. Tundra, 2014. ISBN 978-177049624-8 Subj: ABC books. Animals. Seasons.

Wick, Walter. *Can you see what I see? Christmas* photos by author. Scholastic, 2015. ISBN 978-054583183-3 Subj: Format, unusual – board books. Holidays – Christmas. Picture puzzles. Rhyming text.

Hey, Seymour! a search and find fold-out adventure photos by author. Scholastic, 2015. ISBN 978-054550216-0 Subj: Format, unusual – toy & movable books. Picture puzzles. Rhyming text.

Wigger, J. Bradley. *Thank you, God* ill. by Jago. Eerdmans, 2014. ISBN 978-080285424-7 Subj: Nature. Religion.

Willems, Mo. *The pigeon needs a bath* ill. by author. Disney/Hyperion, 2014. ISBN 978-142319087-5 Subj: Activities – bathing. Birds – pigeons.

Williams, Brenda. *Outdoor opposites* ill. by Rachel Oldfield. Barefoot, 2015. ISBN 978-178285094-6 Subj: Camps, camping. Concepts – opposites. Songs.

Williams, Pharrell. *Happy!* ill. by Kristin Smith. Putnam, 2015. ISBN 978-039917643-2 Subj: Emotions – happiness. Songs.

Willis, Jeanne. *Boa's bad birthday* ill. by Tony Ross. Andersen, 2014. ISBN 978-146773450-9 Subj: Animals. Birthdays. Gifts. Reptiles – snakes.

Slug needs a hug! ill. by Tony Ross. Andersen, 2015. ISBN 978-146779309-4 Subj: Animals –

slugs. Character traits – appearance. Family life – mothers. Hugging. Rhyming text.

Wilson, Karma. *Bear counts* ill. by Jane Chapman. Simon & Schuster/Margaret K. McElderry, 2015. ISBN 978-144248092-6 Subj: Animals – bears. Animals – mice. Counting, numbers. Rhyming text.

Bear sees colors ill. by Jane Chapman. Simon & Schuster/Margaret K. McElderry, 2014. ISBN 978-144246536-7 Subj: Animals. Animals – bears. Concepts – color. Rhyming text.

Duddle Puck: the puddle duck ill. by Marcellus Hall. Margaret K. McElderry, 2015. ISBN 978-144244927-5 Subj: Birds – ducks. Character traits – being different. Farms. Noise, sounds. Rhyming text.

Wilson, N. D. *Ninja boy goes to school* ill. by J. J. Harrison. Random House, 2014. ISBN 978-037586584-8 Subj: Imagination. School. Sports – martial arts.

Winstead, Rosie. *Sprout helps out* by author. Dial, 2014. ISBN 978-080373072-4 Subj: Behavior – messy. Character traits – helpfulness. Family life.

Winter, Jeanette. *Malala, a brave girl from Pakistan / Iqbal, a brave boy from Pakistan* ill. by author. Simon & Schuster/Beach Lane, 2014. ISBN 978-148142294-9 Subj: Character traits – bravery. Character traits – freedom. Foreign lands – Pakistan. Violence, nonviolence.

Mr. Cornell's dream boxes ill. by author. Simon & Schuster/Beach Lane, 2014. ISBN 978-144249902-7 Subj: Art. Careers – artists. Character traits – shyness. Dreams. Memories, memory.

Winter, Jonah. *How Jelly Roll Morton invented jazz* ill. by Keith Mallett. Roaring Brook, 2015. ISBN 978-159643963-4 Subj: Careers – musicians. Ethnic groups in the U.S. – African Americans. Music. Musical instruments – pianos.

Joltin' Joe DiMaggio ill. by James Ransome. Atheneum, 2014. ISBN 978-141694080-7 Subj: Sports – baseball.

Lillian's right to vote: a celebration of the Voting Rights Act of 1965 ill. by Shane W. Evans. Random/Schwartz & Wade, 2015. ISBN 978-038539028-6 Subj: Ethnic groups in the U.S. – African Americans. Prejudice. U.S. history.

Winters, Kari-Lynn. *Bad pirate* ill. by Dean Griffiths. Pajama, 2015. ISBN 978-192748571-2 Subj: Animals – dogs. Character traits – helpfulness. Character traits – selfishness. Family life – daughters. Family life – fathers. Pirates.

Winthrop, Elizabeth. *Lucy and Henry are twins* ill. by Jane Massey. Amazon/Two Lions, 2015. ISBN 978-147782629-4 Subj: Family life – brothers & sisters. Multiple births – twins. Rhyming text.

Witter, Bret. *Tuesday tucks me in: the loyal bond between a soldier and his service dog* (Montalván, Luis Carlos)

Woelfle, Gretchen. *Mumbet's Declaration of Independence* ill. by Alix Delinois. Carolrhoda, 2014. ISBN 978-076136589-1 Subj: Character traits – freedom. Ethnic groups in the U.S. – African Americans. Slavery. U.S. history.

Wohnoutka, Mike. *Dad's first day* ill. by author. Bloomsbury, 2015. ISBN 978-161963473-2 Subj: Family life – fathers. School – first day.

Little puppy and the big green monster ill. by author. Holiday House, 2014. ISBN 978-082343064-2 Subj: Activities – playing. Animals – dogs. Monsters.

Won, Brian. *Hooray for hat!* ill. by author. Houghton, 2014. ISBN 978-054415903-7 Subj: Animals. Animals – elephants. Behavior – bad day, bad mood. Clothing – hats.

Wood, Audrey. *The full moon at the napping house* ill. by Don Wood. Houghton, 2015. ISBN 978-054430832-9 Subj: Animals. Cumulative tales. Family life – grandmothers. Sleep.

Wood, Douglas. *When a grandpa says "I love you"* ill. by Jennifer A. Bell. Simon & Schuster, 2014. ISBN 978-068981512-6 Subj: Emotions – love. Family life – grandfathers.

Woodward, Molly. *The babies and doggies book* (Schindel, John)

Wright, Johana. *The orchestra pit* ill. by author. Roaring Brook/Neal Porter, 2014. ISBN 978-159643769-2 Subj: Musical instruments – orchestras. Reptiles – snakes.

Wunderli, Stephen. *Little Boo* ill. by Tim Zeltner. Holt, 2014. ISBN 978-080509708-5 Subj: Gardens, gardening. Holidays – Halloween. Plants. Seeds.

Yaccarino, Dan. *Billy and Goat at the state fair* ill. by author. Knopf, 2015. ISBN 978-038575325-8 Subj: Animals – goats. Fairs, festivals. Friendship.

Doug unplugs on the farm ill. by author. Knopf, 2014. ISBN 978-038575328-9 Subj: Farms. Robots.

Yankey, Lindsey. *Bluebird* ill. by author. Simply Read, 2014. ISBN 978-192701833-0 Subj: Birds – bluebirds. Character traits – confidence. Weather – wind.

Sun and Moon ill. by author. Simply Read, 2015. ISBN 978-192701860-6 Subj: Emotions – envy, jealousy. Moon. Self-concept. Sun.

Yarlett, Emma. *Orion and the Dark* ill. by author. Candlewick/Templar, 2015. ISBN 978-076367595-0 Subj: Bedtime. Emotions – fear.

Yee, Kristina. *Miss Todd and her wonderful flying machine* (Poletti, Frances)

Yee, Wong Herbert. *My autumn book* ill. by author. Holt, 2015. ISBN 978-080509922-5 Subj: Nature. Rhyming text. Seasons – fall.

Yeoman, John. *Three little owls* (Luzzati, Emanuele)

Yim, Natasha. *Goldy Luck and the three pandas* ill. by Grace Zong. Charlesbridge, 2014. ISBN 978-158089652-8 Subj: Animals – pandas. Behavior – sharing. Folk & fairy tales. Holidays – Chinese New Year.

Yolen, Jane. *How do dinosaurs stay safe?* ill. by Mark Teague. Scholastic, 2015. ISBN 978-043924104-5 Subj: Dinosaurs. Rhyming text. Safety.

Sing a season song ill. by Lisel Jane Ashlock. Creative Editions, 2015. ISBN 978-156846255-4 Subj: Rhyming text. Seasons.

The stranded whale ill. by Melanie Cataldo. Candlewick, 2015. ISBN 978-076366953-9 Subj: Animals – whales. Death. Emotions – sadness.

You nest here with me by Jane Yolen and Heidi E. Y. Stemple ill. by Melissa Sweet. Boyds Mills, 2015. ISBN 978-159078923-0 Subj: Bedtime. Birds. Rhyming text.

Yoon, Salina. *Found* ill. by author. Bloomsbury, 2014. ISBN 978-080273559-1 Subj: Animals – bears. Behavior – lost & found possessions. Character traits – responsibility. Emotions.

Penguin and Pumpkin ill. by author. Walker Books for Young Readers, 2014. ISBN 978-080273732-8 Subj: Birds – penguins. Family life – brothers. Farms. Seasons – fall.

Penguin's big adventure ill. by author. Bloomsbury, 2015. ISBN 978-080273828-8 Subj: Activities – traveling. Animals – polar bears. Birds – penguins. Foreign lands – Arctic.

Stormy night ill. by author. Bloomsbury, 2015. ISBN 978-080273780-9 Subj: Animals – bears.

Bedtime. Emotions – fear. Family life. Weather – storms.

Tap to play! ill. by author. HarperCollins/Balzer & Bray, 2014. ISBN 978-006228684-0 Subj: Games. Imagination. Participation.

Young, Cybèle. *Nancy knows* ill. by author. Tundra, 2014. ISBN 978-177049482-4 Subj: Animals – elephants. Behavior – forgetfulness. Memories, memory.

Some things I've lost ill. by author. Groundwood, 2015. ISBN 978-155498339-1 Subj: Art. Behavior – lost & found possessions. Behavior – resourcefulness. Concepts – change. Format, unusual – toy & movable books. Imagination.

Young, Jessica. *Spy Guy: the not-so-secret agent* ill. by Charles Santoso. Houghton Mifflin Harcourt, 2015. ISBN 978-054420859-9 Subj: Careers – detectives. Character traits – perseverance. Crime. Family life – fathers.

Yuly, Toni. *Early bird* ill. by author. Feiwel and Friends, 2014. ISBN 978-125004327-6 Subj: Birds.

Night owl ill. by author. Feiwel and Friends, 2015. ISBN 978-125005457-9 Subj: Animals – babies. Birds – owls. Noise, sounds.

Yum, Hyewon. *The twins' little sister* ill. by author. Farrar, 2014. ISBN 978-037437973-5 Subj: Babies, toddlers. Family life – sisters. Multiple births – twins.

Zagarenski, Pamela. *The whisper* ill. by author. Houghton Mifflin Harcourt, 2015. ISBN 978-054441686-4 Subj: Activities – storytelling. Books, reading. Imagination. Magic.

Zapf, Marlena. *Underpants dance* ill. by Lynne Avril. Dial, 2014. ISBN 978-080373539-2 Subj: Activities – dancing. Behavior – resourcefulness. Clothing – underwear. Family life – sisters.

Zeltser, David. *Ninja baby* ill. by Diane Goode. Chronicle, 2015. ISBN 978-145213542-7 Subj: Babies, toddlers. Family life – new sibling. Sports – martial arts.

Zoboli, Giovanna. *The big book of slumber* ill. by Simona Mulazzani. Eerdmans, 2014. ISBN 978-080285439-1 Subj: Animals. Bedtime. Lullabies. Rhyming text.

Zoehfeld, Kathleen Weidner. *Secrets of the seasons: orbiting the sun in our backyard* ill. by Priscilla Lamont. Knopf, 2014. ISBN 978-051770994-8 Subj: Seasons. Sun.

Zommer, Yuval. *The big blue thing on the hill* ill. by author. Candlewick/Templar, 2015. ISBN 978-076367403-8 Subj: Animals. Character traits – cooperation.

Title Index

Titles appear in alphabetical sequence with the author's name in parentheses, followed by the page number of the full listing in the Bibliographic Guide. For identical title listings, the illustrator's name is given to further identify the version. In the case of variant titles, both the original and differing titles are listed.

A

An A from Miss Keller (Polacco, Patricia), 110
A is for awesome (Clayton, Dallas), 81
The ABC animal orchestra (Saaf, Donald), 114
ABC insects (American Museum of Natural History), 71
ABC school's for me! (Katz, Susan B.), 97
ABCs on wings (Olivera, Ramon), 107
Abuelo (Dorros, Arthur), 85
Ace Dragon Ltd (Hoban, Russell), 93
Ada Byron Lovelace and the thinking machine (Wallmark, Laurie), 124
The adventures of Beekle (Santat, Dan), 115
Adventures with barefoot critters (White, Teagan), 125
Albert the muffin-maker (May, Eleanor), 104
Alexander, who's trying his best to be the best boy ever (Viorst, Judith), 123
Alice from Dallas (Sadler, Marilyn), 115
Alice Waters and the trip to delicious (Martin, Jacqueline Briggs), 104
All aboard! (Dotlich, Rebecca Kai), 85
All different now (Johnson, Angela), 96
All fall down (Barrett, Mary Brigid), 74
All for a dime! a Bear and Mole story (Hillenbrand, Will), 93
All my stripes (Rudolph, Shaina), 114
All year round (Leduc, Emilie), 99
Ally-Saurus and the first day of school (Torrey, Richard), 121
Alone together (Bloom, Suzanne), 76
Alphabet school (Johnson, Stephen T.), 96
Alphabet trains (Vamos, Samantha R.), 123
Alphabetabum (Raschka, Chris), 111
Always (Dodd, Emma), 85
An ambush of tigers (Rosenthal, Betsy R.), 113
And away we go! (Migy), 104
And Nick (Gore, Emily), 90
And then comes Christmas (Brenner, Tom), 77
And two boys booed (Viorst, Judith), 123
Andrew draws (McPhail, David), 103
Angelina's big city ballet (Holabird, Katharine), 93
Angelina's Cinderella (Holabird, Katharine), 93
The animals' Santa (Brett, Jan), 77
Anna's heaven (Hole, Stian), 93
Any questions? (Gay, Marie-Louise), 89

Archie the daredevil penguin (Rash, Andy), 112
Archie's vacation (Gordon, Domenica More), 90
Are we there, Yeti? (Anstee, Ashlyn), 72
Armond goes to a party (Carlson, Nancy), 79
Around the clock! (Chast, Roz), 80
As an oak tree grows (Karas, G. Brian), 97
Ask me (Waber, Bernard), 123
At the old haunted house (Ketteman, Helen), 97
At the same moment, around the world (Perrin, Clotilde), 109
Aw, nuts! (McClurkan, Rob), 102
Awake beautiful child (Rosenthal, Amy Krouse), 113
Axel Scheffler's Flip flap safari (Scheffler, Axel), 116

B

B. Bear and Lolly: catch that cookie! (Livingston, A. A.), 100
B. Bear and Lolly: off to school (Livingston, A. A.), 100
B is for bear (Viano, Hannah), 123
Baa, baa, black sheep (Cabrera, Jane), 79
Babar on Paradise Island (Brunhoff, Laurent de), 78
The babies and doggies book (Schindel, John), 116
Baby Bear (Nelson, Kadir), 106
Baby bedtime (Fox, Mem), 88
Baby love (DiTerlizzi, Angela), 85
Baby loves to boogie! (Kirwan, Wednesday), 97
Baby party (O'Connell, Rebecca), 107
Baby penguins love their Mama (Guion, Melissa), 91
Baby Pig Pig talks (McPhail, David), 103
The baby swap (Ormerod, Jan), 108
The baby tree (Blackall, Sophie), 76
Baby's got the blues (Shields, Carol Diggory), 117
The backwards birthday party (Chapin, Tom), 79
Bad bye, good bye (Underwood, Deborah), 122
Bad dog (McPhail, David), 103
Bad dog, Flash (Paul, Ruth), 109
Bad pirate (Winters, Kari-Lynn), 126
Baking day at Grandma's (Denise, Anika), 84
The Bambino and me (Hyman, Zachary), 94
Baseball is . . . (Borden, Louise), 76
Bats in the band (Lies, Brian), 100
Be safe around fire (Heos, Bridget), 92
Bea in The Nutcracker (Isadora, Rachel), 95

C

G

H

J

K

L

M

P

Q

R

S

Y

Z

Illustrator Index

Illustrators appear alphabetically in boldface followed by their titles. Names in parentheses are authors of the titles when different from the illustrator. Page numbers refer to the full listing in the Bibliographic Guide.

A

Abbot, Judi. *I love Mom* (Walsh, Joanna), 124
Train!, 71
Agee, Jon. *It's only Stanley*, 71
Alakija, Polly. *Counting chickens*, 71
Alarcao, Renato. *Soccer star* (Javaherbin, Mina), 95
Alexander, Claire. *Monkey and the little one*, 71
Allen, Elanna. *Eva and Sadie and the best classroom ever!* (Cohen, Jeff), 81
Eva and Sadie and the worst haircut ever! (Cohen, Jeff), 81
Allen, Rick. *Winter bees and other poems of the cold* (Sidman, Joyce), 117
Allyn, Virginia. *Mother Goose's pajama party* (Smith, Danna), 118
Anderson, Brian. *Monster chefs*, 71
Anderson, Derek. *Hot Rod Hamster: monster truck mania!* (Lord, Cynthia), 101
Ten pigs, 71
Anderson, Tara. *Nat the cat can sleep like that* (Allenby, Victoria), 71
Ang, Joy. *Mustache Baby meets his match* (Heos, Bridget), 92
Anstee, Ashlyn. *Are we there, Yeti?*, 72
Antony, Steve. *Betty goes bananas*, 72
Green lizards vs. red rectangles, 72
Please, Mr. Panda, 72
The Queen's hat, 72
Appelhans, Chris. *Sparky!* (Offill, Jenny), 107
Apple, Margot. *Sheep go to sleep* (Shaw, Nancy), 117
Appleton, Polly. *Happy birthday Sophie!* (Sirett, Dawn), 118
Arndt, Michael. *Cat says meow and other animalopoeia*, 72
Arnold, Tedd. *A pet for Fly Guy*, 72
Vincent paints his house, 72
Asch, Frank. *Pizza*, 72
Ashdown, Rebecca. *Bob and Flo*, 72
Ashlock, Lisel Jane. *Sing a season song* (Yolen, Jane), 127
Asquith, Ros. *Max the champion* (Stockdale, Sean), 120
Atteberry, Kevan. *Bunnies!!!*, 72

Auch, Mary Jane. *The buk buk buk festival*, 73
Auerbach, Adam. *Edda*, 73
Austin, Mike. *Fire Engine No. 9*, 73
Junkyard, 73
Nellie Belle (Fox, Mem), 88
Avilés, Martha. *Nonna's Hanukkah surprise* (Fisman, Karen), 87
Avril, Lynne. *I'm gonna climb a mountain in my patent leather shoes* (Singer, Marilyn), 118
Ruby Valentine and the sweet surprise (Friedman, Laurie), 88
Underpants dance (Zapf, Marlena), 127
Azarian, Mary. *Before we eat* (Brisson, Pat), 77

B

Bach, Annie. *Monster party!*, 73
Bagley, Jessixa. *Boats for Papa*, 73
Bailey, Ella. *No such thing*, 73
Baker, Keith. *Little green peas*, 73
Ballesteros, Carles. *Día de los muertos* (Thong, Roseanne Greenfield), 121
Bang, Molly. *Buried sunlight*, 73
When Sophie's feelings are really, really hurt, 73
Barclay, Eric. *Counting dogs*, 73
Barner, Bob. *Sea bones*, 74
Sharks have six senses (Waters, John F.), 124
Baroncelli, Silvia. *Be safe around fire* (Heos, Bridget), 92
Barrager, Brigette. *Sleeping Cinderella and other princess mix-ups* (Clarkson, Stephanie), 80
Uni the unicorn (Rosenthal, Amy Krouse), 113
Barrett, Angela. *The most wonderful thing in the world* (French, Vivian), 88
Barrett, Ron. *Cats got talent*, 74
Barrette, Doris. *When the wind blew* (Jackson, Alison), 95
Barroux. *Tickly toes* (Hood, Susan), 93
Barton, Bethany. *I'm trying to love spiders*, 74
Barton, Byron. *My bike*, 74
My bus, 74
Barton, Patrice. *I pledge allegiance* (Mora, Pat), 105
Little sleepyhead (McPike, Elizabeth), 103
Uh-oh! (Crum, Shutta), 82

About the Author

REBECCA L. THOMAS recently retired as an elementary school librarian, Shaker Heights City Schools, Ohio. She is the author of numerous reference books, including the *Popular Series Fiction* set for Libraries Unlimited (2009) and *Across Cultures* (Libraries Unlimited, 2007).